TECHNICAL CHANGE AND ECONOMIC GROWTH

T0382702

In memory of my parents
Aikaterini and Michael Korres

Technical Change and Economic Growth
Inside the Knowledge Based Economy

GEORGE M. KORRES
University of the Aegean, Greece
and
University of Leeds, UK

Second Edition

LONDON AND NEW YORK

First published in paperback 2024

First published 2008 by Ashgate Publishing

Published 2016 by Routledge
4 Park Square, Milton Park, Abingdon, Oxon OX14 4RN

and by Routledge
605 Third Avenue, New York, NY 10158

Routledge is an imprint of the Taylor & Francis Group, an informa business

Publisher's Note
The publisher has gone to great lengths to ensure the quality of this reprint but points out that some imperfections in the original copies may be apparent.

British Library Cataloguing in Publication Data
Korres, George M.
  Technical change and economic growth : inside the knowledge
  based economy
  1. Technological innovations - Economic aspects - European
  Union countries 2. European Union countries - Economic
  conditions
  I. Title
  338'.064'094

Library of Congress Cataloging-in-Publicatin Data
Korres, George M.
  Technical change and economic growth : inside the knowledge based economy / by
George M. Korres.
     p. cm.
  Includes bibliographical references and index.
  ISBN 978-1-84014-992-0
  1. Technological innovations--Economic aspects--European Union countries. 2. Euro -
pean Union countries--Economic conditions. 3. Technological innovations--Economic
aspects--Greece. 4. Greece--Economic
Conditions--1974- 5 . Production functions (Economic theory) I.Title .

  HC240.9.T4K67 2008
  338'.064094--dc22

                                                                    2008007608

ISBN: 978-1-84014-992-0 (hbk)
ISBN: 978-1-03-283871-7 (pbk)
ISBN: 978-1-315-24169-2 (ebk)

DOI: 10.4324/9781315241692

Contents

List of Figures

List of Tables

Preface

The growing importance of technological change in world production and employment is one of the characteristics of the last four decades. Technological change does not only determine growth but also affects international competition and modernisation of an economy. It is difficult to record and analyse the results from research and technological policy. It is well known that the adoption and diffusion of new technologies affect structure and competitiveness of the whole economy. The choice of technology depends upon a good number of factors. It depends upon the availability of technologies, the availability of information to the decision maker, the availability of resources, the availability of technology itself and its ability to be successfully adopted in order to accommodate the particular needs and objectives.

Only recently technology has been distinguished from science policy. "Science policy" is concerned with education and knowledge. "Technological policy" is concerned with the adoption and use of techniques, innovation and diffusion of techniques. The division between the areas and variables of science policy and technology policy is not so clear. For instance, education and the stock of knowledge play an important role in influencing the rate of innovation and diffusion of technology. Usually, the technological policy should aim to create a favourable "psychological climate" for the development of research and innovations; such as: different financial incentives, support in education and training programmes, provision technical services etc.

Survey on technological innovation has adopted methodologies and definitions from the Oslo and Frascati Manuals on technological innovation. It should be helpful to recall the definition of technological innovation suggested to firms surveyed by: "the set of knowledge, professional skills, procedures, capabilities, equipment, technical solutions required to manufacture goods or provide services". Whereas, innovation in process is "the adoption of technologically new methods in production or new methods to provide services. Several changes concerning equipment, production organisation or both may be required".

UNESCO, OECD and EUROSTAT divisions organised the systematic collection, analysis publication and standardization of data concerning science and technological activities. The first experimental questionnaires were circulated to member states by UNESCO in 1966 and standardised periodical surveys were established in 1969. The collection of R&D data of regional statistics implied a lot of problems in comparison to data of national statistics. For the collection of regional statistics, we should consideration local differences and difficulties. In addition, we can use either "local-units" or "local-economic-units". R&D and innovation activities are directly related to economic and regional growth. The outcome of international innovation and diffusion process is uncertain; this process may generate either a pattern in which some countries may follow diverging trends or a pattern in which countries converge towards a common trend. Economic development may be analysed as a disequilibrium process characterized by two conflicting forces:

- innovation which tends to increase economic and technological differences between countries; and
- diffusion (or imitation) which tends to reduce them.

A causal reading of recent economic history suggests two important trends in world economy: firstly, technological change and innovations are becoming important contributors to economic growth and to well-being. Secondly, nations in the world economy are becoming increasingly open and interdependent. These two trends are related. Rapid communication and close contacts among innovations in different countries facilitate the process of invention and the spread of new ideas.

Rapid changes in technology imply some effects on socio-economic integration through world trading system. Therefore, it is not surprising that there is a relation among productivity and technology, on the one hand, while international competitiveness is closely related to world trading system on the other.

One of the most important economic events of the last decades in Europe has been the process of European economic integration. Economic theory, however, is unclear with respect to the effects of economic integration. There are many theories on economic integration, but their conclusions differ widely. Next to investigating the effects of integration from a theoretical point of view, it is also important to assess these effects empirically.

This book performs such an empirical analysis. It uses the unique example of the EU to analyse whether convergence or divergence occurred between the EU. Of course, convergence and divergence may occur in numerous ways. Regional conditions are dynamic. Furthermore, there is a wide range of circumstances. Some places may have little difficulty warranting public policy attention. Elsewhere, there are many different regional problems, such as: lagged adjustment to changing economic circumstances, cumulative decline of services, loss of environmental quality, excessive in-migration, community desire for faster economic expansion than currently prevails and temporary shocks.

Several other policy difficulties that policy-makers encounter are competitive federalism, inter and intra-governmental coordination, and the issue of policy instability. Regional development is a difficult policy arena in which all tiers of government have had limited success. Problems also differ according to the scale of analysis: federal, state or local. The factors that contribute to this diversity are themselves numerous and diverse.

The book argues that regional economic development ultimately depends on technical change, social and human capital and civic entrepreneurship, among others. If so, technology in all its facets will be the crucial ingredient in regional improvement, in contrast with the usual regional pleas for better infrastructure, health care and banking facilities.

The long-term growth and employment depend less on the short-term allocative efficiency measures than on a set of long-term policies aimed at enhancing the knowledge base of economies, through increased investment in the knowledge infrastructure, the knowledge distribution system and the human knowledge component, human resources, education, training and organisational change. While different terminology is used in each country (electronic highways in the USA; information society in Europe), all the indicators point to a rapid increase in the knowledge base of economy is closely associated with (electronic) networking.

One important aspect is related to both distributional aspects of innovation and technical change and to some specific characteristics of information and communication technologies which "exclude" all those who are unconnected to information infrastructure. During 1990s, most technology employment analysis focused on the complexity of the many interactions linking the introduction of new technologies, changes in work organisation, skill mismatches and sectoral employment growth and displacement. Thus, to use Schumpeter's expression, the employment impact of technical change was associated with a process of "creative destruction", involving a process of job destruction in some of the older occupations, technologies, firms and industries. It could also involve changes in the international division of labour.

Based on past experience, however, job losses resulting from the application of new technologies always appeared to be more than compensated for by the parallel process of job creation in new occupations, technologies, firms, industries and services.

In other words, and from historical point of view, there has always been a process of employment growth in industrialised countries, albeit accompanied by a reduction in working hours. Ultimately, technical change has led to higher real incomes, greater employment opportunities and more leisure time. Knowledge can be implemented by human capital and is the key for economic and social development.

Technological gap models represent two conflicting forces: innovation, which tends to increase productivity differences among countries, and diffusion, which tends to reduce them. According to the Schumpeterian theory, growth differences are seen as the combined results of these forces. Research on why growth rates differ has a long history which goes well beyond growth accounting exercises.

Countries that are technologically backward have a potentiality to generate more rapid growth even greater than that of the advanced countries, if they are able to exploit new technologies which have already been employed by the technological leaders. The pace of catching up depends on diffusion of knowledge, rate of structural change, accumulation of capital and expansion of demand. Member states lagging behind in growth rates can succeed in catching up, if they are able to reduce the technological gap. An important aspect of this is that they should not rely only on the combination of technology imports and investment, but they should also increase their innovation activities and improve locally produced technologies, such examples are new industrialised countries like Korea and Singapore.

The book is intended to provide a basic understanding of the current issues and the problems of knowledge economy, technical change, innovation activities; it will also examine many aspects and consequences of regional integration that are obscure or yet to be explored. Most of this research has been presented in variety conferences, seminars, and workshops; some sections have already been published as Departmental papers and in several Journals. After general issues in these fields have been addressed the discussion will turns to empirical and theoretical aspects of technical change, productivity, economic growth, European policy and technology policy. In particular, with its wide range of topics, methodologies and perspectives, the book offers stimulating and wide-ranging analyses that will be of interest to students, economic theorists, empirical social scientists, policy makers and the informed general reader.

The book consists of five main chapters. Chapter 1 is devoted to definitions and measurement of innovation activities and knowledge economy. Three main topics related to such matters will be discussed in this chapter and are as presented below:

- How the definitions of technological innovation and the knowledge based economy should be applied? Several factors should be actually taken into account, including: the relation between technological and non-technological innovations.
- What are the characteristics of research and development (R&D)?
- How can we apply and estimate the main implications and the effects of these variables?
- What do we want to measure?
- How do we want to measure it?
- Where do we want to measure it?: Technological product and process – TPP – innovations

Chapter 2 investigates the neoclassical growth theory and models of innovation activities and the knowledge based economy. This chapter attempts to analyse and model the new economy, within the framework of knowledge and innovation activities; It also attempts to estimate socio-economic effects of technical change, using both a theoretical and an empirical approach. Moreover, this chapter reviews the main statistical measures for research, scientific and technological activities, using various models, through the input-output analysis and the catching-up and production-cost function models, in order to measure the implication on productivity and the growth effects. We would like to tackle upon the following issues in this chapter:

- Why is innovation important for economic development?
- How can we model innovation activities and knowledge-based economy?
- How can we estimate the effects of innovation activities and the knowledge-based economy?

Chapter 3 deals with the main issues of: technical change, knowledge economy and productivity growth. This chapter attempts to identify the R&D activities and also to investigate the estimation-methods, the techniques of scientific and technological activities and the measurement problems for productivity growth. Some of the main questions addressed in this chapter try to answer the questions below:

- How can we model and measure innovation and knowledge for productivity growth?
- What are the main effects of innovation activities and knowledge- based economy on productivity growth?

Chapter 4 investigates the role of FDIs (Foreign Direct Investments) in the context of national systems of innovation. This chapter attempts to investigate how the way in which "knowledge" can be developed and disseminated and the particular effects on socio-economic effects on modernisation, competitiveness and integration process.

Finally, Chapter 5 deals with the challenges and the institutional matters for the European policy-makes encounter and the effects on regional growth and economic integration, including technology policy, other related policies, the distribution of EU funds, regional development and productivity problems. To do this, it examines critically the claims of regional disadvantage and examines the factors that influence regional economic and social conditions. We would also like to tackle upon the following four issues in this chapter:

- Why is innovation important for European regional economic development?
- Why is the regional dimension important for innovation promotion?
- What has our policy response been so far and what lessons have we learnt from it?
- Finally, what are our action lines for the future?

I would like to thank Dr. Ekaterini Nikolarea, University of the Aegean, for her help in English-proofing this project. Finally, I would also like to thank the anonymous reviewer of the volume, and above all, my publisher for the great encouragement and support.

George M. Korres
Leeds, UK
2007

List of Abbreviations

BERD	Business Expenditures in Research and Development
CEC	Commission of European Communities
CIS	Community Innovation Survey
CITP	Corporate Income Tax Rate
CSFs	Community Structural Funds
EAGGF	Guidance European Agricultural Guidance and Guarantee Fund
EC	European Community
EIMS	European Innovation Monitoring System
EMU	European Monetary Union
EPO	European Patent Office
ERA	European Research Area
ERDF	European Regional Development Fund
ESF	European Social Fund
EU	European Union
FDIs	Foreign Direct Investments
FIFG	Financial Instrument for Fisheries Guidance
GBAORD	Government Appropriations or Outlays for Research and Development
GDP	Gross Domestic Product
GERD	Gross Expenditures in Research and Development
GFCF	Gross Fixed Capital Formation
GNP	Gross National Product
GUF	General University Funds
HDI	Human Development Index
HRST	Human Researchers in Science and Technology
IC	Industrial Concentration
ICT	Information Technology and Communications
IDAs	Individual Development Accounts
IMF	International Monetary Fund
IMPs	Integrated Mediterranean Programmes
ISC	International Standard Classification
IT	Information Technology
KBE	Knowledge-based Economy
LD	Law Decree
LFRs	Less Favoured Regions
MERCOSUR	South American Common Market
MIPs	Million Instructions per Second

MNEs	Multinational Enterprises
NAFTA	North American Free Trade Agreement
NUTS	Nomenclature of Territorial Units for Statistics
OECD	Organisation for Economic Co-operation and Development
PAET	Five-year Plan for Research and Technology
PAVE	Programme for the Development of Industrial Research
PENED	Programme to Boost Scientific Potential
PPS	Purchase Power Parity
RCA	Revealed Comparative Advantage
R&D or (RD)	Research and Development
RDH	Research and Development Activities per Inhabitant
RDI	Research Development Intensity.
RDP	Regional Domestic Product
RSE	Research Scientists Engineers
R&T	Research and Technology
RTD	Research, Technology and Development
RTD&I	Research and Technological Development and Innovation
SEA	Single European Act
SGRT	Secretariat General of Research and Technology
SMEs	Small Medium Enterprises
SNSS	Secretariat of National Statistical Service
UN	United Nations
UNCTAD	United Nations Conferences on Trade and Development
WTO	World Trade Organization

Chapter 1
Knowledge Economy and Innovation Activities: An Approach to Definitions and Measurement

1. Introduction

Scientific and technological innovation may be considered the transformation of an idea into a new or improved product introduced to the market, into a new or improved operational process used in industry and commerce, or into a new approach to a social service. The word "innovation" can have different meanings in different contexts and the one chosen will depend on the particular objectives of measurement or analysis. So far, international norms for data collection proposed in the Oslo Manual have been developed only for technological innovation.

Technological innovations comprise new products and processes and significant technological changes in products and processes. An innovation has been implemented if it has been introduced to the market (product innovation) or used within a production process (process innovation). Therefore, innovations involve a series of scientific, technological, organizational, financial and commercial activities. R&D is only one of these activities and may be carried out at different phases of the innovation process, acting not only as the original source of inventive ideas but also as a form of problem-solving which can be called at any point up to implementation.

This chapter deals with *"technologically"* new or improved products and processes. The meaning of the label "technological", as applied to products and processes, and its precise scope in surveys and studies, can be unclear. This is particularly true in an international context. It is not always easy to distinguish between the special meaning attributed here and the dictionary definitions of the word which may differ subtly between countries, as well as the nuances of the word to which respondents may react. For example, it was felt that in the service industries "technological" might be understood as "using high-tech plant and equipment".

Innovation is a complex and multifaceted phenomenon. Technological innovation – even in its broad sense used in the Oslo Manual – is only a part of a set of activities firms carry out to keep or improve their competitiveness. From a statistical point of view, it is not an easy task to identify when technological innovation activities take place or to collect data on activities related to innovation, including scientific research. It is not surprising that several problems have been recorded during the implementation of the survey on innovation. The two most important are the following:

- proposed definitions on technological innovation may not have been fully understood by firms;
- data on technological innovation of firms appear to be substantially different from those referred to manufacturing firms and should be carefully interpreted.

Innovation is about taking risks and managing changes. It is about economics over and above research, science and technology. Some have defined it as "profitable change", others as economic exploitation of new ideas; a more business-related definition could be: "Innovation means harnessing creativity to invent new or improved products, equipment or services which are successful on the market and thus add value to businesses" (Guy de Vaucleroy, European Business Summit, Brussels June 2000).

Moreover, according to Joseph Schumpeter:

Innovation is at the root of the evolution of the economic system and its main engine for change and 'creative destruction'.

According to the Oslo Manual, a probable definition of *technological innovation* suggested to firms surveyed by: "the set of knowledge, professional skills, procedures, capabilities, equipment, and technical solutions required to manufacture goods or provide services". The *innovation in process* is "the adoption of technologically new methods in production or new methods to provide services. Several changes concerning equipment, production organization or both may be required".

Three main topics related to such difficulties will be discussed in this chapter:

- how definitions of technological innovation should be applied; several factors should be actually taken into account, including: the relation between technological and non-technological innovations;
- what the characteristics of Research and Development (R&D) are; and also
- how we can apply and estimate the main implications and the effects through these variables.

The appendix at the end of this book gives a description from the main definitions, measurement and methodological approaches on innovation, research, scientific and technological activities.

2. Knowledge and Innovation Activities

2.1 Defining the Leading Indicators

Joseph Schumpeter is often mentioned as the first economist to have drawn attention to the importance of innovation and to having defined five types of innovation; ranging from introducing a new product to changes in industrial organization. The Oslo Manual clarifies the definition of the two more technical definitions, but it still appears that "innovation" is not easy to define precisely.

In principle, according to Schumpter's theory, we may consider that innovation can result from technology transfer or the development of new business concepts. It can be therefore technological, organizational or presentational. It is clear there are links between research and innovation, with the research laboratory being the optimal starting point.

Technology transfer is the process by which existing knowledge and capabilities developed with public R&D funding are used to fulfil public and private needs. It is the share of knowledge and facilities among public institutions and private organizations to increase productivity generate new industry, improve living standards and public services. Technology transfer from public research institutions can occur either through mechanisms -such as scientific publications, training of students, and continuing education of engineers already working in industry- or through specific measures taken.

The *Oslo Manual* (OECD 1997a) defines technological product and process innovations as those implemented in technologically new products and processes and in significant technological improvements in products and processes.

Technological product and process (TPP) innovations comprise implemented technologically new products and processes and significant technological improvements in products and processes. A TPP innovation has been implemented if it has been introduced to the market (product innovation) or used within a production process (process innovation). TPP innovations involve a series of scientific, technological, organizational, financial and commercial activities. The TPP innovating firm is one that has implemented technologically new or significantly technologically improved products or processes during the period under review.

Technological product innovation can take two broad forms:

- *Technologically new products* A technologically new product is a product whose technological characteristics or intended uses differ significantly from those of previously produced products. Such innovations either can involve radically new technologies, or can be based on combined existing technologies in new uses, or can be derived from the use of new knowledge.
- *Technologically improved products* A technologically improved product is an existing product whose performance has been significantly enhanced

or upgraded. A simple product may be improved (in terms of better performance or lower cost) by the use of higher-performance components or materials or a complex product consisting of a number of integrated technical sub-systems, which may be improved by partial changes to one of the sub-systems.

The distinction between a technologically new product and a technologically improved product may pose difficulties for some industries, notably in services.

Technological process innovation is the adoption of technologically new or significantly improved production methods, including methods of product delivery. These methods may involve changes in equipment, or production organization, or a combination of these changes, and may be derived from the use of new knowledge. The methods may be intended to produce or deliver technologically new or improved products, which cannot be produced or delivered using conventional production methods, or essentially to increase the production or delivery efficiency of existing products.

Table 1.1 illustrates the innovation and not-innovation activities. Innovation indicators measure aspects of the industrial innovation process and the resources devoted to innovation activities. They also provide qualitative and quantitative information about the factors that enhance or hinder innovation, the impact of innovation, the performance of the enterprise and about the diffusion of innovation. The variables commonly used for S-R&T activities are:

- R&D expenditure
- R&D personnel
- Patents of New Technologies

The concept of Scientific and Technological Activities has been developed by OECD and UNESCO and EUROSTAT. According to 'International Standardization of Statistics on Science and Technology', we can consider as scientific and technological activities as: "The systematic activities which are closely concerned with the generation, advancement, dissemination and application of scientific and technical knowledge in all fields of scientific and technology. These include activities on R&D, scientific and technical education and training and scientific and technological services".

Furthermore, we can distinguish R&D activities from Scientific and Technical Education and Training and Scientific and Technological Services.

Table 1.1 Innovation and non-innovation activities

			Innovation		Not innovation
			New to the World	New to the Firm	Already in the Firm
Innovation	Technologically new	Product			
		Production Process			
		Delivery Process			
	Significantly technologically improved	Product			
		Production Process			
		Delivery Process			
		Organisation			
Non Innovation	No significant change. Change without novelty or other creative improvements	Product			
		Production Process			
		Delivery Process			
		Organisation			

Source: OECD (2002a).

"Scientific and Technical Education and Training activities comprising specialised non-university higher education and training, higher education and training leading to a university degree, post-graduate and further training, and organised lifelong training for scientists and engineers", while Scientific and Technological Services consider as comprising: "scientific and technological activities of libraries, museums, data collection on socio-economic phenomena, testing, standardization and quality control and patent and license activities by public bodies".

There is a huge literature studying the effects of innovation activities. However, only a small part of it studies the effects of innovation activities to a regional level. One of the major problems with the measurement of innovation activities is the availability of disaggregate data and the lack of information at a regional level (in particular, for the less advanced technological countries).

According to the definition provided by UNCTAD, technology can be considered as: "the essential input to production which can embodied either in capital and in intermediate goods or in the human labour and in manpower or finally in information which is provided through markets" (United Nations 1983).

Nevertheless, we can distinguish between *technology transfer* and *technology capacity* (that is the flow of *knowledge* as against the *stock of knowledge*), and *technology of innovation* (which indicates the type of technology that enables the country's recipients to establish a new infrastructure or upgrade obsolete technologies).

The most widely used definitions of research and innovation activities are provided by the *Frascati-Manual*. In an effort to standardise definitions and data collection on research expenditures, the Organisation of Economic Cooperation and Development (OECD) has proposed in the so-called *Frascati Manual* (1981, and 1989) that: "Research and Experimental Development comprise creative work undertaken on a systematic basis in order to increase the stock of knowledge ... and the use of this stock of knowledge to devise new applications".

Within this general definition, *pure research* broadly corresponds to activities aimed at enhancing knowledge growth, whereas *applied research* involves the search for applications. *Development* concerns the activities of design, implementation, and prototype manufacturing of the new applications themselves.

From a statistical point of view, while when measuring research and innovation activities there are two inputs:

- The people who work in research activities and
- The expenditures related to research and technological activities.

Research data usually refer to research expenditures (such as gross research expenditures) or innovation criteria (such as the number of external patent applications and the national patent applications) and to the scientific criteria (such as research and scientific personnel).

Expenditure on research activities may be spent within the statistical unit (*intramural*) or outside (*extamural*). According to the OECD, *intramural expenditures* are defined as: "All expenditure on research activities performed within a statistical unit or sector of the economy, whatever the source of funds. Expenditures made outside the statistical-unit or sector but in support of intramural R&D (such as, purchase of supplies of R&D) are included. In addition, for R&D purposes, both current and capital expenditures are measured, while depreciation payments are excluded".

The main disadvantage of R&D input series expressed in monetary terms is that they are affected by differences in price levels over time and across countries.

Compared to the output measures, the input measures do not offer qualitative or other efficiency indicators for current innovation activities and scientific manpower inputs. Scientific and technological indicators may also be used to measure the effects of a given technology on the welfare of a specific target group of people.

R&D is an activity during which there are significant transfers among units, organizations and sectors. R&D activities are usually classified under the following three headings:

.

- *Basic research*, which can be defined as: "Experimental or theoretical work undertaken primarily to acquire new knowledge of the underlying foundations of phenomena and observable facts, without any particular application or use in view".
- *Applied research*, which is: "Original investigation undertaken in order to acquire new knowledge, which however is directed primarily towards a specific practical aim or objective".
- *Experimental development*, which can be defined as: "Systematic word, drawing on existing knowledge gained from research and practical experience, that is directed to producing new materials, products and devices, to installing new processes, systems and services and also to improve substantially those already produced or installed".

The European Commission uses slightly different variation of these definitions and makes the following classification:

- *Fundamental research*, which is similar to the Basic Research as defined by OECD (in Frascati Manual (1981) and (1989));
- *Basic industrial R&D*, which is concerned with the development of industrial technology;
- *Applied R&D*, which refers to the application of technologies to the new products.

The figures of GERD (*Gross Expenditures of Research and Development*) include those research and technological activities which are performed within a country, but they exclude payments for research and technological activities which are made abroad.

The figures of *Gross National Expenditure on R&D* (GNERD) comprises the aggregate total expenditure on research and innovation activities financed by the institutions of a country during a given period and include the research activities performed abroad but financed by the national institutions; R&D performed within a country but funded from abroad should be excluded. In addition, according to Frascatti Manual, OECD, the *Gross Domestic Expenditure on R&D* (GERD) can be defined as the total expenditures on R&D performed on the national territory during a given period.

Beside R&D, six fields of innovative activities may often be distinguished in the innovation process:

- *Tooling-up and industrial engineering* cover acquisition of and changes in production machinery and tools and in production and quality control procedures, methods, and standards required to manufacture the new product or to use the new process.
- *Manufacturing start-up and preproduction development* may include product or process modifications, retraining personnel in the new techniques

or in the use of new machinery, and trial production if it implies further design and engineering.

- *Marketing for new products* covers activities in connection with launching of a new product. These may include market tests, adaptation of the product to different markets and launch of advertising, but will exclude the building of distribution networks for market innovations.
- *Acquisition of disembodied technology* includes acquisition of external technology in the form of patents, non-patented inventions, licenses, disclosure of know-how, trademarks, designs, patterns, and services with a technological content.
- *Acquisition of embodied technology* covers acquisition of machinery and equipment with a technological content connected with either product or process innovations introduced by the firm.
- *Design* is an essential part of the innovation process. It covers plans and drawings aimed at defining procedures, technical specifications, and operational features necessary to the conception, development, manufacturing and marketing of new products and processes. It may be a part of the initial conception of the product or process, as for instance, research and experimental development, but it may also be associated with tooling-up, industrial engineering, manufacturing start-up, and marketing of new products.

Measurement of the *personnel employed on research activities* involves, firstly, the identification of what types of personnel should be initially included, and, secondly, the measurement of research activities in the full time equivalent. Personnel is a more concrete measure and, since labour costs normally account for 50-70% of total R&D expenditures, it is also a reasonable short-term indicator of efforts devoted to R&D. Personnel can be defined as: "All the persons directly on R&D, as well as those providing direct services such as R&D, managers, administrators and clerical staff. In particular, *Research personnel* can be considered either as the number of *researchers, scientists and engineers*, or the *technicians and equivalent staff*".

According to OECD (1981):

- *Researchers, scientists and engineers* are usually those who are: "Engaged in the conception or creation of new knowledge, products, processes, methods and systems".
- *Technicians and equivalent staff* include those: "Who participate in R&D projects by performing S&T tasks normally under the supervision of scientific and engineers".

R&D personnel data are not affected by differences in currency values. However, there are some problems with the classification of full-time with the equivalent and person-years-on-R&D.

Technological balance can be considered as what measures a country's balance of payments and receipts concerning the sale and purchase of knowledge and technological information.

Patent data applications can be considered as partial proxy measures of the output of R&D in the form of inventions. Information about the country concerned is completed with data for *external patent applications (EPA)* by the residents of the country for patents in other countries. The data cover applications processed through national and international patent offices

Finally, we can define as *patents*: "The right which is granted by a government to an inventor in exchange for the publication of the invention and entitles the inventor for an agreed period to prevent any third party from using the invention in any way".

International technological competitiveness has become an increasingly important issue. However, *high technology* is not a well-defined issue in economics. For some authors *high technology* is defined by R&D intensity and R&D activities. OECD, UN and US Department of Commerce use the classification of high technology industries which is based on the criterion of R&D expenditures. The International Trade Classification, the Lower Saxony Institute for Economic Research and the Fraunhofer Institute for Systems and Innovation Research have designed a new list of R&D intensive products.

Table 1.2 presents the product groups considered to have been fall into high technology categories; this list divides the R&D intensive sector into two parts: *the leading edge products* and *the high level technology products*. *Leading edge technology* includes the products that are subject to protectionism, such as aeronautics, and nuclear energy, whereas, the *high level products* include the mass consumption products. Patent statistics measure innovation activities, while R&D data measures both innovation and imitating activities. From *the patent index*, it seems that the (absolute) technological difference is bigger than that indicated by research expenditures.

The use of research and technological data imply a lot of problems with the collection and measurement. The problems of data quality and comparability are characteristic for the whole range of data on dynamic socio-economic activities. However, most of the research and technological indicators capture technological investment in small industries and in small firms only imperfectly. Usually, only manufacturing firms with more than 10,000 employees have established some research and technological laboratories, while industrial units with less than 1,000 employees usually do not have any particular research activities. Finally, the research and technological statistics concentrate mostly on the manufacturing sectors, while neglecting some service activities.

Table 1.2   Classification of R&D intensive products

(SITC) PRODUCT GROUP	(SITC) PRODUCT GROUP
Leading-edge technology	High-level technology
(516) Advanced organic chemicals	(266) Synthetic fibres
(525) Radioactive materials	(277) Advanced industrial abrasives
(541) Pharmaceutical products	(515) Heterocyclic chemistry
(575) Advanced plastics	(522) Rare inorganic chemicals
(591) Agricultural chemicals	(524) Other precious chemicals
(714) Turbines and reaction engines	(531) Synthetic colouring matter
(718) Nuclear, water, wind power generators	(533) Pigments, paints, varnishes
(752) Automatic data processing machines	(542) Medicaments
(764) Telecommunications equipment	(551) Essential oils, perfume, flavour
(774) Medical electronics	(574) Polyethers and resins
(776) Semi-conductor devices	(598) Advanced chemical products
(778) Advanced electrical machinery	(663) Mineral manufacturers, fine ceramics
(792) Aircraft and spacecraft	(689) Precious non-ferrous base metals
(871) Advanced optical instruments	(724) Textile and leather machinery
(874) Advanced measuring instruments	(725) Chapter and pulp machinery
(891) Arms and ammunition	(726) Printing and bookbinding machinery
	(727) Industrial food processing machines
	(728) Advanced machine-tools
	(731) Machine tools working by removing
	(733) Machine tools without removing
	(735) Parts for machine tools
	(737) Advanced metalworking equipment
	(741) Industrial handling equipment
	(744) Other non-electrical machinery
	(746) Boll and roller bearings
	(751) Office machines, word-processing
	(759) Advanced parts for computers
	(761) Television and video equipment
	(762) Radiobroadcast, radio telephony goods
	(763) Sound and video recorders
	(772) Traditional electronics
	(773) Optical fibre and other cables
	(781) Motor vehicles for persons
	(782) Motor vehicles for goods transport
	(791) Railway vehicles
	(872) Medical instruments and appliances
	(873) Traditional measuring equipment
	(881) Photographic apparatus and equipment
	(882) Photo and cinematographic supplies
	(884) Optical fibres, contact, other lenses

Source: Grupp, H. (1995).

The collection of R&D data of regional statistics implies a lot of problems in comparison to data of national statistics. For the collection of regional statistics, we should take into account the local differences and difficulties. R&D units can operate in more than one regions and we should allocate these activities between regions. Usually, regional statistics focus on the three first levels of NUTS (Nomenclature of Territorial Units for Statistics). The reliability of R&D and innovation regional statistics is directly connected with and depends on estimation-methods and application of statistical techniques.

Another important question about R&D and innovation regional statistics is the confidentiality and the collection-method of data-set that may be cover the whole or the majority of local-units. For statistical methods focused on a regional level, we can use either "local-units" (as for instance, enterprises, office, manufacturing etc.) or "local-economic-units" (NACE codes, which is a division of national codes of European member states).

Therefore, we can use the first method "top-to-the-bottom method" for the collection of aggregate R&D data (corresponds to the whole country) and, after that, for the distribution of these figures into a regional-level. The disadvantage of this method is that there is not a direct collection of data from the regions.

The second method "bottom-to-the-top method" for the collection of dissaggregate R&D data (for the whole regions) is based on the direct-collection at a regional-level and, after that, on the summation of these figures in order to obtain the aggregate-total R&D data (for the whole country). The advantage of this method is that there is a consistency in the summary of figures between regional and national level.

Resources allocated to a country's R&D efforts are measured while the two indicators: R&D expenditure and personnel are used. For R&D expenditure, the main aggregate data used for international comparisons is gross domestic expenditure on R&D (GERD), which represents a country's domestic R&D-related expenditure for a given year. The R&D data are compiled on the basis of the methodology of the Frascati Manual 2002 (OECD, Paris 2002).

Furthermore, diffusion is defined as the way in which innovations spread, through market or non-market channels, from their first implementation anywhere in the world, to other countries and regions and to other industries/markets and firms. In order to map innovation activities and draw a picture both of some of the links involved and of the level of diffusion of advanced technologies, the following topics are proposed.

2.2 Leading Measures

R&D input and output
R&D covers both formal R&D in R&D units and informal or occasional R&D in other units. However, interest in R&D depends more on the new knowledge and innovations and their economic and social effects than on the activity itself.

Unfortunately, while indicators of R&D output are clearly needed to complement input statistics, they are very difficult to define and produce.

The output of R&D or science and technology (S&T) in general can be measured in several ways. Innovation surveys are an attempt to measure outputs and the effects of innovation process in which R&D plays an important role. A manual of innovation surveys has been issued and revised by OECD.

Scientific and Technological Activities (STA)
UNESCO has developed a broad concept of STA (Scientific and Technological Activities) and included in its "Recommendation concerning the International Standardisation of Statistics on Science and Technology" (UNESCO 1978). In addition to R&D, scientific and technological activities comprise scientific and technical education and training (STET) and scientific and technological services (STS). The latter include, for example, S&T activities of libraries and museums, translation and editing of S&T literature, surveying and prospecting, data collection of socio-economic phenomena, testing, standardization and quality control, client counselling and advisory services, patent and licensing activities by public bodies. R&D (defined similarly by UNESCO and OECD) is thus to be distinguished from both STET (Scientific and Technical Education and Training) and STS (Scientific and Technological Services).

R&D and Technological Innovation
Technological innovation activities are the scientific, technological, organisational, financial and commercial steps, including investments in new knowledge, which actually, or are intended to, lead to the implementation of technologically new or improved products and processes. R&D is only one of these activities and may be carried out different phases of the innovation process. It may act not only as the original source of inventive ideas but also as a means of problem solving which can be called upon at any point of implementation.

Besides R&D, other forms of innovative activities may be distinguished in the innovation process. According to the *Oslo Manual* (OECD 1997a), these are "acquisition of disembodied technology and know-how, acquisition of embodied technology, tooling up and industrial engineering, industrial design, other capital acquisition, production start-up and marketing for new or improved products".

Measures of R&D Inputs: R&D Personnel
The measurement of personnel employed in R&D involves three exercises:

- identifying which types of personnel should be initially included
- measuring their number
- measuring their R&D activities in full-time equivalent (person-years)

All persons employed directly in R&D should be counted, as well as those providing direct services such as R&D managers, administrators and clerical staff. For statistical purposes, two inputs are measured: R&D expenditures and R&D personnel. Both inputs are normally measured on an annual basis, how much spent during a year, how many person-years used during a year. Both series have their strengths and weaknesses, and, in consequence, both are necessary to secure an adequate representation of the effort devoted to R&D.

Data on the utilisation of scientific and technical personnel provide concrete measurements for international comparisons of resources devoted to R&D. It is recognised, however, that R&D inputs are only one part of the input of a nation's human resources to the public welfare; scientific and technical personnel contribute much more to industrial, agricultural and medical progress with their involvement in production, operations, quality control, management, education and other functions. The measurement of these stocks of scientific and technical manpower is the subject of the *Canberra Manual* (OECD 1995). The focus in this Manual is the measurement and classification of R&D resources instead. For R&D personnel data, the problem lies in reducing such data to full-time equivalent (FTE) or person-years spent on R&D. The national R&D effort requires a wide variety of personnel. Because of the range of skills and education required, it is essential to classify R&D personnel into categories.

R&D Expenditures
Expenditure on R&D may be made within the statistical unit (intramural) or outside it (extramural) R&D expenditure data should be compiled on the basis of performers' reports of intramural expenditures. Intramural expenditures are all expenditures for R&D performed within a statistical unit or sector of the economy, whatever the source of funds. Expenditures made outside the statistical unit or sector but supporting intramural R&D (as for instance, purchase of supplies for R&D) are included; both current and capital expenditures are included.

Research and experimental development (R&D) comprise creative work undertaken on a systematic basis in order to increase the stock of knowledge, including knowledge of man, culture and society, and the use of this stock of knowledge to devise new applications. R&D is a term covering three activities: basic research, applied research, and experimental development.

The basic measure is "*intramural expenditures*"; that is expenditures for R&D performed within a statistical unit or sector of the economy. Another measure, "extramural expenditures", covers payments for R&D performed outside the statistical unit or sector of the economy. For R&D purposes, both current costs and capital expenditures are measured. In the case of government sector, expenditures refer to direct rather than indirect expenditures; depreciation costs are excluded.

R&D is an activity involving significant transfers of resources among units, organisations and sectors and especially between government and other performers. It is important for science policy advisors and analysts to know who finances R&D and who performs it. The main disadvantage of expressing R&D input series in monetary terms is that they are affected by differences in price levels between countries and over time. It can be shown that current exchange rates often do not reflect the balance of R&D prices between countries and that in times of high inflation general price indexes do not accurately reflect trends in the cost of performing R&D.

Labour costs. These comprise annual wages and salaries and all associated costs or fringe benefits – such as bonus payments, holiday pay, contributions to pension funds and other social security payments, payroll taxes, etc. Labour costs of persons providing indirect services and which are not included in the personnel data (such as security and maintenance personnel or the staff of central libraries, computer departments, or head offices) should be excluded and included in other current costs. Only the actual "salaries"/stipends and similar expenditures associated with postgraduate students should be reported.

Other current costs. These comprise non-capital purchases of materials, supplies and equipment to support R&D performed by the statistical unit in a given year. Examples are: water and fuel (including gas and electricity); books, journals, reference materials, subscriptions to libraries, scientific societies and so on; imputed or actual cost of small prototypes or models made outside the research organisation; materials for laboratories (chemicals, animals, etc.). Administrative and other overhead costs (such as interest charges and office, post and telecommunications, and insurance costs) should also be included, if necessary, prorated to allow for non-R&D activities within the same statistical unit. All expenditures on indirect services should be included here, whether carried out within the organisation concerned or hired or purchased from outside suppliers.

Gross Domestic Expenditure on R&D (GERD)
GERD is total intramural expenditure on R&D performed on the national territory. GERD includes R&D performed within a country and funded from abroad but excludes payments made abroad for R&D.

Classification Systems for R&D
To understand R&D activity and its role, one must examine it in terms of the organisations performing and funding R&D (institutional classification) and in terms of the nature of the R&D programs themselves (functional distribution).

Globalisation of R&D and R&D Co-operation
Various studies have shown that R&D activities are more and more a worldwide activity and that a bigger share of R&D is performed in co-operation with individual researchers, research teams and research units. Multinational enterprises play an increasing role as does R&D co-operation between university and other research units and enterprises, both formally, via organisations such as the European Union (EU) or the European Organisation for Nuclear Research (CERN), or informally, via multilateral and bilateral agreements. There is a clear need for more information on these trends.

Research and Experimental Development (R&D): R&D Surveys, Reliability of Data and International Comparability

It is hard to generalise about how much such estimates are necessary or how much they affect the reliability of the data, as the situation will vary from country to country. Nevertheless, it is generally the case that "subjective" estimation by respondents is probably greatest for the breakdown between basic research, applied research and experimental development, while the use of "rule of thumb" estimation by survey agencies is probably greatest for R&D in the higher education sector.

Table 1.3 Type of variables, titles and sources for the measurement of scientific and technological activities

Type of main variables	Titles and sources
Research and Development (R&D)	**Frascati Manual**: "Standard Practice of Research and Experimental Development" and **Frascati Manual Supplement**: "Research and Development Statistics and Output Measurement in the Higher Education Sector".
Technology Balance of Payments	**OECD**: "Manual for the Measurement and Interpretation of Technology Balance of Payments Data"
Innovation	**Oslo Manual**: OECD Proposed Guidelines for Collecting and Interpreting Technological Innovation Data
Patents	**OECD-Patent Manual**: "Using Patent Data as Science and Technology Indicators"
Scientific and Technical Personnel	**OECD-Canberrra Manual**: "The Measurement of Human Resources Devoted to Science and Technology"
High Technology	**OECD**: "Revision of High Technology Sector and Product Classification"
Bibliometrics	**OECD**: "Bibliometric Indicators and Analysis of Research Systems, Methods and Examples" (Working Chapter – Yoshika Okibo).
Globalisation	**OECD**: "Manual of Economic Clobalisation Indicators"
Education Statistics	**OECD**: "OECD Manual for Comparative Education Statistics"
Education Classification	**OECD**: "Classifying Educational Programmes: Manual for Implementation in OECD countries"
Training Statistics	**OECD**: "Manual for Better Training Statistics: Conceptual Measurement and Survey Issues"

Source: OECD (2001c).

Research and experimental development (R&D) comprise creative work undertaken on a systematic basis in order to increase the stock of knowledge, including knowledge of human beings, culture and society, and the use of this stock of knowledge to devise new applications.

Table 1.3 illustrates some of the main type of variables in relation to the measurement of scientific and technological activities and the Titles and Sources from which they derived. However, R&D statistics is not enough. Within the context of the knowledge-based economy, it has become increasingly clear that such data need to be examined within a conceptual framework that relates them both to other types of resources and to the desired outcomes of given R&D activities. Similarly, R&D personnel data need to be viewed as part of a model for the training and use of scientific and technical personnel. R&D covers three activities:

- basic research,
- applied research and
- experimental development.

Basic research is "experimental or theoretical work undertaken primarily to acquire new knowledge of the underlying foundation of phenomena and observable facts, without any particular application or use in view". Basic research analyses properties, structures, and relationships to formulate and test hypotheses, theories or laws. The results of basic research are not sold; they are rather published in scientific journals or circulated to interested colleagues. Occasionally, basic research may be "classified" for security reasons.

Applied research is also "original investigation undertaken in order to acquire new knowledge". It is, however, directed primarily towards a specific practical aim or objective. The results of applied research are intended primarily to be valid for a single or limited number of products, operations, methods, or systems. Applied research develops ideas into operational form. The knowledge or information derived from it is often patented but may also be kept secret.

Experimental development is "systematic work, drawing on existing knowledge gained from research and/or practical experience, which is directed to producing new materials, products or devices, to installing new processes, systems and services, or to improving substantially those already produced or installed". R&D covers both formal R&D in R&D units and informal or occasional R&D in other units".

Table 1.4 reports the three main types of research namely basic research, applied research and experimental research in the Social Sciences and Humanities.

Table 1.4 Three types of research in social sciences and humanities

Basic research	Applied research	Experimental development
Study of causal relations between economic conditions and social development	Study of the economic and social causal of agricultural workers rural districts to towns, for the purpose	Development and testing of a program of financial assistance to prevent rural immigrants to large cities
Study of the social structure and the socio-occupational mobility of a society	Development of a model using the data obtained in order to foresee future consequences of recent trends in social mobility	Development and testing of a program to stimulate spread mobility among certain social and ethic groups
Study of the role of the family in different civilizations past and present	Study of the role and position of the family in a specific country or a specific region at the present time for the purpose of preparing relevant social measures	Development and testing of a program to maintain family structure in low income working groups
Study of the reading process in adults and children	Study of the reading process for the purpose of developing new method of teaching children and adults to read	Development and testing of a special reading program among immigrant children
Ding Study of the international factors influencing national economic development	Study of the national factors determining the economic development of a country in a given period with a view to formulating an operational model for modifying government foreign trade policy	–
Study of specific aspects of a particular language	Study of the of the children aspects of a language for the purpose of devising a new method of teaching that language or of translating from or into that language	–
Study of the historical development of a language.	–	–
Study of sources of all kinds (i.e. manuscripts, documents, buildings, etc), in order to better comprehend historical phenomena (for instance, political, social, cultural development of a country, biography of an individual etc)	–	–

Source: UNESCO (1984) "Manual for Statistics on Scientific and Technological Activities".

Business Enterprise R&D Expenditure (BERD)
Business enterprise R&D (BERD) covers R&D activities carried out in the business sector by performing firms and institutes, regardless of the origin of funding. While the government and higher education sectors also carry out R&D, industrial R&D is most closely linked to the creation of new products and production techniques, as well as with a country's innovation efforts. The business enterprise sector includes: all firms, organisations and institutions whose primary activity is production of goods and services for sale to the general public at an economically significant price.

Characteristics of GBAORD
GBAORD (Government Appropriations or Outlays for R&D) measures the funds committed by the federal/central government for R&D (including those by international organisations) to be carried out in one of the four sectors of performance – business enterprise, government, higher education, private non-profit sector – at home or abroad. These data are usually based on budgetary sources and reflect the views of funding agencies. They are generally considered less internationally comparable than the performer-reported data used in other tables and graphs; yet they have the advantage of being more time and reflecting current government priorities, as expressed in the breakdown of socio-economic objectives. A first distinction can be made between defence programs, which are concentrated in a small number of countries, and civil programs, which can be broken down as follows:

- Economic development: agricultural production and technology; industrial production and technology; infrastructure and general planning of land use; production, distribution and rational utilisation of energy.
- Health and environment: protection and improvement of human health, social structures and relationships, control and care of the environment, exploration and exploitation of the Earth.
- Exploration and exploitation of space.
- Non-oriented research.
- Research financed by General University Funds (GUF). The estimated R&D content of block grants to universities.

Patent Statistics
A patent is an intellectual property related to inventions in the technical field. A patent may be granted to a firm, an individual or a public body by a patent office. An application for a patent has to meet certain requirements: the invention has to be novel, involve a (non-obvious) inventive step and be applied to industry. A patent is valid in a given country for a limited period (20 years).

For purposes of international comparison, statistics on patent applications are preferable to statistics on patents granted because of the lag between application date and grant date, which may be up to ten years in certain countries.

Patent indicators based on simple counts of patents filed at an intellectual property office are influenced by various sources of bias, such as weaknesses in international comparability (home advantage for patent applications) or high heterogeneity in patent values within a single office.

The Technology Balance of Payments (TBP)

Technology Balance of Payments (TBP) registers the international flow of industrial property and know-how. The following operations are included in the TBP: patents (purchases, sales); licences for patents; know-how (not patented); models and designs; trademarks (including franchising); technical services; finance of industrial R&D outside national territory.

The "contribution to the trade balance" makes it possible to identify an economy's structural strengths and weaknesses via the composition of international trade flows. It takes into account not only exports, but also imports, and tries to eliminate business cycle variations by comparing an industry's trade balance with the overall trade balance. It can be interpreted as an indicator of "revealed comparative advantage", as it indicates whether an industry performs relatively better or worse than the manufacturing total, whether the manufacturing total itself is in deficit or surplus.

If there were no comparative advantage or disadvantage for any industry i, a country's total trade balance (surplus or deficit) should be distributed across industries according to their share in total trade. The "contribution to the trade balance" is the difference between the actual and the theoretical balance, as expressed in the following equations:

$$(X_i - M_i) - (X - M)\frac{(X_i + M_i)}{(X + M)}$$

where $(X_i - M_i)$ = observed industry trade balance

and $(X - M)\dfrac{(X_i + M_i)}{(X + M)}$ = theoretical trade balance

A positive value for an industry indicates a structural surplus and a negative one a structural deficit. The indicator is additive and individual industries can be grouped together by summing their respective values: by construction, the sum over all industries is zero.

3. Measurement of Leading Indicators of Knowledge and Innovation Activities

There are two main approaches to collecting data about innovations:

- The "subject approach" survey starts from the innovative behaviour and activities of the firm as a whole. The idea is to explore the factors influencing the innovative behaviour of the firm (strategies, incentives and barriers to innovation) and the scope of various innovation activities, and above all to get some idea of the outputs and effects of innovation. These surveys are designed to be representative of each industry as a whole, so the results can be grossed up and comparisons can be made between industries.
- The other survey approach involves the collection of data about specific innovations (usually a "significant innovation" of some kind, or the main innovation of a firm) – the "object approach". This starts by identifying a list of successful innovations, often on the basis of experts' evaluations or new product announcements in trade journals. The suggested approach is to collect some descriptive, quantitative and qualitative data about the particular innovation at the same time as data is sought about the firm.

The main expenditure aggregate used for international comparison is gross domestic expenditure on R&D (GERD), covering all expenditures for R&D performed on national territory in a given year. It thus includes domestically performed R&D, which is financed from abroad, but excludes R&D funds paid abroad, notably to international agencies. The corresponding personnel measure does not have a special name; it covers total personnel working on R&D (in FTE), on national territory, during a given year. International comparisons are sometimes restricted to researchers (or university graduates), because they are considered to be the true core of the R&D system.

As OECD documents mentioned, the national surveys providing R&D data that are reasonably accurate and relevant to national users' needs may not be internationally comparable. This may simply be because national definitions or classifications deviate from international norms. The situation is more complex when the national situation does not correspond to the international norms.

We can use these measures, in order to estimate to evaluate the effects on capacity, efficiency and growth. To measure *technological capacity, efficiency of the research and scientific structure*, and their effects on economic and regional growth it is necessary to use some of the above international indicators related to research, scientific and technological data. These indicators aim to evaluate innovation activities and technological infrastructure at a national level. In particular, the use of these indicators gives an overall view of *technological capabilities* and facilitates comparison between and within countries.

Table 1.5 R&D intensity* and export specialisation in high technology industries, 1999**

Countries	Export specialisation	R&D intensity
Canada	13.0	1.2
United States	38.3	3.0
Japan	30.7	3.2
Korea	34.2	1.3
Denmark	18.8	1.8
Finland	24.1	2.6
France	23.1	2.2
Germany	18.5	2.7
Ireland	46.0	1.1
Italy	10.6	0.8
Netherlands	25.1	1.6
Norway	10.7	1.2
Spain	9.3	0.6
Sweden	27.0	3.9
United Kingdom	32.4	2.1

Note: * Manufacturing R&D expenditures/manufacturing production. ** High technology exports/manufacturing exports.
Source: OECD, STAN and ANBERD databases, May 2001.

The use of research and technological data imply a lot of problems with the collection and measurement. The problems of data quality and comparability are characteristic for a whole range of data about dynamic socio-economic activities. However, most research and technological indicators capture technological investment in small industries and firms only imperfectly. Usually, only manufacturing firms with more than 10,000 employees have established some research and technological laboratories, while industrial units with less than 1,000 employees do not usually have any particular research activities. Finally, research and technological statistics concentrate mostly in the manufacturing sectors, while usually neglecting some service activities.

The collection of R&D data of regional statistics implies a lot of problems in comparison to data of national statistics. For the collection of regional statistics, we should take into the local differences and the difficulties. R&D units can operate in more than one region, and we should allocate these activities among regions. Usually, regional statistics focus on the three first levels of NUTS (Nomenclature of Territorial Units for Statistics).

The reliability of R&D and innovation regional statistics is directly connected and depends on estimation-method and the application of statistical technique. Another important question on R&D and innovation regional statistics is the confidentiality and the collection-method of data-set that may be cover the whole or the majority of local-units. For the statistical methods focused on a regional level, we can use either "local-units" (for instance, enterprises, office, manufacturing etc.) or "local-economic-units" (NACE codes, which are a division of national codes of European member states). Therefore, we can use the first method "top-to-the-bottom method" for the collection of aggregate R&D data (for the whole country) and, after that, for the distribution of these figures to a regional-level; the disadvantage of this method is that there is not a direct collection of data from the regions.

The second method "bottom-to-the-top method" for the collection of dissaggregate R&D data (for whole regions) is based on the direct collection at a regional-level and, after that, on the summation of these figures in order to obtain the aggregate-total R&D data (for the whole country); the advantage of this method is that there is a consistency in the summary of figures between regional and national level. Table 1.5 illustrates both the R&D intensity and the export specialisation for high technology industries. Furthermore, Table 1.6 shows the annual average growth rate of exports in high and medium-high technology industries.

Data about European Patent Applications refers to those fields designated to European Patent Office (EPO); the data presented are based on a special extraction from the European Patent Office and, therefore, the figures of total national patent applications are somewhat different from the national totals presented by European Patent Office itself.

Major sources of these data come from the OECD, the United Nations and the EU and local authorities. Since 1965, the statistics divisions of the OECD and UNESCO have organised the systematic collection, publication and standardisation of research and technological data. We can collect and present data both for Business, Government and Private non-profit sectors.

The *Business Enterprise Sector* includes all firms, organisations and institutions whose primary activity is the market production of goods or services (other than higher education) for sale to the general public at an economically significant price, and the private non-profit institutes mainly serving them. The core of the sector is made up of private enterprises (corporations or quasi-corporations) whether or they do not make profit. Among these enterprises these may be found some firms for which R&D is the main activity (commercial R&D institutes and laboratories). Any private enterprises producing higher education services should be included in the higher education sector. In addition, this sector includes public enterprises (public corporations and quasi-corporations owned by government units) mainly engaged in market production and sale of the kind of goods and services which are often produced by private enterprises, although, as a matter of policy, the price set for goods and services may be less than the full cost of production. This sector also includes non-profit institutions (NPIs) who are market producers of goods and services other than higher education.

Table 1.6 Annual average growth rate of exports in high and medium-high technology industries, 1990-1999

	High- and medium-high technology	Total manufacturing
Mexico	29.4	26.4
Ireland	17.6	13.3
Iceland	17.2	3.7
Turkey	15.1	9.7
Greece	10.6	2.4
New Zealand	10.1	3.2
Portugal	9.8	4.7
Spain	9.5	8.2
Australia	9.1	5.4
Canada	9.1	8.0
Finland	8.6	5.0
United States	8.5	7.9
Sweden	6.9	4.7
OECD	6.5	5.4
Belgium-Luxembourg	6.2	4.4
United Kingdom	6.0	4.9
France	5.9	4.5
Netherlands	5.9	3.4
Austria	5.8	4.6
EU	5.7	4.4
Norway	5.4	2.6
Denmark	4.8	3.2
Italy	4.7	4.0
Japan	4.2	4.0
Germany	4.0	3.1
Switzerland	3.8	3.2

Source: OECD, STAN database, May 2001.

The *Government Sector* consists of all departments, offices and other bodies furnished but normally do not sell to the community those common services, other than higher education, which cannot otherwise be conveniently and economically provided and administer the state and the economic and social policy of the community.

Public enterprises are included in the business enterprise sector, and NPIs controlled and mainly financed by government. Private non-profit sector includes both private or semi-public organisations and individuals and households. However, all enterprises serving government, those being financed and controlled by government, those offering higher education services or controlled by institutes of higher education should be excluded. Higher education comprises of all universities, colleges of technology and other institutes of post-secondary education. Finally, data from abroad includes all institutions and individuals located outside the political frontiers of a country, and all international organisations (except business enterprise) including facilities and operations within the frontiers of a country. Apart form the OECD and the UN research departments, there is another committee (the *Scientific and Technical Research Committee*) dealing with research and innovation statistics. The research and scientific indicators not only provide a view of the innovation and research structure of a given country but also indicate its *technological strength and capacity*.

Various research and technological indicators attempt to explain *technological relationships* at a specific point of time or for a whole period. The aim is to measure the nature, the capacity and the efficiency of scientific and technological activities both at a national level and at a sectoral level.

Table 1.7 illustrates in high-tech exports, the exports of high technology products as a share of total exports. This indicator is calculated as share of exports of all high technology products of total exports. High Technology products are defined as the sum of the following products: Aerospace, computers, office machinery, electronics, instruments, pharmaceuticals, electrical machinery and armament. The total exports for the EU do not include the intra-EU trade.

Technological indicators related to *output measures* are more meaningful than those related to *input measures* (such as the number of scientists and engineers which are involved in research activities or the number of research institutions), since the later say little about the achieved research.

Table 1.7 High-tech exports: Exports of high technology products as a share of total exports

	2000	2001	2002	2003	2004	2005	2006
EU: (27 countries)	21.39	21.23	18.88	18.56	18.49	18.78	16.67
Belgium	8.69	8.98	7.49	7.42	7.12	7.05	6.64
Bulgaria	1.64	1.77	2.56	2.91	2.54	2.91	3.34
Czech Republic	7.78	9.1	12.32	12.37	13.66	11.67	12.74
Denmark	14.43	13.99	15.02	13.45	13.32	14.86	12.83
Germany	16.08	15.8	15.15	14.76	15.36	14.79	13.62
Estonia	25.12	17.1	9.84	9.38	10.07	10.31	8.13
Ireland	40.54	40.8	35.35	29.91	29.08	29.54	28.88
Greece	7.46	6.19	6.56	7.52	7.12	5.97	5.72
Spain	6.37	6.11	5.71	5.91	5.7	5.65	4.72
France	25.47	25.6	21.88	20.74	20.07	19.07	17.84
Italy	8.53	8.58	8.21	7.1	7.08	6.94	6.42
Cyprus	3.04	3.99	3.46	4.2	15.89	31.56	21.35
Latvia	2.25	2.24	2.27	2.75	3.21	3.21	4.2
Lithuania	2.55	2.92	2.44	3.02	2.72	3.2	4.65
Luxembourg	20.56	27.91	24.71	29.63	29.46	37.99	40.59
Hungary	23.11	20.42	20.83	21.84	21.72	19.65	20.22
Malta	64.4	58.13	56.53	55.49	55.9	50.84	54.61
Netherlands	22.82	22.28	18.74	18.81	19.1	20.25	18.27
Austria	14.04	14.64	15.71	15.31	14.74	12.8	11.34
Poland	2.84	2.71	2.45	2.71	2.73	3.2	3.11
Portugal	5.57	6.94	6.36	7.48	7.49	6.81	6.96
Romania	4.63	4.97	3.09	3.31	3.08	3.11	3.85
Slovenia	4.46	4.83	4.86	5.8	5.2	4.26	4.48
Slovakia	2.87	3.17	2.63	3.28	4.68	6.4	5.37
Finland	23.48	21.14	20.9	20.58	17.77	22.05	18.13
Sweden	18.71	14.23	13.71	13.12	14.14	13.62	12.77
UK	28.89	29.79	28.64	24.42	22.8	22.14	26.48

Source: OECD, STAN database, May 2001.

Table 1.8 Researchers per thousand total employment, 2001

	Total of which business enterprise researchers	Others	Country share of total OECD researchers, 2000
Italy	1.1	1.7	2.0
Portugal	0.5	3.0	0.5
Greece	0.6	3.2	0.4
Poland	0.6	3.2	1.6
Hungary	1.1	2.8	0.4
Slovak Republic	1.1	3.4	0.3
Austria	3.0	1.8	0.6
Spain	1.2	3.8	2.3
Ireland	3.3	1.7	0.3
Netherlands	2.5	2.7	1.2
United Kingdom	3.2	2.3	5.0
EU	2.9	2.9	28.8
Canada	3.3	2.8	2.8
South Korea	4.7	1.7	3.2
OECD	4.1	2.4	–
Germany	4.0	2.7	7.7
Denmark	3.3	3.6	0.6
France	3.4	3.8	5.1
Australia	1.7	5.5	2.0
Belgium	4.1	3.4	0.9
New Zealand	1.9	5.8	0.3
United States	6.9	1.7	38.3
Norway	4.2	4.4	0.6
Japan	6.5	3.7	19.2
Sweden	6.4	4.2	1.2
Finland	9.0	6.8	1.0

Source: OECD, ANBERD and STAN databases.

Table 1.9 Estimates of the share of OECD gross domestic expenditure on R&D (GERD) and of total number of researchers by OECD country/zone

	Gross domestic expenditure on R&D (GERD)				Total number of researchers		
	1991	1995	2000	2001	1991	1995	2000
Canada	2.3	2.6	2.7	2.7	2.8	3.1	–
Mexico	–	0.4	–	–	–	0.7	–
United States	43.5	41.9	43.9	43.7	41.0	36.8	–
Australia	1.2	1.4	1.3	–	2.1	2.1	2.0
Japan	18.0	17.9	16.3	16.1	20.5	19.6	19.2
South Korea	1.9	2.9	3.1	3.4		3.6	3.2
New Zealand	0.1	0.1	–	–	0.2	0.2	–
Austria	0.6	0.6	0.7	0.7	–	–	–
Belgium	0.8	0.9			0.8	0.8	–
Czech Republic	0.5	0.3	0.3	0.3	–	0.4	0.4
Denmark	0.4	0.5	–	–	0.5	0.6	
Finland	0.4	0.5	0.7	0.7	0.6	0.6	1.0
France	6.8	6.3	5.4	5.4	5.4	5.4	5.1
Germany	9.6	9.0	8.9	8.4	10.1	8.2	7.7
Greece	0.1	0.1			0.3	0.3	–
Hungary	0.2	0.2	0.2	0.2	0.6	0.4	0.4
Iceland	0.0	0.0	0.0	0.0	0.0	0.0	–
Ireland	0.1	0.2	0.2	0.2	0.2	0.2	0.3
Italy	3.3	2.6	2.6	–	3.1	2.7	2.0
Netherlands	1.4	1.5	1.4	–	–	1.2	1.2
Norway	0.4	0.4	–	0.4	0.6	0.6	–
Poland	–	0.4	0.4	0.4	–	1.8	1.6
Portugal	0.2	0.2	0.2	0.2	0.4	0.4	0.5
Slovak Republic	0.2	0.1	0.1	0.1	–	0.3	0.3
Spain	1.2	1.1	1.3	1.3	1.7	1.7	2.3
Sweden	1.1	1.4	–	1.5	1.1	1.2	–
Switzerland	1.1	1.0	0.9	–	0.7	0.7	0.8
Turkey	0.4	0.3	0.4	–	0.5	0.6	0.7
United Kingdom	5.1	4.9	4.5	4.6	5.3	5.2	–
European Union	30.9	29.8	29.1	28.9	31.1	29.0	28.8
Total OECD	100.0	100.0	100.0	100.0	100.0	100.0	100.0

Source: OECD, ANBERD and STAN databases.

Table 1.10 EPO (European Patent Office) Patent applications by priority year and by inventor's country of residence

	1991	1999	Average annual growth rate 1991-1999	Share in OECD applications to the EPO		Number of EPO patent applications per million population	
				1991	1999	1991	1999
Canada	548	1,493	13.3	0.93	1.50	19.6	48.9
Mexico	14	40	14.1	0.02	0.04	0.2	0.4
United States	17,401	28,109	6.2	29.45	28.32	68.7	100.7
Australia	399	885	10.5	0.67	0.89	22.9	46.4
Japan	11,804	17,454	5.0	19.98	17.58	95.3	137.8
South Korea	168	972	24.6	0.28	0.98	3.9	20.9
New Zealand	44	135	15.2	0.07	0.14	12.5	35.5
Austria	655	1,043	6.0	1.11	1.05	83.9	128.9
Belgium	596	1,277	10.0	1.01	1.29	59.6	124.9
Czech Republic	28	60	9.9	0.05	0.06	2.7	5.8
Denmark	364	802	10.4	0.62	0.81	70.7	150.7
Finland	417	1,367	16.0	0.71	1.38	83.1	264.6
France	4,961	7,050	4.5	8.40	7.10	84.9	116.9
Germany	11,285	20,397	7.7	19.10	20.55	141.1	248.5
Greece	25	48	8.7	0.04	0.05	2.4	4.4
Hungary	56	107	8.4	0.09	0.11	5.4	10.5
Iceland	10	35	16.5	0.02	0.04	39.7	125.6
Ireland	64	216	16.5	0.11	0.22	18.1	57.5
Italy	2,285	3,638	6.0	3.87	3.67	40.3	63.1

Table 1.10 continued

	1991	1999	Average annual growth rate 1991-1999	Share in OECD applications to the EPO		Number of EPO patent applications per million population	
				1991	1999	1991	1999
Luxembourg	30	60	9.0	0.05	0.06	77.4	138.5
Netherlands	1,439	2,873	9.0	2.43	2.89	95.5	181.7
Norway	173	356	9.4	0.29	0.36	40.6	79.7
Poland	19	32	6.4	0.03	0.03	0.5	0.8
Portugal	10	36	16.7	0.02	0.04	1.1	3.5
Slovak Republic	0	15	–	0.00	0.02	0.0	2.9
Spain	322	714	10.5	0.55	0.72	8.3	18.0
Sweden	923	2,119	11.0	1.56	2.13	107.1	239.2
Switzerland	1,593	2,424	5.4	2.70	2.44	234.3	339.2
Turkey	4	22	22.8	0.01	0.02	0.1	0.3
United Kingdom	3,452	5,492	6.0	5.84	5.53	60.1	93.8
European Union	26,827	47,130	7.3	45.40	47.48	73.0	125.0
OECD Total	59,089	99,268	6.7	100.00	100.00	56.0	88.4
World	60,020	101,731	6.8	–	–	–	–

Source: OECD, ANBERD and STAN databases.

Table 1.11 Scientific publications per million population, 1999

	Scientific publications per million population, 1999	Country share of scientific publications in the OECD total, 1999
Mexico	23	0.5
Turkey	42	0.6
Luxembourg	67	0.0
Poland	117	1.0
South Korea	143	1.5
Portugal	148	0.3
Slovak Republic	161	0.2
Hungary	191	0.4
Czech Republic	195	0.4
Greece	206	0.5
Italy	297	3.8
Spain	310	2.7
Ireland	329	0.3
Japan	378	10.6
OECD	402	100.0
Iceland	411	0.0
Austria	442	0.8
France	454	6.1
Germany	454	8.3
EU	462	38.6
Belgium	479	1.1
Norway	582	0.6
United States	586	36.3
New Zealand	623	0.5
Canada	645	4.4
Australia	658	2.8
Netherlands	660	2.3
United Kingdom	678	8.8
Denmark	776	0.9
Finland	779	0.9
Sweden	940	1.8
Switzerland	979	1.6

Source: OECD, ANBERD and STAN databases.

Table 1.12 Evolution of gross domestic expenditure on R&D, average annual growth rate for 1995-2001

	Evolution of gross domestic expenditure on R&D	R&D expenditure in billions of (current) PPP dollars, 2001 or latest available year
Slovak Republic	-9.7	0.4
Switzerland	1.3	5.6
Australia	1.8	7.7
United Kingdom	2.3	29.4
France	2.4	35.1
Italy	2.7	15.5
Japan	2.8	103.8
Netherlands	2.9	8.4
Germany	3.3	53.9
European Union	**3.7**	**186.3**
Poland	4.0	2.6
New Zealand	4.4	0.8
Norway	4.4	2.7
Total OECD	**4.7**	**645.4**
United States	5.4	282.3
Canada	5.6	17.4
Czech Republic	5.9	2.0
Austria	5.9	4.4
Belgium	6.0	4.9
Spain	6.5	8.2
Sweden	7.2	9.9
Denmark	7.2	3.2
Ireland	7.5	1.4
Korea	7.5	22.3
Hungary	8.5	1.3
Portugal	10.1	1.5
Finland	11.3	4.7
Greece	12.0	1.1
Mexico	14.1	3.5
Turkey	15.4	2.7
Iceland	17.0	0.3

Source: OECD, ANBERD and STAN databases.

Table 1.13 R&D expenditures by source of financing, percentage share in national total (2001)

	Business enterprises	Other (other national and non-national sources)	Government	Not available
Mexico	24	15	61	–
Greece	24	27	49	–
Poland	31	4	65	–
Portugal	32	6	61	–
New Zealand	34	15	51	–
Hungary	35	10	54	2
Austria	39	19	41	–
Canada	42	27	31	–
Turkey	43	6	51	–
Italy	43	6	51	–
Australia	46	8	46	0
Iceland	46	20	34	–
United Kingdom	46	24	30	–
Spain	47	13	40	–
Netherlands	50	14	36	–
Norway	52	9	40	–
Czech Republic	52	4	44	–
France	53	9	39	–
Slovak Republic	56	3	41	–
EU	56	9	35	–
Denmark	59	9	31	1
OECD	64	5	29	3
Germany	66	2	32	–
Ireland	66	11	23	–
Belgium	66	11	23	–
United States	68	5	27	–
Switzerland	69	8	23	–
Finland	71	4	26	–
Sweden	72	7	21	–
South Korea	72	3	25	–
Japan	73	9	18	–

Source: OECD, ANBERD and STAN databases.

Table 1.14 Growth of HRST occupations, average annual growth rate, 1995-2002

	HRST occupations	Total employment
Poland	-1.1	-2.3
Hungary	-1.0	0.7
Portugal	-0.6	1.7
Slovak Republic	1.0	-0.2
Switzerland	1.0	0.7
Czech Republic	1.7	-0.1
Germany	2.0	0.3
United States	2.0	1.0
Austria	2.1	0.1
France	2.1	1.0
Belgium	2.2	1.1
Finland	2.3	2.5
United Kingdom	2.5	1.1
Greece	2.6	0.4
Canada	3.0	2.1
New Zealand	3.1	1.0
Australia	3.1	1.8
South Korea	3.4	1.2
Sweden	3.4	2.1
Denmark	3.5	0.6
Netherlands	3.9	2.5
Italy	4.3	1.0
Luxembourg	5.4	2.3
Iceland	5.6	2.4
Ireland	7.1	4.5
Norway	7.6	0.5
Spain	8.4	4.0

Source: OECD, ANBERD and STAN databases.

According to the previous analysis, we are providing some data for inter-country comparisons for knowledge and technological background, innovation activities and growth process. Tables 1.8 – 1.15 illustrate researchers per thousand total employment, estimates of the share of OECD gross domestic expenditure on R&D (GERD) and of total number of researchers by OECD country/zone, the EPO (European Patent Office) patent applications by priority year and by inventor's country of residence, scientific publications per million population, the evolution of gross domestic expenditure on R&D as an average annual growth rate for the period 1995-2001, the R&D expenditures by source of financing, percentage share in national total, and the growth of HRST occupations as an average annual growth rate for the period 1995-2002, respectively.

Table 1.15 Researchers per thousand employed, full-time equivalent

	1999	2000	2001	2002	2003	2004
Belgium	7.4	7.5	7.8	7.4	7.5	7.7
Czech Republic	2.8	2.9	3.1	3.1	3.3	3.4
Denmark	6.9	–	7	9.2	9.1	9.5
Finland	14.5	15.1	15.8	16.4	17.7	17.3
France	6.8	7.1	7.2	7.5	7.8	–
Germany	6.6	6.6	6.7	6.8	7	–
Greece	3.7	–	3.7	–	3.9	–
Hungary	3.3	3.8	3.8	3.9	3.9	3.8
Ireland	4.9	5	5.1	5.3	5.5	5.8
Italy	2.9	2.9	2.9	3	2.9	–
Japan	9.9	9.7	10.2	9.9	10.4	10.4
Luxembourg	–	6.2	–	–	6.6	7.1
Netherlands	5.1	5.2	5.5	4.6	4.5	–
Poland	3.6	3.5	3.7	3.8	4.5	4.6
Portugal	3.3	3.4	3.5	3.8	4	–
Slovak Republic	4.5	4.9	4.7	4.5	4.7	5.2
Spain	3.9	4.7	4.7	4.8	5.2	5.5
Sweden	9.6	–	10.6	–	11	–
United States	9.3	9.3	9.5	9.6	–	–
EU 15 total	5.6	5.7	5.9	6	6.1	–
OECD total	6.5	6.6	6.8	6.9	–	–

Source: OECD, ANBERD and STAN databases.

Table 1.16 Classification of scientific and research capabilities

Groups of S&T capabilities	Countries
Group A	Most underdeveloped countries (without S&T capabilities)
Group B	Most developing countries (with some fundamental elements of S&T base)
Group C	New and semi-industrialised countries (for instance, Greece, Israel Finland, Singapore, New Zealand and so on (with S&T base established)
Group D	Industrialised countries: (advanced EEC states) with effective S&T base

Source: UNESCO, "Science and Technology in Developing Countries – Strategies-1990s".

Furthermore, we can classify four-groups using four different scientific criteria of UNESCO so to be able to measure and to evaluate the *technological efficiency and capabilities strength*. Table 1.16 illustrates the classification according to scientific and research criteria. The first criterion refers to *scientists and engineers engaged in research activities per million inhabitants (full-time equivalents)*. For instance, according to this criterion, we can classify Greece in the third group of the new industrialised countries (those which had established a research and scientific apparatus).

Using the second criterion of research and development personnel in higher education per thousand inhabitants (full-time equivalent), Greece belongs to the second group of the developing countries (the countries which had established some initial elements of innovation activities). The third criterion refers to the *third level students per 100,000 inhabitants*. According to this criterion, Greece belongs to the fourth group of industrialised countries (that is, the countries with an effective scientific and technological apparatus).

According to the fourth measure of the *percentage of manufacturing in GDP and the growth of manufacturing in the value added*, Greece is classified in the third group of the new industrialised countries (that is, those countries which had established a scientific apparatus). Finally, using the measure of *scientific and capabilities strength*, Greece belongs to the second group of developing countries (that is, those countries which have established some initial elements of research and technological apparatus).

Finally, with regard to *non-technological innovation*, it covers all those innovation activities which are excluded from technological innovation; that is it includes all innovation activities of firms which do not relate to the introduction of a technologically new or substantially changed good or service or to the use of a technologically new or substantially changed process. Major types of non-technological innovation are likely to be organisational and managerial innovations. Purely organisational and managerial innovations are excluded from technological innovation surveys. These types of innovation will only be included in innovation surveys if they occur as part of some technological innovation project. The minimum set of data that need to be collected in an innovation survey is:

- the type of non-technological innovation;
- economic benefits flowing from a non-technological innovation activity;
- expenditures on non-technological innovation activity;
- the purpose of the non-technological innovation activity; and
- the source of ideas/information for the non-technological innovation activity.

3.1 Measuring Investment in Knowledge Economy

Investment in knowledge is defined and calculated as the sum of expenditure on R&D, on total higher education from both public and private sources and on software. Simple summation of the three components would lead to overestimation of the investment in knowledge owing to overlaps (R&D and software, R&D and education, software and education). Therefore, before calculating total investment in knowledge, the data must be reworked to derive figures that meet the definition. The R&D component of higher education, which overlaps R&D expenditure, has been estimated and subtracted from total expenditure on higher education (both public and private sources).

Not all expenditure on software can be considered investment. Some should be considered as intermediate consumption. Purchases of packaged software by households and operational services in firms are estimated. The software component of R&D, which overlaps R&D expenditure, is estimated when information from national studies and subtracted from software expenditure is used. Due to a lack of information, it was not possible to separate the overlap between expenditure on education and on software; however, the available information indicates that this overlap is quite small.

A more complete picture of investment in knowledge would also include parts of expenditure on innovation (expenditure on the design of new goods), expenditure by enterprises on job-related training programs, investment in organisation (spending on organisational change, etc.), among others. However, due to the lack of available data, such elements could not be included.

Knowledge-economy is closely related to the Information Technology (IT) and Information Communication Technology (ICT). *IT* covers both hardware and software. Their development and diffusion is believed to have had a major impact on the pattern of production and employment in a wide range of industries. In the case of hardware, it may be interesting not only to know when a company innovates by first introducing a technologically new or improved piece of IT equipment but also the IT proportion of its total stock of equipment including subsequent purchases of further machines of the same model.

3.2 The B Index

The amount of tax subsidy to R&D is calculated as 1 minus the B index. The B index is defined as the present value of before-tax income necessary to cover the initial cost of R&D investment and to pay corporate income tax, so that it becomes profitable to perform research activities. Algebraically, the B index is equal to the after-tax cost of an expenditure of USD 1 on R&D divided by one minus the corporate income tax rate. The after-tax cost is the net cost of investing in R&D, taking into account all the available tax incentives.

$$\mathrm{B}index = \frac{(1-A)}{(1-\tau)}$$

where A = the net present discounted value of depreciation allowances, tax credits and special allowances on R&D assets; and t = the statutory corporate income tax rate (CITR). In a country with full write-off of current R&D expenditure and no R&D tax incentive scheme, $A = t$, and consequently $B = 1$. The more favourable a country's tax treatment of R&D, the lower its B index.

The B index is a unique tool for comparing the generosity of the tax treatment of R&D in different countries. However, its computation requires some simplifying assumptions. It should therefore be examined together with a set of other relevant policy indicators. Finally, these calculations are based on reported tax regulations and do not take into account country-specific exemptions and other practices.

B indexes have been calculated with the assumption that the "representative firm" is taxable, so that it may enjoy the full benefit of the tax allowance or credit. For incremental tax credits, calculation of the B index implicitly assumes that R&D investment is fully eligible for the credit and does not exceed the ceiling if there is one. Some detailed features of R&D tax schemes (for instance, refunding, carry-back and carry-forward of unused tax credit, or flow through mechanisms) are therefore not taken into account.

The effective impact of the R&D tax allowance or credit on the after-tax cost of R&D is influenced by the level of the CITR. An increase in the CITR reduces the B index only in those countries with the most generous R&D tax treatment. If tax credits are taxable (as in Canada and the United States), the effect of the CITR on the B index depends only on the level of the depreciation allowance. If the latter is over 100% for the total R&D expenditure, an increase in the CITR will reduce the B index. For countries with less generous R&D tax treatment, the B index is positively related to the CITR.

4. Policy Implications and Summary

As a driving force, innovation points firms towards ambitious long-term objectives. Innovation also leads to the renewal of industrial structures and is behind the emergence of new sectors of economic activity. In brief, innovation is:

- the renewal and enlargement of the range of products and services and the associated markets;
- establishment of new methods of production, supply and distribution;
- introduction of changes to management, work organisation, and working conditions and skills of the workforce.

Research, development and the use of new technologies – in other words, the technological factor – are key elements in innovation, but they are not the only ones. Incorporating them means that the firm must make an organisational effort by adapting its methods of production, management and distribution. Human resources are thus the essential factor. In this respect, initial and ongoing training plays a fundamental role in providing the basic skills required and in constantly adapting them. Many studies and analyses show that a better-educated, better-trained and better-informed workforce helps to strengthen innovation. The ability to involve the workforce to an increased extent and from the outset, in technological changes and their implications for the organisation of production and work must be considered a deciding factor.

Innovation in work organisation and the exploitation of human resources, together with the capacity to anticipate techniques and trends in demand and the market, are frequently necessary preconditions for the success of the other forms of innovation. Innovation in processes increases the productivity of the factors of production by increasing production and/or lowering costs. It provides room for flexible pricing and increased product quality and reliability. Competition makes this quest for productivity an ongoing activity: successive improvements are a guarantee of not falling behind. Replacement of equipment is increasingly accompanied by changes to and improvements in methods, such as in organisation. Radical changes, which are rarer, completely transform the methods of production and sometimes pave the way for new products.

Innovation in terms of products (or services) makes for differentiation vis-à-vis competing products, thus reducing sensitivity to competition on costs or price. Improved quality and performance, better service, shorter response times, more suitable functionality and ergonomics, safety, reliability, etc., are all elements which can be strengthened by innovation and which make all the difference for demanding customers. Here again, progressive innovation is predominant. Radical innovation in products, for its part, opens up new markets. Properly protected and rapidly exploited, it confers for a certain time a decisive advantage for the innovator. In association with business start-ups (and the subsequent development of the businesses), it gives a country or a supranational group temporary domination of the growth markets, thereby ensuring a renewal of the economic fabric

Innovation is at the heart of the spirit of enterprise: practically all new firms are born from a development which is innovative, at least in comparison to its existing competitors on the market. If it is subsequently to survive and develop, however, firms must constantly innovate – even if only gradually. In this respect, technical advances are not themselves sufficient to ensure success. Innovation also means anticipating the needs of the market, offering additional quality or services, organising efficiently, mastering details and keeping costs under control.

Innovation and technology management techniques – such as the quality approach, participative management, value analysis, design, economic intelligence, just-in-time production, re-engineering, performance ratings etc. give the firms concerned an undeniable competitive advantage.

This chapter has attempted to identify the R&D activities and investigate estimation-methods, techniques of scientific and technological activities and measurement problems. According to 'International Standardisation of Statistics on Science and Technology', we can estimate the most important inputs and outputs of scientific and technological activities and also the Scientific and Technical Education and Training and Scientific and Technological Services. The term of "Research and Development Statistics" covers a wide range of statistical series measuring the resources devoted to R&D stages, R&D activities and R&D results. It is important for science policy advisors to know who finances R&D and who performs it.

Series of R&D statistics are only a summary of quantitative reflection of very complex patterns of activities and institutions. In the case of international comparisons, the size aspirations and institutional arrangements of the countries concerned should be taken into consideration. One way of constructing reliable indicators for international comparisons is to compare R&D inputs with a corresponding economic series, for example, by taking GERD as a percentage of the Gross Domestic Product. However, its quite difficult to make detailed comparisons between R&D data and those of non-R&D series both because of the residual differences in methodology and because of defects in the non-R&D data.

UNESCO, OECD and EUROSTAT divisions organised the systematic collection, analysis publication and standardisation of data concerning science and technological activities. The first experimental questionnaires were circulated to member states by UNESCO in 1966 and standardised periodical surveys were established in 1969.

The collection of R&D data of regional statistics suggests problems in comparison to data from national statistics. For the collection of regional statistics, we should take into the local differences and the difficulties. In addition, we can use either the "local-units" or the "local-economic-units". The first method "top-to-the-bottom method" focused on the collection of aggregate R&D data (for the whole country) and after that on the distribution of these figures into a regional-level; the disadvantage of this method is that there is not a direct collection of data from the regions or the second method "bottom-to-the-top method" for the collection disaggregate R&D data (for the whole regions) based on the direct-collection at a regional-level and after that on the summation of these figures in order to obtain the aggregate-total R&D data (for the whole country).

Technological progress has become virtually synonymous with long- run economic growth. It raises a basic question about the capacity of both industrial and newly industrialised countries to translate their seemingly greater technological capacity into productivity and economic growth. Usually, there are difficulties with the estimation the relation between technical change and productivity. Technological change may have accelerated but, in some cases, there is a failure to capture the effects of recent technological advances in productivity growth or a failure to account for the quality changes of previously introduced technologies.

In literature, there are various explanations for the slow-down in productivity growth for OECD countries. One source of the slow-down may be substantial changes in the industrial composition of output, employment, capital accumulation and resource utilisation. The second source of the slow-down in productivity growth may be that technological opportunities have declined; otherwise, new technologies have been developed but the application of new technologies to production has been less successful. Technological factors act in a long run way and should not be expected to explain medium run variations in the growth of GDP and productivity.

Chapter 2

Modelling Knowledge Economy and Innovation Activities with the Context of New Growth Theory

1. Introduction

Innovation activities contribute essentially to the regional dimension and growth. The technological infrastructure and innovation capabilities affect not only the regional growth but also the whole periphery and economy. In the last decades, OECD introduced measures and indexes, concerning the Research and Development Expenditures, patents etc., that measure innovation activities. However, there are many problems and questions regarding the measurement of innovation activities at a regional level. This chapter attempts to analyse the whole framework of innovation statistics and in particular to examine the measurement and the statistical estimation of innovation activities. Within this context, it also aims to emphasise and review appropriate techniques, the most common methods and particular problems.

Technical change and innovation activities have an important role for growth and sustainable development. There is a huge literature on the role and economic impact of invention and innovation activities; many studies investigate the relationship between productivity, technical change, welfare, growth and regional development. Locally produced technologies may affect and determine the rate of regional growth. It is important to estimate the effects of technical change and innovation activities. However, how can we determine and measure innovation activities and technical change? This chapter attempts to analyse the framework of innovation statistics, to examine the major indexes and measures for innovation activities. The notion of a production function has been used for a long time. In the theoretical literature, in the first edition of his 1980 famous text *Principles of Economy*, Alfred Marshall emphasised theoretical relationships between production function and factor demands. However, empirical analysis has lagged considerably behind theoretical developments.

We can classify two categories of the concept of technology; first, there is the *neoclassical conception of technology* in the form of a production function and, secondly, there is what might be termed the *pythagorean concept of technology*, in terms of patent statistics, etc. The *pythagorean conception of technology* is based on contributions from fields as diverse as economics, history of science, sociology and theoretical physics (Merton 1935, May 1996, Moravcsik 1973, Schmookler

1966). Both the *neoclassical* and *pythagorean* viewpoints have been the subject of a great deal of literature.

Technological knowledge indicates the manner in which resources can be combined to yield outputs of goods and services. Most countries have relied either on the *disembodied innovative capacity* (measured as a proxy of R&D intensity) or as the *technology embodied in investment* (measured as a proxy of capital formation per employee). Technological knowledge can be embedded in the designs of equipment and machinery, the skills or even in technical literature.

Technical change can be considered as a change that affects a set of existing techniques where the new knowledge affects the output (*disembodied technical change*) or a change that affects through the introduction of new techniques where the new techniques replace the old ones. On the other hand, in *disembodied technical change* the output that can be produced by any technical feasible factor combination is greater than before; thus given the input levels, the output is *augmented* and can be represented by an upward shift in the output surface. On the other hand, the *embodied technical change* implies incremental improvements in the output yield; we can consider that the *embodied technical change* is a kind of *biased technical change*. The adoption of the new techniques may depend on the elasticities of factor supplies. If new inventions and techniques are embodied in new machinery, that implies new capital should be more productive than the older one.

This chapter attempts to review the theory to analyse the framework of more contemporary cost functional forms. We will begin with an historical overview of literature, notably with the famous Cobb-Douglas model and the constant elasticity of substitution (CES); we will them move to the more flexible forms of Generalised Leontief and translog function.

2. New Growth Debate

Solow (1994) writes "I think that the real value of endogenous growth theory will emerge from its attempt to model the endogenous component of technological progress as in integral part of the theory of economic growth. Here the pioneer was Romer (1990). Many others have followed his lead: my short list includes Grossman and Helpman (1991), Aghion and Howitt (1992), Stokey (1992) and Young (1991) (1993), but there are others."

Solow (1956) expanded the work by John Stuart Mill and developed *neoclassical growth models. Neoclassical growth theory* as developed by Solow and his followers dominated over the literature of *long term or trend movements* in per capita income for more than three decades. The starting *neoclassical growth models* of Solow are important studies for economic growth and convergence. In these models, the rate of exogenous technical progress is the key parameter determining the steady state growth rate of per capita income. Since Solow 1956, technological change is regarded as one of the main sources of economic growth. According to the neoclassical models based on the assumptions of marginal productivity, technological change (or labour growth) is needed to compensate for the negative productivity effects of capital accumulation.

The recent debate about the determinants of output growth has concentrated mainly on the role of knowledge, typically produced by a specific sector of the economy. This approach considers the economy in a three sector framework (Romer 1990a, 1990b), where the R&D sector produces knowledge to be used as an input by firms producing capital goods. Output growth rate is indigenously determined by the allocation of human capital in research and manufacturing sectors and is not affected by other crucial variable such as the unit cost of production of new capital goods.

Schumpeter and Schmooker supported that productivity growth is related to an economy's structure and policies; from one hand, they tried to explain the links between industrial innovation and economic growth, while from the other hand, they also tried to explain the market conditions and innovation rates. Many of the early models treated technological progress as an exogenous process driven by time.

Technological progress has often been treated as an exogenous process in the long-run economic analysis. This treatment would be appropriate for studying the growth of industrial economies, if advances in industrial know-how are followed automatically by fundamental scientific discoveries and if basic research is guided mostly by non-market forces. This would seem an appropriate assumption if advanced technical knowledge stems largely from activities that take place outside of the economic sector. The view that innovation is driven by basic research, which is implicit in the models with exogenous technology, was made explicit by Shell (1967). He introduced a public research sector that contributes technical knowledge to profit-entities in the Solow economy. Arrow viewed technological progress as an out-growth of activities in the economic realm. Romer (1986) discussed the possibility that learning-by-doing might be a source of sustained growth, maintained this treatment of technological progress as wholly the outgrowth of an external economy. Romer (1987b) has described a competitive equilibrium where ongoing growth in per capita income is sustained by endogenous technological progress. Many others have followed his lead, such as, Grossman and Helpman (1991a), Aghion and Howitt (1992), Stokey (1995) and Young (1993) (1998).

However, recent work by Harrigan (1995) shows that there are systematic differences across countries in industry outputs that cannot be explained by differences in factor endowments. While there are many possible explanations for this result, such an explanation is that technology is not the same across countries. This is a hypothesis which has gained greater attention from international economists recently, including Trefler (1993, 1995), Dollar and Wolff (1993) and Harrigan (1997a). If technology is not the same across countries, then much of the theoretical work in neoclassical trade theory is irrelevant to applied research on cross-country comparisons, and much applied research that assumes identical technology (for example, many applied general equilibrium models and factor endowment regressions) is incorrectly specified.

In general, this chapter is a brief overview of theoretical foundations of models with endogenous technical change. In particular, in this chapter we attempt to analyse two types of technological change: the first type *generates new technologies*, while the second type *generates quality improvements*.

3. Theoretical Approach to the Endogenous Theory

The concept of endogenous technological change has resulted in the so-called "new growth theory". The literature of endogenous growth provide us with better insights in the causes and effects of technological change as a determinant of economic growth. We can distinguish two different types of technological change. On the other hand, an increase in the number of technologies (the embodied technological change or, otherwise, the product-innovation); and on the other hand a quality improvement of existing technologies (the disembodied technological change or otherwise the process-innovation). In order to present the different approaches of endogenous technical change which can be found in the literature, we will essentially follow the exposition scheme proposed by Barro and Sala-i-Martin (1995) in distinguishing three main models of endogenous growth motivated by endogenous technological change: models based on expanding product variety; Shumpeterian models based on improvements in the quality of products;, and models based on human capital accumulation. Taking an exogenous rate of technological change and keeping it constant over a long-period of time might neglects the fact that new technologies depend on R&D expenditures, investment decisions and economic policy.

Schumpeter and Schmooker supported that productivity growth is related to an economy's structure and policies. On the other hand, they tried to explain the links between industrial innovation and economic growth, while, on the other hand, they tried to explain the market conditions and innovation rates too.

3.1 New Technologies and Product Innovations

The seminal works on endogenous growth theory of Romer (1990a), Grossman and Helpman (1991a), Young (1993) consider innovations as means of expanding the variety of available goods. These models treat R&D activity like other production activities, which converts primary inputs, as capital and labour, into knowledge. Young (1993) adds another dimension to the research process: she stressed the importance of learning-by-doing before the adoption of any innovation.

Let us adopt the presentation of the encompassing model by Romer (1996), or by Aghion and Howitt (1998), in order to emphasise the main features of such theoretical explanations of growth through an endogenous technological change. Two sectors are considered: the first one produces the "final good", and the second is the "Research and Development" sector whose activity aims to increase the level of technology.

For instance, the speed of elevation of the technological level depends on both the aggregate amount of research the number of researchers involved, and the current level of technology. The total amount of knowledge in the economy, an indicator of human capital or, in Romer's model, as the number of new intermediate products or designs.

In the simplest case where there is no accumulation of capital (and no capital in the production functions), one shows that the growth rate of economy is equal to the growth rate of the level of technology A_t, denoted g_A, which satisfies the following equation: $\overset{*}{g}_A = (\gamma n + (\theta-1)g_A)g_A$

- if $\theta \leq 1$ that is if the technological progress is less than proportional to the existent level of technology, the economy grows increasingly then decreasingly until a steady state when its growth rate is reached: the output per capita can't grow without population growth, and, surprisingly, this rate of technological progress is independent from the quantity of labour involved in R&D activities.
- if $\theta \geq 1$, the growth rate of knowledge and, subsequently the growth rate of the output per capita always increases.

Assuming that H represents the human capital, K is physical capital and A is the existing level of technology. Human capital can be used both for the production of the final goods Y and the generation of new technologies, which use the human capital and the stock of knowledge. Therefore, the equation for the generation of technology can be written as follows:

$$\frac{dA}{dt} = \delta v H A,$$

where: v is the fraction of total-stock of human capital devoted to R&D and δ is a productivity-parameter.

Research sector is human-capital intensive and technology- intensive, while physical capital K does not enter the technology-equation; it is used in the production of final goods only:

$$Y = [(1-v)H]^\alpha \sum_{i=1}^{A} (x_i)^{1-\alpha},$$

where x_i represents the amount of capital of type i.

In this context, growth is driven by technological change that results from the research and development activities of profit-maximising firms. An important implication of this mechanism is that the government policies and, especially, subsidies to R&D may influence the long-run rate of economic growth. However, Jones emphasises the growth rate of the economy should be proportional to the number of researchers – which is not confirmed by statistical observation. He assumes that the absolute productivity of innovators remains constant, unsensitive to past innovation, and this assumption results in the fact that, as technology advances, an increasing quantity of resources have to be devoted to innovative activity to sustain a given growth rate. The growth rate in this model depends only on parameters which are usually taken as exogenous and is independent of policy changes like subsidies to R&D or to capital accumulation; growth is only "semi-endogenous".

At the same direction, Young (1998) proposes a model of endogenous innovation in which a rise in the profitability of innovative activities could lead to an increased variety of technologies which consequently will increase the level of utility of the representative consumer and a rise in the scale of the market could raise the equilibrium quantity of R&D without increasing the economy's growth rate.

3.2 Existing Technologies and Process Innovations

Aghion and Howitt (1992) built an endogenous growth model involving creative destruction, in the Schumpeterian tradition (Schumpeter 1934), very close to the model by Grossman and Helpman (1991a). There are three sectors in the economy: producing respectively the intermediate good, the final good and research. Technical progress appears as a rise of the productivity of the intermediate good in the production of the final good, because each innovation produced by the research sector improves the quality of the intermediate good.

This model can easily be presented in a simple way. Let the current level of aggregate productivity be denoted by A, the amount of intermediate product by x, the production function of the final good y is given by:

$$y = AF(x) \quad \text{where} \quad F' \geq 0, \ F'' \leq 0$$

The productivity in the final good sector is increased by each innovation, by a factor y, so that after t innovations:

$$A_t = A_0 y^t$$

This model takes into consideration the inherent uncertainties associated with scientific and industrial research: technological advances are essentially stochastic. The arrival of an innovation is here uncertain, its probability of arrival being characterised by a Poisson process depending positively on the number of researchers: the time interval between two innovations is a random variable. The endogenous number of researchers depends negatively on interest rate, positively on the size of the innovation and the size of the qualified labour population. This kind of endogenous growth model embodies two kinds of externalities: a positive intertemporal externality, because a given innovation raises productivity not only in the present period, but also in the following periods, and a negative externality, because each new innovation makes the previous one obsolete.

Technological change can be modeled as an increase in the quality of a fixed number of already existing technologies. We can rewrite the production function, according to the lines used by Barro and Sala-i-Martin (1995) as follows:

$$Y = [(1-v)H]^{\alpha} \sum_{i=1}^{A} (qx_i)^{1-\alpha},$$

where the number of technologies A is regarded as fixed. The increase in the quality q increases the total efficiency of capital-goods x_i and therefore increases the total output Y. The engine of growth is no-longer the increase in the number of technologies, but the increase in the quality of existing technologies. The relevant technology generation equation is now:

$$\frac{dq}{dt} = \delta v H q,$$

We are assuming that only human-capital is needed to improve the quality of existing technologies. Human capital is a scale-variable in the sense that an exogenous increase in the stock of human capital increases the growth rate of quality improvements.

3.3 Human Capital

By "human-capital" we mean a set of specialised skills that agents can acquire by devoting time to an activity called "schooling": the more time that an individual spends in school, the greater is the measure of human capital that the individual acquires. A variety of approaches to training and education process could be combined with the underlying models of technological change.

The accumulation of human capital *h* by an individual is specified by a "production function of human capital" (which embodies an intertemporal externality, but not an interindividual one), where *u* is the fraction of time spent by him on the production of final good, and thus (1-*u*) is the fraction of time spent on the acquisition of knowledge or skills:

$$h' = \delta(1-u)h$$

The production function of the final good combines physical capital *K*, specific human capital *h* and average level of human capital h_a (representing here an interindividual positive externality: the higher is the average level of knowledge, the more efficient is any individual); all agents being assumed identical, $h_a = h$:

$$Q = AK^{\beta}(uh)^{1-b}h = AK^{\beta}(uh)^{1-\beta}h^{\gamma}$$

The optimal rates of growth of human capital (g_h^*) and production (g^*) are respectively:

Cross-country regressions reveal the special role that human capital plays in growth process (Mankiw *et al.* (1992), for example). Human capital is defined as the sum of the abilities specific to individuals; it is often seen as the accumulation of effort devoted to schooling and training that is, as an accumulable factor in some models, the engine of growth. Lucas (1988) proposed the first endogenous growth model based on human capital, which will be here quickly presented (following Amable, 1994). In Romer's model (1990), the steady state growth rates of A, K and Y were equal. This means that since $Y = \alpha A + (1-\alpha)K$, the marginal rate of productivity (MGP) of human capital equals:

$$MGP = \frac{\partial Y}{\partial(vH)} = \frac{\partial A}{\partial(vH)} = \delta,$$

where vH corresponds to the amount of human-capital allocated to the production of new technologies.

Following the framework in which technological change is generated by improving existing technologies, it follows that: $Y = (1-\alpha)q + (1-\alpha)K$, the marginal rate of productivity of human capital equals:

$$MGP = \frac{\partial Y}{\partial(vH)} = \left(\frac{1-\alpha}{\alpha}\right)\frac{\partial q}{\partial(vH)} = \left(\frac{1-\alpha}{\alpha}\right)\delta = \delta',$$

where vH corresponds to the amount of human-capital allocated to the generation of better-quality. The factor of

$$\left(\frac{1-\alpha}{\alpha}\right)$$

appears because of the different way of quality improvement and the amount of new technologies influence the production-process.

Table 2.1 illustrates the characteristics of the main previously reviewed models, in a way which emphasise the main features to keep in any future empirical modelling work.

Table 2.1 Some insights and characteristics of endogenous growth rate

References-models	Type of innovation process	Factors influencing positively the growth rate	Factors influencing negatively the growth rate
Romer (1986)	Process Innovation through knowledge accumulation	Accumulation of knowledge	Discount-rate
Lucas (1988)	Process Innovation through capital accumulation	Effectiveness of investment in human capital	Elasticity of substitution: discount-rate
Romer (1990)	Process Innovation through addition of new intermediate goods	Efficiency in the research sector	Elasticity of substitution: discount-rate
Grossman and Helpman (1991)	Process Innovation through improvements in quality of consumer good	Size of innovation and efficiency of research	Discount-rate
Aghion and Howitt (1992)	Process Innovation through stochastic improvements for intermediate goods.	Size of innovation and efficiency of research	Interest-rate

Source: Korres (2003).

R&D expenditures are often used as an indicator of the technological change, but most studies are limited to the link between productivity and R&D engaged in the sector itself, but they are not R&D used by the sector, while being engaged by other productive sectors. The efforts of research and development is often only caught by the amount of expenditures involved, but patents data would be more appropriate to capture the efficiency of R&D process. The productive potential of the research process has thus decreased ratio patents / R&D become lower, but the link between innovation and factor productivity remains strong.

In most empirical works, an accumulated stock of R&D is included in the production function as an additional input. This R&D stock stands for a measure of the current level of knowledge: it ought to proxy for the number of varieties of intermediate products in Romer's model or for the aggregate quality index of goods in Aghion and Howitt's model (Barro and Sala-i-Martin 1995). It should be considered that technological externalities between different productive sectors: empirical studies stress the importance of inter-industrial externalities for explaining the growth of productivity growth.

3.4 Productivity, R&D and Environment

Most literature on environmental policy and economic growth (Jorgenson and Wilcoxen 1990, for example) assumes that technological progress is exogenous and, thus, is not affected by environmental policy. Hence, Bovenberg and Smulders (1996) argue that the experience of industrial countries shows that active environmental policies, such as taxes or introduction of pollution permits, induce major technological advances in new technologies, and that environmental quality enhances the productivity of inputs into production by providing non-extractive services. In the computable general equilibrium model by Jorgenson and Wilcoxen (1990), the technical progress is not exactly endogenous; it is rather modelled in an interesting way which we should mention here: introducing standard exponential temporal biases of technical progress in a macroeconomic model would necessarily lead in the long term the saved inputs to "vanish", which can be avoided by modelling the temporal bias with a logistic trend.

4. Modelling Knowledge and Estimation of Innovation and Scientific Activities

There is a huge literature suggesting and demonstrating that research and scientific indicators make an important contribution to the growth at the firm, industry and national levels. Most studies have investigated the relation between productivity, employment, growth and R&D.

4.1 Input-output Framework: Technological Change within the Input-output Framework

The structural decomposition analysis can be defined as a method of characterising major shifts within an economy by means of comparative static changes. The basic methodology has introduced by Leontief (1953) for the structure of the US economy and has been extended in several ways. Carter (1960) has incorporated some dynamic elements with a formal consideration of the role of investment in embodied technical change. Chenery, Syrquin and others (1963) has added elements of trade into this framework.

Growth decomposition analysis uses input-output techniques, because they capture the flows of goods and services between different industries. Input-output methods exploit the inter-linkages effects and search for the components of growth. In addition, input-output techniques allow us to calculate the contribution of *technical change* to output growth. The principal argument of the method of inter-industry analysis is to show explicitly the interdependence of growth rates in different sectors of the economy. Usually, two different compositional indicators are used to analyse the extent of structural change, the annual growth rate of real output in each industry and the share of national real output accounted for each industry.

Input-output tables are available both in current and constant prices. Following Kubo et al. (1986), we can consider the *basic material balance condition* for the gross output of a sector as given by:

$$X_i = W_i + F_i + E_i - M_i \quad \text{(material balance equation)} \tag{2.1}$$

where X_i = the gross output:
W_i = the intermediate demand for the output of sector i by sector j,
F_i = the domestic final demand for the output of sector i,
E_i = the export demand, and
M_i = the total imports classified in sector i.

The gross output of sector i is the sum of output to intermediate demand plus the domestic final demand plus the exports less the imports. In the matrix notation the *material balance condition* becomes:

$$X = AX + F + E - M = (I-A)^{-1}(F+E-M) \tag{2.2}$$

where $(I-A)^{-1}$, the inverse of the coefficients matrix, captures the indirect as well as the direct flows of intermediate goods.

Holding one part of the material balance equation constant and varying the other components over time, the change in an industry's output can be decomposed into the following factors:

- technical change (corresponding to changes in the inverted I-A matrix);
- changes in final demand;
- changes in the structure of exports; and
- changes in the structure of imports.

At an aggregate level, this equation provides a comprehensive picture of structural change for each country. It does not explain why the structure of an economy changes, but it describes how it comes about and measures the relative importance each factor in each industry's growth. Growth effects are analysed in order to reveal how much output in each industry would have changed with the same growth rate for each element in the final demand category. When growth rates differ between the final demand categories, the resulting growth rates for the industrial output will also vary.

Positive or negative effects of structural change affect final demand categories. Technological change plays an important role for the expansion and decline of sectors. Technology intensity and real growth rates of output can be used to classify individual industries into different performance groups. These groups can then be used to describe the patterns of structural change and to make comparisons among various countries.

The effects of technical change are analysed in order to find out how much the use of primary inputs has changed, due to changes in the endogenous factors of the model. Furthermore, the effects of technical change on industrial output are analysed in order to reveal how much output in each industry has changed, because input-output coefficients have altered.

A way of measuring changes in input-output coefficients is to compute the weighted average changes in input-output coefficients of various sectors and to compare matrices at two different points of time. For instance, we can use the following formula (4.3) to compute the weighted indexes:

$$T_j = \frac{1}{\frac{1}{2}\Sigma(X_{ij}^2 + X_{ij}^1)}\Sigma[\frac{(A_{ij}^2 - A_{ij}^1)}{(A_{ij}^2 + A_{ij}^1)}(X_{ij}^2 + X_{ij}^1)] \qquad (4.3)$$

where A_{ij}^2 is the elements of matrix of input-output coefficients for the second period:

A_{ij}^1 is the elements of matrix of input-output coefficients for the first period,

X_{ij}^2 is the matrix of interindustry transactions for second period at constant 1975 prices,

X_{ij}^1 is the matrix of interindustry transactions for first period at constant 1975 prices.

This index measures the overall input changes in each of the n production sectors due to technological changes, changes in the prices, and product mix (the so called *Rasmussen index* of structural change).

The total change in sectoral output can be decomposed into sources by category of demand. The total change in output equals the sum of the changes in each sector and can also be decomposed either by sector or by category of demand.

The relations (with the two intermediate terms combined), can be shown as following:

$$DD_1 + EE_1 + IS_1 + IO_1 = \Delta X_1$$
$$DD_2 + EE_2 + IS_2 + IO_2 = \Delta X_2$$

$$\cdot \quad \cdot \quad \cdot \quad \cdot \quad \cdot$$
$$\cdot \quad \cdot \quad \cdot \quad \cdot \quad \cdot$$
$$\cdot \quad \cdot \quad \cdot \quad \cdot \quad \cdot$$

$$DD_n + EE_n + IS_n + IO_n = \Delta X_n$$
$$\Sigma DD_i + \Sigma EE_i + \Sigma IS_i + \Sigma IO_i = \Sigma \Delta X_i = \Delta X$$

where DD_i=domestic demand expansion in sector i:
EE_i=export expansion in sector i,
IS_i=import substitution of final and intermediate goods in sector i,
IO_i=input-output coefficients in sector i,
ΔX_i=change in the output of sector i.

Reading down the columns gives the sectoral composition of each demand category, while reading across the rows gives the decomposition of changes in sectoral demand by different demand categories. When comparisons across countries and time periods are made, it is convenient to divide the entire table by $\Sigma \Delta X_i$, so that all components across sectors and demand categories sum to 100. Alternatively, it is sometimes convenient to divide the rows by ΔX_i and then to look at the percentage contribution of each demand category to the change in sectoral output.

At this stage, we can give an *alternative model*, which is known as the *deviation model* and measures changes in the relative shares of output. The deviation model starts from balanced growth, where it is assumed that all sectors grow at the same rate equal to the growth rate of total output.

The same industry can be driven by different factors in different countries. Since industrial production depends on different forces such as: the existence of natural resources, human capital, trade policies, rates of economic growth and innovation levels.

Table 2.2 Decomposition formulas*

Sources of growth:	*Variable*	*being*	*decomposed*	
	Output ΔX	Val.Add. ΔV	Imports ΔM	Empl. ΔL
Domestic-final-demand expansion (F.E.)				
Export expansion (E.E.)	$B_0 \hat{u}^f_0 \Delta F$	$v_0 B_0 \hat{u}^f_0 \Delta F$	$(m11f_0 + m^w_0 A_0 B_0 \hat{u}^f_0) \Delta F$	$l_0 B_0 \hat{u}^f_0 \Delta F$
Import-substitution of final goods (I.S.F.)	$B_0 \Delta E$	$v_0 B_0 \Delta E$	$m^w_0 A_0 B_0 \Delta E$	$l_0 B_0 \Delta E$
Import- substitution of intermediate goods (I.S.W.)	$B_0 \Delta \hat{u}^f F_1$	$v_0 B_0 \Delta \hat{u}^f F_1$	$(I - m^w_0 A_0 B_0) \Delta m^w W_1$	$l_0 B_0 \Delta \hat{u}^f F_1$
Technical change (I.O.A.)	$B_0 \Delta \hat{u}^w W_1$	$v_0 B_0 \Delta \hat{u}^w W_1$	$(I - m^w_0 A_0 B_0) \Delta m^w W_1$	$l_0 B_0 \Delta \hat{u}^w W_1$
Change in value-added-ratio (I.O.V.)	$B_0 \hat{u}^w_0 \Delta A X_1$	$v_0 B_0 \hat{u}^w_0 \Delta A X_1$	$(m^w_0 + m^w_0 A_0 B_0 \hat{u}^w_0) \Delta A X_1$	$l_0 B_0 \hat{u}^w_0 \Delta A X_1$
Labour-productivity-growth (I.O.L.)	-----	$\Delta v X_1$	-----	-----
Labour-productivity-growth (I.O.L.)	-----	-----	-----	$\Delta l X_1$

Note: * The previous analysis can be extended to value added, employment, and imports.
Source: OECD Document: "Structural change and Industrial performance", 1992.

Table 2.3 illustrates the sources of output growth for selected countries in order to draw some comparisons. Decomposition analysis shows that the sources of output growth varied from country to country. In most countries, domestic final demand is the primary force for output growth; domestic final demand is a significant factor in Japan, Korea, Norway and Israel. In addition, exports are contributing to growth. The effects of imports are negative for all countries.

Table 2.3 Sources of output growth for selected countries (percentage)

	D.D.E.	E.E.	I.S.	I.O.C.	Total
Greece: 1960-1980	78.43	28.37	-4.91	-3.71	100
Greece: 1960-1970	98.67	14.50	-7.55	-5.63	100
Greece: 1970-1980	60.26	38.07	-0.29	1.95	100
Japan: 1914-1935	73.8	26.7	-0.5	-0.1	100
Japan: 1935-1955	90.8	-13.8	15.6	7.4	100
Japan: 1955-1960	87.9	8.0	-4.1	8.3	100
Japan: 1960-1965	90.8	15.1	-2.1	-3.8	100
Japan: 1965-1970	82.6	14.9	-3.2	5.7	100
Korea: 1955-1963	74.5	10.0	21.4	-6.0	100
Korea: 1963-1970	81.8	21.9	-1.8	-1.9	100
Korea: 1970-1973	51.9	55.7	-3.2	-4.4	100
Taiwan: 1956-1961	54.3	23.9	15.1	6.7	100
Taiwan: 1961-1966	61.3	37.6	-1.1	2.2	100
Taiwan: 1966-1971	52.7	49.5	-0.2	-2.0	100
Israel: 1958-1965	76.7	25.6	3.1	-5.4	100
Israel: 1965-1972	69.1	42.0	-18.9	7.9	100
Norway:1953-1961	60.7	40.4	-10.6	9.5	100
Norway:1961-1969	60.2	49.1	-13.3	4.0	100

Note: D.D.E. = Domestic Demand Expansion, E.E. = Export Expansion, I.S. = Import Substitution, I.O.C. = changes of Input-Output Coefficients.
Source: The data for Greece comes from the results of the above analysis (in % units), while the data for other countries is from Shujiro Urata: "Economic growth and structural change in the Soviet Economy 1952-1972" in paper 19 of Maurizio Ciaschini: "Input-Output Tables".

The comparison of changes in output shares and differences in growth rates reveals the direction and the pace of structural change. Japan represents the most clear example of structural change. High technology sectors increase rapidly and contribute significantly to manufacturing's share of total output. In Japan the low technology sector show the second largest loss of output share of all countries examined.

Table 2.4 indicates the sources of growth in real output for various countries. This Table illustrates a typical example of decomposition of gross output for manufacturing in constant prices. Domestic Final Demand and Exports are the most important sources for the expansion of output growth.

Table 2.4 Sources of growth in real output of all industrial sectors*

Country/Period (constant prices)	Annual average growth rate (%)	Domestic final demand expansion	Export expansion	Domestic final demand expansion	Imports intermediate goods	Input-output coef (tech. change)
France: 1972-1985 (1980)	1.32	1.03	1.61	-0.48	-0.59	-0.25
Germany:1978-1986 (1980)	0.97	0.55	1.77	-0.40	-0.63	-0.32
Greece:1960-1980 (1975)	4.13	2.69	1.17	-0.21	-0.12	0.61
Japan: 1970-1985 (1975)	4.40	2.66	2.04	0.00	-0.05	-0.26
UK: 1968-1984 (1980)	0.19	0.82	0.98	-0.65	-0.81	-0.15
USA: 1972-1985 (1982)	1.57	2.23	0.60	-0.40	-0.38	-0.48

Note: * The values of Greece derived as an average from the sectors of Industrial Intermediate goods, Industrial Manufacturing goods, Industrial Consumer goods.

Source: OECD study of "Structural change and Industrial performance", 1992, Paris.

Table 2.5 Sources of change in real output shares for manufacturing

	Total change output share (%)	Domestic final demand expansion	Export expansion	Imports of final goods	Imports of intermeadiate goods	Tech. change (IOC)
France: (1972-1985)						
High Technology	1.72	0.81	1.34	-0.29	-0.29	0.15
Medium Technology	-0.52	-0.46	1.63	-0.76	-0.95	0.02
Low Technology	-5.18	-2.35	1.52	-1.29	-1.68	-1.38
Germany: (1978-1986)						
High Technology	0.87	0.31	0.94	-0.26	-0.25	0.13
Medium Technology	0.44	-0.34	1.84	-0.37	-0.86	0.18
Low Technology	-3.63	-1.31	0.74	-0.69	-0.99	-1.38
Japan: (1970-1985)						
High Technology	7.25	2.58	3.41	0.11	0.04	1.11
Medium Technology	1.02	-2.29	3.00	0.01	-0.12	0.43
Low Technology	-6.92	-4.34	0.38	-0.11	-0.29	-2.55
Un.Kingdom (1968-84)						
High Technology	0.49	0.52	1.49	-1.02	-0.72	0.21
Medium Technology	-4.09	-0.40	0.65	-1.84	-2.66	0.16
Low Technology	-7.97	-2.88	-0.44	-1.32	-1.96	-1.38
United States(1972-85)						
High Technology	2.40	1.87	0.80	-0.34	-0.24	0.31
Medium Technology	-1.52	0.05	0.34	-0.77	-0.66	-0.47
Low Technology	-3.95	-1.05	0.42	-0.63	-0.78	-1.91

Source: "Structural change and industrial performance: Growth decomposition in seven OECD economies" OECD, 1992, Paris, Section 4.

Table 2.5 summarises the sources of change in the real output shares of manufacturing (high, medium and low technology sectors) for various countries. Domestic Final Demand Expansion contributed substantial to the low and medium technology industries, while technical change contributed positively for high and medium technology industries and negatively for low technology industries and for manufacturing sector.

Table 2.6 indicates the Primary sources of change for the fastest and slowest output growth industries.

Table 2.6 Primary sources of change for fastest and slowest output growth industries*

(Fast/slow)	Domestic final demand	Exports expansion	Imports final products	Imports intermediate inputs	Technology
France (1972-1985)	7/2	3/1	0/1	0/3	0/3
Germany (1978-1986)	3/0	6/1	0/1	0/3	0/3
Greece** (1960-1980)	9/0	9/0	2/7	4/5	5/4
Japan (1970-1985)	6/1	2/0	0/0	0/1	2/8
United Kingdom (1968-1984)	5/1	3/0	0/3	0/3	2/3
USA (1972-1985)	10/1	0/0	0/4	0/0	0/5

Note: * The values of the nominator indicate the number of fastest growth sectors, while the values of the dominator indicate the number of the slowest growth sectors for each source.
** The values for Greece derive from the previous analysis.
Source: OECD, "Structural change and industrial performance: growth decomposition in seven OECD countries" 1992, Paris.

4.2 Catching Up Models

A higher level of innovation activities tend to have a higher level of value added per worker (or a higher GDP per head) and a higher level of innovation activities than others. Following technological-gap arguments, it would be expected that the more technologically advanced countries would be the most economically advanced (in terms of a high level of innovation activities and in terms of GDP per capita). The level of technology in a country cannot be measured directly. A proxy measure can be used to give an overall picture of the set of techniques invented or diffused by the country of the international economic environment. For productivity measure, we can use the real GDP per capita as an approximate measure. The most representative measures for *technological inputs and outputs* are indicators of patent activities and research expenditures.

For the level of productivity, we can use as a proxy real GDP per capita (GDPCP). For the measurement of *national technological level*, we can also use some approximate measures. For instance, we can again use the traditional variables of *technological input* and *technological output* measures (GERD and EXPA). The majority of empirical studies in estimations between productivity growth and R&D follow a standard linear model. In the present context we use a similar approach. The reason is that even though there is a dynamic relationship, data limitations (the lack of time series annual data on R&D activities for most countries) prevent the application of some complex models.

We can test the basic technological gap model (with and without these variables) reflecting the structural change in order to decide to what degree these variables add something to the other explanatory variable of the model. We will use the external patent applications (EXPA) and gross expenditures on research and development (GERD) as proxies for the growth of the national technological activities, GDP per capita (GDPCP) (in absolute values at constant prices) as a proxy for the total level of knowledge appropriated in the country (or *productivity*). Investment share (INV) has been chosen as an indicator of growth in the capacity for economic exploitation of innovation and diffusion; the share of investment may also be seen as the outcome of a process in which institutional factors take part (since differences in the size of investment share may reflect differences in institutional system as well). For the structural change we used approximation changes in the shares of exports and agriculture in GDP.

We have tested the following version of the models:

GDP (or PROD)=f[GDPCP, EXPA (or GERD), INV] basic model   (2.1a)

GDP (or PROD)= f[GDPCP, EXPA (or GERD), INV, EXP]   (2.2b)

GDP = f[GDPCP, EXPA (or GERD), INV, TRD]   (2.3c)

The first model may be regarded as a pure *supply model*, where economic growth is supposed to be a function of the level of economic development GDPCP (GDP per capita with a negative expected sign), the growth of patenting activity (EXPA with a positive sign) and the investment share (INV with a positive sign). However, it can be argued that this model overlooks differences in overall growth rates between periods due to other factors and especially differences in economic policies. We can easily investigate the relationship between these two approximate measures using cross-section data on average growth rates in the period 1973-1997 for the EU member states.

The correlation between productivity and patenting is much closer than that between productivity and research expenditure. When an econometric analysis of the technological gap models is conducted, it is important to include the most relevant variables. For the level of productivity, as a proxy we can use real GDP per capita (GDPPC). For the national technological level we can use some approximate measures; for instance. we can again use the traditional variables of technological input and technological output (GERD and EXPA).

### Table 2.7	Relationship between productivity and innovation in EU member states, 1973-1997

Relation between productivity and patents:
GDPPC = 5547.23 + 529.695EXPA
t =	(7.455)	(4.544)	$R^2 = 0.28$ (adj.df 0.22). DW = 2.05
Rho (autocorrelation coefficient) = -0.0962, t = -0.344. SEs and variance shown are heteroskedastic consistent estimates.

The logarithm models:
LGDPPC = 8.068 + 0.564LEXPA
t =	(21.099)	(2.336)	$R^2 = 0.23$ (adj.df 0.16). DW = 1.69
Rho (autocorrelation coefficient) = 0.705, t = 0.223. SE's and variance shown are heteroskedastic consistent estimates.
LLGDPPC = 2.160 + 0.783LLEXPA
t = (128.747)	(2.868)	$R^2 = 0.31$ (adj. df 0.24). DW = 1.81
Rho (autocorrelation coefficient) = -0.032, t = -0.101. SEs and variance shown are heteroskedastic consistent estimates.

The relation between productivity and gross expenditures on research and development:
GDPPC = 9584.54 - 366.10GERD
t =	(5.738)	(-1.324)	$R^2 = 0.76$ (adj. df 0.52). DW = 1.644
Rho (autocorrelation coefficient) = 0.131, t = 0.475. SEs and variance shown are heteroskedastic consistent estimates.

The logarithm models:
LGDPPC = 9.424 - 0.384LGERD
t =	(25.721) (-1.529)	$R^2 = 0.091$ (adj.df 0.02) DW = 1.24
Rho (autocorrelation coefficient) = 0.347, t = 1.352. SEs and variance shown are heteroskedastic consistent estimates.
LLGDPPC = 2.200 - 0.0647LLGERD
t =	(141.439)	(-1.586)	$R^2 = 0.087$ (adj.df 0.017) DW = 1.177
Rho (autocorrelation coefficient) = 0.385, t = 1.525. SEs and variance shown are heteroskedastic consistent estimates.

Note: GDPPC = GDP per capita average for the period 1973-1997, absolute values in constant (1985) prices (US$000) for per capita GDP; EXPA = average annual growth rates for external patent applications for the period 1973~1997. GERD = average annual growth rates for the period for gross expenditure on research and development; LGDP, LPROD, LEXPA, LGERD, LEXP, LINV, LTRD, LLGERD, LLGDPCP are the above variables in a logarithmic form.

Following the model by Fagerberg (1987, 1988, 1994), we can test the basic technological gap model (with and without these variables), reflecting structural change in order to determine the degree to which these variables have added something to the other explanatory variable of the model. We shall use external patent applications (EXPA) and gross expenditure on research and development (GERD) as proxies for the growth of national technological activities, and GDP per capita (GDPPC) (in absolute values at constant prices) as a proxy for the total level of knowledge appropriated in the country (or productivity).

Investment share (INV) has been chosen as an indicator of an improvement in the capacity for economic exploitation of innovation and diffusion; the share of investment may also be seen as the outcome of a process in which institutional factors take part (since differences in the size of investment share may reflect differences in the institutional system).

Table 2.7 shows the model for the EU member states, including as additional variables exports (as a share of GDP) and the terms of trade. This indicates that growth has been influenced by changes in the terms of trade (terms of trade shock).

The export variable also has the expected sign and the results support the hypothesis of structural change as a source of economic growth. The second model takes account of structural changes using as a proxy the share of exports in GDP.

The third model uses an additional variable that reflecting changes in the macroeconomic conditions and suggests that growth rates are seriously affected by changes in the terms of trade. All reflecting models are tested for the EU member states.

The basic model is tested for the variables of GDP, GDP per capita, external patent applications and investment as a share of GDP. The explanatory power (or the overall goodness of fit of the estimated regression models) is not very high, but this is not surprising for cross-sectional data.

However, there is a problem with interdependence between variables. For this reason we shall focus on the relationship between productivity and innovation. Most variables have the expected signs.

The introduction of the terms of trade variable into the basic model led to a negative sign for the innovation variables (GERD and EXPA); indicating that the economic slowdown after 1973 can be better explained in terms of trade shock. However, some results are not statistically significant and the explanatory power is not very high.

In both cases we use the same approach; that is we first use the basic model and then we introduce the terms of trade and export variables. It is worth noting that for the technologically advanced member states the estimated coefficients display the expected signs except for exports (EXPA) and gross expenditure on R&D (GERD).

Table 2.8 The basic model tested for the EU member states, 1973-1997

The basic model including patents:
GDP = 2.824 - 0.002GDPPC + 0.10EXPA + 0.027INV
t = (1.53)   (-3.30)   (2.30)   (0.32) R^2 = 0.52 (adj. df 0.39). DW = 1.52
Rho (autocorrelation coefficient) = 0.385, t = 1.475. SEs and variance shown are
heteroskedastic consistent estimates.
The logarithm model:
LGDP = 1.499 - 0.384LGDPPC + 0.155LEXPA + 0.806LINV
t = (0.593)   (-2.569)   (0.930)   (1.340) R^2 = 0.56 (adj. df 0.42). DW = 1.36
Rho (autocorrelation coefficient) = 0.297, t = 0.985. SEs and variance shown are
heteroskedastic consistent estimates.

The basic model including patents:
PROD = 0.453 - 0.00015GDPPC - 0.0198EXPA + 0.174INV
t =   (-0.386)   (-3.979)   (-0.245)   (3.012) R^2 = 0.64 (adj. df 0.54). DW = 1.49
Rho = 0.301. SEs and variance shown are heteroskedastic consistent estimates.
The logarithmic model:
LPROD = -0.566 - 0.384LGDPPC - 0.131LEXPA + 1.558LINV
t =   (-0.220)   (-2.519)   (-0.770)   (2.541) R^2 = 0.75 (adj. df 0.66). DW = 1.38
Rho (autocorrelation coefficient) = 0.241, t = 0.786. SEs and variance shown are
heteroskedastic consistent estimates.

The basic model including the gross expenditures on research and development:
GDP = 1.775 - 0.00129GDPPC + 0.0142GERD + 0.0646INV
t =   (0.92)   (-1.86)   (0.21)   (0.75) R^2 = 0.40 (adj. df 0.24). DW = 2.30
Rho (autocorrelation coefficient) = -0.153, t=-0.539. SEs and variance shown are
heteroskedastic consistent estimates.
The logarithm model:
LGDP = 0.619 - 0.275LGDPPC + 0.00625LGERD + 0.837LINV
 t = (0.246)   (-2.098)   (0.0396)   (1.408) R^2 = 0.47 (adj. df 0.33). DW = 2.38
Rho (autocor.coefficient) = -0.228, t = -0.815. SEs and variance shown are
heteroskedastic consistent estimates.

The basic model including the gross expenditures on research and development:
PROD = 0.349 - 0.00018GDPPC - 0.0716GERD + 0.168INV
t = (0.231)   (-3.413)   (0.933)   (2.677) R^2 = 0.66 (adj. df 0.57). DW= 1.43
Rho (autocorrelation coefficient)=0.301. SEs and variance shown are heteroskedastic
consistent estimates.
The logarithmic model:
LPROD = -0.404 - 0.421LGDPPC - 0.0345LGERD + 1.568LINV
t = (-0.130)   (-2.585)   (-0.176)   (2.126) R^2 = 0.61 (adj. df 0.50) DW=1.79
Rho (autocorrelation coefficient) = -0.0131, t = -0.0402. SEs and variance shown are
heteroskedastic consistent estimates.

Note: GDP = annual average growth rates for real gross domestic product; PROD = annual
average growth rates for product (defined as labour product GDP per person employed);
GDPPC = average absolute values in constant (1985) prices (US$000) for GDP per capita;
EXPA = annual average growth rates for external patent applications. GERD = annual
average growth rates for gross expenditures on research and development; EXP = annual
average growth rates for exports as a share of GDP; INV = annual average growth rates for
investment as a share of GDP; TRD = annual average growth rates for the terms of trade.
LGDP, LPROD, LEXPA, LGERD, LEXP, LINV and LTRD are the above variables in a
logarithmic form.

The results do not support the hypothesis of structural changes as independent causal factors of economic growth. These results can be seen as supporting the view that the influence of a change in outward orientation towards growth depends on international macroeconomic conditions (since random shocks and crises and slow growth in world demand in the 1970s restrained the growth of outward-oriented countries).

4.3 An Historical Overview of Initial Functional Forms

Paul Douglas was very devoted paid much attention to explain the movements of labour productivity and real wages over time (Cobb Charles and Paul H. Douglas (1928), "A Theory of Production", American Economic Review, Supplement Vol. 18, pp. 139-165). Douglas wanted to test the marginal productivity theory. The important issue for him was if labour was in fact paid the value of its marginal product. Furthermore Cobb and Douglas assumed that production was characterised by constant returns to scale. They related empirically in a logarithmic form the value added output to the inputs of capital and labour for the US manufacturing based on annual data for the period 1899-1922.

$$\ln Y = \ln A + \alpha_K \ln K + \alpha_L \ln L$$

where: Y are the output (value added), and K, L is capital and labour respectively.

The assumption of constant returns to scale (or otherwise the homogeneity of degree one) imply the restriction for the parameters $\alpha_K + \alpha_L = 1$. The non-logarithmic form is $Y = A K^\alpha L^\beta$, and multiplying by $\lambda > 1$, we have: $\lambda^\mu Y = A(\lambda K^\alpha)(\lambda L^\beta) = AK^\alpha L^\beta \lambda^{\alpha+\beta}$. This function is homogeneous of degree $\mu=\alpha+\beta$ and when $\mu =1$ then $\alpha+\beta=1$. Rearranging the above logarithmic equation of labour productivity to the capital/labour ratio:

$$\ln(Y/L) = \ln A + \alpha_K \ln (K/L)$$

The corresponding non-logarithmic form with constant returns to scale using for the empirical implementation has the following form:

$$Y = A K^\alpha L^{1-\alpha}$$

Rearranging the above non-logarithmic equation, taking the partial derivatives of Y with respect to K and L and equating the marginal products with the real input prices and solving, we can obtain:

$$\alpha_K = \frac{P_K K}{PY} \quad \text{and}$$

$$\alpha_L = 1 - \alpha_K = \frac{P_L L}{PY}$$

Cobb and Douglas argued that if markets were competitive, if marginal products equated to the real prices and if production technology following the constant returns to scale, then the least squares estimates of the parameters α_K and α_L should be equal approximately to the value shares of capital and labour.

Nevertheless, other economists were more interested in measuring substitution elasticities among inputs. They defined the substitution elasticity between capital and labour as following:

$$\sigma = \frac{\partial \ln(K/L)}{\partial \ln(F_L/F_K)} = \frac{\partial \ln(K/L)}{\partial \ln(P_L/P_K)}$$

where: F_K and F_L are the marginal products of capital and labour respectively.

For the Cobb-Douglas function the substitution of elasticity (σ) always equals to unity. Using the theory of cost and production Ragnar Frisch was attempted to measure the substitution elasticities between the inputs and estimated a substitution coefficient (the ratio of marginal productivities) between the inputs (Frisch Ragnar (1935) "The principle of substitution: an example of its application in the chocolate industry", *Nordisk Tidsskrift for Teknisk Okonomi*, 1:1, pp. 12-27.).

Later, an extension of the Cobb-Douglas function was introduced by Kenneth Arrow, Hollis Chenery, Bagicha Minhas, and Robert Solow. In their model, Arrow, Chenery, Minhas, and Solow tried to search in which functional form the substitution of elasticity (σ) will be constant but not constrained to unity. They concluded in the following equation:

$$\ln(K/L) = \text{constant} + \sigma \ln(F_K/F_L)$$

where the second term (F_K/F_L) indicates the marginal rate of substitution.

The above function indicates the well-known Constant Elasticity of Substitution (CES) production function with constant returns to scale, which can be expressed as follows:

$$Y = A[\delta K^{-\rho} + (1-\delta)L^{-\rho}]^{-1/\rho}$$

where the substitution of elasticity $\sigma = 1/(1+\rho)$

There is a limiting case in which $\rho \to 0, \sigma \to 0$, the Cobb-Douglas function is a limiting form of the CES function. In fact, the Constant Elasticity of Substitution, CES, production function has appeared in the literature a quarter century earlier than Cobb-Douglas production function. The CES production function has been derived from consumer demand analysis. Abraham Bergson used the following function (Bergson (Burk) Abraham (1936) "Real Income, Expenditure Proportionality, and

Frisch's New Method of Measuring Utility", Review of Economic Studies, Vol. 4:1, October, pp. 33-52):

$$Y^{-\rho} = A\left(\sum_{i=1}^{n} \delta_i X_i^{-\rho}\right)$$

Nerlove estimated a three input Cobb-Douglas cost function (namely, capital, labour and fuels) with returns to scale to be other than constant; his empirical analysis indicated that the returns to scale were increasing rather than being constant (Bergson (Burk) Abraham (1936) "Real Income, Expenditure Proportionality, and Frisch's New Method of Measuring Utility", Review of Economic Studies, Vol. 4:1, October, pp. 33-52). However, Nerlove was unsatisfied with the restricted assumptions of Cobb-Douglas function according to which the substitution of elasticities required to be equal to unity and by CES which implied some other restrictions for the substitution of elasticities; that is, it required to be constant and equal to each other.

Lucas et al. have attempted to reconcile the seemingly disparate cross-sectional and time-series estimates of substitution of elasticity (σ) (Lucas Robert (1969) "Labour-Capital Substitution in US Manufacturing" in Arnold C. Harberger and Martin J. Bailey eds. *The Taxation of Income from Capital*, Washington, DC: The Brooking Institution, pp. 223-274).

In 1961 in their book *Agricultural Production Function*, Earl Heady and John Dillon experimented with Taylor's series expansion introduced the second-degree polynomial in logarithms that added quadratic and cross-terms to the Cobb-Douglas function (Heady Earl and John L. Dillon (1961) *Agricultural Production Functions*, Ames, Iowa: Iowa State University Press). They estimated the production function directly using least square methods and called this procedure production function contour fitting. They reported the least squares estimates of a square root transformation that included the generalised linear production function introduced by Erwin Diewert in 1971 (Diewert Erwin (1971) "An Application of the Shepard Duality Theorem: A Generalized Linear Production Function", *Journal of Political Economy*, Vol. 79:3, May/June, pp. 482-507). Diwert's Generalized Leontief Functional Form was the first in the theory of dual cost and production.

Daniel McFadden focused on the theory and its applications of duality in production (Daniel McFadden (1978) *Production Economics: A Dual Approach to Theory and Applications*, Vol. 1, Amsterdam, North Holland). He examined both the use of duality theory and the problem of generating more flexible functional forms with more than two or three inputs and less restrictive forms than the Cobb-Douglas and CES specifications.

Moreover, several other empirical results have been reported in literature in 1971. Nervlove surveyed empirical findings (Nerlove Marc (1967) "Recent Empirical Studies of the CES and Related Production Functions" in Murray Brown ed., *The Theory and Empirical Analysis of Production*, Studies in Income and Wealth, Vol. 32, New York, Columbia University Press for the National Bureau of Economic Research, pp. 55-122), and, in 1973, Berndt summarised additional empirical findings (Berndt Ernst (1976) "Reconciling Alternative Estimates of the Elasticity of Substitution", *Review of Economics and Statistics*, Vol. 58:1, February, pp. 59-68).

A decade later (1970), Laurits Christensen, Dale W. Jorgenson, and Lawrence J. Lau introduced a flexible functional form, the "translog production function", a form that placed no restrictions on the substitution of elasticities (Christensen Laurits, Dale W. Jorgenson and Lawrence J. Lau (1971) "Conjugate Duality and the Transcendental Logarithmic Production Function", *Econometrica*, Vol. 39:4, July, pp. 255-256, and Christensen Laurits, Dale W. Jorgenson and Lawrence J. Lau (1973) "Conjugate Duality and the Transcendental Logarithmic Production Function", *Review of Economics and Statistics*, Vol. 55:1, February, pp. 28-45). The translog function was a second order Taylor's series in logarithms and was identical to the production function considered by Heady some decades earlier. It should be mentioned however that Heady emphasised only the primal production function; he did not consider the dual cost or even the specifications of the profit function.

Lastly, Boskin and Lau introduced another flexible functional form "the meta-production function", that is an extension of translog production function and can be employed with the panel or pool data (Boskin, M.J. and Lau, L.J. (1992) "Capital, Technology and Economic Growth", Chapter 2 in Rosenberg, Landau and Mowery (ed.) *Technology and the Wealth of Nations*, Stanford University Press). This function form places no *a priori* restrictions on the substitution possibilities among the inputs of production. It also allows scale economies to vary with the level of output. This feature is essential because it enables the unit cost curve to attain the classical shape.

Econometric applications of cost and production functions differ in their assumptions. In the regression of the production function, output is endogenous and input quantities are exogenous. In the dual cost function, the production costs and the input quantities are endogenous. When output and input prices can be considered as exogenous, then it is better to apply a cost function that has input prices as regressors, rather than a production function in which input quantities are the right-hand variables (Zellner Arnold, Jan Kmenta and Jaques Dreze (1966) "Specification and Estimation of Cobb-Douglas Production Function Models", *Econometrica*, Vol. 34:3, October, pp. 784-795).

Empirical research on estimating cost and production function relationships has a long history, trying to explain the average labour productivity, and the interrelationship between inputs and outputs, to estimate the substitution elasticities among inputs and, finally, to estimate the returns to scale. The production function parameters can be uniquely recovered from estimation of the demand equations derived from the dual cost function (A cost function is dual in the sense that it embodies all the parameters of the underlying production function; see Berbdt Ernst (1991) *The Practice of Econometrics: Class and Contemporary*, Addison-Wesley Publishing Company).

The empirical analysis of input demands and input substitution patterns provides an example of the strong links between economic theory and econometric implementation. The econometric techniques that we employ deal with estimation of parameters in systems of equations.

In addition, the implementation of a multi-product cost functions can permit a richer analysis of the effects on costs and factor demands of various changes in the composition and levels of output; some recent examples of empirical implementation of multi-product cost functions can be found among others in Douglas Caves and Lauritis Christensen.

4.3.1 The Generalised Leontief Function

There is a number of ways to approach the estimation of production function and technical progress. The aim of this section is to examine the theory of *Generalised Leontief production function* and the translog cost function. The *Generalised Leontief functional form* which proposed by Diewert has been established as a useful alternative for the long-run production studies. We can consider the following *Generalised Leontief functional form* for a cost function. Using the following equation:

$$C(w_K, w_L, Y, T) = \alpha_0 + \alpha_Y Y + \alpha_{YY} Y^2 + \sum_{i=1}^{n} \alpha_i w_i + \sum_{i=1}^{n} \sum_{j=1}^{n} \gamma_{ij} w_i^{1/2} w_j^{1/2} +$$

$$\sum_{i=1}^{n} \gamma_{it} w_i^{1/2} T + \gamma_t \sum_{i=1}^{n} w_i^{1/2} T + \gamma_{YY} \sum_{i=1}^{n} w_i^{1/2} Y^2 + \gamma_{iT} \sum_{i=1}^{n} w_i^{1/2} T^2 Y + \gamma_{TT} T^2 + \gamma_{YT} T$$

where C is the total cost, Y is the output, wij the prices of n inputs (i, j = 1,........,n), Qij the n input quantities, and T is the time trend, with the constant returns to scale that can be written as:

$$C = Y \left[\sum_{i=1}^{n} \sum_{j=1}^{n} \gamma_{ij} (w_i w_j)^{1/2} \right] \qquad (2.1)$$

where C is the total cost, Y is the output, w_{ij} the prices of n inputs (i, j = 1,........,n), and Q_{ij} the n input quantities, with $\gamma_{ij} = \gamma_{ji}$ (i,j=1,2,...., n). The parameters γ_{ij} are such that (a) $\gamma_{ij} = \gamma_{ji}$ and (b) $\gamma_{ij} \geq 0$ (for i, j=1,2,..,n).

Let us assume that we have n inputs, as w_i (i=1,...,n), with the n input quantities Q_i, and the total cost indicating by C and the output by Y.

We assume that the output and the input prices Y and w_{ij} are exogenous, while the input quantities Q_{ij} are endogenous.

The cost C defined by equation (2.1) is linearly homogeneous in input-prices w and has N(N=1)/2+2N+3 independent d parameters, just the right number to be flexible functional form (Diwert and Wales, 1987 and Diewert Erwin and Terence

J. Wales (1987) "Flexible Functional Forms and Global Curvature Conditions", *Econometrica*, Vol. 55:1, January, pp. 43-68).

The first set of N(N+1)/2 independent terms on the right had side of equation (2.1) correspond to the *"Generalised Leontief cost function"* for a constant returns to scale technology with no technological progress (Diewert) (Diewert Erwin (1971) "An Application of the Shepard Duality Theorem: A Generalized Linear Production Function", *Journal of Political Economy*, Vol. 79:3, May/June, pp. 482-507 and also, Diewert Erwin (1974) "Applications of Duality Theory" in Michael D. Intriligator and David A. Kendrick eds., *Frontiers of Quantitative Economics*, Vol. II, Amsterdam. North Holland, pp. 106-171).

The ith input demand function which correspond to equation (1) can be obtained by differentiating C with respect to w_i (using the *"Shephard's lemma"*).

$$X_i(w, Y, T) = \sum_{i=1}^{n} \gamma_{ij} w_i^{1/2} w_j^{1/2} Y + \gamma_i + \gamma_{it} TY + \gamma_t T + \gamma_{YY} Y^2 + \gamma_{TT} T^2 Y$$

with (i=1,2,,...n).

The *Generlaised Leotief linear function* can also be written as: $Y = H(A_{11}K + A_{12}K^{1/2}L^{1/2} + A_{22}L)$, where, Aii's are parameters and H is a single value increasing function. We also assume the *homotheticity hypothesis* for H (Yasushi Toda).

The function $w_i^{1/2} w_j^{1/2}$ is concave in w and as a nonnegative sum of concave functions is concave. That function is a nondecreasing in γ follows from the nonnegativity of the parameters γ_{ij}. If all $\gamma_{ij}=0$ (for i, j) then the above equation reduces to a linear production function.

The production function given by equation exhibits constant returns to scale; we can generalize equation to any degree of returns to scale by:

$$c = f\left(\sum_{i=1}^{n} \sum_{i=j}^{n} \gamma_{ij} w_i^{1/2} w_j^{1/2} \right)$$

(2.1')

where, $\gamma_{ij} = \gamma_{ji} \geq 0$ and f is a continuous monotonically increasing function which tends to plus infinity and has f(0)=0.

The *"Generalized Leontief cost function"* and the *"Generalized linear production function"* are very useful by providing a second-order approximations to an arbitrary twice differentiable cost function (or production function) at a given vector of factor prices or at a given vector of inputs using minimal number of parameters.

In order to be able to obtain equations that are responsible to estimation, it is convenient to employ the shephard's lemma which states that the optimal cost-minimising demand for input i can simply be derived from differentiating the cost function with respect to w_i.

Therefore, if we differentiate the equation (2.1) with respect to w_i yielding the equation (2.2) and dividing the equation by Y, then yielding the optimal input-output equation (2.3) denoted by α_i:

$$\alpha_i = \frac{X_i}{Y} = \sum_{j=1}^{n} \gamma_{ij} \, (w_i/w_i)^{1/2} \tag{2.2}$$

$$\frac{\partial C}{\partial w_i} = X_i = Y \left[\sum_{j=1}^{n} \gamma_{ij}(w_i w_j)^{1/2} \right] \tag{2.3}$$

when, $i = j$ then $(w_j/w_i)^{1/2}$ is equal to 1 and the γ_{ij} is a constant term in the input-output equation.

Assuming two inputs, such as K = the capital and L = the labour and also Y = the output. The "*Generalised Leontief cost-minimising*" equations are the followings:

$$\alpha_K = \frac{K}{Y} = \gamma_{KK} + \gamma_{KL}(w_L / w_K)^{1/2} \tag{2.3'}$$

$$\alpha_L = \frac{L}{Y} = \gamma_{LL} + \gamma_{KL}(w_K / w_L)^{1/2} \tag{2.4}$$

The estimates of all parameters in the "*Generalised Leontief cost function*" can be obtained by estimating only the input-output demand equations (3) and (4); this occurs because there is no intercept term in the "*Generalised Leontief cost function*" owing to the assumption of the constant returns to scale. Finally, if $\gamma_{ij} = 0$ for all i and j, then the input-output demand equations are independent of the relative input prices and all the cross-price elasticities are equal to zero.

Although equation by equation OLS estimation might appear attractive since the input demand functions (2.3') and (2.4) are linear in the parameters, these demand equations have cross-equation symmetry constraints. Even these constraints hold in the population, for any given sample equation-by-equation OLS estimates will not reveal such restrictions; for example, γ_{KL} in the K/Y equation estimated by OLS will not necessarily equal γ_{LK} estimated in the L/Y equation (for a more detailed analysis see Berbdt Ernst (1991) *The Practice of Econometrics: Class and Contemporary*, Addison-Wesley Publishing Company). Constant returns to scale restrictions imply the symmetry restrictions (the cost shares sum to one).

To implement the "*Generalised Leontief model*" empirically, a stochastic framework must be specified. An additive disturbance term is appended to each of the input-output equations and is typically assumed that the resulting disturbance vector is independently and identically normally distributed with mean vector zero and constant, nonsingular covariance matrix Ω.

An attractive feature of the "*Generalised Leontief cost function*" is that they place no a-priory restrictions on the substitution elasticities. The elasticity of factor substitution measures the responsiveness of the ratio of factor inputs to changes in the ratio of the marginal product of the inputs.

The Hicks-Allen partial elasticities of substitution for a "*general dual cost function*" (between inputs i and j in a general functional form with n inputs) can be expressed as:

$$\sigma_{ij} = (C * C_{ij}) / (C_i * C_j),$$

where the subscripts i and j refer to the first and the second partial derivatives of the cost function with respect to the input prices w_i and w_j.

In particular, for "*Generalised Leontief cost function*" the cross-substitution elasticities are given:

$$\sigma ij = \frac{1}{2} \frac{C\gamma_{ij}(w_i w_j)^{-1/2}}{Y\alpha i\alpha j} \tag{2.5}$$

where i, j = 1,........, n (with $i \neq j$).

While the own-substitution elasticities are given as following:

$$\sigma ii = \frac{-\dfrac{1}{2} C \displaystyle\sum_{\substack{j=1 \\ j \neq 1}}^{n} \gamma_{ij}(w_j^{1/2} w_i^{-3/2})}{Y\alpha_i^2} \tag{2.6}$$

where i, j = 1,........, n.

We will be able to estimate the price elasticities with the output quantity, while assuming that all the other input prices are fixed. The familiar price elasticities are given by:

$$\varepsilon_{ij} = \frac{\partial \ln X_i}{\partial \ln w_j} = \left(\frac{\partial X_i}{\partial w_j}\right)\left(\frac{w_j}{X_i}\right)$$

(see Berbdt Erns (1991) *The Practice of Econometrics: Class and Contemporary*, Addison-Wesley Publishing Company).

We can also use the calculation of the following formula:

$$\varepsilon_{ij} = S_i * \sigma_{ij},$$

where S_i is the cost share of the jth input in the total production costs.

For the "*Generalised Leontief cost function*" the cross-prices elasticities are computed as following:

$$\varepsilon_{ij} = \frac{1}{2} \cdot \frac{\gamma_{ij}(w_i / w_j)^{-1/2}}{\alpha i} \tag{2.7}$$

where i, j = 1,........, n (with $i \neq j$).

While the own-prices elasticities are computed as follows:

$$\varepsilon_{ij} = \frac{-\dfrac{1}{2} \displaystyle\sum_{\substack{j=1 \\ j \neq 1}}^{n} \gamma_{ij}(w_i / w_j)^{-1/2}}{\alpha_i} \tag{2.8}$$

where i, j = 1,........, n. In order the own-prices elasticity to be negative it is necessary the summation portion of equation (2.8) to be positive.

Because the equations (2.7) and (2.8) of elasticity computations are based on the estimated parameters, and the predicted or fitted values of C and α_i, α_j, it is necessary to check the elasticity calculations which always must be hold:

$$\sum_{j=1}^{n} \varepsilon_{ij} = 0 \quad \text{, (with i = 1,...,n)}$$

(see Berbdt Ernst (1991) *The Practice of Econometrics: Class and Contemporary*, Addison-Wesley Publishing Company).

Since the input prices and α_i vary between observations, then the estimators of σ_{ij} and ε_{ij} will also differ between observations. The price elasticities are not symmetric that means $\varepsilon_{ij} \neq \varepsilon_{ji}$ unlike the Hicks-Allen elasticities and our assumption of $\sigma_{ij} = \sigma_{ji}$. According to equations (2.5) (2.6) (2.7), and (2.8) the input i and j are substitutes, independent or complement inputs depending on whether the estimated γ_{ij} is positive, zero, or negative values. To ensure as its required by theory that the estimated cost function is monotonically increasing and strictly quasi-concave in input prices, we must verify that the fitted values for all the input-output equations are positive and that the n x n matrix of the σ_{ij} substitution elasticities is negative semi-definite at each observation. Because the computed elasticites depend on the estimated parameters and therefore are stochastic, the estimated elasticities have also variances and covariances, we should calculate these variances.

4.3.2 Modelling Technological Progress in a Production Function

The cost function approach does not dominate the production function approach; the choice depends on the parameters to be estimated. For example, for reasons much the same as the ones given above, the production function approach is preferable when estimates of factor productivity is sought. A production function is by definition a relationship between outputs and inputs. For a single country, say ith, the production function may be written as:

$$y_{it} = F_i(X_{i1t}, X_{i2t}, \ldots\ldots, X_{imt}, t),$$

where: y_{it} is the quantity of output produced per producer unit and X_{ijt} is the quantity of the jth input employed per producer unit (j=1,2,....m) in the ith country for the period.

This model contributes substantially and upgrade the methodologies adopted therein. It is possible to distinguish several different aspects of this procedure. For instance:

- The model was first proposed by Jorgenson D.W. and Fraumeni B.M. (1983). Their main innovation was that they estimated the rate of technical change along with income share equations as functions of relative input prices. The shares and the rate of technical change are derived from a translog production function.
- The procedure is decomposed i the estimated technical change of three components: *pure technology*, which is only the time element times a coefficient; *non-neutral* component, which shows how time trend influences the usage of inputs; *scale augmenting* component, which suggests how time affects the economies of scale. The sum of these three components give the growth of *multifactor productivity*.
- In addition, we can relax the assumption of constant returns to scale by estimating the initial cost function along with factor shares and the rate of technological change, and so provides the evidence for the existence of *scale economies*.

In a cross section study, technology can be regarded as given in each country, but this is clearly not in the case when we consider a single country over a period of time. The country's production function will shift as new and more efficient techniques are adopted. A major problem with time series data is to distinguish between increases in output resulting from movements along the production function (for instance, from increased inputs) and increases in output which occur because of shifts in the production function resulting from the technical progress. The problem of simultaneous equation bias is present with time-series data as with cross sectional data. However, there is a more serious problem with time series data that of the technical progress or innovation over time. With cross sectional data, the identification problem can arise if product and factor prices show any marked tendency to change at similar rates over time, as this may leave price ratios constant; see also Thomas R.L. 1993.

The concept of a production function plays an important role in both micro- and macro-economics. At the macro level, it has been combined with the marginal productivity theory to explain the prices of the various factors of production and the extent to which these factors are utilised. The production function has been used as a tool for assessing what proportion of any increase in the output over time can be attributed first to increase in the inputs of factors in the production, second to the increasing returns to scale and third to *technical progress*.

Most studies of the production function (Solow 1957, Griliches 1967) have been handled under one or more traditionally maintained hypothesis of *constant returns of scale, neutrality of technical progress* and *profit maximisation* with competitive output and input markets. Therefore, the validity or otherwise of each of these hypotheses affects the measurement of technical progress and the decomposition of economic growth into its sources.

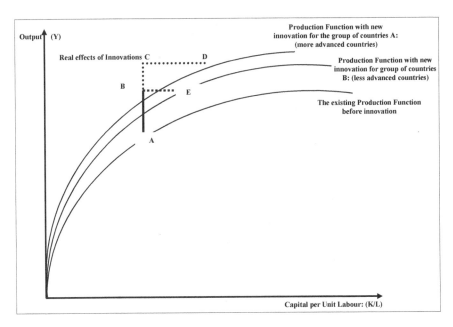

Figure 2.1 Technical change and innovation in production function
Source: Korres, G., 2003.

Following Landau's analysis, we can assume that there is a production function that relates output to capital per unit of labour and that the economy is at the point A, where labour force growth is static and investment is at an average level. When a new technology is introduced, there is an upward shift of the production function. Of course, the shift of the production function will be different across different countries. This shift of the production function implies additional output per person, and this most likely can lead to extra savings and consequently to more capital per worker, which means that economy will move along the production function. Figure 2.1 shows that the economy reaches the point E for less advanced countries and point D for more advanced countries. The real effects of innovation can now be measured by the distances AE and AD respectively.

The methodology of a translog function is based on a two-input (capital and labour) case dual translog cost function (Christensen, Jorgenson and Lau 1971, 1973), the derived factor shares and on the rate of technical change for all twenty industrial sectors. All these variables are functions of relative prices and time. Implicitly, it is assumed that total cost and input shares are translog functions of their corresponding prices and time. Technology is in fact endogenous in our sectoral models and is parametrically rather than residually estimated.

Implementing Jorgenson and Fraumeni's methodology, we fitted the models so that they embrace all of these theoretical requirements. Since perfect competition is assumed, the input prices are exogenously determined. The translog cost function can be written:

$$lnc^v(w_K, w_L, Y, T) = \alpha_0^v + \alpha_y^v lny^v + \frac{1}{2}\alpha_{yy}^v(lny^v)^2 + \sum_{i=1}^{n}\alpha_i^v lnw_i^v + \frac{1}{2}\sum_{i=1}^{n}\sum_{j=1}^{n}\gamma_{ij}^v lnw_i^v lnw_j^v + \sum_{i=1}^{n}\gamma_{iy}^v lnw_i^v lny^v$$

$$\gamma_T^v T + \frac{1}{2}\gamma_{TT}^v T^2 + \sum_{i=1}^{n}\gamma_{iT}^v lnw_i^v T + \gamma_{yT}^v \ln y^v T \tag{2.1}$$

where C= total cost, Wi (i= K,L)=input prices (price of capital and labour), Y= value-added, and T= technical change index.

Since we use the averages, we have to transform the cost function, the share equations and the rate of technical change as (for simplicity purposes, we can drop the superlative index which declares the number of sectors):

$$\overline{lnc}^v(\overline{w}_K, \overline{w}_L, \overline{Y}, T) = \alpha_0^v + \alpha_y^v \overline{lny}^v + \frac{1}{2}\alpha_{yy}^v (\overline{lny}^v)^2 + \sum_{i=1}^{n}\alpha_i^v \overline{lnw_i}^v + \frac{1}{2}\sum_{i=1j=1}^{n}\gamma_{ij}^v \overline{lnw_i}^v \overline{lnw_j}^v$$

$$+\sum_{i=1}^{n}\gamma_{iy}^v \overline{lnw_i}^v \overline{lny}^v + \gamma_T^v T + \frac{1}{2}\gamma_{TT}^v T^2 + \gamma_{iT}^v \overline{lnw_i}^v T + \gamma_{yT}^v \overline{lny}^v T + \overline{e}_\varepsilon^v \tag{2.2}$$

$$\bar{S}_i^v(w_K, w_L, Y, T) = \alpha_i^v + \sum_{i=1}^{n} \gamma_{ij}^v \overline{lnw_j}^v + \gamma_{iy}^v \overline{lnY}^v + \gamma_{iT}^v T + \bar{e}_i^v \qquad (2.3)$$

$$-\bar{S}_T^v(w_k, w_L, Y, T) = \gamma_T^v + \gamma_{TT}^v T + \sum_{i=1}^{n} \gamma_{iT}^v \overline{lnw_i}^v + \gamma_{yT}^v \overline{lnY}^v + \bar{e}_T^v \qquad (2.4)$$

where the share equation and the rate of technical change take the form:

Where v = 1,...,20 and i = K, L, are the average error terms. The share equations have the following form: S_K (share of capital)=$(P_K*Q_K)/TC$ and S_L (share of labour)=$(P_L*Q_L)/TC$, where $P_{K,L}$ is the price of capital and the price of labour, $Q_{K,L}$ is the capital and labour and TC is the total cost.

The Allen-Uzava partial elasticities of substitution, σ_{ij}, and price elasticities of input demands, P_{ij} are given by following equations:

$$\sigma_{ij} = (\gamma_{ii} + S_i^2 - S_i)(S_i^2), \quad i = K, L \ i = j$$

$$\qquad (2.5) \text{ and}$$

$$\sigma_{ij} = (\gamma_{ij} + S_i S_j)(S_i S_j), \quad i,j = K, L \ i \neq j$$

where the own-partial elasticities of substitution, σ_{ii}, are expected to be negative. The cross-partial elasticities of substitution can be either positive, suggesting substitutability between inputs, or negative, suggesting input complementarity.

$$P_{ij} = \sigma_{ij} S_j, i = K, L \ i \neq j$$

$$\qquad (2.6) \text{ and}$$

$$P_{ii} = \sigma_{ii} S_i, i = K, L \ i = j$$

Several comments should be made on these substitution elasticity estimates. First, parameter estimates and fitted shares should replace the γ's and S's, when computing estimates of the σ_{ij} and P_{ij}. This implies that, in general, the estimated elasticities will vary across observations. Second, since the parameter estimates and fitted shares have variances and covariances, the estimated substitution elasticities also have stochastic distributions. Third, the estimated translog cost function should be checked to ensure that it is monotonically increasing and strictly quasi-concave in input prices, as required by theory. For monotonicity, it is required that the fitted shares all be positive, and for strict quasi-concavity the (n x n) matrix of substitution elasticities must be negative semidefinite at each observation. Moreover, we may calculate the scale elasticities (which is the percentages change of the total cost after the change one percentage in the output). As Giora Hanoch (1975) has shown that scale elasticities are computed as the inverse of costs with respect to output. More specifically, *scale* =$1/e_{cy}$ where $e_{cy}= \partial lnc/\partial lny$, that is, for the translog function:

$$\bar{e}_{cy}^v = a_y + a_{yy} \overline{lnY}^v + \sum_i^n \gamma_{ij} \overline{lnP_i}^v + \gamma_{YT} \overline{T} \qquad (2.7)$$

A number of additional parameter restrictions can be imposed on the translog cost function, corresponding to further restrictions on the underlying technology model. For the translog cost function to be homothetic, it is necessary and sufficient that $\gamma_{iy} = 0 \; \forall \; i = 1,...,n$. Homogeneity of a constant degree in output occurs if, besides these homotheticity restrictions, we have $\gamma_{yy} = 0$. In this case, the degree of homogeneity equals $1/\alpha_y$. Constant returns to scale of the dual production function occurs when, in addition to the above homotheticity and homogeneity restrictions, $\alpha_y = 1$.

One potential problem with estimation of scale economies, however, is that α_y and γ_{YY} parameters do not appear in the share equations, and so these parameters cannot be estimated, if only the share equation system (equations 2.2, 2.3, 2.4) is used. To estimate the above model of the average cost functions along with the share of one input and the rate of technical change, we have adopted the three stage least squares --with endogenous lag variables-- (for instance, lag shares, lag prices of capital, labour and output). This method requires the usage of instrumental variables. We picked up the lagged variables of capital stock, price of capital, value added, price of output, number of employees and the price of labour. To interpret the estimates of these parameters, it is useful to recall that if the production function is increases in capital and labour inputs then the average value shares are non negative.

The specification of the cost-function does not impose any restriction on technological change and returns to scale. Invoking Shephard's lemma obtains the familiar cost shares, which together with the above equations, provide the basis for the estimation:

$$\frac{\partial \ln C^v}{\partial T} = -S_T^v(w_k, w_L, Y, T) \tag{2a}$$

where

$$S_i^v(w_K, w_L, Y, T) = \alpha_i^v + \sum_{i=1}^{n} \gamma_{ij}^v lnw_j^v + \gamma_{iy}^v ln\,Y^v + \gamma_{iT}^v T \tag{2b}$$

The rate of technical change in each sector is given as the negative of the rate of growth of sectoral cost with respect to time, holding input prices constant. Doing this, we can get:

$$\frac{\partial \ln C^v}{\partial T} = -S_T^v(w_k, w_L, Y, T) \tag{2c}$$

$$-S_T^v(w_k, w_L, Y, T) = \gamma_T^v + \gamma_{TT}^v T + \sum_{i=1}^{n} \gamma_{iT}^v lnw_i^v + \gamma_{yT}^v ln\,Y \tag{2d}$$

or s.t.: $\gamma_{ij} = \gamma_{ji}$, $i \neq j$, $i,j = K,L$, $v = 1,...,20$ is the number of sectors.

$$\Sigma \alpha_i = 1 \; ; \Sigma \gamma_{ij} = \Sigma \gamma_{ji} = 0$$

$$\Sigma \gamma_{it} = 0; \text{ and } \Sigma \gamma_{yi} = 0$$

(2e)

The restrictions (equations e) imposed on the cost function, the cost-shares and on the rate of technological change imply that the share equations satisfy:

$$\Sigma \alpha_i = 1 \; ; \Sigma \gamma_{ij} = \Sigma \gamma_{ji} = \Sigma \gamma_{iy} = \Sigma \gamma_{it} = 0$$

The second order parameters, for instance γ_{KK}, γ_{LL} and γ_{KL} are defined as the constant share elasticities which are derived from the differentiation of the factor shares with respect to logarithmic prices. The coefficients γ_{KT} and γ_{LT} are the biases of technical change and they are given by differentiating the rate of technical change with respect to input prices. If we differentiate again the rate of technical change equation (c) with respect the time then we get γ_{TT}, which shows the rate of change of the negative of the rate of technical change.

The function C has to be non-decreasing in input prices so the factor shares have to be non-negative throughout the sample period. If we denote as (S) the matrix of shares and (H) the Hessian matrix of the second order terms, then we may represent the matrix of share elasticities, say Q, in the form:

$$Q = (1/C) \; P*H*P - ss' + S$$

where

$$P = \begin{bmatrix} w_K & 0 \\ 0 & w_L \end{bmatrix} \quad S = \begin{bmatrix} S_K & 0 \\ 0 & S_L \end{bmatrix} \quad s = \begin{bmatrix} S_K \\ S_L \end{bmatrix}$$ Now, concavity implies that the cost function has to have a negative semi-definite H matrix. If we rewrite equation (Q), we can get:

$$(1/C) \; P*H*P = Q + ss' - S$$

which is negative semidefinite, if and only if, H matrix is negative semidefinite. This is very useful outcome because it gives right to represent the unknown parameters using the Cholesky factorisation:

$$Q + ss' - S = L*D*L'$$

where L is a unit lower triangular matrix and D is a diagonal matrix with non-positive terms. Implementing the above transformation permits to the share elasticities matrix and to guarantee concavity in the sample period.

The idea here is to estimate the rate of technical change along with the share equations but what is the quantity of S_T? Although it is unobserved, we may circumvent this problem by considering the *translog price index* for the rate of technical change. We may say that the technical change between any two points of time, T and T-1 is given by the subtraction from the growth of total cost the growth of each input price weighted by their corresponding average shares:

$$-\overline{S}_T^v = [(\; lnc - (T)^v - lnc - (T-1)^v) - \textstyle\sum_{i=1}^n \overline{S}_i^v (lnw_{i(T)}^v - lnw_{i(T-1)}^v)\;] \qquad (2f)$$

where T = time (i = K, L and v = 1,...,20 the number of sectors).

Within the same context we may derive the average shares as:

$$\overline{S}_i^v = \frac{1}{2} [\; S_{i(T)}^v + S_{i(T-1)}^v \;] \qquad (2g)$$

T = time (i = K, L and v = 1,...,20 the number of sectors).

The above restrictions also imply an adding up condition of the share equation system (2.2) such as:

$$\textstyle\sum_i \overline{S}_i^v = 1$$

This adding up feature of the share equation has several important econometric implications, to which we now turn our attention.

$$\overline{e}_c^v = \frac{1}{2} (\; e_{c(T)}^v + e_{c(T-1)}^v\;) \qquad (2h)$$

$$\overline{e}_i^v = \frac{1}{2} (\; e_{i(T)}^v + e_{i(T-1)}^v\;) \qquad (2j)$$

$$\overline{e}_T^v = \frac{1}{2} (\; e_{T(T)}^v + e_{T(T-1)}^v\;) . \qquad (2k)$$

First, since the shares always sum to unity and only n-1 of the share equations are linearly independent, for each observation the sum of the disturbances across equations must always equal zero. Second, because the shares sum to unity at each observation, when the symmetry restrictions are not imposed, the residuals across equations will sum to zero at each observation; that is,

$$\overline{e}_K^v + \overline{e}_L^v = 0$$

Finally, from the translog function reduces to the constant returns into scale Cobb-Douglas function when, in addition to all the above restrictions, each of the $\gamma_{ji}=0$ i, j=1,...,n.

4.3.3 Theoretical Background of a Meta-Production Function

This approach enables us to identify not only the returns to scale and the rate of technical progress in each economy but also their biases, if any. The estimated aggregate *meta-production function* can be used as the basis for a new measurement of technical progress as well as a new measurement of the relative contributions of capital, labour and technical progress to economic growth. The concept of a *meta-production function* is theoretically attractive because it is based on the simple hypothesis that all countries (producers) have potential access to the same technology. The production function applies to standardised (or efficiency equivalent) quantities of outputs and inputs; that is,

$$Y^*_{it} = F(K^*_{it}, L^*_{it}) \quad i = 1,2,....,n \tag{2.1}$$

where: Y^*_{it}, K^*_{it}, L^*_{it} are the quantities of output, capital and labour respectively of the ith country at the time t, and n is the number of countries. Furthermore,

$$Y'_{it} = A_{i0}(t)Y_{it}, \; K'_{it} = A_{i0}(t)K_{it}, \; L'_{it} = A_{i0}(t)L_{it} \; (i=1,2,...,n) \tag{2.1'}$$

In terms of the measured quantities of outputs, the production function may be rewritten as:

$$Y_{it} = A_{i0}(t)^{-1}F(K'_{it}, L'_{it}) \; (i=1,2,....,n) \tag{2.2}$$

so that the complementary factor of output-augmentation $A_{i0}(t)$ has the interpretation of the possibly time varying level of technical efficiency of the production, in the ith country at time t. These augmentation factors are not likely to be identical across the countries and this can be a result of different factors (such as differences in the composition of outputs, in the quality and in infrastructure). The commodity augmentation factors are assumed to have the constant exponential form with respect to time:

$$Y'_{it} = A_{i0}exp(B_{i0}t)Y_{it}, \; K'_{it} = A_{i0}exp(B_{iK}t)K_{it}, \; L'_{it} = A_{i0}(B_{iL}t)L_{it}, (i=1,..,n) \tag{2.3}$$

where: A_{i0}'s, A_{ij}'s, B_{i0}'s, B_{ij}'s, are constants.

The used inputs are the capital K and labour L and the translog function in terms of *efficiency-equivalent* output and inputs takes the following form:

$$nY^*_{it} = lnY_0 + \alpha_K lnK^*_{it} + \alpha_L lnL^*_{it} + \gamma_{KK}(lnK^*_{it})^2/2 + \gamma_{LL}(lnL^*_{it})^2/2$$
$$+ \gamma_{KL}(lnK^*_{it})(lnK^*_{it}) \tag{2.4}$$

substituting in equation (2.4) the terms of Y^*_{it}, K^*_{it}, L^*_{it} of equations (2.2), we can get:

$$lnY_{it}=lnY_0+lnA^*_{it}+\alpha^*_{iK}lnK_{it}+\alpha^*_{iL}lnL_{it}+\gamma_{KK}(lnK_{it})^2/2+\gamma_{LL}(lnL_{it})^2/2+$$
$$\gamma_{KL}(lnK_{it})(lnL_{it})+\beta^*_{i0}t+(\gamma_{KK}\beta_{iK}+\gamma_{KL}\beta_{iL})(lnK_{it})t+(\gamma_{KL}\beta_{iK}+\gamma_{LL}\beta_{iL})(lnL_{it})t$$
$$+(\gamma_{KK}\beta^2_{iK}+\gamma_{LL}\beta^2_{iL}+2\gamma_{KL}\beta_{iK}\beta_{iL})t/2 \qquad (2.5)$$

where A^*_{i0}, α^*_{iK}, α^*_{iL}, β^*_{i0} are the country specific constants; the parameters γ_{KK}, γ_{KL} and γ_{LL} are independent of i of the particular country.

The parameters γ_{KK}, γ_{KL}, γ_{LL} are independent of i that is, of the particular individual country and they must be identical across the countries. This is the *common link* between the aggregate functions of different countries, and this tests the hypothesis that there is a single aggregate meta-production function for all countries. The parameter corresponding to the $t^2/2$ term for each country is not independent; it is rather determined given the γ_{KK}, γ_{KL}, γ_{LL}, β_{iK}, and β_{iL} and this test the second hypothesis that technical progress may be represented in the constant exponential commodity-augmentation form. Consequently, the above equation (**2.2**) can test the maintained hypotheses of constant returns to scale, the neutrality of technical progress and the profit maximisation with competitive output and input markets. In addition to the aggregate *meta-production function*, we can also consider the behavior of the share of labour costs in the value of output:

$$w_{it}L_{it}/p_{it}Y_{it}$$

where: w_{it} is the wage rate and p_{it} is the nominal price of output at time t.

Under profit maximisation with competitive output and input markets, the assumption of profit maximisation with respect to labour implies that the elasticity of output with respect to labour which is equal to the share of labour cost in the value of output. We can also test the hypothesis of profit maximisation with respect to labour and, if this hypothesis does not hold, then the parameters of equation (**2.3**) will not be the same as those in the aggregate meta-production function. A similar analysis can be derived for the capital:

$$r_{it}K_{it}/p_{it}Y_{it}$$

where r_{it} is the interest rate and p_{it} is the price of output at time, in order to test the hypothesis of profit maximisation with respect to capital. Finally, the following equation gives the same approach to the time: for a more detailed analysis, see Boskin and Lau 1993.

$$w_{it}L_{it}/p_{it}Y_{it}=\partial lnY_{it}/\partial lnL_{it}=\alpha^*_{iL}+\gamma_{KL}lnK_{it}+\gamma_{LL}lnL_{it}+(\gamma_{KL}\beta_{iK}+\gamma_{LL}\beta_{iL})t \qquad (2.6)$$

$$r_{it}K_{it}/p_{it}Y_{it}=\partial lnY_{it}/\partial lnK_{it}=\alpha^*_{iK}+\gamma_{KK}lnK_{it}+\gamma_{KL}lnL_{it}+(\gamma_{KK}\beta_{iK}+\gamma_{KL}\beta_{iL})t \qquad (2.7)$$

The restrictions imposed on the inputs' shares imply that the parameters must satisfy the following properties:

- Meta-production function is *homogeneous* of degree one in input quantities; that is:

$$\Sigma\alpha_i = 1 \; ; \; \Sigma\alpha_{ij} = \Sigma\alpha_{ji} = \Sigma\gamma_{iT} = 0$$

The above restrictions are necessary, if we want the function to be well defined.

- Another crucial property for the twice-differentiable function to content is the *concavity principle*.

Apart from the above restrictions there is also an adding up condition of the share equation system, such as, see also Jorgenson:

$$\Sigma S_i = 1$$

Regarding the Allen-Uzava partial elasticities of substitution, σ_{ij}, and price elasticities of input demands, they are expressed by the following equations:

$$\sigma_{ij} = (\gamma_{ii} + S_i^2 - S_i)/(S_i^2), \; i = K, L \; i = j \qquad (2.8) \text{ and}$$

$$\sigma_{ij} = (\gamma_{ij} + S_i S_j)/(S_i S_j), \; i,j = K, L \; i \neq j \qquad (2.9)$$

The choice of a particular algebraic form of the production function is associated with the question of substitution between different inputs. The elasticity of technical substitution can be defined as the division of the percentage change in k by the percentage change in α or, otherwise:

$$\sigma = d(K/L)/(K/L)/d(MP_K/MP_L)/(MP_K/MP_L)$$

where k = K/L (capital / labour ratio) and $\alpha = MP_K/MP_L$ (ratio of the marginal products of capital and labour respectively). If the elasticity of factor substitution is high, then this implies that the marginal rate of substitution does not change relative to changes in the capital / labour ratio. In case that $\sigma = +\infty$, then the isoquant will be a straight line, and when $\sigma = 0$ then the isoquant curve would be right-angled; for a more detailed analysis see Sato and Suzawa (1983).

The own-partial elasticities of substitution, σ_{ii}, are expected to be negative. The cross-partial elasticities of substitution can be either positive, suggesting substitutability between inputs, or negative, suggesting input complementarity.

$$P_{ij} = \sigma_{ij} S_i \; (i = K, L \; i \neq j) \qquad (2.10) \text{ and}$$

$$P_{ii} = \sigma_{ii} S_i \; (i = K, L \; i = j) \qquad (2.11)$$

Whereas using productivity growth capital is associated with a positive bias of productivity growth for the capital input, implementing that an increase in the price of capital input diminishes the rate of productivity growth, capital saving productivity growth implies that productivity growth increases with the price of capital input.

4.3.4 An Estimation of technical change using a translog Production Function for European Member States

The aggregate cost (or production) function is based on a cost function (or a production function), which is characterised by constant returns to scale:

$$C=F(P_K, P_L, Y, T) \tag{2.1}$$

where: P_K, P_L, Y, T indicate the price of capital input, labour input, the value added and time. The translog cost function can be written (where ij=K,L):

$$\ln C(P_K, P_L, Y, T) = \alpha_0 + \alpha_y \ln y + \frac{1}{2}\alpha_{yy}(\ln y)^2 + \sum_{i=1}^{n}\alpha_i \ln P_i + \frac{1}{2}\sum_{i=1}^{n}\sum_{j=1}^{n}\gamma_{ij} \ln P_i \ln P_j$$

$$+\sum_{i=1}^{n}\gamma_{ij} \ln P_i \ln y + \gamma_T T + \frac{1}{2}\gamma_{TT}T^2 + \sum_{i=1}^{n}\gamma_{iT} \ln P_i T + \sum_{i=1}^{n}\gamma_{yT} \ln yT$$

We use aggregate data assuming that input prices are endogenous in order to estimate the *translog share equation system* and avoid the simultaneous equation problems; we employ three stage least squares with an instrumental variable estimator provided that appropriate instruments are available. The aggregate data we use are available for forty years 1950-1990, as reported from IMF. Output measured as value added. Labour is measured as the number of employees and capital is measured as the capital stock. As price of capital we use the long-term interest rate and as price of labour wages and salaries. To estimate the above model of the average cost functions along with the share of one input and the rate of technical change, we adopt the three stage least squares, using instrumental variables with endogenous lag variables, such as lag shares, lag prices of capital, labour and output and some exogenous variables, such as export and import prices and consumer prices.

Parameters α_K and α_L can be interpreted as the average value shares of capital and labour inputs. Parameters γ_T and α_y indicate the average (negative) rate of technical change and the average share of output in total cost and parameter γ_T can also be interpreted as the average rate of productivity growth.

Parameters γ_{KK}, γ_{KL}, γ_{LL} can be interpreted as constant share elasticities. These parameters describe the implications of patterns of substitution for the relative distribution of output between capital and labour. A positive share elasticity implies that the corresponding value share increases with an increase in quantity. A share elasticity equal to zero implies that the corresponding value share is independent of quantity. The bias estimates γ_{KT} and γ_{LT} describe the implications of patterns of productivity growth for the distribution of output. A positive bias implies that the corresponding value increases with time, while a negative bias implies that the value share decreases with time. Finally, a zero bias implies that the value share is independent of time. An alternative and equivalent interpretation of the biases is that they represent changes in the rate of productivity growth with respect to proportional changes in input quantities.

The parameter γ_T can be interpreted as the average rate of productivity growth, while parameters γ_K and γ_L can be interpreted as the average value shares of capital and labour inputs.

The results of multivariate regression appear in Tables 2.9 and 2.10, where the numbers in brackets, are t-statistics. The countries included are France, Germany, Italy, Netherlands and United Kingdom (the first category of more advanced member states) and Greece, Ireland and Spain (the second category of less advanced member states).

Parameter α_Y has a positive value which indicates the average value share of output in the total cost (except for Britain and Ireland). Parameter γ_{YT} indicates how time affects the growth of output (*the rate of technical change or the acceleration rate*); this parameter has negative values for both Ireland and the United Kingdom.

The parameter γ_{KL} indicates the substitution patterns between the two factors (capital and labour); because we assumed a two factor cost function, we do not expect capital and labour to be complements. In this sense, capital and labour are substitutes as parameter γ_{KL} is negative. Actually, parameter γ_{KL} is negative for all countries, except for the case of France, where it is positive but not statistically significant.

Parameter α_{YY} (the *flexibility cost*) indicates how marginal cost will change with a change in the level of output; for three countries (England, Germany and Ireland) the marginal cost increases as the output expands.

Parameters γ_{KY} and γ_{LY} indicate share elasticities with respect to the output (scale biases); in other words, they show how an input's share would be affected by a change at the level of output. Parameters γ_{KT} and γ_{LT} suggest technical change biases, and represent a change of factor share with respect to time. Parameter γ_{YT} measures the impact of technical change in the growth of output and indicates that the technical change in England and Ireland decreases aggregate the output.

Table 2.9 Parameter estimations time series of translog-cost function for selected european countries (1950-1990)

	α_0	α_Y	α_{YY}	α_K	α_L	γ_T	γ_{KK}	γ_{LL}	γ_{TT}	γ_{YT}	γ_{KY}	γ_{KL}	γ_{KT}	γ_{LY}	γ_{LT}
England	193 (3.44)	-575 (-3.4)	152 (3.41)	-0.16 (-0.4)	1.163 (3.41)	13.40 (3.33)	0.214 (24)	0.214 (24)	0.083 (3.23)	-3.54 (-3.3)	0.123 (1.31)	-0.21 (-24)	0.026 (1.02)	-0.12 (-1.3)	-0.2 (-1.0)
France	-223 (-1.8)	134.8 (1.89)	-39.7 (-1.9)	2.548 (23.8)	-1.54 (-14)	-5.26 (-1.9)	-0.02 (-0.7)	-0.02 (-0.7)	-0.05 (-2.3)	1.552 (2.0)	-0.55 (-20)	0.02 (0.7)	0.01 (17)	0.55 (20)	-0.01 (-17)
Greece	-37.8 (-2.3)	26.81 (2.5)	-8.06 (-2.4)	-0.74 (-16)	1.741 (37.8)	-1.33 (-2.7)	0.213 (26.9)	0.213 (26.9)	-0.09 (-1.7)	0.357 (2.4)	0.280 (18.8)	-0.21 (-26)	-0.01 (-1.0)	-0.28 (-18)	0.014 (1.0)
Germany	1.71 (0.6)	0.763 (0.5)	0.194 (0.4)	-0.24 (-1.4)	1.249 (7.11)	-0.37 (-0.6)	0.168 (13)	0.168 (13)	-0.03 (-0.4)	0.071 (0.4)	0.160 (3.5)	-0.16 (-13)	0.002 (0.19)	-0.16 (-3.5)	-0.02 (-0.4)
Italy	-33.0 (-0.6)	22.31 (0.7)	-6.45 (-0.6)	-0.66 (-7.5)	1.661 (18.9)	-1.03 (-0.7)	0.226 (20.8)	0.226 (20.8)	-0.09 (-0.6)	0.287 (0.7)	0.248 (6.89)	-0.20 (-20)	0.003 (1.1)	-0.24 (-6.8)	-0.03 (-1.1)
Ireland	85.27 (0.7)	-46.1 (-0.6)	13.32 (0.64)	-4.3 (-13)	5.33 (17)	1.10 (0.44)	0.229 (14.6)	0.229 (14.6)	0.010 (0.37)	-0.34 (-0.4)	1.155 (13.1)	-0.22 (-14)	-0.01 (-4.6)	-1.15 (-13)	0.013 (4.6)
Netherlands	-104 (-2.0)	61.5 (2.0)	-17.1 (-1.9)	0.219 (1.26)	0.780 (4.51)	-2.02 (-1.9)	0.203 (10)	0.203 (10)	-0.01 (-1.5)	0.558 (1.85)	-0.01 (-0.2)	-0.20 (-10)	0.09 (4.4)	0.013 (0.2)	-0.09 (-4.4)
Spain	-21.2 (-2.9)	16.8 (3.6)	-5.4 (-3.8)	0.502 (7.9)	0.497 (7.8)	-0.85 (-4.2)	0.086 (5.9)	0.086 (5.9)	-0.01 (-4.2)	0.284 (4.4)	-0.06 (-4.5)	-0.08 (-5.9)	0.08 (10)	0.06 (4.5)	-0.08 (-10)

Note: The numbers in the brackets are t-statistics.

Source: Korres, G., 2008.

Table 2.10 Substitution, price elasticities and technical change (1959-1990)

	σ_{LL}	σ_{KK}	σ_{KL}	P_{LL}	P_{KK}	P_{LK}	P_{KL}	c/l	TCH1	TCH2	TCH3	MFP	Scale
England	-0.122	-0.103	0.109	-0.048	-0.047	0.048	0.047	c.s	15.204	0.0027	-15.21	-0.0095	0.584
France	-1.500	-0.68	1.001	-0.596	-0.403	0.596	0.403	c.u	-6.449	0.0375	6.405	-0.0587	0.233
Greece	-0.016	-0.074	0.054	-0.021	-0.033	0.021	0.033	c.s	-1.538	-0.002	1.416	-0.124	0.403
Germany	-0.417	-0.209	0.283	-0.165	-0.117	0.165	0.117	c.s	-0.385	0.0003	0.297	-0.086	0.321
Italy	-0.059	-0.059	0.057	-0.028	-0.028	0.028	0.028	c.s	-1.243	0.0004	1.169	-0.074	0.405
Ireland	-0.052	-0.044	0.047	-0.024	-0.022	0.024	0.022	c.s	1.3318	-0.021	-1.40	-0.096	0.608
Netherlands	-0.195	-0.160	0.172	-0.090	-0.082	0.090	0.082	c.s	-2.360	0.0074	2.328	-0.024	2.903
Spain	-0.563	-0.758	0.651	-0.301	-0.349	0.301	0.349	c.s	-1.119	0.0059	1.163	0.0503	0.317

Note: σ_{LL}, σ_{KK}, σ_{KL} = substitution elasticities, P_{LL}, P_{KK}, P_{KL} = price elasticities, TCH1, TCH2, TCH3 = technical change, MFP, Scale = multifactor productivity and scale, respectively. The proxy overall growth of technical change is examined by ST. Finally, c/l=capital-labour saving (where c.u. is the capital-using (or labour saving)); according to David and Van De Klundert (1965), technical progress is capital-saving if and only if the elasticity of substitution between capital and labour is less than unity in absolute value.

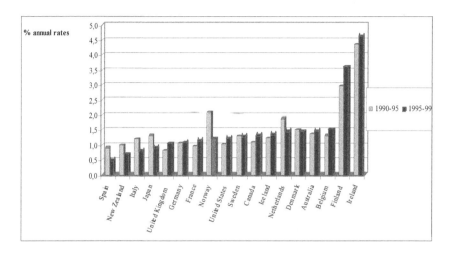

Figure 2.2 Trends in multi-factor productivity, business sector, 1990-1999

Table 2.10 illustrates estimates of substitution and price elasticities. The elasticity of substitution (σ_{KL}) for the production function is equal to:

$$\sigma_{ij} = (\gamma_{ij} + S_i S_j)/S_i S_j.$$

If σ_{KL} is greater than zero then inputs are substitutes for this country; otherwise if σ_{KL} is less than zero then they are complements. The price elasticities can be defined as:

$$P_{ij} = (\gamma_{ij} + S_i S_j)/S_i.$$

Multifactor productivity MFP (or the rate of technical change) is decomposed into three parts, pure technology, non- neutral technology and scale augmenting technology. The *multifactor productivity* is negative for all countries (except Spain) which means technological change reduces total costs.

An initial investigation of the aggregate function allows for the possibility that the growth of conventional inputs may be *non-neutral* in the sense that the marginal productivity of those inputs does not increase at the same rate through time. An interesting question is to see whether technical progress is *capital or labour augmenting* and if it is *capital (or labour) saving* in the sense that the demand for capital (labour) relative to the labour (capital) at a given quantity of output is reduced as a result of the technical progress.

Neutrality of technical change implies that the *rate of technical progress* is independent of capital and labour. *Non-neutrality of technical progress* implies that the *rate of technical progress* at time t will vary depending on the quantities of capital and labour inputs at time t and to that extent may be regarded as endogenous. According to our estimates, we can divide technical change into *neutral technical change* and *non-neutral technical change* (where time affects capital and labour inputs). Neutral technical change is indicated by TCH1 for the various countries. Non neutral technical change is indicated by TCH2.

Table 2.11 Trends in multi-factor productivity growth, 1990-1995 and 1995-1999*

	1990-1995	1995-1999
Ireland	4.4	4.6
Finland	3.0	3.6
Belgium	1.3	1.6
Australia	1.4	1.5
Denmark	1.5	1.5
Netherlands	1.9	1.5
Iceland	1.2	1.4
Canada	1.1	·1.3
Sweden	1.3	1.3
United States	1.0	1.2
Norway	2.1	1.2
France	0.9	1.1
Germany	1.1	1.1
United Kingdom	0.8	1.0
Japan	1.3	0.9
Italy	1.2	0.8
New Zealand	1.0	0.7
Spain	0.9	0.5

Notes: * Adjusted for hours worked, based on trend series and time-varying factor shares. Series end in 1997 for Austria, Belgium, Italy and New Zealand; 1998 for Australia, Denmark, France, Ireland, Japan, Netherlands and United Kingdom. Data for Germany start in 1991.
Source: OECD calculations, based on data from the OECD Economic Outlook No. 68. See S. Scarpetta et al., Economics Department Working Paper No. 248, 2000 for details; May 2001.

Figure 2.1 shows the multifactor productivity growth for the Business Sector, for the period 1990-1999 for our estimations. Labour productivity is a partial measure of productivity; it relates output to only one input in the production process, albeit an important one. More complete measures of productivity at the economy-wide level relate output growth to the combined use of labour and capital inputs. Table 2.11 illustrates the trends in multifactor productivity for selected countries for the period of 1990-1999.

4.3.5 An Estimation of Technical Change Using a Translog Production Function for Greek Manufacturing Sectors

Technical progress (through production functions) plays a crucial role in the theory of economic growth. A production function specifies a long-run relationship between inputs and outputs and technical progress is an essential factor underlying the growth of per capita income. There are a number of ways to approach the estimation of production functions and technical progress. A shift in the production function over time is generally considered to represent technical progress through greater efficiency in combining inputs. These shifts are achieved in a variety of ways, including changes in the coefficients of labour and capital.

The characteristics of technical change may be shown by the shifts of the unit isoquant towards the origin over time. A greater saving in one input than in others will result in a bias in technical change. The relative contribution of factors to the production process is measured by the elasticity of substitution. Then, a bias in technical change will be represented by a modification in the position of the isoquant and will lead, for example, to greater labour savings for all techniques. All these specific themes are under inquiry here within an inter-sectoral environment and comparison.

Finally, we attempt to infer some policy implications, if possible, as well as to indicate the leading manufacturing sectors throughout the time period 1959-1990, due to the data restrictions. This section consists of two parts: the first contains a detailed description of the theoretical model adopted and an estimation technique. The second part shows the estimated results and tests against the underlying microeconomic theory. We have estimated only the period between 1959 to 1990, due to restrictions on the available data-set and the application of a new adjusted recalculation system since after 1991.

The aim of this section is to examine the nature of technological progress and factor substitution using the *translog production function* for the annual time-series data of Greek industrial sectors for the period 1959-1990. In particular, this section presents an estimate of technical progress and the contributions of each source of growth (namely: capital, labour and technical progress), without maintaining these assumptions.

One of the problems in estimating the rate of technical change and the elasticity of substitution is to accurately specify the production function and the type of technical progress. There is a big difference, though between the models adopted here and models of *induced* technical change. The sectoral cost functions have to be homogeneous of degree one, monotonic or non-decreasing and concave in input prices. In particular, this section analyses cost structures and technical change in twenty Greek manufacturing sectors with double digit codes (ISIC).

There are only few attempts for Greek sectoral analysis, such as those by Kintis (1973, 1978), Ioannides and Caramanis (1979) and Panas (1986). All of them tried to investigate the patterns of input substitution as well as to derive a measure for technical change and technological biases. They modelled producers' behaviour using simply the constant elasticity of substitution (CES) and a Cobb-Douglas functional form applied to period 1958-1975. Ioannides and Caramanis employed a translog cost function assuming constant returns to scale fitted to period 1958-1978. Furthermore, they did not take into account possible scale biases which may affect not only sectoral decisions but also policy-makers' orientation.

The data used for our estimations come from annual industrial surveys (AIS) and statistical yearbooks (SY) of the National Statistical Service of Greece (NSSG). *The data we use refer to large industries* (which correspond to companies with 20 or more employees). However, there is a restriction on data-set. Some of the series (such as capital-stock and output) are up to 1990. In particular, for the series of output since 1990, there is a new re-calculation adjusted system using another basis for the large industries, while the series of capital-stock are given by CEPR (Center of Economic Planning and Research) up to 1990. For these reasons, we have estimated the function and the variables up to 1990.

Table 2.12 Parameter estimations (time-series translog-cost function): Greece (1959-1990)

	α_0	α_Y	α_{YY}	α_K	α_L	γ_T	γ_{KK}	γ_{LL}	γ_{TT}	γ_{YT}	γ_{KY}	γ_{KL}	γ_{KT}	γ_{LY}	γ_{LT}
20	2.0 (7.0)	2.6 (5.0)	-1.4 (-1.8)	0.51 (6.9)	0.49 (6.6)	-0.1 (-2.8)	0.01 (0.4)	0.01 (0.4)	-0.03 (-1.4)	0.21 (1.5)	-0.1 (-2.1)	-0.01 (-0.4)	0.17 (2.6)	0.10 (2.1)	-0.1 (-2.6)
21	-0.60 (-1.3)	4.59 (4.4)	-2.28 (-1.2)	0.80 (8.4)	0.20 (2.1)	-0.42 (-2.2)	0.017 (0.8)	0.017 (0.8)	-0.05 (-0.8)	0.34 (0.9)	-0.06 (-1.6)	-0.01 (-0.8)	0.013 (2.3)	0.062 (1.6)	-0.01 (-2.35)
22	0.63 (0.5)	1.98 (1.5)	-0.5 (-0.7)	0.40 (2.6)	0.60 (4.0)	-0.05 (-0.3)	-0.03 (-0.1)	0.090 (2.7)	-0.02 (-1.7)	0.094 (0.9)	-0.10 (-2.5)	0.03 (0.1)	0.015 (3.4)	-0.03 (-1.8)	-0.086 (-1.7)
23	0.710 (1.7)	3.195 (4.4)	-1.19 (-1.2)	0.64 (5.4)	0.36 (3.1)	-0.24 (-2.0)	-0.03 (-0.1)	-0.03 (-0.1)	-0.01 (-0.5)	0.132 (0.7)	-0.10 (-2.5)	0.037 (0.1)	0.015 (3.4)	0.104 (2.5)	-0.015 (-3.4)
24	3.42 (22)	0.91 (2.5)	-1.10 (-2.5)	0.16 (5.7)	0.84 (32)	0.055 (0.6)	0.096 (7.7)	0.096 (7.7)	-0.03 (-1.9)	0.201 (2.1)	-0.05 (-0.3)	-0.09 (-7.7)	0.012 (3.8)	0.05 (0.3)	-0.012 (-3.8)
25	3.84 (37)	0.55 (0.9)	-0.49 (-0.5)	0.18 (3.8)	0.82 (17)	0.049 (0.5)	0.088 (3.8)	0.088 (3.8)	-0.02 (-0.7)	0.101 (0.6)	-0.04 (-1.6)	-0.08 (-3.8)	0.19 (5.3)	0.044 (1.6)	-0.019 (-5.3)
26	2.93 (27)	1.566 (4.7)	0.057 (0.6)	0.24 (5.8)	0.76 (18)	-0.03 (-0.1)	0.042 (1.9)	0.042 (1.9)	0.060 (0.2)	-0.04 (-0.2)	-0.08 (-3.4)	-0.04 (-1.9)	0.019 (3.9)	0.089 (3.4)	-0.019 (-3.95)
27	1.906 (2.6)	1.558 (1.2)	0.179 (0.1)	0.01 (0.7)	0.99 (9.8)	-0.06 (-0.3)	0.130 (4.9)	0.130 (4.9)	0.019 (0.4)	-0.07 (-0.3)	0.166 (0.4)	-0.13 (-4.9)	0.104 (1.8)	-0.01 (-0.4)	-0.010 (-1.8)
28	3.24 (5.4)	-0.10 (-0.9)	0.849 (0.6)	0.19 (1.5)	0.81 (6.7)	0.169 (1.0)	0.107 (3.1)	0.10 (3.1)	0.163 (0.4)	-0.12 (-0.6)	0.064 (1.2)	-0.10 (-3.1)	0.071 (0.7)	-0.06 (-1.2)	-0.071 (-0.7)
29	2.240 (5.4)	1.832 (3.4)	0.511 (0.9)	0.15 (2.9)	0.85 (18)	-0.04 (-0.7)	0.055 (2.7)	0.05 (2.7)	0.253 (1.7)	-0.14 (-1.7)	0.010 (0.4)	-0.05 (-2.7)	0.069 (2.0)	-0.01 (-0.4)	-0.069 (-2.01)
30	3.124 (14)	1.146 (1.4)	-0.23 (-0.7)	0.25 (3.2)	0.75 (10)	-0.01 (-0.7)	0.120 (4.0)	0.12 (4.0)	-0.01 (-0.1)	0.080 (0.1)	-0.16 (-2.7)	-0.12 (-4.0)	0.043 (3.6)	1.60 (2.7)	-0.043 (-3.6)
31	4.214 (5.8)	-0.13 (-0.1)	-0.16 (-0.4)	0.51 (6.0)	0.49 (5.7)	0.515 (0.4)	0.058 (1.8)	0.05 (1.8)	-0.01 (-1.6)	0.070 (1.2)	0.015 (0.2)	-0.05 (6.0)	0.022 (0.1)	-0.01 (-0.2)	-0.022 (-0.1)

Table 2.12 continued

	α_0	α_Y	α_{YY}	α_K	α_L	γ_T	γ_{KK}	γ_{LL}	γ_{TT}	γ_{YT}	γ_{KY}	γ_{KL}	γ_{KT}	γ_{LY}	γ_{LT}
32 *	0.98 (0.9)	3.609 (2.3)	-2.92 (-1.3)	0.76 (6.0)	0.24 (1.9)	-0.19 (-0.7)	(*)	(*)	-0.11 (-1.6)	0.555 (1.4)	-0.16 (-3.0)	(*)	0.032 (3.6)	0.160 (3.0)	-0.032 (-3.6)
33	2.056 (5.4)	1.726 (2.0)	0.786 (0.5)	0.36 (5.9)	0.64 (10)	-0.05 (-0.4)	0.052 (3.2)	0.052 (3.2)	0.039 (0.9)	-0.19 (-0.8)	-0.06 (-2.4)	-0.05 (-3.2)	0.017 (5.4)	0.060 (2.4)	-0.017 (-5.4)
34	3.259 (13)	0.324 (0.5)	-0.21 (-0.2)	0.22 (2.2)	0.78 (8.3)	0.132 (1.2)	0.167 (5.4)	0.167 (5.4)	-0.01 (-0.4)	0.075 (0.3)	-0.06 (-1.4)	-0.16 (-5.4)	0.031 (4.0)	0.060 (1.4)	-0.031 (-4.0)
35	2.419 (12)	2.543 (5.7)	-0.56 (-0.5)	0.30 (4.2)	0.70 (10)	-0.18 (-2.8)	0.086 (3.5)	0.086 (3.5)	0.036 (0.1)	0.027 (0.1)	-0.05 (-1.6)	-0.08 (-3.5)	0.021 (3.4)	0.054 (1.6)	-0.021 (-3.43)
36	0.582 (1.1)	5.707 (5.6)	-5.09 (-3.8)	0.30 (3.7)	0.70 (8.7)	-0.69 (-4.4)	0.079 (3.1)	0.079 (3.1)	-0.12 (-3.4)	0.777 (3.6)	-0.03 (-1.2)	-0.07 (-3.1)	0.014 (3.0)	0.038 (1.2)	-0.014 (-3.0)
37	1.562 (1.4)	3.072 (0.9)	-0.03 (-0.7)	0.62 (5.3)	0.38 (3.3)	-0.22 (-0.4)	0.103 (2.9)	0.103 (2.9)	0.030 (0.2)	0.028 (0.3)	-0.23 (-5.1)	-0.10 (-2.9)	0.051 (6.8)	0.239 (5.1)	-0.051 (-6.8)
38	2.332 (7.3)	3.414 (4.4)	-2.39 (-1.5)	0.40 (5.2)	0.60 (8.0)	-0.29 (-2.5)	0.084 (4.6)	0.084 (4.6)	-0.05 (-0.8)	0.342 (1.1)	-0.05 (-1.2)	-0.08 (-4.6)	0.023 (2.5)	0.052 (1.2)	-0.023 (-2.5)
39 *	1.809 (7.2)	1.629 (9.0)	-0.33 (-6.0)	0.40 (6.7)	0.60 (10)	(*)	0.026 (1.3)	0.026 (1.3)	(*)	(*)	0.077 (0.4)	-0.02 (-1.3)	(*)	-0.07 (-0.4)	(*)
20-39	5.560 (6.94)	-1.61 (-1.6)	1.04 (1.5)	1.27 (1.6)	0.87 (11.4)	-0.23 (-2.4)	0.155 (4.68)	0.155 (4.68)	0.010 (1.71)	0.128 (2.93)	0.020 (0.31)	-0.15 (-4.6)	0.004 (0.09)	-0.02 (-0.3)	-0.0042 (-0.09)

Note: The numbers in brackets indicating the t-statistic. Note: * Parameters in sector (32) are not presented due to the convexity restrictions, while parameters in sector (39), by definition, there is no technical change in the 39 sector (miscellaneous). According to the ISIC classification, we have the branches (brackets show the categories): (20) food (21) beverages (22) tobacco (23) textiles (24) footwear and wearing apparel (25) wood and cork (26) furniture (27) paper (28) printing -publishing (28) leather (30) rubber and plastic products (31) chemicals (32) petroleum (33) non-metallic mineral products (34) basic metal industry (35) metal products (36) machinery and appliances (37) electrical supplies (38) transport equipment (39) miscellaneous industry.

Source: Korres, G., 2007.

Output is measured as value added in the large enterprises, as reported by AIS and SY. Labour is measured as number of employees. Wage rate and salaries correspond to the total labour cost for the large industry. The price of labour was derived from dividing the total labour cost by the number of employees. The price of capital stock was derived by dividing the value added minus the total labour cost by the capital stock figures. Data on value added and wage rates have been deflated to the constant prices in 1985.

There are data are available for twenty industrial sectors for 32 years (1959-1990). A function of manufacturing sector as a whole estimated using the same data, and each variable is *weighted* by its shares and calculate the averages. The capital-stock derived from the data-set of CEPR (Center of Economic Planning and Research) calculated by Skountzos and Mathaios for the period up to 1990. The capita-stock include residential buildings, non-residential buildings, other construction and works, transport equipment, machinery and other equipment, public sector and private sector. Finally, there are no available series-data for energy input, so we have used two input-model for the period 1957-1990.

To solve the equation system we should use the *Zellne's seemingly unrelated estimator* (the so called *ZEF or SUR – seemingly unrelated regression estimator* or otherwise the *minimum chi-square estimator*). The *iterative Zellner efficient estimator* is termed as *IZEF* and yields parameter estimates that are numerically equivalent to those of the maximum likelihood estimator (ML). The ZEF system estimator yields different parameter estimates from those form equation by equation OLS. This happen because the input-output equation contains different regressors, and in addition, we would expect disturbances across input-output equations to be contemporaneously correlated, implying that the covariance matrix would be non-diagonal.

We adopt an alternative estimate using 3SLS; we also employ the instrumental variables estimation techniques (as instrumental variables we are used logarithms of lagged variables of prices of capital and labour, output and time). The steps in estimation of the model are the following: we estimate the total cost as a function of capital and labour inputs and prices. We construct capital and labour shares, using prices, inputs and total cost. Using the Shephard's lemma (for instance, for the cost and labour shares) in order to derive the input demands and to solve parametrically the equations of capital and labour shares. We use instrumental variables (logarithms of lagged variables), and we solve by 3SLS. With these parameters, we estimate the two-factor cost shares (such as, S_L, S_K). We calculate the substitution elasticities from the preceding parameters using the equations (2.5) (or similarly the equations (2.6)) for price elasticities.

Table 2.13 Substitution, price elasticities, technical change and scales, 1959-1990

	σ_{LL}	σ_{KK}	σ_{KL}	P_{LL}	P_{KK}	P_{LK}	P_{KL}	c/l	TCH1	TCH2	TCH3	MFP	Scale
Foodstuffs (20)	-0.839	-1.101	0.957	-0.44	-0.51	0.44	0.51	c.u	-0.812	-0.00058	0.745	-0.0679	0.858
Beverages (21)	-4.222	-0.184	0.875	-0.72	-0.15	0.72	0.15	c.u	-1.385	0.017460	1.233	-0.1348	0.655
Tobacco (22)	-1.699	-0.102	0.412	-0.33	-0.08	0.33	0.08	c.u	-0.450	0.010289	0.383	-0.0561	0.724
Textiles (23)	-1.077	-0.963	1.014	-0.52	-0.49	0.52	0.49	c.s	-0.518	0.008332	0.480	-0.0299	1.545
Footwear and wearing (24)	-0.267	-1.177	0.554	-0.22	-0.28	0.22	0.28	c.u	-0.668	-0.00399	0.600	-0.0721	1.182
Wood and cork (25)	-0.299	-1.228	0.596	-0.17	-0.37	0.17	0.37	c.u	-0.305	-0.00866	0.301	-0.0124	1.298
Furniture (26)	-0.278	-2.207	0.777	-0.20	-0.57	0.20	0.57	c.u	0.0994	-0.02033	-0.13	-0.0533	0.964
Paper (27)	-0.347	-0.639	0.459	-0.19	-0.26	0.19	0.26	c.u	0.2635	0.008485	-0.30	-0.0361	1.501
Printing-publishing (28)	-0.676	-0.483	0.564	-0.30	-0.25	0.30	0.25	c.u	0.4473	0.000461	-0.43	0.00994	1.366
Leather (29)	-0.285	-1.855	0.723	-0.20	-0.51	0.20	0.51	c.u	0.3845	-0.00143	-0.45	-0.0751	2.076
Rubber and plastics (30)	-0.416	-0.645	0.508	-0.22	-0.28	0.22	0.28	c.u	-0.344	0.001361	0.276	-0.0667	0.644
Chemical (31)	-1.383	-0.427	0.731	-0.46	-0.26	0.46	0.26	c.u	-0.248	0.001290	0.272	0.02507	4.445
Petroleum (32)	-2.631	-0.403	1.000	-0.17	-0.28	0.17	0.28	c.s	-2.133	0.058802	2.048	-0.0255	0.209
Non-Metallic products (33)	-0.697	-0.904	0.789	-0.36	-0.42	0.36	0.42	c.u	0.6072	0.009445	-0.66	-0.0498	0.941
Basic metal industries (34)	-0.307	-0.129	0.189	-0.11	-0.07	0.11	0.07	c.u	-0.1874	0.023929	0.264	0.10102	1.579
Metal products (35)	-0.587	-0.738	0.653	-0.30	-0.34	0.30	0.34	c.u	-0.1273	-0.00067	0.0916	-0.0363	1.228
Machinery and appliances (36)	-0.486	-0.952	0.672	-0.28	-0.39	0.28	0.39	c.u	-2.7787	0.001201	2.7022	-0.075	1.986

Table 2.13 continued

	σ_{LL}	σ_{KK}	σ_{KL}	P_{LL}	P_{KK}	P_{LK}	P_{KL}	c/l	TCH1	TCH2	TCH3	MFP	Scale
Electrical supplies (37)	-1.070	-0.275	0.529	-0.34	-0.17	0.34	0.17	c.u	-0.172	0.000704	0.0999	-0.065	0.464
Transport equipment (38)	-1.214	-0.339	0.615	-0.40	-0.21	0.40	0.21	c.u	-1.1805	0.008928	1.1000	-0.071	3.947
Miscellaneous Manuf/ind. (39)	-0.634	-1.265	0.890	-0.36	-0.52	0.36	0.52	c.u	(*)	(*)	(*)	(*)	1.582
All manufacturing:	-0.285	-0.385	0.309	-0.14	-0.16	0.14	0.16	c.u	-0.126	0.0009419	0.12283	-0.00227	0.8977

Note: σ_{LL}, σ_{KK}, σ_{KL} = indicate the substitution elasticities, P_{LL}, P_{KK}, P_{KL} = indicate the price elasticities, TCH1, TCH2, TCH3 = indicate the technical change, MFP, Scale = indicate the multifactor productivity and scale, respectively. Finally, c/l = indicate the capital-labour saving (where c.u. is the capital-using (or labour saving)); according to David and Van De Klundert (1965) the technical progress is capital-saving if and only if the elasticity of substitution between capital and labour is less than unity in absolute values.
Source: Korres, G., 2007.

The duality property between cost and production functions was first introduced by Shephard (1953). Given a cost function satisfying certain regularity conditions, we can derive a production function which in turn may be used to derive our original cost function; see in Diewert and Wales (1987). A disturbance term must specified in each of the input-output equations, and it is also assumed that the disturbance vector is independently and identical normally distributed with mean vector zero and constant non-singular covariance matrix W. These disturbance terms could simply reflect optimisation errors on the part of industries (Berndt 1991). Since input-demand functions are linear in parameters and these demand equations have cross-equation symmetry constrains, then the OLS estimation equation by equation appears more attractive. However, we can use the *Zellner's seemingly unrelated estimator* (ZEF which called and *seemingly unrelated regression estimator (SUR) or the minimum ch-square estimator*).

The different parameter estimates from those form equation by equation OLS result from:

- disturbances across the input-output equations are simultaneously correlated, imply that the disturbance covariance matrix is non-diagonal;
- each input-output equation contains different regressors.

For these reason, the ZEF estimator will provide more efficiently estimates of parameters rather that the OLS. The *Zellner's seemingly unrelated estimator* (ZEF) uses equation by equation OLS to obtain an estimate of the disturbance covariance matrix and then does generalise the least squares; see also Berndt (1991). A common procedure to reduce collinearity with time series data is to implement first-difference data and then to work with the first-difference data. Logarithmic first-differenced, since $\ln y_t - \ln y_{t-1}$ equals $\ln(y_t / y_{t-1})$, which for small changes can be interpreted as the percentage change in y from period t-1 to period t. This way of computing percentage change is also attractive in that $\ln(y_t / y_{t-1})$, always yields a value between $(y_t - y_{t-1})/ y_{t-1}$ and $(y_t - y_{t-1})/ y_t$. Using the annual data from 1959 to 1990, we have computed the logarithmic first differences to avoid the problem of multicollinearity.

Table 2.14 Parameter estimations cross-section of translog-cost function in 1959-1990, Greece

	α_0	α_Y	A_{YY}	α_K	α_L	γ_T	γ_{KK}	γ_{LL}	γ_{TT}	γ_{YT}	γ_{KY}	γ_{KL}	γ_{KT}	γ_{LY}	γ_{LT}
59	5.5	-1.6	1.04	0.127	0.87	-0.23	0.155	0.15	0.105	0.128	0.202	-0.15	0.004	-0.20	-0.0042
	(6.9)	(-1.6)	(1.5)	(1.67)	(11.4)	(-2.4)	(4.68)	(4.68)	(1.71)	(2.93)	(0.31)	(-4.6)	(0.09)	(-0.3)	(-0.09)
60	5.40	-1.15	0.608	0.125	0.874	-0.24	0.143	0.143	0.101	0.124	0.57	-0.14	0.006	-0.05	-0.0061
	(6.7)	(-1.1)	(0.92)	(1.73)	(12)	(-2.6)	(5.06)	(5.06)	(1.84)	(2.88)	(1.03)	(-5.0)	(0.15)	(-1.0)	(-0.15)
61	4.01	0.682	-0.45	0.217	0.782	-0.08	0.197	0.197	-0.01	0.048	-0.07	-0.19	-0.01	0.072	0.016
	(5.3)	(1.02)	(-0.9)	(3.48)	(12)	(-0.7)	(5.83)	(5.83)	(-0.1)	(1.36)	(-1.1)	(-5.8)	(-0.4)	(1.19)	(0.438)
62	4.18	-0.27	0.268	0.239	0.760	0.033	0.227	0.227	-0.09	0.031	-0.10	-0.22	-0.01	0.108	0.019
	(5.9)	(-0.4)	(0.68)	(4.16)	(13)	(0.35)	(10)	(10)	(-1.8)	(0.99)	(-2.5)	(-10)	(-0.6)	(2.55)	(0.64)
63	3.89	-0.17	0.132	0.171	0.828	0.059	0.177	0.177	-0.01	0.055	0.021	-0.17	0.028	-0.02	-0.028
	(2.2)	(-0.8)	(0.10)	(1.9)	(9.4)	(0.39)	(6.57)	(6.57)	(-1.6)	(0.84)	(0.03)	(-6.5)	(0.81)	(-0.3)	(-0.819)
64	3.72	0.49	-0.38	0.122	0.877	0.010	0.159	0.159	-0.08	0.061	0.047	-0.15	0.051	-0.04	-0.051
	(2.2)	(0.25)	(-0.3)	(1.34)	(9.63)	(0.07)	(6.14)	(6.14)	(-1.1)	(1.0)	(0.80)	(-6.1)	(1.48)	(-0.8)	(-1.48)
65	5.214	-0.77	0.221	0.086	0.913	-0.12	0.142	0.142	-0.02	0.102	0.092	-0.14	0.075	-0.09	-0.075
	(2.24)	(-0.3)	(0.17)	(0.67)	(7.04)	(-0.7)	(-5.1)	(5.1)	(0.32)	(1.55)	(1.28)	(-5.1)	(1.81)	(-1.2)	(-1.81)
66	2.873	0.941	-0.32	-0.17	1.173	0.083	0.167	0.167	-0.08	0.017	0.190	-0.16	0.083	-0.19	-0.083
	(1.44)	(0.48)	(-0.3)	(-1.7)	(12)	(0.56)	(9.92)	(9.92)	(-1.4)	(0.30)	(4.2)	(-9.9)	(2.9)	(-4.2)	(-2.97)
67	2.644	1.652	-0.73	-0.04	1.045	-0.04	0.178	0.178	-0.01	0.030	0.123	-0.17	0.032	-0.12	-0.032
	(0.87)	(0.56)	(-0.5)	(-0.3)	(7.54)	(-0.2)	(5.46)	(5.46)	(-0.2)	(0.52)	(1.77)	(-5.4)	(0.87)	(-1.7)	(-0.87)
68	3.124	1.202	-0.51	-0.06	1.069	-0.07	0.182	0.182	0.002	0.030	0.142	-0.18	0.013	-0.14	-0.013
	(1.19)	(0.48)	(-0.4)	(-0.8)	(12)	(-0.5)	(10)	(10)	(0.03)	(0.66)	(3.63)	(-10)	(0.59)	(-3.6)	(-0.59)
69	3.057	1.235	-0.64	0.047	0.952	-0.02	0.165	0.165	-0.03	0.043	0.082	-0.16	0.060	-0.08	-0.060
	(0.74)	(0.32)	(-0.3)	(0.45)	(9.0)	(-0.1)	(8.4)	(8.4)	(-0.5)	(0.78)	(1.62)	(-8.4)	(2.46)	(-1.6)	(-2.46)
70	-5.47	8.003	-3.21	-0.04	1.041	0.137	0.129	0.129	-0.05	-0.02	0.173	-0.12	0.023	-0.17	-0.0231
	(-0.9)	(1.6)	(-1.5)	(-0.2)	(7.07)	(0.75)	(5.52)	(5.52)	(-0.9)	(-0.5)	(2.66)	(-5.5)	(0.85)	(-2.6)	(-0.85)

Table 2.14 continued

	α_0	α_Y	A_{YY}	α_K	α_L	γ_T	γ_{KK}	γ_{LL}	γ_{TT}	γ_{YT}	γ_{KY}	γ_{KL}	γ_{KT}	γ_{LY}	γ_{LT}
71	-2.24 (-0.4)	5.343 (1.23)	-2.03 (-1.1)	0.126 (0.78)	0.873 (5.42)	-0.43 (-0.3)	0.205 (6.85)	0.205 (6.85)	-0.01 (-0.3)	0.029 (0.6)	0.075 (1.04)	0.126 (0.78)	0.034 (1.55)	-0.07 (-1.0)	-0.0346 (-1.55)
72	-9.60 (-1.8)	11.19 (2.81)	-4.25 (-2.8)	0.407 (1.88)	0.592 (2.74)	-0.04 (-0.4)	0.245 (7.51)	0.245 (7.51)	0.031 (1.0)	0.013 (0.37)	-0.39 (-0.4)	-0.24 (-7.5)	0.054 (1.96)	0.039 (0.44)	-0.0548 (-1.96)
73	16.99 (1.70)	-8.05 (-1.2)	2.658 (1.17)	0.017 (0.07)	0.982 (4.25)	-0.15 (-0.6)	0.161 (4.74)	0.161 (4.74)	-0.09 (-0.1)	0.060 (0.91)	0.140 (1.62)	-0.16 (-4.7)	0.020 (0.73)	-0.14 (-1.6)	-0.0204 (-0.73)
74	2.149 (0.21)	1.699 (0.26)	-0.56 (-0.2)	-0.23 (-1.1)	1.233 (6.3)	-0.03 (-0.1)	0.152 (8.55)	0.152 (8.55)	-0.09 (-1.8)	0.046 (0.62)	0.226 (3.59)	-0.15 (-8.5)	-0.05 (-0.1)	-0.22 (-3.5)	0.00051 (0.019)
75	9.261 (6.22)	-1.65 (-0.2)	0.245 (0.11)	-0.67 (-2.5)	1.678 (6.22)	-0.57 (-1.7)	0.122 (4.9)	0.122 (4.9)	-0.02 (-0.5)	0.180 (1.90)	0.360 (4.3)	-0.12 (-4.9)	-0.01 (-0.5)	-0.36 (-4.3)	0.01719 (0.57)
76	49.11 (2.81)	-22.6 (-2.2)	5.89 (1.98)	-0.08 (-0.2)	1.089 (3.26)	-1.28 (-4.1)	0.154 (6.28)	0.154 (6.28)	0.014 (3.51)	0.314 (3.82)	0.168 (1.76)	-0.15 (-6.2)	-0.0 (-0.6)	-0.16 (-1.7)	0.1541 (6.28)
77	15.98 (1.37)	-5.78 (-0.8)	1.57 (0.87)	0.350 (5.65)	0.649 (10)	-0.05 (-0.6)	0.209 (53.2)	0.209 (53.2)	0.006 (1.11)	0.014 (0.60)	0.038 (2.28)	-0.20 (-53)	0.006 (0.15)	-0.03 (-2.2)	-0.0006 (-0.15)
78	25.27 (0.97)	-11.2 (-0.8)	3.112 (0.86)	0.090 (0.02)	0.990 (2.30)	0.387 (0.69)	0.198 (6.59)	0.198 (6.59)	-0.02 (-0.4)	-0.09 (-0.7)	0.131 (1.24)	-0.19 (-6.5)	-0.01 (-0.8)	-0.13 (-1.2)	0.0188 (0.88)
79	-98.8 (-0.8)	43.45 (0.82)	-8.92 (-0.7)	-1.04 (-0.8)	2.048 (1.73)	1.987 (2.23)	0.180 (3.64)	0.180 (3.64)	-0.11 (-0.2)	-0.45 (-2.2)	0.368 (1.35)	-0.18 (-3.6)	0.003 (0.10)	-0.36 (-1.3)	-0.0003 (-0.01)
81	-56 (-3.5)	27.57 (3.94)	-6.14 (-3.8)	-0.84 (-1.3)	1.840 (3.02)	-0.24 (-1.0)	0.142 (3.18)	0.142 (3.18)	-0.05 (-2.0)	0.064 (1.42)	0.321 (2.50)	-0.14 (-3.1)	0.013 (0.38)	-0.32 (-2.5)	-0.0012 (-0.38)
82	-36.7 (-1.5)	17.01 (1.7)	-3.42 (-1.6)	-1.28 (-2.1)	2.28 (3.8)	0.34 (0.9)	0.98 (2.37)	0.98 (2.37)	-0.01 (-1.8)	-0.04 (-0.6)	0.386 (3.19)	-0.09 (-2.3)	0.035 (0.93)	-0.38 (-3.1)	-0.0355 (-0.933)
83	-9.61 (-0.3)	7.037 (0.54)	-1.56 (-0.5)	-1.60 (-3.2)	2.609 (5.29)	-1.09 (-1.7)	0.081 (1.94)	0.081 (1.94)	0.098 (1.20)	0.210 (1.84)	0.441 (4.69)	-0.08 (-1.9)	0.058 (1.92)	-0.44 (-4.6)	-0.0581 (-1.9)

Table 2.14 continued

	α_0	α_Y	A_{YY}	α_K	α_L	γ_T	γ_{KK}	γ_{LL}	γ_{TT}	γ_{YT}	γ_{KY}	γ_{KL}	γ_{KT}	γ_{LY}	γ_{LT}
84	-51.7	22.76	-4.50	-1.33	2.336	-0.51	0.110	0.110	-0.02	0.114	0.369	-0.11	0.069	-0.36	-0.0693
	(-4.5)	(5.16)	(-5.1)	(-3.2)	(5.74)	(-2.1)	(3.91)	(3.91)	(-0.8)	(2.76)	(4.82)	(-3.9)	(2.14)	(-4.8)	(-2.14)
85	-124	51.15	-10	-2.41	3.413	-1.49	-0.01	-0.01	-0.01	0.305	0.544	0.011	0.026	-0.54	-0.0260
	(-6.4)	(6.6)	(-6.4)	(-7.1)	(10)	(-2.9)	(-0.8)	(-0.8)	(-1.7)	(3.62)	(8.5)	(0.81)	(0.81)	(-8.5)	(-0.81)
86	-85.4	34.96	-6.63	-0.48	1.483	-0.91	0.151	0.151	0.004	0.167	0.215	-0.15	0.037	-0.21	-0.0377
	(-5.7)	(6.41)	(-6.5)	(-1.0)	(3.12)	(-2.6)	(6.43)	(6.43)	(0.11)	(3.0)	(2.60)	(-6.4)	(1.0)	(-2.6)	(-1.02)
87	-61.3	25.5	-4.77	-0.63	1.633	-1.33	0.163	0.163	0.092	0.223	0.249	-0.16	0.038	-0.24	-0.0381
	(-2.7)	(3.15)	(-3.1)	(-1.1)	(2.92)	(-2.7)	(4.7)	(4.7)	(1.39)	(2.90)	(2.64)	(-4.7)	(1.06)	(-2.6)	(-1.06)
88	-40.8	16.73	-2.93	-0.46	1.461	-0.86	0.144	0.144	0.067	0.140	0.205	-0.14	0.041	-0.20	-0.0410
	(-1.8)	(2.20)	(-2.2)	(-0.7)	(2.24)	(-1.8)	(3.47)	(3.47)	(0.99)	(2.04)	(2.05)	(-3.4)	(1.20)	(-2.0)	(-1.20)
89	-22	9.64	-1.61	-0.59	1.598	-0.60	0.117	0.117	0.038	0.098	0.219	-0.11	0.035	-0.21	-0.0358
	(-0.6)	(0.83)	(-0.8)	(-0.7)	(1.97)	(-1.1)	(2.30)	(2.30)	(0.47)	(1.26)	(1.83)	(-2.3)	(1.0)	(-1.8)	(-1.05)
90	20.36	-4.42	0.73	-1.48	2.486	-0.98	0.060	0.060	0.013	0.141	0.341	-0.06	0.040	-0.34	-0.0402
	(0.54)	(-0.3)	(0.37)	(-1.5)	(2.52)	(-1.8)	(1.07)	(1.07)	(1.85)	(1.86)	(2.42)	(-1.0)	(1.18)	(-2.4)	(-1.18)

Note: Numbers in brackets indicate the t-statistic. This analysis indicate all industries by year (variables are weighted shares).
Source: Korres, G., 2007.

Table 2.15 Substitution and price elasticities, technical change and scale for period 1959–1990

	σ_{LL}	σ_{KK}	σ_{KL}	P_{LL}	P_{KK}	P_{LK}	P_{KL}	c/l	TCH1	TCH2	TCH3	MFP	Scale
1959	-0.285	-0.385	0.309	-0.142	-0.166	0.142	0.166	c.s	-0.126	0.00094	0.128	-0.00255	0.189
1960	-0.409	-0.411	0.368	-0.185	-0.187	0.181	0.187	c.s	-0.138	0.00139	0.133	-0.00352	-2.995
1961	14.605	-0.150	0.553	-0.488	-0.064	0.488	0.064	c.s	-0.093	-0.0037	0.066	-0.03094	-7.709
1962	5.8562	-0.013	0.277	-0.279	0.0027	0.279	-0.0027	c.s	-0.0697	-0.0043	0.046	-0.02797	3.108
1963	-0.226	-0.212	0.215	-0.111	-0.103	0.111	0.1038	c.s	-0.0777	0.00573	0.078	0.006551	2.519
1964	-0.371	-0.286	0.294	-0.157	-0.137	0.157	0.137	c.s	-0.0890	0.00957	0.094	0.015205	7.379
1965	-0.461	-0.379	0.375	-0.196	-0.178	0.196	0.178	c.s	-0.1481	0.01151	0.173	0.036977	-2.99
1966	-0.276	-0.273	0.256	-0.128	-0.127	0.128	0.127	c.s	-0.0044	0.01364	0.032	0.041807	1.271
1967	-0.265	-0.220	0.224	-5.039	-4.194	4.270	-0.117	c.s	-0.0588	0.00567	0.058	0.005280	2.094
1968	-0.190	-0.189	0.183	-0.092	-0.090	0.092	0.0902	c.s	-0.0679	0.00225	0.061	-0.00351	1.713
1969	-0.245	-0.247	0.242	-0.123	-0.118	0.089	0.0882	c.s	-0.0694	0.01020	0.097	0.038471	2.057
1970	-0.524	-0.355	0.398	-0.212	-0.180	0.218	0.180	c.s	0.07531	0.00316	-0.06	0.009342	-35.9
1971	0.0462	-0.082	0.058	-0.019	-0.038	0.019	0.038	c.s	-0.0613	0.00384	0.076	0.018688	1.933
1972	0.231	0.0714	-0.08	0.058	0.0311	-0.05	-0.03	c.s	-0.0168	0.00488	0.036	0.024108	0.149
1973	-0.38	-0.224	0.260	-0.14	-0.113	0.146	0.113	c.s	-0.1671	0.00173	0.182	0.017306	-0.87
1974	-0.45	-0.276	0.308	-0.17	-0.135	0.173	0.135	c.s	-0.1391	-0.0002	0.151	0.012476	2.613
1975	-0.61	-0.466	0.455	-0.24	-0.210	0.245	0.210	c.s	-0.6081	-0.0004	0.598	-0.01030	0.319
1976	-0.39	-0.319	0.321	-0.16	-0.153	0.168	0.153	c.s	-1.1302	-0.0002	1.112	-0.01809	-0.54
1977	-0.02	-0.081	0.067	-0.02	-0.038	0.028	0.038	c.s	-0.0520	0.00005	0.052	0.000384	0.518
1978	-0.03	-0.136	0.124	-0.05	-0.067	0.057	0.067	c.s	0.38514	-0.0001	-0.38	0.000020	-2.76
1979	-0.29	-0.20	0.229	-0.12	-0.103	0.125	0.103	c.s	1.97499	-0.0006	-1.96	0.011265	-0.31

Table 2.15 continued

	σ_{LL}	σ_{KK}	σ_{KL}	P_{LL}	P_{KK}	P_{LK}	P_{KL}	c/l	TCH1	TCH2	TCH3	MFP	Scale
1981	-0.45	-0.39	0.385	-0.20	-0.183	0.201	0.183	c.s	-0.2967	-0.0011	0.291	-0.00613	0.152
1982	-0.51	-0.80	0.559	-0.25	-0.305	0.254	0.305	c.s	0.22542	-0.0039	-0.20	0.019652	5.761
1983	-0.69	-0.80	0.639	-0.31	-0.324	0.314	0.324	c.s	-0.9872	-0.0007	1.101	0.022614	-0.49
1984	-0.53	-0.54	0.488	-0.24	-0.248	0.240	0.248	c.s	-0.5470	-0.0008	0.576	0.021308	0.932
1985	-1.08	-1.69	1.054	-0.49	-0.558	0.496	0.558	c.s	-1.6270	-0.0040	1.593	-0.03803	0.008
1986	-0.41	-0.28	0.331	-0.17	-0.153	0.178	0.153	c.s	-0.9117	-0.0052	0.908	-0.00870	-0.10
1987	-0.35	-0.25	0.283	-0.15	-0.132	0.150	0.132	c.s	-1.2344	-0.0058	1.245	0.005730	0.149
1988	-0.47	-0.35	0.011	-0.19	-0.167	0.193	0.167	c.s	-0.7942	-0.0068	0.812	0.011590	-0.851
1989	-0.63	-0.48	0.488	-0.26	-0.227	0.260	0.227	c.s	-0.5666	-0.0064	0.587	0.014652	0.705
1990	-0.84	-0.84	0.739	-0.37	-0.366	0.372	0.366	c.s	-0.8402	-0.0008	0.865	0.016348	2.812

Note: σ_{LL}, σ_{KK}, σ_{KL} = indicate the substitution elasticities, P_{LL}, P_{LL}, P_{KK}, P_{KL} =indicate price elasticities, TCH1, TCH2, TCH3 = indicate technical change, MFP, Scale = indicate multifactor productivity and scale, respectively. Finally, c/l = indicate the capital-labour saving (where c.u. is capital-using (or labour saving)): according to David and Van De Klundert (1965), technical progress is capital-saving if and only if the elasticity of substitution between capital and labour is less than unity in absolute values.

Source: Korres, G., 2008.

Table 2.16 Comparison of the elasticities of substitutions

ISIC	σ_{KL}	σ_{KL} (1)	σ_{KL} (2)	σ_{KL} (3)	σ_{KL} (4)
Foodstuffs (20)	0.957	0.944	0.460	0.663	-10.11
Beverages (21)	0.875	0.877	0.745	0.503	2.457
Tobacco (22)	0.412	0.676	0.990	0.462	2.278
Textiles (23)	1.014	0.162	0.592	1.279	1.420
Footwear and wearing(24)	0.554	0.635	0.753	0.012	1.277
Wood and cork (25)	0.596	0.448	0.981	0.350	2.899
Furniture (26)	0.777	1.017	0.545	0.246	200.0
Paper (27)	0.459	0.851	–	–	1.852
Printing-publishing (28)	0.564	–	0.177	–	1.656
Leather (29)	0.723	0.852	0.625	0.775	1.855
Rubber and plastics (30)	0.508	0.855	0.772	0.588	1.608
Chemicals (31)	0.731	0.885	–	–	3.953
Petroleum (32)	1.000	1.027	0.545	0.342	12.658
Non-Metallic products (33)	0.789	–	0.421	–	2.571
Basic metal industry (34)	0.189	1.002	0.464	0.532	15.873
Metal products (35)	0.653	0.440	0.558	1.425	3.922
Machinery and appl.(36)	0.672	0.719	0.401	0.220	1.751
Electrical supplies (37)	0.529	0.191	0.736	0.387	-9.804
Transport equipments (38)	0.615	0.325	0.933	–	–
Miscellaneous manf. / ind. (39)	0.890	–	–	–	–

Source: Korres, G., 2008.

Since input prices and β_i vary over observations, then substitution and price elasticities σ_{ij}, P_{ij} estimates will also differ over observations. As required by the theory, fitted values for all input-output equations are positive and the (n x n) matrix of the σ_{ij} substitution elasticities is negative and semi-definite at each observation implying that the estimated cost function is monotonically increasing and strictly quasi-concave in input prices.

All parameters are being presented in the Table 2.12. This Table provides the empirical estimations for the translog cost function over the period 1959-1990. In particular, coefficients $\{\alpha_K, \alpha_L\}$ are the average values of input shares for each sector; we have discarded the superscript v for convenience. The interpretation of parameters $\{\gamma_T, \alpha_Y\}$ which represent the average of the negative rate of the technical change and the average share of output in the total cost is similar. Parameters $\{\gamma_{KK}, \gamma_{LL}, \gamma_{KL}\}$ imply the share elasticities with respect to input prices and are constant.

Coefficients $\{\gamma_{KT}, \gamma_{LT}, \gamma_{TT}\}$ express technical change biases and the rate of acceleration of the technical change correspondingly. Our next set of parameters $\{\gamma_{KY}, \gamma_{LY}\}$ provide an indication of the scale biases, given that the underlying function is not homothetic; they show the growth of output influences the input shares. So, a positive number implies that input i is relatively more as output grows. Coefficient α_{YY} shows rate of outputs' acceleration. Parameter γ_{YT} tells us how time affects growth of output.

The preceding parameters have been estimated for twenty industrial sectors in Greek manufacturing but in sector 39 (Miscellaneous manufacturing industry) the rate of technical change is set equal to zero by definition. Several comments should be made on the preceding results. Let us start with the analysis of the parameters $\{\alpha_K, \alpha_L, \alpha_Y \gamma_T\}$. The average factor shares are positive as required by monotonicity for all twenty sectors. Apart from sectors 28 and 31, α_Y has a positive value and shows the average value share of output in the total cost, whereas the negative rate of technological change is negative in five sectors and positive in nineteen.

The next set of the estimated coefficients we are going to discuss is $\{\gamma_{KK}, \gamma_{LL}, \gamma_{KL}\}$. They imply the substitution patterns between the two factors. Second order parameters, for instance γ_{KK}, γ_{LL} and γ_{KL}, are defined as constant share elasticities which are derived from differentiating factor shares with respect to logarithmic prices. Coefficients γ_{KT} and γ_{LT} are biases of technical change and derived from differentiating the rate of technical change with respect to input prices. If we differentiate again the rate of technical change equation with respect the time, then we get γ_{TT}, which shows the rate of change of the negative of the rate of technical change.

We should note that, because a two-factor cost-function is assumed, we do not expect capital and labour to be complements. Then in this case producers could have been able to increase their output without any cost. In this sense, capital and labour are substitutes as parameter γ_{KL} is negative for seventeen sectors and positive but not significant in two. The rest, γ_{KK}, γ_{LL}, show how the use of an input responds to a shift in its price. By the law of demand, these should have been negative but they are not. Although these differences suggest violations in convexity, this is not so since values of own substitution elasticities for nineteen sectors are non-positive for every point within the sample period. This means that capital and labour inputs are price responsive. In sector 32, we have convexity violations so we imposed it, by using the method OLS described above. The cost of this imposition is that we set these parameters equal to zero.

Parameters $\{\gamma_{KY}, \gamma_{LY}\}$ indicate share elasticities with respect to output. In other words, they show how an input' share would be affected after a change at the level of output. In five sectors 27, 28, 29, 31 and 39, share of capital increases with an increase of output and in fifteen sectors it decreases. Exactly the opposite is true with labour input. The parameter α_{YY} represents cost flexibility or how marginal cost will change with a change at the level of output. In five sectors 26, 27, 28, 29 and 33, marginal cost increases as the output expands.

Parameters $\{\gamma_{KT}, \gamma_{LT}\}$ suggest technical change biases. They represent the change of a factor share with respect to time. In all nineteen sectors (not forgetting that for sector 39 $\gamma_{KT}=\gamma_{LT}=0$) γ_{KT} is positive, implying that the usage of capital increases over time. At the same time, all sectors have the tendency to be labour saving, because of technical change. Coefficient γ_{YT} shows the impact of technical change on growth of output.

More specifically, in sectors 26, 27, 28, 29 and 33, technical change decreases with sectoral output. Last parameter γ_{TT} shows the rate of acceleration of the negative rate of technical change. In seven 26, 27, 28, 29, 33, 35 and 37 sectors, the acceleration rate is positive which implies that technical change decreases with time whereas in the rest twelve it increases.

Table 2.13 provides estimations for mean substitution and price elasticities. We decomposed multifactor productivity (MFP) or rate of technical change in three parts; pure technology, non-neutral technology, and scale augmenting technology. In the last column of this Table, we furnished Hannoch's measure for scale economies. Finally, Tables 2.14 and 2.15 illustrate the results from the cross-section analysis.

First, the mean own substitution and price elasticities are negative as required; that is, factor demands are price responsive. Furthermore, in twelve sectors 20, 24, 25, 26, 27, 29, 30, 32, 33, 35, 36 and 39, the share of capital is influenced relatively more after a change in the price of labour. In other words, the demand for capital is less inelastic for the above twelve sectors than the labour demand is. Consequently, these industrial Greek sectors are willing, for instance, to give up comparatively easier some capital inflows in order to substitute with relatively cheaper labour inputs. *Technological capability and the efficiency of the country* remained at low levels. The transfer of technological inputs is *orientated to the traditional sectors*, which correspond to the less intensive research activities. If we take qualitative research characteristics into account, such as, the quality control, the overall situation of the country rather worsens than improving. A worth-note characteristic is the extremely low level of innovation activities of the private sector. The major part of research activities derive from funding of public sector. Linkages between *theoretical and productive research* are very loose, implying an additional barrier for the improvement of technological apparatus of the country. Finally, the administration of national research centres and in universities has proved rather inefficient in passing on research results and innovation activities to the industrial production. The Greek industry is very vulnerable to foreign competition and one of the main causes for this is the weak technological performance and the lack of indigenous produced technologies. In order to change this situation, the Greek industry should utilise imported technologies more creatively in the future rather than it did in the past.

Second, we provide a measure of the scale economies (Scale). In twelve sectors 23, 24, 25, 27, 28, 29, 31, 34, 35, 36, 38 and 39, we observed increasing returns to scale. This suggests that these sectors are able to increase their outputs at a relatively faster rate than in their total costs.

More simply, these twelve sectors function on the left-hand side of the minimum point of the U shaped average cost. So, they can still exploit high returns by expanding their production until their marginal cost gets equal to the average cost (under the assumption of perfect competition). In three industries 20,

26 and 33, values of scale economies are very close to unity 0.86, 0.96 and 0.94 respectively, so without making a significant mistake, we can assume constant returns to scale for these sectors. In five industries left 21, 22, 30, 32 and 37 (plus all manufacturing) we decisively conclude the existence of diseconomies of scale, implying that these industries function in an inefficient way. Their marginal cost is greater than their average cost.

Third, the multifactor productivity (MFP) is positive for only three sectors 28, 30 and 34; this means that in the rest of sixteen sectors, technological change reduces total costs at a rough average of 6% throughout the sample period. In addition, we performed a decomposition of the shadow value of time (MFP) in TCH1, TCH2 and TCH3. In particular, TCH1 is negative in fourteen sectors, which suggests that the pure technology -the technology which is attributed more to the time trend- reduces total costs in fourteen industrial sectors by an average 8%.

The non-neutral part of technical change TCH2 is in fourteen sectors positive, implying that technology makes the usage of inputs relatively more intense as the years pass by and so the total costs increase on average 0.1%. At last, we have the scale augmenting part TCH3. It is positive in fourteen sectors and implies that technology increases sectoral output and total cost by almost 1.5%.

Table 2.16 shows the comparison of elasticities of substitution and technological progress between this study and previous studies for the Greek economy. The index of substitution elasticities in the first column indicates the results from our estimations. The index of substitution elastcities in second column indicates the estimation-results of Panas' paper (1986), covering the period 1958-75 and gives estimations for 17-sectors of Greek economy. The index of substitution elastcities in the third column indicates estimation-results from Kintis' paper (1978), covering the period 1958-1973 and give estimations for 14-sectors of the Greek economy. The estimation-results of this study are *closer* to the results of Kintis and Panas. Of course, the methods and the data set used are quite different. According to these, the capital input in the case of Greek manufacturing industries grew faster than output and also confirms the existence of *over capitalisation*. Consequently, more and more capital-intensive methods are adopted and imply that capital grew more than is required which can lead to negative capital augmentation.

We estimate a translog cost function for twenty Greek manufacturing sectors double digit (ISIC). Due to the restrictions of data-set, estimations cover the period 1959-1990. We tried to estimate the technical change which was decomposed in three parts:

i.   pure technology,
ii. non-neutral technology and
iii. scale augmenting component

Scale economies are also allowed. We test and reject the hypothesis of homotheticity, homogeneity and constant returns to scale. First we estimate the parameters of cost-function with share inputs and then price elasticities and elasticities of substitution. Second, we decompose the multifactor productivity (MFP) or the rate of technical change in three parts: the pure technology, the non-neutral technology, and scale augmenting technology.

Based on previous discussion, the main conclusions and recommendations of this paper can be summarised below:

The interpretation of parameter-coefficients $\{\alpha_K, \alpha_L\}$, $\{\gamma_T, \alpha_Y\}$, $\{\gamma_{KK}, \gamma_{LL}, \gamma_{KL}\}$, $\{\gamma_{KT}, \gamma_{LT}, \gamma_{TT}\}$ and, finally, $\{\gamma_{KY}, \gamma_{LY}\}$ are the average values of input shares for each sector; the average of the negative rate of technical change and the average share of output in total cost, share elasticities with respect to input prices which they are constant, technical change biases and rate of acceleration of technical change and, finally, scale biases, showing the growth of output influences and input shares, respectively. Coefficients γ_{KT} and γ_{LT} are biases of technical change and derived from differentiating the rate of technical change with respect to input prices. If we differentiate again the rate of technical change equation with respect to time, then we get γ_{TT} which shows the rate of change of the negative of the rate of technical change.

The above parameters have been estimated for twenty industrial sectors in Greek manufacturing. Parameters $\{\alpha_K, \alpha_L, \alpha_Y \gamma_T\}$ showing the average factor shares are positive as required by monotonicity for all twenty sectors; that is producers would have been able to increase their output without any cost. Parameters γ_{KK}, γ_{LL} showing how the use of an input responds to a shift in its price and, according to the law of demand, these should showed have been negative, but they are not. Parameters $\{\gamma_{KY}, \gamma_{LY}\}$ indicating the share elasticities with respect to output and they show how an input' share, would be affected after a change at the level of output. In five sectors 27, 28, 29, 31 and 39, the share of capital increases with an increase of output and in fifteen sectors it decreases, while the opposite is true with labour input. Finally, according to the parameter γ_{TT}, the rate of acceleration of the technical change, showing that in seven 26, 27, 28, 29, 33, 35 and 37 sectors the acceleration rate is positive, implies that technical change decreases with time, whereas in the rest twelve it increases.

In conclusion, according to our results, technology is proxied by the use of time trend for the estimation of *translog cost function* for the sectors of Greek manufacturing. Although time trend functions only as a rough representative of true underlying determinants of technological change, it is the best we could do given the lack of satisfactory data set. Results indicate that most of industrial sectors (except for sectors 23 and 32) are capital using intensive (or labour saving) and can be interpreted in accordance with the previous analysis that technological inputs (such as imported capital goods and transferred technologies) are not appropriate to the local necessities and does not fit the availability of market resources. To see the difficulties that Greek manufacturing has in adjusting itself to new technologies, we may use the measure of scale economies as a guide. It is evident that Greek manufacturing to a large extent exhibits increasing returns. Hence, these industries have the potential for further improvement. If this is the case, they could contribute to Greek economic development.

5. Policy Implications and Summary

Neoclassical theory suggests that convergence will be taken across countries in either growth rates or income levels. Poor countries will perform lower capital-labour ratios, implying a higher marginal product of capital. Given equal rates of labour force growth, technical progress and domestic savings, their capital stock will exceed and they will tend to converge with richer countries; as convergence will occur, growth rates of poorer countries should be greater. However, convergence in *neoclassical theory* will not occur if differences exist across countries in the production function. *Endogenous growth theory* suggests that it is possible that there would be sustained differences in both rates and levels of growth of national income.

Both diffusion and neoclassical models suggest the convergence to a unique equilibria. However, neither considers the possibility of multiple convergent equilibria; this has come out of new endogenous growth models. Romer provide important insights for the relation between growth and R&D and place them with a general equilibrium growth model.

The so-called *new growth theories* argue that greater investment (both in physical and human capital) creates externalities and economies of scale effects. These theories emphasise the role of economy returns for scale, expenditure on R&D, human capital formation and the role of investment on diffusion and technical change. Higher rates of gross investment could raise the rate of growth of productivity by increasing the rate of substitution of the old by new capital. Solow focused his attention on the process of capital formation.

On the other hand, *new growth theories* examine the way in which some countries been able to grow with no apparent tendency to slow down and try to explain why some countries exhibited medium or long term accelerations or decelerations in their growth. Romer makes technological change endogenous by assuming that technology is a public good and private investment in capital increases the level of technology available to entrepreneurs; higher investment rate will accelerate the economic growth.

Theoretical and empirical models of *endogenous growth* emerged in the 1980s. The approach of *endogenous growth* suggests that growth rates are not exogenous rather depend on internal allocation processes; this arises rather because of non-decreasing returns to scale or because of the production externalities. *Endogenous growth* differs from *neoclassical growth models* because it assumes that economic growth is an endogenous outcome of an economic system and not the result of forces that infringe from outside. *Endogenous growth theory* has the advantage of explaining the forces that give rise to technological change rather than following the assumption of *neoclassical theory* that such change is exogenous. *Endogenous growth models* emphasise the role of international trade; they suggest that high productivity growth is possible in poor countries as a result of the diffusion of knowledge already available in industrial countries. Since Solow (1956), technological change has been regarded as one of the main sources of economic growth. Neoclassical models are assuming marginal productivity, technological change (or labour growth) are needed to compensate for the negative productivity effects of capital accumulation.

In this chapter, we have attempted to analyse the determinant factors of technological change. In the steady state of technological change, we can present both types of technological change: the actual amounts of basic research and quality improvement depend on the different marginal growth productivity of human capital between basic research and quality improvements.

In literature, there are various explanations for the slow-down in productivity growth. One source of the slow-down may be substantial changes in the industrial composition of output, employment, capital accumulation and resource utilisation. The second source may be that technological opportunities have declined and furthermore the application of new technologies to production has been less successful. Technological factors act in long run and should not be expected to explain medium-run variations in the growth of GDP and productivity.

Technological gap models represent two conflicting forces: innovation, which tends to increase the productivity differences between countries, and diffusion, which tends to reduce them. In the Schumpeterian theory, growth differences are seen as the combined results of these forces. Research on *why growth rates differ* has a long history which goes well beyond growth accounting exercises.

In this chapter, we have also attempted to analyse the theoretical background and the evaluation form of a flexible functional form. Using a flexible functional form we can estimate the technical change which may decompose in three parts:

- pure technology;
- non-neutral technology; and
- scale augmenting component; scale economies are also allowed.

We have tested and rejected the hypothesis of homotheticity, homogeneity and constant returns to scale. First we estimated parameters of cost-function with share inputs and then the price elasticities and elasticities of substitution. Furthermore, we may decomposed the multifactor productivity (MFP) or the rate of technical change in three parts: pure technology, non-neutral technology, and scale augmenting technology.

The substitution effect is linked with the characteristics of production technology. It increases with the possibility of substitution between factors of production. Such possibilities are measured by their elasticity of substitution, a concept which most directly reflects the technical constraints inherent in production processes.

Chapter 3
Knowledge Economy, Technical Change and Productivity Growth

1. Introduction

This chapter investigates the relationship between productivity and technological change. The question that we shall address in this chapter is whether a slow down in productivity can be explained by the slow-down of innovation activities. This chapter attempts to measure technical change in order to measure the effects of economic growth for European member states. It introduces the reader, first, to some basic elements and concepts central to the understanding of this approach. The characteristics of the innovation process such as its nature and sources as well as some factors shaping its development are examined. Particular emphasis is laid on the role of technical change and dissemination based on the fundamental distinction between codified and tacit forms. These concepts recur throughout the chapter and particularly in discussions about the nature and specifications of systems approach. The chapter concludes summarising some major findings of the discussion and pointing to some directions for future research activities.

Many studies have suggested that there is an interrelation between technological development and productivity (see, for example, Abramovitz 1986; Fagerberg 1987, 1988, 1994), and economists have analysed different possible views of why productivity growth has declined. These alternative explanations can be grouped into the following categories:

- the capital factor; for instance, investment may have been insufficient to sustain the level of productivity growth;
- the technology factor; for instance, a decline in innovation might have affected productivity growth;
- the increased price of raw materials and energy;
- government regulations and demand policies that affect the productivity level;
- skills and experience of the labour force may have deteriorated or workers may not work as hard as they used to;
- products and services produced by the economy may have become more diverse; and
- productivity levels may differ greatly across industries.

This chapter attempts to measure the relationship between technology and productivity or, more precisely, to investigate the correlation between technological development and the decline in productivity growth. We shall empirically test technological and catching-up models, using data mainly for the EU member states.

2. Theory and Measurement of Productivity Growth

Productivity is a relationship between production and the means of production, or, more formally, a relation of proportionality between the output of a good or service and inputs used to generate that output. This relationship is articulated through the given technology of production. There are two general types of studies that have calculated international TFP differentials:

a. Studies of value added
b. Studies of gross output

Among the studies which calculate TFP using a value added output measure are Dollar and Wolff (1993), Dollar, Wolff and Baumol (1988), Maskus (1991), van Ark (1993), and van Ark and Pilat (1993). The first three of these researchers use overall GDP price levels to deflate sectoral outputs. The second class of studies of TFP uses data on gross output, and deflates all inputs (capital, labour, materials, energy, etc) in a symmetric way. This procedure was pioneered by Jorgenson and various co-authors, and is undoubtedly the most theoretically appealing and least restrictive method of making productivity comparisons.

2.1 Productivity Growth and Technological Change

Productivity growth is crucially affected by technological change. Their relationship is so close that the two terms are often used interchangeably. Productivity is a wider concept. Even though a crucial one, technological change is only one of the many factors which affect productivity growth; others being social, cultural, educational, organisational and managerial factors. Better management of workers and machinery and appropriate incentive structures can increase production and/or reduce costs. But these are different from technological change.

It is not easy or straightforward to disentangle the effects of technological change from social and cultural factors. One simple way to conceptualise the differences is the way suggested by Spence (1984). On the other hand, if changes concern primarily people, then they may reasonably be considered as being *social* in nature. On the other hand, if they appear to be fundamentally about material products and related processes, then they can be more easily viewed as *technological*.

2.2 Technology and Technological Change

At this point, it is appropriate to ask what technological change means. A prior question is "what is technology"? Unfortunately, there is no simple answer to this question. We confine ourselves to one directly related to our study. In the standard neo-classical economic model, technology refers to a collection of techniques or ways of specifying how much of various outputs can be produced when given quantities of various inputs are used. In most textbook cases this is simplified as a single output production function which specifies the maximum quantity of output predicable from given quantities of labour and capital. Technology is then production function. It is generally represented graphically with the help of level curves or isoquants. Technological progress in this simple framework is a shift upwards of the production function, or shift downwards of the representative isoquant. An alternative way is to look at cost functions which relate levels of cost of production to level of output and to factor prices. In many cases, cost functions are easier to characterise production functions. Data for cost functions is more easily available.

Given input prices, we can view technological improvement as a downward shift of cost function. Technology has two aspects, called "embodied" or "disembodied". The former is identified with "hardware" and consists of tools, machinery, equipment and vehicles, which together make up the category of capital goods. The other is identified with "software" and encompasses the knowledge and skills required for the use, maintenance, repairs, production, adaptation and innovation of capital goods. These are often called the "know-how and the know-why of processes and products". Technological change does not affect all factors equally. When it does, it is considered neutral technical change. Otherwise, it may have a specific factor using or factor saving bias.

The terms "technological change" and "technical change" are used interchangeably in the literature under review, both being indicators of a shift in the production function. It would have been useful to reserve the latter term to indicate change in techniques or processes. The terms "technological progress" and "technical progress" are synonymous with "technological change" and "technical change" respectively, all change being considered as being for the better.

2.3 Production Function and Productivity Growth

As indicated above, the notion of a production function is central for the meaning of technology. It is consequently crucial for the measurement of productivity. A production function is a technological relationship which specifies the maximum level of output of a good which can be obtained from a given level of one or several inputs. In its general form, two-input production function can be written as

$$V_t = f(K_t, L_t) \tag{3.1}$$

where V_t = level of net output (value added).
K_t = capital input (or service of factor capital)
L_t = labour input
t = time

2.4 Partial or Single Factor Productivity

Partial or single factor productivity (PP) of labour or capital is indicated by the ratio V/L, or V/K for instance, output per unit, or the average product of the factor concerned. Productivity defined this way is merely the inverse of factor intensity. An increase in this ratio, while assuming that other things remaining the same, implies an increased efficiency of input use, whereby the same level of output can be produced by a smaller quantity of given input. However, when other things cannot be assumed to be the same, the interpretation of these output factor ratios as indicators of productivity becomes problematic. For example, an increase in labour productivity may only reflect capital deepening – a rise in the K/L ratio. In such cases it becomes necessary to compute total factor productivity.

2.4.1 Total Factor Productivity

Total factor productivity (TFP) extends the concept of single factor productivity such as output per unit labour or capital to more than one factor. Thus, TFP is the ratio of gross output to a weighted combination of inputs. For the case of production function shown above, TFP at time t would be given by:

$$A_t = \frac{V_t}{g(K_t, L_t)}$$

(3.2)

where A_t : Index of TFP at time t.
g the aggregation procedure is implicit in the specific production function adopted.

Different functional forms of production functions imply different aggregation procedures or weighting schemes for combining factor inputs.

2.4.2 Total Productivity (TP) versus Total Factor Productivity (TFP)

At this stage, choice exists in regards to the specification of output as value added (V) as in equation (1) above or gross value of output (Y). In the latter case, material and energy inputs are explicitly accounted for in both the left and the right-hand sides in the production function. This would give rise to the following general functional form which has recently come to be known as KLEM type production function.

$Y_t = g(K_t, L_t, E_t, M_t, t)$

where: Y_t = level of gross output per unit of time,
K_t = capital input (or service of factor capital)
L_t = labour input
E_t = input of energy
M_t = material inputs
t = time

The choice between the two form depends on what one believes to be the correct measure of output. It also depends on whether one thinks the production function to be separable in factor and material inputs or not. The above functional forms give rise to alternative concepts of productivity. One can define the productivity measure associated with the value added (V) production function as total factor productivity (TFP) and that associated with gross output (Y) production function as total productivity (TP).

In the survey which follows it will be seen that the majority of studies have been conducted using production functions with value added as output and with K and L as inputs.

2.4.3 Description of Main Variables and Data for TFP

Real Output: The OECD has recently compiled data on nominal output, valued added, employment, and gross fixed capital formation (GFCF) from a number of existing data sources to form a single internally consistent source for disaggregated cross-country comparisons. Making the OECD data internationally comparable requires currency conversion, being the most problematic part of any international comparison. Using purchasing power parity (PPP) GDP deflators is the most common procedure, but this creates bias in industry level comparisons since it implicitly assumes that there are no relative price differences across countries.

Capital: Given the series on real investment, the capital stock is a function of past investment flows. The choice of function is both important and somewhat arbitrary, since it is not feasible to gather information on useful asset lives and depreciation patterns across industries and countries. Follow many researchers and construct the capital stock as a distributed lag of past investment flows:

$$k_{cjt} = \sum_{n=1}^{T} (1 - \delta)^{n-1} i_{j,t-n}$$

where k_{cjt} is the capital stock of industry j in country c at the beginning of year t, $\delta < 1$ is the discount factor, and i is real investment during year t. Note that the capital stock in year t does not include year t investment, but only up through year t-1. An alternative method is to use the so-called delayed linear scrapping rule: a newly purchased capital good is added to the capital stock, and after a period of S years a constant proportion $1/(M+1)$ is scrapped each year:

$$k_{cjt} = \sum_{n=1}^{S} i_{cj,t-n} + \sum_{n=S+1}^{S-M} i_{cj,t-n} \cdot \left[1 - \frac{n-S}{M+1}\right]$$

Labour: Labour can be derived from industry employment figures in the STAN data. Because employment is an imperfect indicator of labour input, two adjustments are made to these data. First, the employment data are converted into 40-hour work-week equivalents using average hours worked in manufacturing. Second, the data are disaggregated into three occupational categories (professional/technical, managerial, and other) using the proportions of each occupation in manufacturing. The occupational categories are aggregated into total labour we can also use a translog index:

$$I = I_1^{\alpha_1} I_2^{\alpha_2} I_3^{\alpha_3}$$

where the subscripts refer to the three occupational categories and country-industry-year subscripts are omitted for readability. The weights α_1, α_2, and α_3 sum to unity and are constructed from each occupation's share in total labour cost. Analogously to the total cost shares used in the TFP index we can use the following weights to construct the index of labour for country c in year t:

$$\alpha_m = \left(s_m + \bar{s}_m\right)/2$$

where s_m is the share of occupation m in total cost for a particular country-industry-year observation and $\bar{s}_m$ is the arithmetic mean of s_m across observations. Construction of the labour cost shares s_m requires data on wages.

Total Factor Productivity: The TFP levels can be calculated from the above data of value added y, employment l, and capital stocks k. The TFP calculations usually require the assumption of constant returns to scale throughout. Furthermore, we can also assume that value added can be modeled as a function of the capital stock and employment, and that these inputs are measured perfectly and in the same units for each observation. For a particular industry in county c, we can consider the real value added y, as a constant returns to scale function of the real capital stock k_c, and the level of employment l_c:

$$y_c = f_c(k_c, l_c) = f_c(x_c)$$

A formula to compare country-year b relative to country-year c is

$$TFP_{bc} = \left[\prod_{j=1}^{N} \left(\frac{y_{bj}}{\bar{y}_j}\right)^{P_{bj}} \cdot \left(\frac{\bar{y}_j}{y_{cj}}\right)^{P_{cj}}\right] \cdot \left(\frac{\bar{l}}{l_b}\right)^{o_b} \left(\frac{\bar{k}}{k_b}\right)^{1-\sigma_b} \left(\frac{l_c}{\bar{l}}\right)^{\sigma_c} \left(\frac{k_c}{\bar{k}}\right)^{1-\sigma_c}$$

where: y_{cj} = real value-added in country c by sector j

$\rho_{cj} = (r_{cj} + \bar{r}_j \, r_j)/2$, where r_{cj} is the share of total value-added in country c accounted for by sector j.

l_c = total labour employed in country c (that is, summed over all N sectors)

k_c = total capital stock in country c (that is, summed over all N sectors)

$o_c = (s_c + \bar{s})/2$, where s_c is labour's share in total cost in country c.

Overbars indicate averages over all the observations in the sample. Subscripts b and c can refer to any two distinct observations, such as two different countries during the same year, two different countries in different years, or the same country in different years.

2.5 Approaches to Measurement of Productivity Growth

There are three principal approaches to measurement of productivity growth. These are

- The index number approach,
- The parametric approach,
- The non-parametric approach.

In the present survey, we focus primarily on studies which have estimated productivity growth using the first approach. Wherever appropriate, the results from the estimation of cost and production functions have been mentioned to support alternative explanations of the results of the first approach. The non-parametric approach which is based on linear programming models of relative efficiency is not reviewed here.

2.5.1 Index Number Approach

In this approach the observed growth in output is sought to be explained in terms of growth in factor inputs. The unexplained part or the residual is attributed to growth in productivity of factors. It consists in assuming a certain functional form for the producers' production function and then deriving an index number formula that is consistent (exact) with the assumed functional form. Preferred functional forms are the flexible ones. These indexes differ from each other on the basis of underlying production function or the aggregation scheme assumed. Following are some of the most commonly used indexes.

2.5.2 Kendrick Index

Kendrick's index of total factor productivity for the case of value added as output, and two inputs can be written as

$$A_t = \frac{V_t}{(r_0 K_t + w_0 L_t)} \tag{3.3}$$

where,

A_t is the value of index in a given year,

V_t is the value of gross output,

w_0 and r_0 denote the factor rewards of labour and capital respectively in the base year.

The index measures average productivity of an arithmetic combination of labour and capital with base year period factor prices. It assumes a linear and a homogeneous production function of degree one. Besides constant returns to scale and neutral technical progress, it assumes an infinite elasticity of substitutability between labour and capital. The index can be generalised to allow for more than two factors. If a sufficiently long time series for this index can be constructed, then a trend rate of growth can be estimated econometrically. From the time series of Kendrick index, yearly series (gt) can be formed by writing growth between successive years as

$$g_{t+1}^K = (A_{t+1} - A_t) / A_t$$

The growth rates thus obtained can be appropriately averaged for sub-periods.

2.5.3 Solow Index

Solow's measure of productivity growth for two input case is given by (4)

$$g_{t+1}^S = \left[\frac{V_{t+1} - V_t}{V_t} \right] - \left[\frac{L_{t+1} - L_t}{L_t} + \frac{K_{t+1} - K_t}{K_t} \right] \tag{3.4}$$

where V_j = measure of output.

This measure is based on general neo-classical production function. It assumes constant returns to scale, Hicks-neutral technical change, competitive equilibrium and factor rewards being determined by marginal products. Under these conditions, the growth of total factor productivity is the difference between the growth of value added and the rate of growth of total factor inputs. The latter is in the form of a Divisia index number for instance, a weighted combination of the growth rates, the weights being the respective shares. If we assumed specific Cobb-Douglas production function, with unit elasticity of output (unlike in the general functional form above) and took base year factor shares as weights, we would get Domar's geometric index of TFPG.

Assuming $A_1 = 1$, a time series of Solow index of productivity (A_t) can be formed from the formula:

$$A_{t+1} = A_t * (1 + g_{t+1}^S)$$

2.5.4 Malmquist Index

Over twenty-five years ago, Malmquist (1983) proposed a quantity index for use in consumption analysis. The index scales consumption bundles up or down, in a radial fashion, to some arbitrarily selected indifference surface. In this context Malmquist's scaling factor turns out to be Shephard's (1953) input distance function, and Malmquist quantity indexes for pairs of consumption bundles can be constructed from ratios of corresponding pairs of input distance functions.1 Although it was developed in a consumer context, the Malmquist quantity index recently has enjoyed widespread use in a production context, in which multiple but cardinally measurable outputs replace scalar-valued but ordinally measurable utility. In producer analysis, Malmquist indexes can be used to construct indexes of input, output or productivity, as ratios of input or output distance functions. The period t output-oriented Malmquist productivity index is

$$M_0^t(x^t, y^t, x^{t+1}, y^{t+1}) = D_0^t(x^{t+1}, y^{t+1}) / D_0^t(x^t, y^t).$$

$M_0^t(x^t, y^t, x^{t+1}, y^{t+1})$ compares (x^{t+1}, y^{t+1}) to (x^t, y^t) by scaling y^{t+1} to Isoquant $\text{P}^t(\text{x}^{t+1})$, that is, by using period t technology as a reference. Although $D_0^t(x^t, y^t) \leq 1$, it is possible that $D_0^t(x^t, y^t) > 1$, since period t+1 data may not be feasible with period t technology. Thus $M_0^t(x^t, y^t, x^{t+1}, y^{t+1}) \gtreqless 1$ according as productivity change is positive, zero or negative between periods t and t+1, from the perspective of period t technology. The period t output-oriented Malmquist productivity index decomposes as:

$$M_0^t(x^t, y^t, x^{t+1}, y^{t+1}) = \Delta TE(x^t, y^t, x^{t+1}, y^{t+1}) * \Delta T^t(x^t, y^t, x^{t+1}, y^{t+1}) =$$

$$= \frac{D_0^{t+1}(x^{t+1}, y^{t+1})}{D_0^t(x^t, y^t)} \bullet \frac{D_0^t(x^{t+1}, y^{t+1})}{D_0^{t+1}(x^{t+1}, y^{t+1})},$$

where $\Delta TE(*)$ refers to technical efficiency change and $\Delta T^t(*)$ refers to technical change.

2.5.5 Translog Index

Translog measure of TFPG is given by:

$$g_{t+1}^T = \ln\left[\frac{Y_{t+1}}{Y_t}\right] - \left[\left[\frac{s_{t+1}^L + s_t^L}{2}\right] * \ln\left[\frac{L_{t+1}}{L_t}\right] + \left[\frac{s_{t+1}^K + s_t^K}{2}\right] * \ln\left[\frac{K_{t+1}}{K_t}\right]\right] \quad (3.5)$$

This expresses TFP as the difference between growth rate of output and weighted average of growth rates of labour and capital input. This is equivalent to Tornquist's discrete approximation to continuous Divisia index. The index is based on the translog function which describes the relationship both between outputs and inputs and between the aggregate and its components. The homogeneous translog functional form is flexible in the sense that it can provide a second order approximation to an arbitrary twice continuously differentiable linear homogeneous function. This functional form helps overcome the problem which arises with the Solow index where discrete set of data on prices and quantities need to be used in a continuous function. This index also imposes fewer a priori restrictions on the underlying production technology. The index can be generalised for more than two inputs.

Like in the previous case, from year to year changes in productivity growth one can construct a time series of the translog index as follows:

$$A_{t+1} = A_t * (1 + g^T_{t+1})$$

2.6 Parametric Approach

Parametric approach consists in econometric estimation of production functions to infer contributions of different factors and of an autonomous increase in production over time, independent of inputs. This latter increase, which is a shift over time in the production function, can be more properly identified as technological progress. It is one of the factors underlying productivity growth. An alternative to estimation of production functions is estimation of cost functions using results from the duality theory. Below we give some commonly used specifications of production functions.

2.6.1 Cobb-Douglas Specification

The general form of Cobb-Douglas Function has the following form:

$$V = A_0 e^t L K \qquad (3.6)$$

Where, V, L, K and t refer to value added, labour, capital and time. a and b give factor shares respectively for labour and capital. A_0 describes initial conditions. Technological change takes place at a constant rate l. It is assumed to be disembodied and Hicks-neutral, so that when there is a shift in the production function, K/L ratio remains unchanged at constant prices. In log-linear form this function can be written as:

$$\log V = a + \alpha \log L + \beta \log K + \lambda_t \qquad (3.7)$$

The estimated value of l provides a measure of technological progress, which is often identified with total factor productivity growth.

2.6.2 Constant Elasticity of Substitution (CES) Specification

The general form of Constant-Elasticity of Substitution Function has the following form:

$$V = A_0 e^t \left(L^{-\delta} + (1 - \lambda) K^{-\rho} \right)^{-\nu} \tag{3.8}$$

where l is the efficiency parameter, δ the distribution parameter, ρ the substitution parameter and u is the scale parameter. The elasticity of substitution $\sigma = 1/(1 + \rho)$ varies between 0 and μ. Technical change is Hicks neutral and disembodied. The value of λ (a measure of technical progress) can be estimated using a non-linear estimation procedure, or by using the following Taylor-series linear approximation to the CES function:

$$\ln V = \ln A_0 + \lambda t + \nu\delta \ln L + \nu(1 - \delta) \ln K - (1/2)\rho\nu\delta(1 - \delta)(\ln L - \ln K)^2 \tag{3.9}$$

This function can be estimated by OLS.

2.6.3 Transcendental Logarithmic (TL) Specification

The general form of Transcendental Function has the following form:

$$\log V = \alpha_0 + \beta_L (\log L) + \beta_K (\log K) + \frac{1}{2} \beta_{LL} (\log L)^2 + \frac{1}{2} \beta_{KK} (\log K)^2$$

$$+ \beta_{LK} (\log L)(\log K) + \beta_{Lt} (\log L)t + \beta_{Kt} (\log K)t + \frac{1}{2} \beta_{tt} t \tag{3.10}$$

where α's and β's are the parameters of the production function.

The rate of technical progress or total factor productivity growth is given by:

$$\frac{\log V}{t} = \alpha_t + \beta_{tt} t + \beta_{Lt} (\log L) + \beta_{Kt} (\log K) \tag{3.11}$$

where: α_t is the rate of autonomous total factor productivity growth.
β_{tt} is the rate of change of TFPG, and
β_{Lt}, β_{Kt} define the bias in TFPG.

If both β_{Lt} and β_{Kt} are zero, then the TFPG is Hicks-neutral type. If β_{Lt} is positive then the share of labour increases with time and there is labour using bias. Similarly, a positive β_{Kt} will show a capital using bias.

2.6.4 Direct Estimation of Cost Functions

Due to results of duality theory, one may estimate a cost function instead of production function to calculate technical progress. In its general form, a four-factor cost function can be written as:

$$C = C(P_L, P_K, P_E, P_M, Q, t) \tag{3.12}$$

Specific forms of cost functions corresponding to each of the above functional forms can be derived. We give below the translog cost function which has many desirable properties sought out by researchers and which has been used most commonly in recent years.

2.6.5 The Translog Cost Function

The general form of Translog Function has the following form:

$$\log C = \beta_i + \sum_i \beta_i \log p_i + \frac{1}{2} \sum_i \sum_j \log p_i \log p_j + \beta_Q \log Q +$$
$$+ \frac{1}{2} \beta_{QQ} (\log Q)^2 + \beta_{Qt} \log Q \log t + \beta_t \log t + \frac{1}{2} \beta_{tt} (\log t)^2 +$$
$$+ \sum_i \beta_{Qi} \log Q \log p_j + \sum_i \beta_{ti} \log t \log p_i$$

Using Shepherd's lemma one can estimate demands for individual factors and shares in total cost of individual factors as follows:

$$\frac{\log C}{\log p_i} = \frac{x_i p_i}{C} = S_i = \beta_i + \sum_j \beta_{ij} \log p_j + \beta_{Qi} \log Q + \beta_{ti} \log t$$

Rate of technical progress (λ_t) is given by

$$(t) = \frac{\log C}{t} = \frac{1}{t} \left(\beta_t + \beta_{tt} \log t + \beta_{Qt} \log Q + \sum_j \beta_{ti} \log p_i \right)$$

Technical progress has a factor i using bias if $\beta_{ti} > 0$. It is neutral with respect to factor i if $\beta_{ti} = 0$ and it is factor i saving if β_{ti} is < 0.

Schmookler (1966), Kendrick (1991), and Abramovitz (1986) have studied the interaction between technological change and productivity. In these studies, factor prices were used to weight the various inputs in order to obtain a measure of total input growth. The approach developed by Abramovitz (1986), Solow (1957) and Denison (1962) involves the decomposition of output growth into its various sources, which can be defined as the growth accounting and residual method. Growth accounting tries to explain changes in real product and total factor productivity based mainly on a comparison between the growth of inputs (capital and labour) and the growth of output. One part of actual growth cannot be explained and has been classified as 'unexplained total factor productivity growth' (or the so called residual).

2.6.6 Catching-up Models

There are many different approaches to the measurement of productivity. The calculation and interpretation of the different measures are not straightforward, particularly for international comparisons. OECD estimates of productivity adjusted for the business cycle: For its recent work on economic growth, the OECD developed estimates of productivity growth adjusted for the business cycle. Most productivity measures are procyclical; they tend to accelerate during periods of economic expansion and decelerate during periods of recession. This is partly due to measurement: variations in volume output tend to be relatively accurately reflected in economic statistics, but variations in the rate of utilisation of inputs are at best only partially picked up. Even if capacity utilisation is accurately measured, the standard model of productivity fits the realities of the business cycle somewhat awkwardly. Much economic and index number theory relies on long-term, equilibrium relationships involving few unforeseen events of economic actors.

The economic model of productivity measurement is therefore easier to implement and interpret during periods of continued and moderate expansion than during a rapidly changing business cycle. It is therefore appropriate to examine productivity growth over longer periods of time or to adjust productivity estimates for cyclical fluctuations. Usually, TFP is the total factor productivity that is a weighted average of the growth in labour and capital productivity. Whereas, the capital productivity is the ratio of output to capital and the labour productivity is the output per employed person.

For structural change we use as an approximation changes in the share of exports and agriculture in GDP. Technological gap models, as developed here, can say little about how to boost the level of innovation activities or improve diffusion and innovation. We test the following versions of models:

GDP (or PROD) = f [GDPPC, EXPA (or GERD), INV] (the basic model)

GDP (or PROD) = f [GDPPC, EXPA (or GERD), INV, EXP]

GDP = f [GDPPC, EXPA (or GERD), INV, TRD]

However, it can be argued that this model overlooks differences in overall growth rates between periods due to other factors and more particularly differences in economic policies. As expected, the best results are obtained for the logarithmic models which imply a steeper curve. Patenting data reflect the innovation process, while both the research indexes reflect the imitation and the innovation process.

The research and development data reflect imitation, innovation and diffusion activities. The relation between productivity (as measured by per capita GDP) and innovation activities should be expected to be log linear, rather than linear and steeper for the patent data than for the index based on research data.

3. Innovation Activities, Growth and Productivity: Recent Trends and Evidence

Productivity growth is the basis of efficient economic growth. Economic growth has been defined as the process of a sustained increase in the production of goods and services with the aim of making available a progressively diversified basket of consumption goods to population Scarcity of resources, which includes physical, financial and human resources, has been recognised as a limiting factor on the process of economic growth. While output expansion based on increased use of resources is feasible, it is not sustainable.

Therefore, efficiency or productivity of resources becomes a critical factor in economic growth. These terms, which will be defined more precisely in the following section, indicate ability to obtain a given amount of good or service by using a lesser amount of input. Productivity growth, therefore, is critical for ensuring sustained increase in the production of goods and services. Economic growth is traditionally been associated with industrialisation. At least that is what makes the diversity in the basket of consumption goods and services possible, when trading possibilities are limited. But industrialisation at the initial stages has the effect of making resource scarcities more acute, making it all the more necessary that available resources are utilised more productively.

Role of productivity growth in the process of economic growth became clear when it was found that accumulation of productive factors (capital and labour) could explain only a fraction of actual expansion of output in the 1950s. Empirical work on the American economy by Tinbergen (1992), Schmookler (1966), Fabricant (1954), Abramovitz (1956), Kendrick (1961), Solow (1957) and Denison (1962) showed that between 80 to 90% of observed increase in output per head could not be explained by increase in capital per head and was attributed to productivity growth. Further, Terleckyi (1974), Scherer (1982a, 1982b) and Griliches (1980) showed that technological advancement was a major source of productivity improvement for the American industry.

While productivity growth and technological change affect the use of all factors, it is important to single out energy for a separate treatment. Energy is essential for economic growth and rapid increases in economic activity associated with accelerating economic growth lead to large increases in demand. As economic growth progresses and the economy moves away from agricultural to industrial modes of production, energy intensity, that is, energy use per unit of GDP, first increases and then declines.

Productivity growth in the manufacturing sector in general and in the energy intensive industries in particular has the effect of moderating the growth of energy demand. The degree of this moderation of course depends on magnitude and the nature of technological change. If technological change is neutral, in the sense that it affects all inputs equally, the degree of moderation will depend on the overall growth of technological progress. On the one hand, if it has an energy saving bias, there will be significant degree of moderation. On the other hand, if technological change has an energy using bias, the economy is likely to experience a rapid increase in energy demand, requiring explicit policy initiatives.

Growth accounting tries to explain changes in real product and total factor productivity based mainly on a comparison between the growth of inputs (capital and labour) and the growth of output. One part of actual growth cannot be explained and has been classified as 'unexplained total factor productivity growth' (or the so called residual). In particular, following the decomposition analysis by Solow (1957), many alternative factors can explain the path of economic growth. According to Solow's findings, technology has been responsible for 90% of the increase in labour productivity in the twentieth century United States. The unexplained decline in productivity growth can thus be regarded as resulting from a collapse in technological activities. This may have happened because the availability of technological opportunities has been temporarily or permanently reduced.

Furthermore, technological gap theories (Abramovitz 1986; Fagerberg 1987, 1988, 1994) relate the technological level and innovation activities to the level of economic growth. According to these theories, countries where more innovation activities take place tend to have a higher level of value added per worker (or a higher per capita GDP). The size of the productivity factor differs substantially across countries with Japan and France having the highest rates for their respective time periods and the US and the UK having the lowest. Table 3.1 presents a macro and micro approach for the measurement of productivity.

Table 3.1 Macro and micro-approaches to measuring productivity

Question	Measure (Agency)	Information Needs	Methodology	Current Status	Gaps and Challenges

Micro Approach: (establishment, enterprise (firm), or enterprise segment)

Question	Measure (Agency)	Information Needs	Methodology	Current Status	Gaps and Challenges
Impact	Productivity	Output Inputs: Labour (for instance, payroll hours) Other Inputs (for instance, capital services, materials, energy) E-commerce, e-Business	Model-based estimates of labour and multi-factor productivity at the business using: Economic Annual, quarterly, and monthly	Several completed for manufacturing New studies for selected other sectors just started Subject to gaps and measurement challenges	Gaps: Limited information (for instance, detail on inputs) in sectors outside manufacturing None on use of e-business processes Challenges: Capturing changes to the structure of firms, such as vertical integration and contracting -out.

Macro Approach: (industry, sector, nation)

Question	Measure (Agency)	Information Needs	Methodology	Current Status	Gaps and Challenges
Impact	Productivity	Output Inputs: Labour (for instance, hours) Other Inputs (for instance, capital services, materials, energy) E-commerce, e-Business	Model-based estimates of labour and multi-factor productivity at the industry and national level. Economic Annual, quarterly, and monthly Other non-Census Data	Labour productivity estimated for all sectors MFP not estimated for services	Gaps: Lack of detailed information on inputs calculate MFP for industries outside manufacturing. Challenges: Measures of inputs, Outputs, prices.

Source: Atrostic, B.K., Colecchia, A. and Pattinson, B., 2000.

Table 3.2 Recent trends in productivity growth, 1980-1999

	Trend growth in GDP per hour worked				Trend growth in multi-factor productivity			
	Total economy, percentage change at annual rate				Business sector, percentage change at annual rate			
	1980-90	1990-99	1990-95	1995-99	1980-90	1990-99	1990-95	1995-99
Canada	1.1	1.3	1.3	1.4	0.5	1.2	1.1	1.3
Mexico	–	-0.6	-1.0	-0.1	–	–	–	–
United States	1.3	1.6	1.3	2.0	0.9	1.1	1.0	1.2
Australia	1.2	2.0	1.8	2.2	0.5	1.4	1.4	1.5
Japan	3.2	2.5	2.6	2.2	2.1	1.2	1.3	0.9
South Korea	6.3	5.1	5.3	4.7	–	–	–	–
New Zealand	–	0.7	0.5	0.9	0.7	0.9	1.0	0.7
Austria	–	–	–	2.9	–	–	–	–
Belgium	2.4	2.3	2.3	2.4	1.7	1.4	1.3	1.6
Czech Republic	–	–	–	1.7	–	–	–	–
Denmark	1.7	1.8	1.9	1.6	0.9	1.5	1.5	1.5
Finland	2.8	2.9	3.0	2.8	2.3	3.3	3.0	3.6
France	2.7	1.8	1.8	1.6	1.8	1.0	0.9	1.1
Germany	2.3	2.0	2.2	1.8	1.5	1.1	1.1	1.1
Greece	1.3	1.4	0.9	2.0	–	–	–	–
Hungary	–	2.7	2.7	2.7	–	–	–	–
Iceland	–	1.5	1.3	1.6	–	1.3	1.2	1.4
Ireland	3.6	4.3	4.0	4.6	3.6	4.5˙	4.4	4.6
Italy	2.6	2.0	2.3	1.6	1.5	1.1	1.2	0.8
Luxembourg	–	5.1	5.5	4.6	–	–	–	–
Netherlands	2.9	1.8	1.9	1.7	2.3	1.7	1.9	1.5
Norway	2.6	2.6	3.1	2.0	1.2	1.7	2.1	1.2
Portugal	–	2.3	2.4	2.2	–	–	–	–
Spain	3.2	1.4	2.0	0.7	2.3	0.7	0.9	0.5
Sweden	1.2	1.7	1.8	1.6	0.7	1.3	1.3	1.3
Switzerland	–	0.8	0.6	1.2	–	–	–	–
United Kingdom	2.3	1.9	1.9	1.9	2.2	0.9	0.8	1.0

Source: OECD calculations, based on data from the *OECD Economic Outlook No. 68*. See Economics Department Working Paper No. 248.

In particular, following the decomposition analysis by Solow (1957), many alternative factors can explain the path of economic growth. According to Solow's findings, technology has been responsible for 90% of the increase in labour productivity in the United States in the twentieth century. The unexplained decline in productivity growth can thus be regarded as resulting from a collapse in technological activities. This may have happened because the availability of technological opportunities has been temporarily or permanently reduced.

Following the technological-gap argument, it would be expected that the more technologically advanced countries would also be the most economically advanced (in terms of innovation activities and per capita GDP). Technology-intensive industries play an increasingly important role in the international manufacturing trade of OECD countries. In the 1990s, OECD exports of high- and medium-high-technology industries grew at an annual rate of around 7%, and their shares in manufacturing exports reached 25% and 40% respectively, in 1999. Substantial differences in the shares of high- and medium-high-technology industries in manufacturing exports are observed across the OECD area, ranging from over 75% in Japan, Ireland, and the United States, to less than 20% in Greece, New Zealand and Iceland. Between 1990 and 1999, the annual growth rate of exports in technology-intensive industries was highest in Mexico (29%), followed by Ireland (18%). A catch-up effect can also be seen in Iceland and Turkey which still have a relatively low share of high- and medium-high-technology industries in manufacturing exports; they experienced annual growth of trade in technology-intensive industries of 17% and 15%, respectively.

High-technology industries represent around 50% of manufacturing exports in Ireland and 27% in Mexico, compared with 38% in the United States, 35% in Switzerland and 32% in Japan. The relatively high export share of technology-intensive goods in Ireland and Mexico does not appear to be the result of domestic R&D efforts. It rather points to the role of foreign affiliates and technological transfers. Both countries import many intermediate goods for assembly, mainly from the United States, and then export finished goods.

Table 3.2 indicates the recent trends in productivity growth for the period 1980-1999. The level of technology in a country cannot be measured directly, but an approximation measure can be used to obtain an overall picture of the set of techniques invented or diffused by that country. We shall use real per capita GDP as an approximate productivity measure. The most representative measures for technological inputs and outputs are patent activities and research expenditures.

Catching-up theory (Abramovitz 1986; Fagerberg 1987) starts with the investigation of growth performance. The main idea is that large differences in productivity among countries tend to be due to unexpected events (for instance wars). According to these studies, the only possible way for technologically weak countries to converge or catch up with advanced countries is to copy their more productive technologies. The outcome of international innovation and diffusion process is uncertain; the process may generate a pattern where some countries follow diverging trends or one where countries converge towards a common trend.

In this literature, economic development is analysed as a disequilibrium process characterised by two conflicting forces:

- innovation, which tends to increase economic and technological differences between countries, and
- diffusion (or imitation), which tends to reduce them. Technological gap theories are an application of Schumpeter's dynamic theory.

Table 3.3 R&D intensity* and export specialisation** in high technology industries, 1999

Countries	Export specialisation	R&D intensity
Canada	13.0	1.2
United States	38.3	3.0
Japan	30.7	3.2
South Korea	34.2	1.3
Denmark	18.8	1.8
Finland	24.1	2.6
France	23.1	2.2
Germany	18.5	2.7
Ireland	46.0	1.1
Italy	10.6	0.8
Netherlands	25.1	1.6
Norway	10.7	1.2
Spain	9.3	0.6
Sweden	27.0	3.9
United Kingdom	32.4	2.1

Notes: * Manufacturing R&D expenditures/manufacturing production. ** High technology exports / manufacturing exports.
Source: OECD, STAN and ANBERD databases.

Table 3.3 illustrates R&D intensity that is Manufacturing R&D expenditures/ manufacturing production and export specialisation that is the High-technology exports/manufacturing exports in high-technology industries 1999. Whereas, Table 3.4 indicates the annual average growth rate of exports in high and medium-high technology industries for the period 1990-1999. Furthermore, Table 3.5 presents the annual average growth rate for the labour productivity growth by industry, for the period 1995-1998. Finally, Table 3.6 illustrates the Labour productivity levels relative to total non-agricultural business sector in the European Union, for the period 1998.

Table 3.4 Annual average growth rate of exports in high and medium-high technology industries, 1990-1999

	High- and medium-high technology	Total manufacturing
Mexico	29.4	26.4
Ireland	17.6	13.3
Iceland	17.2	3.7
Turkey	15.1	9.7
Greece	10.6	2.4
New Zealand	10.1	3.2
Portugal	9.8	4.7
Spain	9.5	8.2
Australia	9.1	5.4
Canada	9.1	8.0
Finland	8.6	5.0
United States	8.5	7.9
Sweden	6.9	4.7
OECD	6.5	5.4
Belgium-Luxembourg	6.2	4.4
United Kingdom	6.0	4.9
France	5.9	4.5
Netherlands	5.9	3.4
Austria	5.8	4.6
EU	5.7	4.4
Norway	5.4	2.6
Denmark	4.8	3.2
Italy	4.7	4.0
Japan	4.2	4.0
Germany	4.0	3.1
Switzerland	3.8	3.2

Source: OECD, STAN database.

One of the main measures is the *research and development intensity index* (RDI), which is defined as: (BERD/GDP)*100, where BERD is business expenditure on R&D. We can also use some other alternative measures, such as GERD/GDP, that is the ratio of gross expenditures on research and development to gross domestic product, or furthermore, GERD/GFCF, that is the ratio of gross expenditures on research and development to gross fixed capital formation.

Table 3.5 Labour productivity growth by industry, 1995-1998 annual average growth rate

	ISIC Rev. 3	United States			Japan			European Union		
		Employment	Real value added	Labour productivity	Employment	Real value added	Labour productivity	Employment	Real value added	Labour productivity
All industries	01-95	2.1	4.6	2.4	0.3	1.5	1.2	1.0	2.4	1.4
Total non-agriculture business sector	10-67,71-74	2.5	5.9	3.3	-0.3	1.4	1.7	1.2	2.6	1.4
Mining and quarrying	10-14	0.7	3.7	3.1	-3.9	-0.9	3.1	-3.5	-1.5	2.1
Food, drink, tobacco	15-16	0.2	-5.4	-5.6	-1.3	-2.1	-0.8	0.3	0.0	-0.4
Textiles, clothing	17-19	-5.3	-3.9	1.6	-4.8	-3.8	1.0	-1.7	-1.4	0.4
Paper, printing	21-22	0.0	-0.4	-0.4	-1.7	-2.1	-0.4	0.1	1.5	1.3
Petroleum refining	23	-1.4	-0.4	1.1	-0.7	3.9	4.6	-1.9	0.9	2.8
Chemicals	24	0.1	2.6	2.5	-0.5	0.7	1.1	-0.9	1.3	2.3
Rubber, plastics	25	1.3	4.6	3.2	-2.1	-3.4	-1.43	1.6	3.3	1.7
Non-metallic minerals	26	1.1	3.1	1.9	-1.9	-2.1	-0.2	-0.5	-0.1	0.4
Basic metals and metal products	27-28	1.2	2.5	1.4	-1.6	-2.7	-1.1	0.4	1.0	0.6
Machinery and equipment	29-33	1.8	14.5	12.4	-0.7	4.7	5.5	0.1	3.0	2.9

Table 3.5 continued

	ISIC Rev. 3	United States			Japan			European Union		
		Employment	Real value added	Labour productivity	Employment	Real value added	Labour productivity	Employment	Real value added	Labour productivity
Transport equipment	34-35	2.2	2.5	0.4	-0.4	-1.9	-1.5	2.0	4.3	2.3
Wood and other manufacturing	20,36-37	1.3	0.5	-0.8	-2.1	0.1	2.2	-0.1	1.0	1.1
Electricity, gas and water supply	40-41	-2.0	-1.6	0.4	0.8	4.3	3.5	-2.6	2.1	4.8
Construction	45	4.5	4.9	0.4	-0.1	-2.0	-1.9	-0.6	-0.4	0.3
Services: Wholesale and retail trade, hotels, restaurants	50-55	1.6	8.5	6.8	0.3	1.1	0.8	1.4	2.4	1.0
Transport and storage	60-63	3.2	4.5	1.3	0.4	-3.4	-3.8	0.8	3.0	2.2
Post and tele-communications	64	2.4	4.5	2.1	0.4	17.7	17.3	-1.1	7.6	8.7
Finance and Insurance	65-67	2.6	7.5	4.8	-1.4	0.6	2.0	0.5	3.1	2.6
Business services	71-74	6.3	7.0	0.6	2.2	6.4	4.1	5.8	5.6	-0.2

Source: OECD, STAN and National Accounts databases.

Table 3.6 Labour productivity levels relative to total non-agricultural business sector, in the European Union, 1998

	EU	Labour productivity annual average growth, 1995-98
Textiles, clothing	0.7	0.4
Wholesale/retail trade, hotels, restaurants	0.7	1.0
Wood and other manufacturing	0.8	1.1
Construction	0.8	0.3
Basic metals and metal products	1.0	0.6
Food, drink, tobacco	1.0	-0.4
Rubber, plastics	1.0	1.7
Business services	1.1	-0.2
Non-metallic minerals	1.1	0.4
Transport and storage	1.1	2.2
Machinery and equipment	1.1	2.9
Paper, printing	1.1	1.3
Transport equipment	1.2	2.3
Finance and Insurance	1.6	2.6
Post and telecommunications	1.7	8.7
Chemicals	1.7	2.3
Mining and quarrying	2.5	2.1
Electricity, gas and water supply	3.1	4.8
Petroleum refining	3.8	2.8

Source: OECD, STAN and National Accounts databases.

Low starting point, low rates of catch-up in the OECD area, cross-country differences in GDP per capita and labour productivity have eroded considerably since the 1950s. Over the 1950s and 1960s, income levels of OECD countries – except Australia, New Zealand and the United Kingdom – were catching up with those of the United States. In the 1970s, that phenomenon was less widespread and the rate of catch-up fell, Korea being the main exception. In the 1980s, there was even less catch-up, as GDP per capita grew more slowly in 19 OECD countries than in the United States. Table 3.7 illustrates the share in total gross value added for medium and high technology manufactures for the period of 1998.

A final group of countries started with low income levels in the 1950s and have caught up little or not at all. It includes Eastern European countries, Mexico and Turkey. Changes in levels of GDP per hour worked show a slightly different pattern. Out of 21 OECD countries for which data are available, only Mexico and Switzerland have not been catching up with US productivity levels almost continuously over the post-war period. Several European countries now stand even with the United States in terms of average labour productivity and some have even surpassed it. Labour productivity levels relative to the total non-agriculture business sector in the European Union for 1998. The ratio of value added to employment provides an indication of which industries yielded relatively high value added per unit of labour input. Although total employment is not the best measure of labour input for this purpose a reasonably clear pattern emerges.

Table 3.7 Share in total gross value added, 1998: High and medium-high technology manufactures

	High-technology manufactures	Medium-high technology manufactures	High- and medium-high technology manufactures
Iceland	–	1.6	1.6
Greece	0.6	1.2	1.8
Norway	0.9	2.6	3.5
New Zealand	–	3.7	3.7
Portugal	1.2	3.2	4.5
Australia	–	5.7	5.7
Netherlands	–	6.2	6.2
Spain	1.3	5.1	6.4
Denmark	2.0	4.4	6.5
Italy	1.6	5.6	7.2
Canada	2.0	5.3	7.3
Austria	2.1	5.2	7.3
France	2.5	4.9	7.4
Slovak Republic	–	7.9	7.9
United Kingdom	3.0	5.1	8.1
Mexico	2.4	5.9	8.3
Belgium	–	8.3	8.3
EU	2.2	6.2	8.4
United States	3.7	4.8	8.5
OECD	3.1	5.7	8.8
Czech Republic	1.4	8.3	9.8
Finland	4.5	5.5	10.0
Sweden	3.5	6.5	10.0
Hungary	3.5	6.8	10.3
Japan	3.6	7.1	10.7
Switzerland	–	11.5	11.5
Germany	2.1	9.6	11.7
South Korea	5.6	7.0	12.6
Ireland	7.6	8.8	16.3

Source: OECD, STAN and National Accounts databases.

The same was true for 20 OECD countries in the 1990s. Japan and Korea had the highest rates of catch-up over the 1950-99 period, with GDP per capita growing by 2.7% and 3.2%, respectively; that is growing more rapidly than in the United States. Most of Western Europe had much lower rates of catch-up, typically below 1% a year. Countries such as Australia, New Zealand, the United Kingdom and Canada were already at relatively high income levels in 1950 and have done little catching up with the United States ever since. Switzerland had a marked decline in relative income levels. Table 3.8 showing the trends of growth in GDP per hour worked for the total economy and for the percentage change at annual rate.

Table 3.8 Trend growth in GDP per hour worked: Total economy, percentage change at annual rate

	1990-1995	1995-1999
South Korea	5.3	4.7
Ireland	4.0	4.6
Luxembourg	5.5	4.6
Austria	–	2.9
Finland	3.0	2.8
Hungary	2.7	2.7
Belgium	2.3	2.4
Japan	2.6	2.2
Australia	1.8	2.2
Portugal	2.4	2.2
Norway	3.1	2.0
United States	1.3	2.0
Greece	0.9	2.0
United Kingdom	1.9	1.9
Germany	2.2	1.8
Netherlands	1.9	1.7
Czech Republic	–	1.7
France	1.8	1.6
Denmark	1.9	1.6
Sweden	1.8	1.6
Italy	2.3	1.6
Iceland	1.3	1.6
Canada	1.3	1.4
Switzerland	0.6	1.2
New Zealand	0.5	0.9
Spain	2.0	0.7
Mexico	-1.0	-0.1

Source: OECD calculations, based on data from the OECD Economic Outlook No. 68. See S. Scarpetta et al., Economics Department Working Paper No. 248, 2000.

By the end of the 1990s, industries predominantly involved in extracting, processing and supplying fuel and energy goods produced the highest value added per labour unit. These industries were more than twice as productive as the average industry. They account for about 5% of total OECD value added and are typically highly capital-intensive. Besides the energy-producing industries, those that yield the most value added per labour unit are those considered technology and/or knowledge intensive. In manufacturing, the chemical industry has the highest relative labour productivity level, while in services, finance, insurance and telecommunications lead the way.

Construction, wholesale and retail trade, hotels and restaurants and textiles show relatively low levels of labour productivity in all three major OECD regions. These industries are typically highly labour-intensive, have a high proportion of low-skilled jobs and are not considered high-technology sectors. OECD economies are also characterised by considerable differences in labour productivity growth. In the second half of the 1990s, labour productivity growth in the three major OECD regions was typically highest in manufacturing of machinery and equipment, in telecommunications and in finances and insurance. Labour productivity growth in some sectors of the economy has been negative over the most recent period. This may reflect cyclical or structural patterns, but may also be due to measurement difficulties.

Labour productivity by industry can be measured in several ways. For the measurement of output; total production or value added are the typical yardsticks. If production (gross output) is used; productivity measures need to cover a combination of inputs, including intermediate inputs (such as materials and energy), labour and capital. If value added is used as the output measure; labour and capital suffice as indicators of factor inputs. The indicators shown here are determined by data availability and simply measure value added per person employed. Further adjustments to labour input, including adjustment for part-time work and hours worked per worker, can be made for certain OECD countries but international comparisons are not yet feasible. For the labour productivity levels, 1998 value added at current prices was used. For the European Union, member countries' value added data were aggregated after US dollar has been applied to GDP PPPs in 1988 – industry-specific PPPs are preferable, but are not available for all sectors and countries.

For value-added volumes (used to estimate labour productivity growth), the European Union series were derived from aggregating member countries' value-added volumes after 1995 US dollar has been applied to GDP PPPs in 1995, the reference year for the volume series being 1995. This is not an ideal practice since some countries, such as France and Sweden are now using annually reweighted chained (rather than fixed-weight) Laspeyres aggregation methods to derive their value-added volumes by industry. Volumes calculated in this manner are generally non-additive.

Table 3.9 Income and productivity levels, 2005 percentage point differences with respect to the United States: Percentage gap in GDP per capita

	Percentage gap with respect to US GDP per capita	Effect of labour utilisation*	Percentage gap with respect to US GDP per hour worked
Turkey	-81	-9	-72
Mexico	-74	-4	-71
Poland	-69	-5	-64
Slovak Republic	-63	-11	-53
Hungary	-59	-5	-54
Portugal	-52	-2	-50
Czech Republic	-52	3	-55
South Korea	-48	12	-59
Greece	-44	-8	-36
New Zealand	-39	3	-42
Spain	-35	-11	-24
EU-19	-33	-13	-21
Italy	-32	-11	-21
OECD	-30	-6	-25
Germany	-29	-20	-9
Euro-zone	-29	-15	-13
France	-28	-29	1
Japan	-27	2	-29
Finland	-25	-8	-17
United Kingdom	-23	-6	-17
Belgium	-22	-32	9
Sweden	-22	-11	-11
Austria	-20	-3	-17
Australia	-19	-2	-17
Canada	-19	2	-20

Notes: * This reflects the joint effect of differences in the demographic structure of countries (the ratio of the working-age population to the total population), in employment rates and in average hours worked per person.

Source: OECD, Productivity database, September 2006; Annual National Accounts and Labour Force Statistics databases, September 2006 <www.oecd.org/statistics/productivity>.

Labour productivity levels by industry are relative to the total non-agriculture business sector. This consists of all industries except agriculture, hunting, forestry and fishing (ISIC 01-05), real estate activities (ISIC 70) and community, social and personal services (ISIC 75-99); includes mainly non-market activities such as public administration, education and health). Table 3.9 illustrates the income and the productivity levels for the period of 2005. The percentage point of differences for PPP (Purchase Power Parity) is based on GDP per capita respecting the United States.

Table 3.10 Estimates of multi-factor productivity (MFP) growth rates, 1980-1998: Average annual growth rates (based on trend series time-varying factor shares)

Countries	MFP growth rate without control for composition / quality changes in labour and capital		MFP growth rate with control for composition / quality changes in labour and capital	
	1980-1990	1990-1998	1980-1990	1990-1998
Australia	0.9	0.9	2.1	2.0
Belgium	1.4	–	1.0	–
Denmark	1.0	0.9	1.8	1.9
Finland	2.4	2.2	3.2	2.8
Greece	0.6	–	0.3	–
Ireland	3.9	3.8	3.9	3.6
Netherlands	2.2	2.2	1.7	1.7
New Zealand	0.7	0.6	1.1	1.2
Norway	1.1	0.9	2.1	1.9
Portugal	1.9	1.9	2.2	–
Spain	2.2	–	0.6	–
Sweden	0.8	0.6	1.3	1.0
Switzerland	–	–	0.2	0.2

Source: OECD, Economic Outlook, 2000, Paris.

Productivity ratios relate a measure of output to one or several inputs to production. The most common productivity measure is labour productivity, which links output to labour input. It is a key economic indicator as it is closely associated with standards of living. Ideally, estimates of labour productivity growth should incorporate changes in hours worked. Figure 3.1 presents GDP per capita and GDP per hour worked for European member states.

Estimates of the increase in GDP per hour worked for OECD countries–adjusted for the business cycle – show that Korea, Ireland and Luxembourg had the highest rates of productivity growth in the 1990s. Switzerland, New Zealand, Spain and Mexico had the lowest. In countries such as Ireland, Australia, the United States, Greece and Germany, labour productivity growth in the second half of the 1990s was substantially higher than in the first half. Table 3.10 indicates the trends in multi-factor productivity growth for the period 1990-1995 and 1995-1999. Labour productivity is a partial measure of productivity; it relates output to only one input in the production process, albeit an important one. More complete measures of productivity at the economy-wide level relate output growth to the combined use of labour and capital inputs.

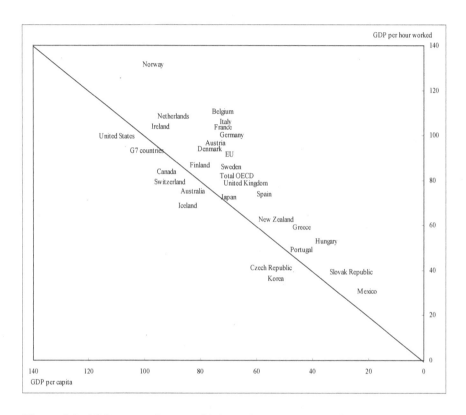

Figure 3.1 GDP per capita and GDP per hour worked (USA = 100), 2002
Source: Based on OECD data.

This measure is called multi-factor productivity (MFP). Growth in MFP is key to long-term economic growth, as it indicates rising efficiency in the use of all available resources. It is also a better reflection of technological progress than the increase in labour productivity, since the latter can also be achieved through greater use of capital in the production process and the dismissal of low-productivity workers. Table 3.11 illustrates the multi-factor productivity (MFP) in annual growth rates in percentage.

Estimates of MFP growth are available for fewer countries than estimates of labour productivity growth, primarily because of the limited availability of data on capital stock.

The estimates show that Ireland and Finland experienced the most rapid MFP growth over the 1990s. In countries such as Ireland, Finland, Belgium, Australia, Canada, the United States, France and the United Kingdom, MFP growth accelerated during the 1990s. In other countries, such as the Netherlands, Norway, Spain and Japan, MFP growth declined.

Table 3.11 Multi-factor productivity, annual growth in percentage

	1995	1996	1997	1998	1999	2000	2001	2002	2003	2004	2005
Australia	1.3	3.6	2.3	2.7	1	-0.5	2.3	0.7	2	-0.4	–
Austria	–	0.9	0.4	2	2.5	2	-0.4	0.2	-	–	–
Belgium	0.8	0.4	1.3	0.4	1.8	1.4	-0.9	1.1	0.9	–	–
Canada	0.9	-0.3	3	1.1	1.8	2.1	-	0.9	-0.2	0.1	1.3
Denmark	1	1.3	0.2	-1.1	-0.1	1.1	-1.5	-0.4	0.7	–	–
Finland	2.3	2.7	3.2	3.5	1.5	3.7	2	1	2	–	–
France	2	-0.1	1.5	1.9	1	2.8	0.2	1.9	0.8	0.4	0.8
Germany	1.7	1.3	1.7	0.7	0.8	1.9	0.9	0.6	0.5	0.6	0.9
Greece	1.1	2.7	4.3	-0.7	0.5	2.7	3.7	2.4	2.2	–	–
Ireland	4.6	4.1	7.6	3.4	4.7	3.7	2.9	4	2.7	–	–
Italy	2.5	-0.7	1.4	-0.8	0.3	1.9	-0.6	-1	-0.9	–	–
Japan	1.4	0.8	1	-0.9	1.2	2.1	0.7	1.3	1.5	2.3	–
Netherl.	1.7	-1.5	1.4	1.6	2.8	0.2	-0.4	0.9	-0.6	–	–
Portugal	–	3.5	3.3	1.4	0.5	3	-0.7	-0.5	-0.1	–	–
Spain	0.3	0.2	-0.1	-0.5	-0.4	-0.4	-0.1	-0.2	0.1	0.1	–
Sweden	1.5	0.7	2.3	1.4	1.2	2.3	-0.1	2.6	2.6	–	–
UK	0.9	1.1	0.9	1.4	1.4	2.6	0.6	1.4	1.9	–	–
USA	-0.3	1.7	1	1.1	1.5	1.3	0.8	2.1	2.3	2.4	1.5

Source: OECD, STAN database.

Table 3.12 Contributions to growth of GDP, 1990-95 and 1995-2001, as percentage points

	Labour input	ICT capital	Non-ICT capital	Multi-factor productivity
Canada				
1990-1995	0.2	0.3	0.7	0.5
1995-2001	1.5	0.7	0.6	0.6
France				
1990-1995	-0.5	0.1	0.7	0.8
1995-2001	0.4	0.3	0.5	1.3
Germany				
1990-1995	-0.8	0.3	0.5	1.3
1995-2001	-0.1	0.4	0.5	0.7
Italy				
1990-1995	-0.8	0.1	0.5	1.4
1995-2001	0.6	0.4	0.6	0.4
Japan				
1990-1995	-0.6	0.3	0.8	0.9
1995-2001	-0.5	0.6	0.5	0.9
United Kingdom				
1990-1995	-1.0	0.3	0.4	2.1
1995-2001	0.8	0.6	0.6	0.8
United States				
1990-1995	0.9	0.5	0.3	0.7
1995-2001	1.0	0.8	0.5	1.1
Australia				
1990-1995	0.8	0.4	0.3	1.7
1995-2001	1.0	0.6	0.2	2.0
Denmark				
1990-1995	0.0	0.3	0.5	1.2
1995-2001	0.8	0.6	0.8	0.5
Finland				
1990-1995	-2.7	0.1	0.1	1.7
1995-2001	1.1	0.3	0.3	2.9
Greece				
1990-1995	0.5	0.3	0.4	0.1
1995-2001	0.5	0.5	0.5	1.9
Ireland				
1990-1995	0.9	0.2	0.2	3.3
1995-2001	3.0	0.6	0.9	4.8

Table 3.12 continued

	Labour input	ICT capital	Non-ICT capital	Multi-factor productivity
Netherlands				
1990-1995	0.0	0.3	0.6	1.2
1995-2001	1.9	0.7	0.6	0.5
Portugal				
1990-1995				
1995-2001	0.6	0.3	0.8	2.0
Spain				
1990-1995	-0.3	0.2	0.8	0.8
1995-2001	2.1	0.5	0.8	0.2
Sweden				
1990-1995	-0.9	0.3	0.5	0.8
1995-2001	0.6	0.6	0.6	1.4

Source: OECD, STAN database.

Table 3.13 Contribution to labour productivity growth by industry, average annual growth rate over 1995-2001

	Business sector services	Manufacturing	Other industries	Total
Spain	0.2	0.1	0.1	0.4
Italy	0.2	0.2	0.3	0.8
Hungary	0.3	1.7	1.2	3.2
New Zealand	0.3	0.6	-0.2	0.8
France	0.4	0.6	0.1	1.1
Japan	0.5	0.8	0.2	1.5
Belgium	0.7	0.8	-0.1	1.4
Denmark	0.9	0.4	0.1	1.4
Netherlands	0.9	0.4	-0.3	1.0
Austria	0.9	0.9	0.3	2.1
Germany	0.9	0.4	0.1	1.5
Sweden	1.0	1.1	0.2	2.3
Canada	1.1	0.5	0.2	1.7
South Korea	1.2	2.8	0.2	4.2
Finland	1.2	1.5	0.2	3.0
Portugal	1.3	0.8	0.1	2.2
United Kingdom	1.3	0.3	-0.1	1.6
Australia	1.4	0.2	0.4	2.0

Table 3.13 continued

	Business sector services	Manufacturing	Other industries	Total
Poland	1.4	2.2	0.6	4.3
Norway	1.6	0.0	1.0	2.5
Greece	1.8	0.3	0.6	2.7
Mexico	1.8	0.6	-0.3	2.1
United States	2.0	0.7	-0.7	2.0

Source: OECD, STAN database.

Table 3.14 Real value added in knowledge-based industries (1995 = 100, base year index)

	1992	1993	1994	1995	1996	1997	1998	1999	2000	2001
Real value added high and medium-high technology manufactures										
United States	79.2	83.1	91.4	100.0	105.9	116.6	127.6	136.5	151.0	145.7
Japan	97.6	93.4	92.2	100.0	107.1	113.4	108.3	116.7	128.7	122.4
Germany	109.7	96.0	99.1	100.0	98.1	102.0	105.7	102.9	108.2	–
France	87.1	83.2	90.9	100.0	101.6	111.2	119.6	128.6	136.8	–
Italy	93.1	86.8	92.6	100.0	99.4	104.3	105.6	108.1	111.9	109.7
United Kingdom	89.4	90.8	96.8	100.0	103.0	104.9	108.7	112.3	118.1	115.1
Knowledge-based market services										
United States	89.3	93.2	95.7	100.0	104.7	113.2	121.8	129.4	138.8	144.1
Japan	87.3	90.5	94.9	100.0	106.1	112.4	118.2	120.2	125.1	132.9
Germany	90.9	95.3	96.1	100.0	104.6	110.4	117.3	129.5	139.5	–
France	100.8	100.7	100.0	100.0	103.4	104.4	107.7	114.1	121.4	124.0
Italy	91.8	96.7	97.4	100.0	104.7	110.0	114.2	120.4	131.5	136.1
United Kingdom	84.0	86.8	93.2	100.0	107.4	118.0	128.3	135.4	145.7	155.9

Source: OECD, STAN database.

Table 3.15 Share of value added in total gross value added. current prices. as a percentage for technology-based industries

	High technology manufactures (2423. 30. 32. 33. 353)	Medium-high technology manufactures (24less2423. 29. 31. 34. 352. 359)	Post and telecommunications services (64)	Finance and insurance services (65-67)	Business activities (excluding real estate activities) (71-74)	Total with 'market' services	Education and health (80. 85)	Total
Canada	2.1	5.8	2.8	6.9	6.9	24.4	11.1	35.5
Mexico	2.4	5.6	1.7	2.3	6.5	18.4	8.9	27.3
United States	3.7	4.2	3.5	8.8	10.3	30.4	11.5	41.9
Australia	3.3	↑	3.1	7.1	11.5	25.0	10.9	35.9
Japan	3.9	6.0	1.6	6.4	7.8	25.7	–	–
Korea	7.0	7.0	2.1	6.6	4.0	26.8	7.6	34.4
Austria	2.1	5.4	2.0	6.8	7.9	24.2	9.8	34.0
Belgium	2.2	5.9	1.6	5.9	–	–	12.9	–
Czech Republic	1.7	8.3	4.3	4.5	6.9	25.7	7.1	32.8
Denmark	2.3	3.9	2.4	5.0	8.1	21.7	15.2	36.9
Finland	6.1	5.0	3.2	3.8	6.1	24.3	12.2	36.5
France	2.4	5.1	2.2	5.0	13.4	28.0	11.4	39.4
Germany	2.4	9.3	2.3	4.5	13.2	31.7	10.2	41.9
Greece	0.5	↑ 1.2	3.3	5.0	7.0	17.1	10.1	27.2

Table 3.15 continued

	High technology manufactures 2423, 30, 32, 33, 353	Medium-high technology manufactures 24less2423, 29, 31, 34, 352, 359	Post and telecommunications services 64	Finance and insurance services 65-67	Business activities (excluding real estate activities) 71-74	Total with 'market' services	Education and health 80, 85	Total
Hungary	11.8	↑	3.8	3.9	8.6	28.1	9.2	37.3
Iceland	2.3		–	6.5	–	–	13.3	–
Ireland	8.6	10.4	–	4.5	–	–	8.3	–
Italy	1.9	5.6	2.3	6.2	9.1	25.0	9.7	34.7
Luxembourg	2.1	↑	–	25.6	8.6	36.3	7.2	43.5
Netherlands	6.0	↑	2.4	6.4	12.0	26.8	11.5	38.3
Norway	1.0	2.4	2.2	3.9	9.4	19.0	13.6	32.6
Poland	6.4	↑	2.1	2.2	–	–	8.4	–
Portugal	1.1	2.8	2.9	6.4	–	–	12.7	–
Slovak Republic	7.7	↑	2.7	3.6	6.0	20.0	7.4	27.5
Spain	1.2	4.8	2.6	5.2	5.9	19.8	10.2	29.9
Sweden	3.7	7.1	2.8	3.8	10.0	27.4	14.8	42.2

Table 3.15 continued

	High technology manufactures 2423, 30, 32, 33, 353	Medium-high technology manufactures 24less2423, 29, 31, 34, 352, 359	Post and telecommunications services 64	Finance and insurance services 65-67	Business activities (excluding real estate activities) 71-74	Total with 'market' services	Education and health 80, 85	Total
Switzerland	9.3	↑	3.0	16.1	8.5	37.0	5.8	42.8
United Kingdom	3.0	4.3	2.9	5.2	12.7	28.2	12.1	40.2
European Union	2.3	6.0	2.4	5.3	11.0	27.0	11.0	38.0
Total OECD	3.2	5.2	2.7	6.7	9.6	27.4	–	–

Source: OECD, STAN database.

Table 3.16 Share of value added in total gross value added. current prices as percentages for aggregate sectors

	Agriculture, hunting, forestry and fishing	Mining and quarrying	Total manufacturing	Electricity gas and water	Construction	Wholesale and retail trade; hotels and restaurants	Transport, storage and communication	Finance, insurance, real estate and business services	Community, social and personal services
	01-05	10-14	15-37	40-41	45	50-55	60-64	65-74	75-99
Canada	2.5	3.8	19.7	2.9	5.2	13.8	7.0	25.4	19.8
Mexico	4.0	1.4	20.1	1.1	5.0	21.2	11.0	18.3	17.8
United States	1.6	1.3	15.8	1.9	4.9	16.0	6.7	29.4	22.5
Australia	3.5	4.6	12.4	2.5	6.7	13.8	8.5	28.7	19.4
Japan	1.4	0.1	19.5	3.5	7.3	12.8	6.0	26.9	22.5
South Korea	5.1	0.4	29.8	2.8	8.1	12.3	7.0	18.3	16.2
New Zealand	6.7	1.2	16.2	2.7	4.3	15.4	7.7	28.0	17.8
Austria	2.2	0.4	20.7	2.3	7.8	16.9	6.9	22.9	20.0
Belgium	1.4	0.2	19.0	2.6	5.0	13.1	6.8	28.1	23.8
Czech Republic	4.3	1.4	26.9	3.9	7.1	16.5	8.1	16.6	15.1
Denmark	2.7	2.9	15.9	1.9	5.2	13.8	8.1	23.8	25.6
Finland	3.6	0.2	25.8	1.7	5.6	11.0	10.3	21.2	20.6
France	2.8	0.2	17.8	2.0	4.6	13.0	6.2	30.3	23.1
Germany	1.2	0.3	22.2	1.8	5.1	12.6	5.9	29.7	21.3
Greece	7.3	0.6	11.3	1.9	7.2	21.4	7.9	22.5	19.9

Table 3.16 continued

	Agriculture, hunting, forestry and fishing	Mining and quarrying	Total manufacturing	Electricity gas and water	Construction	Wholesale and retail trade; hotels and restaurants	Transport, storage and communication	Finance, insurance, real estate and business services	Community, social and personal services
Hungary	4.2	0.3	24.8	3.6	4.6	12.7	9.6	20.8	19.3
Iceland	9.5	0.1	13.2	3.4	8.2	14.7	7.7	19.9	23.4
Ireland	3.8	0.7	33.3	1.2	7.3	12.6	5.1	20.5	15.5
Italy	2.8	0.5	20.6	2.1	4.8	16.7	7.2	26.1	19.1
Luxembourg	0.7	0.1	10.8	1.1	5.7	11.9	10.3	43.8	15.5
Netherlands	2.7	2.6	16.3	1.5	5.7	15.2	7.1	26.4	22.5
Norway	2.0	24.8	10.2	2.2	4.2	10.8	8.1	17.6	20.0
Poland	3.8	2.8	20.6	3.3	8.3	22.1	6.8	14.8	17.5
Portugal	3.9	0.4	19.1	3.0	7.8	18.0	6.8	15.1	25.8
Slovak Republic	4.7	0.9	22.8	4.0	5.4	16.7	10.9	19.9	14.9
Spain	3.5	0.4	18.1	2.2	8.4	19.4	8.1	19.3	20.6
Sweden	1.9	0.2	22.2	2.4	4.0	12.1	8.3	24.6	24.3
Switzerland	1.2	0.2	17.8	2.4	5.2	15.2	5.9	31.5	20.7
Turkey	14.2	1.2	19.3	3.0	5.2	20.1	14.3	12.1	10.6
United Kingdom	1.0	2.9	17.5	1.8	5.0	14.9	7.9	27.4	21.6
European Union	2.2	0.9	19.5	2.0	5.4	14.8	7.0	26.8	21.4
Total OECD	2.3	1.2	18.3	2.3	5.6	15.3	7.0	26.7	21.3

Source: OECD, STAN database.

We can also provide some data for the productivity growth, labour productivity and the knowledge economy. In particular, Tables 3.15-3.16 illustrates the main sources and contributions to growth of GDP as percentage points for period 1990-2001, the contribution to average annual growth rate of labour productivity by industry, the real value added in knowledge-based industries, the share of value added in total gross value added for technology-based industries and the share of value added in total gross value added as a percentage for aggregate sectors correspondingly.

4. Policy Implications and Summary

Technological progress has become virtually synonymous with long-term economic growth. This raises a basic question about the capacity of both industrial and newly industrialised countries to translate their seemingly greater technological capacity into productivity and economic growth. Usually, there are difficulties in estimating the relation between technology change and productivity. Technological change may have accelerated, but in some cases there is a failure to capture the effects of recent technological advances in productivity growth or a failure to account for quality changes in previously introduced technologies. The countries of Europe have a long cultural and scientific tradition and major scientific discoveries and developments in technology are products of European civilisation. There is a close relationship between innovation and productivity levels. However there are large technological disparities between the European member states affecting productivity performance, increases economic disparities and hinders economic integration.

There are various explanations in literature for the slow-down in productivity growth in the OECD countries. One source of the slow-down may be substantial changes in the industrial composition of output, employment, capital accumulation and resource utilisation. Another may be that technological opportunities have declined; or else new technologies have been developed but their application to production has been less successful. Technological factors act in a long-term way and should not be expected to explain medium-term variations in the growth of GDP and productivity.

Technological gap models represent two conflicting forces: innovation, which tends to increase productivity differences between countries; and diffusion, which tends to reduce them. In Schumpeterian theory, growth differences are seen as the combined result of these forces. We have applied an economic growth model based on Schumpeterian logic. This technological gap model provides a good explanation of the differences among various countries.

The empirical estimates suggest that the convergence hypothesis is applicable to industrialised countries. Research on why growth rates differ has a long history that goes well beyond growth accounting exercises. The idea that poorer countries eventually catch up with richer ones was advanced as early as in the nineteenth century to explain continental Europe's convergence with Britain. In the 1960s, one of the most basic model, was the Marx–Lewis model of abundant labour supplies, which explained the divergent growth experience of the Western European countries.

To achieve safe results it is necessary to conduct a cross-country, multisectoral analysis of how technological activities affect different sectors. According to our estimates, there is a relationship between the level of economic growth and the growth of technological activities. Technological activities (best measured by patents) appear to contribute considerably to economic growth, unless it is a negative demand effect. More specifically, our results confirm that there is a close relationship between the level of economic growth (as measured by per capita GDP) and the level of technological development (as measured by the number of external patents). Our results indicate that both imitation and innovation activities have a significant effect on the growth of GDP and productivity. Countries that are technologically backward might be able to generate more rapid growth than even the advanced countries if they were given the opportunity to exploit the technologies employed by technological leaders.

The pace of the catching up depends on diffusion of knowledge, the rate of structural change, accumulation of capital and the expansion of demand. Those member states whose growth rates are lagging behind could catch up if they reduce the technological gap. An important aspect of this is that they should not rely only on technology imports and investment, but should also increase their innovation activities and improve their locally produced technologies (as happened in Korea and Singapore). However, our results confirm that some of the small and medium-sized EU member states have attained high levels of per capita GDP without a large innovation capacity. To explain the differences in growth between these countries in the postwar period a much more detailed analysis of economic, social and institutional structures should be conducted. When we compare the technologically advanced and less advanced member states, it is not difficult to see that the less advanced countries lack experience of large-scale production, technical education and resources.

The catching-up hypothesis is related to economic and technological relations among countries. There are different opportunities for countries to pursue a development strategy that depends on resource and scale factors. In summary, we can say that the introduction of new technologies has influenced industrialisation and economic growth. Of course, for countries with poor technological apparatus the impact of new technologies is much smaller. Finally, it seems that the technological gap between the less and more advanced countries is still widening.

Chapter 4

Foreign Direct Investment (FDIs), National System of Innovations and Diffusion of Knowledge

1. Introduction

Foreign Direct Investment (FDI) inflows and outflows to and from OECD countries have showed continuing rapid growth. Inward investment into OECD countries has grown by 35% and reached US dollars (USD) 684 billion, while outflows have showed an increase of 22% and amounted to USD 768 billion. Some OECD countries have experienced an unprecedented level of inflows (for instance, Japan, Sweden and Germany) and others have recorded historically high outflows (for instance, Denmark, France and Ireland). The increase in investment flows was significant in 1990s, but it was by far exceeded by the growth in mergers and acquisitions (M&A). As in previous years, M&A was the primary vehicle behind the increase in FDI. Last year, Western Europe was the world's leading region for cross-border M&A. The 1990s brought considerable improvements in the investment climate, influenced in part by the recognition of the benefits of FDI.

The change in attitudes, in turn, has led to a removal of direct obstacles to FDI and to an increase in the use of FDI incentives. Continued removal of domestic impediments through deregulation and privatisation has been also widespread. Deregulation and enhanced competition policy made M&A more viable in the telecommunications, electricity, other public utilities and financial services sectors, while privatisation programmes provided opportunities for international investment. The sale of state-owned companies to foreign investors represented a large share of the source of FDI, particularly among new members to the OECD and in some emerging economies.

Entrepreneurship and relevant policies have also got an important local dimension. Indeed, facilitating increasing rates of enterprise creation is an almost universal concern for local authorities who seek to accelerate development or reverse decline in localities, whether disadvantaged or prosperous. Programmes aimed at reducing social distress and unemployment, including chronic unemployment, have been implemented in many countries. New enterprises can procure a range of benefits that contribute to local development, including: increases in employment and incomes; enhanced provision of services for consumers and businesses; and possibly, demonstration and motivational effects. Determinants of rates of enterprise creation at the local level include a statistical analysis based on demographics, unemployment, wealth, the educational and occupational profile of the workforce, the prevalence of other small firms and infrastructure endowment. New firms in particular must often have an innovative edge on their competition in order to survive; this is most directly applicable in younger and high-technology industries where competitive pressure and rates of firm churning are high.

International investment and market access are primary vehicles for the cross-border transmission of innovation which assures growth and wealth creation in participating countries. This participation is based on long term economic processes – such as new market development, job creation, and enterprise – as well as structural changes and adjustment costs. International investment liberalisation within the context of open market frameworks is essential to the diffusion of benefits created by globalisation.

Technological creativity and advancement are key components of not only innovation and growth but also of their sustainability in the long term. Most economy consists of users of a given technology and is concerned chiefly with the breadth of the application of technology outside the sector that invented it. Therefore, R&D is an incomplete indicator for innovative capacity. Liberalisation and macroeconomic adjustment are increasingly motivated by the movement toward globalisation rather than the balance of payments crises of the 1980s, at least in middle-income developing countries and are central for the transmission of the effects of globalisation to the household level.

According to international figures, we may conclude the following points:

- World exports of goods and services increased from 12.1% of output in 1985 to 16.7% in 1994.
- FDI grew much faster, from US$ 50 billion per annum in the first half of the 1980s to US$ 318 billion in 1995.
- FDI in services provides a mechanism (in some sense) for international trade in services that have traditionally been regarded as non-tradable. By the mid-1990s, service sectors accounted for well over half the total stock of FDI (UNCTAD 1997, p. 71).
- Cross-border transactions in financial assets in the United States and Germany increased from less than 10% of GDP in 1980 to 80%, 135% and 170% respectively in 1993.

Foreign direct investment contributed substantially to the transfer of new technologies and consequently to the modernisation and reorientation of the structure of the economies. The main bulk of technology transfer took place either through foreign direct investments (FDIs) (mainly through multinationals MNEs) or through *technological agreements* (for instance, licensing and joint ventures). *Mergers and acquisitions* have played a major role in this direction. Acquisitions have been used by foreign and domestic firms as a tool for strengthening their position in domestic or international markets.

The improvement of technological infrastructure and human resources may improve the quality of life, and have more impact on production and development of a nation. R&D and technical change are directly related to industrial infrastructure, productivity effects and regional development. The term "technological policy" indicates the national technological capabilities and the structure as well as planning of research and development. This chapter attempts to examine the role of "technological policy" and its effects on sustainable development; in particular, the implications on growth and social change. The growing importance of technological change in world production and employment is one of the characteristics of the last four decades. Technological change is not only a determinant of growth but also affects the international competition and the modernisation of a country.

It is difficult to record and analyse the results from a research and technological policy. It is well known that the adoption and diffusion of new technologies affect the structure and the competitiveness level of economy as well as. The choice of technology depends upon a large number of factors. It depends upon the availability of technologies, the availability of information to the decision makers, the availability of resources, the availability of technology itself and its capacity for successful adoption to suit the particular needs and objectives.

The advanced countries, which are among the leaders in technological change and which rely on well-functioning large economies, have tended to put more emphasis on policies aiming to encourage the development of research and technological activities. Technological policy only recently has been distinguished from the science policy. Whereas the "science policy" is concerned with education and the stock of knowledge, "technology policy" is concerned with the adoption and use of techniques, innovation, and diffusion of techniques. The borderline between the areas and variables of science policy and technology policy is blurred. Education and stock of knowledge, for instance, play an important role in influencing the rate of innovation and diffusion of technology. Usually, technological policy should aim to create a favourable "psychological climate" for the development of research and innovations.

New technologies imply some micro effects (that is on firms, and organisations) and some macro effects (that is on industrial sectors) for the whole economy. In addition, new technologies play an important role to productivity and to competitiveness of a country. For instance, the faster the technological progress is, the faster should the factor productivity should rise and the less "cost-push" exert upward pressure on the price level. The principal effects for technological policy can be distinguished in demand and supply sides.

The economic performance of the bulk of manufacturing industries and services that lie outside new technology sectors depends to a large extent on adopting ideas and products developed elsewhere. Since society benefits from research and technology efforts of firms, public policies should provide an environment which stimulates innovation while allowing maximum use of their products. A stable macro-economic environment that encourages investment in creating and adopting new technologies is an important prerequisite. More important, however, are micro-economic policies that induce firms to share information, develop absorptive capacity and increase rates of adoption of new technologies, either directly through subsidies, and financial schemes or indirectly through alteration of the institutional and regulatory environment.

The emergence of knowledge-economy means that there is great focus upon and recognition of the notion that people and their skills are the key to international competitiveness and sustainable growth. At the same time, it implies an increasing pace of change, for which new competencies must be acquired. One important aspect concerns the distributional aspects of innovation and technical change in some specific characteristics of information and communication technologies which "exclude" all those who are disconnected with information infrastructure.

What do we mean and what is the relationship of knowledge-based economy and innovation policy? Both approaches might usefully be related to visions of future innovation policy. This approach requires a vision of future innovation policy to be derived from various lines of analysis and commentary, including such sources as: innovation studies (providing new theories about economics and management of innovation and information about our understanding of innovation performance and impacts), analysis of socio-economic change more generally (providing improved conceptualisation and data about the role of innovation in knowledge based economies), and policy analyses (evaluation studies, and the benchmarking of policy trends across member states. Such a vision of change in the innovation process and trends in innovation policy should generate opportunities for links between innovation and other policy areas.

Those countries that innovate more slowly will find hard to compete in the world market where there are many successful innovators. On the contrary, those countries which innovate fast may also enjoy additional gains in productivity, growth, exports, even from licensing and patent fees. Government policies in new technologies and innovations aims exactly to this point: to reinforce technological capabilities in order to enhance productivity, competitiveness and economic growth of their countries. Government support is usually taken under the form of "direct" and "indirect" measures that is, different grant, loans, tax concessions, and equity capital. This chapter attempts to examine the structure and role of technological policy and their implications on sustainable development and social change. This chapter also deals with the FDIs trends with research activities. In the following sections, FDI trends and research activities are analysed and used to illustrate the role of regional growth.

2. Defining and Measuring Foreign Direct Investments (FDIs)

Efforts in the areas of FDIs and research activities have been associated in the economic literature with higher growth rates, increases in exports and trade, gains in productivity, growth in income and output, bigger business profits and lower inflation, international competitiveness. This section will present and analyse the terminology, classification and the main concepts of Foreign Direct Investment, Research Activities and Innovation.

There are many aspects of technology transfer to be studied, such as through the direct investment, multinational corporations, joint-ventures and the licensing agreements. This section investigates the transfer of technological inputs in Greece (through FDIs, MNEs and licensing agreements). Technology transfer has been variously defined. According to the definition provided by UNCTAD, it can be considered as: "Technology as the essential input to production which can embodied either in capital and in intermediate goods or in the human labour and in manpower or finally in information which is provided through markets" (United Nations).

We can also distinguish among *technology transfer*, *technology capacity* (that is, the flow of *knowledge* and the *stock of knowledge*, respectively), and *technology of innovation* (which indicates the type of technology that gives the capacity to the recipients country's to establish a new infrastructure or to upgrade obsolete technologies). Direct investment is a category in which an international investment made by a resident entity in one economy (direct investor) with the objective of establishing a lasting interest in an enterprise (or, otherwise, the direct investment enterprise) resident in another economy is classified. *Direct investment* involves both the initial transaction between the entities and all subsequent capital transactions between them and among affiliated enterprises, both incorporated and unincorporated.

OECD recommends that direct investment flows be defined as: "A foreign direct investor may be an individual, an incorporated or unincorporated public or private enterprise, a government, a group of related individuals, or a group of related incorporated and/or unincorporated enterprises which has a direct investment enterprise – that is, a subsidiary, associate or branch – operating in a country other than the country or countries of residence of the foreign direct investor or investors".

Moreover, following the IMF definition, we can say that: "Direct investment refers to investment that is made to acquire a stake in an enterprise operating in an economy other than that of the investor, the investor's purpose being to have an effective voice in the management of the enterprise. The foreign entity or group of associate entities that makes the investment is termed the direct investor. The unincorporated or incorporated enterprise (a branch or subsidiary, respectively) in which a direct investment is made is referred to as a direct investment enterprise".

According to the OECD definition: "A foreign direct investor is an individual an incorporated or unincorporated public or private enterprise, a government, a group of related individuals, or a group of related incorporated and/or unincorporated enterprises which has a direct investment enterprise (that is a subsidiary, associated enterprise or branch operating in a country other than the country(ies) of residence of the direct investors)".

Also, *Direct Investment Enterprises* defined as: "Incorporated or unincorporated enterprises in which a single foreign investor either controls ten per-cent or more of the ordinary shares or voting power of an incorporated enterprise (or the equivalent of an unincorporated enterprise) or has an effective voice in the management of the enterprise".

Finally, the OECD definition states that: "Direct investment flows are defined to include for subsidiary and associated companies: the direct investor's share of the company's reinvested earnings plus the direct investor's net purchases of the company's share and loans plus the net increase in trade and other short-term credits given by the direct investor to the company. For branches this includes the increase in unremitted profits plus the net increase in funds received from the direct investor. Finally, loans on short-term balances from fellow subsidiaries and branches to foreign direct investment enterprises, loans by subsidiaries to their direct investors and loans guaranteed by direct investors and defaulted as well as the value of goods leased by direct investors should be included in direct investment, with an exception only for the bank, deposits, bills and short term loans which should be excluded from direct investments".

A direct investment enterprise may be defined as an incorporated or unincorporated enterprise in which a foreign investor owns 10% or more of the ordinary shares or voting power of an incorporated enterprise or the equivalent of an unincorporated enterprise. The numerical guideline of ownership of 10% of ordinary shares or voting stock determines the existence of a direct investment relationship. Some countries may consider that the existence of elements of a direct investment relationship may be indicated by a combination of factors such as:

- representation on the board of directors;
- participation in policy-making processes;
- material inter-company transactions
- interchange of managerial personnel
- provision of technical information
- provision of long-term loans at lower than existing market rates

The concept of Scientific and Technological Activities has been developed by OECD and UNESCO and EUROSTAT. According to "International Standardization of Statistics on Science and Technology", we can consider as scientific and technological activities as: "The systematic activities which are closely concerned with the generation, advancement, dissemination and application of scientific and technical knowledge in all fields of scientific and technology. These include activities on R&D, scientific and technical education and training and scientific and technological services".

Furthermore, we can distinguish R&D activities from Scientific and Technical Education and Training and Scientific and Technological Services. Whereas, "Scientific and Technical Education and Training activities comprising specialised non-university higher education and training, higher education and training leading to a university degree, post-graduate and further training, and organised lifelong training for scientists and engineers", while Scientific and Technological Services are considered as the following main categories: "Scientific and Technological Services comprise scientific and technological activities of libraries, museums, data collection on socio-economic phenomena, testing, standardisation and quality control and patent and license activities by public bodies".

There is a huge literature on the effects of innovation activities. However, only a small part of these studies their effects on a regional level. One of the major problems for the measurement of innovation activities is the availability of disaggregated data and the lack of information in a regional level; this becomes more poignant for less advanced technological countries.

According to the definition provided by UNCTAD, technology can be considered as: "the essential input to production which can embodied either in capital and in intermediate goods or in the human labour and in manpower or finally in information which is provided through markets" (United Nations, 1983).

Major sources of these data come from OECD, the United Nations, the European Union and local authorities. Since 1965, the statistics divisions of OECD and UNESCO have organised the systematic collection, publication and standardisation of research and technological data. We can collect and present data both for Business, Government and Private non-profit sectors. Business Sector – including all firms, private and non-private institutions, organisations whose primary activity – is the production of goods and services for sale to the general public at price intended to cover at least the cost of production; public enterprises are also included in the Business Enterprise sector. Government sector includes all departments, offices and other bodies which normally sell to the community those services which cannot otherwise be conveniently and economically provided. Private non-profit sector includes private or semi-public organisations as well as individuals and households. However, these should be excluded all enterprises which serve government or those which are financed and controlled by government, those which offer higher education services or are controlled by institutes of higher education. Higher education consists of all universities, technology colleges and other institutes of post-secondary education. Finally, data from abroad includes all institutions and individuals located outside the political frontiers of a country, and all international organisations (except business enterprises), including facilities and operations within the frontiers of a country.

Apart form the OECD and the United Nations research departments, there is another committee, the *Scientific and Technical Research Committee*, which deals with research and innovation statistics. Research and scientific indicators not only provide a view of the innovation and research structure of a given country but also indicate its *technological strength and capacity* relative to others.

Various research and technological indicators attempt to explain *technological relationships* at a specific point of time or for a whole period. The aim is to measure the nature, the capacity and the efficiency of scientific and technological activities both at a national and a sectoral level. Technological indicators related to *output measures* are more meaningful than those related to *input measures* (such as the number of scientists and engineers which are involved in research activities or the number of research institutions), since the later say little about the achieved research.

The use of research and technological data imply a lot of problems with the collection and measurement. The problems of data quality and comparability are characteristic for a whole range of data on dynamic socio-economic activities. However, most of research and technological indicators capture technological investment in small industries and firms only imperfectly. Usually only the manufacturing firms with more than 10,000 employees have established some research and technological laboratories, while industrial units with less than 1,000 employees haven't. Finally, research and technological statistics concentrate mostly on manufacturing sectors, usually neglecting some service activities.

3. FDIs and Productivity Growth in the Context of National Systems of Innovation

This section reviews the trends in FDI in some of the major host countries among the emerging economies in the 1990s. The increase in FDI in the OECD area continued in 1999, both in absolute value and as a percentage of GDP. This took FDI activity to a remarkable peak, following almost a decade of continued growth. In 1999, the increase of FDI inflows in Japan, Sweden and Germany were particularly remarkable. Compared with those of previous year, they almost quadrupled in Japan, more than tripled in Sweden and more than doubled in Germany. Spectacular growth rates were also recorded in OECD outflows, with the outgoing FDI of Denmark, France, Ireland, New Zealand and Norway more than doubling compared with 1998. The United States and United Kingdom witnessed high FDI flows in 1999.

These countries were the most prominent home and host countries, accounting for more than half of total OECD inflows and more than 45% of outflows. Investment inflows to the United States grew by almost 50% and by 28% to the United Kingdom. Outflows from these countries increased by 15% and 67% respectively. Table 4.1 illustrates the main figures of FDI for the period 1982-1999. Developed countries attracted $ 636 billion in FDI flows in 1999, nearly three quarters of the world's total. The United States and the United Kingdom were the leaders as both investor and recipients with $199 billion, the United Kingdom became the largest outward investor in 1999.

**Table 4.1 Selected indicators of FDI, 1982-1999
(billions of US$ and percentages)**

	1982	1990	1992	1986-90	1991-95	1996-99	1995	1999
FDI inflows	55	209	565	24.0	28.0	31.9	43.5	27.3
FDI outflows	37	245	600	27.6	15.7	27.0	45.6	16.4
FDI inward stock	594	1761	4772	15.2	9.4	16.2	20.1	15.5
FDI outward stock	567	1716	4759	20.5	10.7	14.5	17.6	17.1

Source: UNCTAD, World Investment Report, 2000.

The driving force behind this trend was transatlantic M&A. The United States strengthened its net capital importing position, while the United Kingdom's balance shows increasingly high net outflows. Inflows into the United States came mainly from Europe. The most important investors were the United Kingdom, Germany and the Netherlands. In 1999, as that of the previous year, the United Kingdom's share represented more than one third of total investments in the United States. As far as the sectoral distribution of investments is concerned, the manufacturing sector (especially machinery industry) and telecommunications were the most prominent absorbers of investments, while the traditionally higher share of the petroleum industry declined over the year.

On the outflow side, Europe is still the most important recipient of US FDI. However, between 1998 and 1999, its share decreased from 61% to 53%. Canada's, Latin America's and especially Asia's shares of outflows increased, with each representing around 15% of total FDI outflows. Asia has been attracting the lion's share of international investment in developing countries for some time. Inward investment into Asia in the 1990s experienced healthy, uninterrupted growth prior to the financial crisis. It recorded a decline in 1998 as the impact of the crisis took effect. Consequently, its share in the global investment flow declined and became almost on a par with that of Latin America.

The Asian financial crisis in the late 1990s had various impacts on the countries of the region, depending on the nature of investment and local economic conditions. Investment in Asia in the 1990s was characterised by the rising prominence of China both as an FDI recipient and investor, and by the growth of intra-regional FDI. China emerged as a popular destination of FDI in the early 1990s, and became the second largest FDI recipient in the world after the United States by 1993. Other main destinations of international investment within Asia in the 1990s are Singapore, Malaysia, Thailand, Indonesia, Hong Kong (China), Taiwan and Philippines.

By 1997, the level of inward investment in newly industrialising economies (NIEs – Taiwan, Singapore and Hong Kong) had almost doubled compared with the beginning of the decade. Flows into Hong Kong (China) and Singapore have not been stable, while Taiwan attracted a steady flow until the crisis. The volume of FDI in Taiwan and Hong Kong (China) declined considerably in 1998, due to the slowdown of the regional economies. OECD investment into Hong Kong (China) turned negative, minus USD 1.1 billion in 1998, from USD 4.3 billion in 1997.

Although it is suggested that China surpassed the United States and Japan to become the largest investor in Hong Kong (China) since the early 1990s, the decline of OECD investment provides a substantial explanation for the shrinking investment. Since the latter part of 1980s, inward investment in ASEAN grew at an impressive rate. The growth was largely led by Japanese investment, triggered by the appreciation of the yen, which pushed Japanese manufacturers out of the home country. The share of Japanese manufacturing investment in ASEAN4 (Malaysia, Indonesia, Philippines, and Thailand) grew from 8% in 1987 to 18% in 1992. Although it has not regained its peak, it has maintained a 16-17% share to date. Malaysia began to support export-oriented investments at an early stage.

Perhaps the biggest beneficiaries of the growth of intra-regional FDI are less developed ASEAN members. In most of these countries, other ASEAN countries play a vital role as investors. Hong Kong (China) has been the biggest investor into China since the inauguration of China's open policy in 1979, consistently accounting for roughly 60% of foreign investment. Contrary to its dynamism in China, Hong Kong (China) is much less active in other Asian countries. At the same time China has emerged as the biggest investor in Hong Kong (China) in the 1990s. In fact, China's outward investment expansion is another noteworthy phenomenon of the 1990s. Chinese investors – mostly state-owned enterprises – have demonstrated diversified interests: there is high concentration of investment in the trade and services sector in Hong Kong (China), whereas the availability of raw materials is seen as the main motive for their investments in Australia and Canada. Chinese investment in the United States is also active, in search of proprietary technology. Market-seeking investment from China can be found in a great variety of locations around the world.

Most of the countries in Latin America have undergone drastic policy reformulation in the 1990s. Macroeconomic stabilisation, trade liberalisation, privatisation programmes, deregulation of policies regarding private investment, and regional integration all contributed to creating a favourable climate for foreign investments. As a result, the level of FDI inflows into the region has increased eightfold compared with those at the end of the 1980s. The healthy growth of FDI in the region throughout the 1990s demonstrates that the confidence of foreign investors has recovered after going through the difficult decade of the post debt-crisis. In fact, the share of the region in global inward investment has at last recovered to the level prior to the debt crisis. The growth of FDI is largely influenced by privatisation programmes throughout the region.

The four largest economies of Latin America – Mexico, Argentina, Brazil and Chile – have been constantly receiving over 70% of the total inward FDI in Latin

America since the 1970s. This trend remained unchanged in the 1990s. It should, however, be kept in mind that the amount of FDI attracted by some of the smaller countries in the region are quite significant when measured against the size of their economies. Although the region as a whole demonstrates a steady growth in FDI flows in the 1990s, the country breakdown shows a rather different picture. Annual investment flows in individual countries depend largely on the completion of large-scale investment projects – be they privatisation, acquisition or a greenfield investment. As a result, most countries' FDI flow in the 1990s has shown large year-to-year fluctuations. The change in the nature of FDI is even more striking. For example, the role of debt-equity swaps in attracting FDI has diminished. In the 1980s, the level of FDI flows to some countries; especially larger recipients were mainly sustained by such swaps. Argentina, Chile and Mexico owed their growth in FDI in the former half of the 1990s largely to their privatisation programmes.

In the latter part of the 1990s Brazil has emerged as the largest FDI recipient in the region as a result of the sell-off of publicly owned entities. Over one-third of investment in the telecommunications and electricity industries – the two high profile industries that also in other countries usually attract foreign investors – was generated by privatisation. The change in investment climate has also affected the sectoral distribution of FDI in the region. Prior to the wave of liberalisation, the majority of investment targeted the manufacturing sector and aimed to penetrate highly protected domestic markets. In the 1990s, however, privatisation and the opening up of industry previously closed to foreign investment induced a much higher growth of investment in the services sector, which is usually market oriented investment. Spain has become very active since the mid-1990s, especially in Mercosur, Chile and the Andean countries. Latin America's share of Spain's total FDI soared from 29% to 72%, between 1990-1998.

A very large proportion of those FDI flows went to the services industry, through privatisation or M&A that became possible thanks to deregulation. Since 1996, Spain has overtaken the United Kingdom as main European investor. Led by MNEs in the more mature economies in the region, outward investment in Latin America increased in the 1990s.

The process of liberalisation, privatisation and deregulation forced some local MNEs into increased domestic competition, which made corporate restructuring inevitable. There are signs that countries in the region may be able to sustain the level of FDI inflows once privatisation is completed.

Experiences elsewhere indicate that as privatisation process comes to an end, infusions of capital continue to occur in order to upgrade existing facilities that have been privatised. Mexico and some Caribbean countries have begun to attract a type of investment that is not related to privatisation but aimed to increase the efficiency of MNEs' international production facilities. This type of investment is particularly concentrated in automotive, computers, electronics and apparel industries. Table 4.2 indicates the Flows of Direct Investment for OECD countries, 1996-2005 (million US$).

Table 4.2 Direct investment flows for OECD countries, 1996-2005 (million US$)

	Inflows			Outflows			
Australia	1996	2004	2005	1996	1999	2004	2005
Austria	5171	42036	-36810	5927	-3192	17488	-39787
Belgium-Luxemb.	4429	3687	8905	1935	2703	7392	9382
Canada	14061	42064	23710	8065	24937	33545	22946
Czech Republic	1428	1533	33824	153	197	43248	34084
Denmark	776	4975	10988	2518	8207	1014	856
Finland	1109	-10721	5020	3596	4194	-10371	8072
France	21942	3539	4558	30395	88324	-1076	2703
Germany	6577	31388	63540	50841	98853	57044	115607
Greece	5888	-15123	32643	–	573	1884	45606
Hungary	2275	2103	606	-3	249	1030	1450
Iceland	82	4657	6700	62	70	1122	1346
Ireland	1888	654	2329	–	18326	2553	6693
Italy	3535	11165	-22759	6465	3038	15813	12931
Japan	228	16824	19498	23424	20730	19273	41536
Korea	2325	7819	2778	4670	4044	30962	45830
Mexico	9185	9246	4339	–	–	4658	4312
Netherlands	15055	18674	18055	31230	45540	4432	6171
New Zealand	3697	442	43604	-1260	1020	17292	119382
Norway	3201	4371	2834	5918	5483	1074	-318
Poland	4498	2547	14464	53	123	3526	3414
Portugal	1368	12355	7724	776	2679	778	1455
Spain	6820	2368	3112	5590	35421	7963	1146
Sweden	5076	24775	22973	4664	18951	60567	38748
Switzerland	3078	-1852	13692	16150	17910	11947	26029
Turkey	722	750	5781	110	645	26851	42754
United Kingdom	26084	2837	9686	34125	199275	859	1048
United States	88977	56253	164499	92694	152152	94929	101080
Total OECD	248882	133162	109754	340977	767814	244128	9072

Note: Data converted using the yearly average exchange rates.
Source: OECD/FDI database – based on national sources.

Germany was the target of a record USD 52 billion inflow. This was due to a merger in the chemical industry, in the course of which the newly established enterprise located its headquarters abroad and acquired the majority stake in the German company. German investments abroad remained of high level of the previous year and were also led by M&A. The most important host countries were the United States and the United Kingdom, accounting for 45% and 23% of German FDI outflows, respectively. As a result, Germany maintained its net investor position in 1999.

The *Netherlands* witnessed a decrease, though inflows and outflows were still high compared with the years before 1998. The country remained an important net outward investor. While still experiencing high inflows, *Spain* became a large investor, mainly due to its increased activity in Latin America. Spanish participation in the privatisation of public utilities and banks in the region was considerable. M&A between companies in the private domain (the most important of which including an Argentinean company) contributed to the high level of flows. As a result, Spain was a net investor for the third consecutive year. In 1999, while remaining a recipient of high gross inflows, *Ireland* doubled its investments abroad compared with 1998; this is also related to the increasing importance of the country as a European platform for overseas companies.

Table 4.3 Cumulative FDI flows in OECD countries, 1990-1999 (million US$)

United States	927,378	United States	876,705	Germany	305,988
United Kingdom	319,726	United Kingdom	566,400	United Kingdom	246,674
France	215,804	Germany	422,455	Japan	222,720
Netherlands	159,523	France	347,839	France	132,035
Sweden	127,633	Netherlands	250,860	Netherlands	91,337
Belgium-Luxem.	123,206	Japan	248,729	Switzerland	84,506
Germany	116,467	Canada	120,113	Italy	33,451
Canada	99,000	Switzerland	119,187	Canada	21,113
Spain	97,780	Belgium-Luxem.	109,350	Finland	17,919
Mexico	81,570	Sweden	102,114	Ireland	9,444
Australia	58,910	Spain	93,236	South Korea	4,366
Italy	37,697	Italy	71,148	Norway	1,460
Switzerland	34,680	Finland	40,760	Denmark	782
Denmark	32,176	Denmark	32,958	Iceland	-96
Poland	30,616	South Korea	29,018	Austria	-2,929
Greece	26,942	Norway	28,131	Spain	-4,544
Norway	26,670	Ireland	26,895	Turkey	-6,029
Japan	26,008	Australia	26,596	Portugal	-7,038
South Korea	24,653	Austria	18,155	Belgium-Luxem.	-13,856

Table 4.3 continued

Finland	22,841	Portugal	10,463	Czech Republic	-14,404
Austria	21,084	New Zealand	5,135	New Zealand	-15,620
New Zealand	20,754	Turkey	2,087	Hungary	-18,357
Hungary	19,618	Hungary	1,261	Sweden	-25,519
Portugal	17,501	Czech Republic	828	Greece	-26,369
Ireland	17,451	Poland	639	Poland	-29,977
Czech Republic	15,233	Greece	573	Australia	-32,314
Turkey	8,116	Iceland	380	United States	-50,673
Iceland	476	Mexico	na	Mexico	-81,570
Total OECD	2,709,512	TOTAL OECD	3,552,013	TOTAL OECD	842,501

Source: OECD, International Direct Investment database.

Table 4.4 FDIs flows

		Net foreign direct investment inflows (% of GDP)		Other private flows (% of GDP)	
High human development		**1990**	**2002**	**1990**	**2002**
22	Israel	0.3	1.6	–	–
23	Hong Kong, China (SAR)	–	7.9	–	–
24	Greece	1.2	(.)	–	–
25	Singapore	15.1	7	–	–
26	Portugal	3.7	3.5	–	–
27	Slovenia	–	8.5	–	–
28	Korea, Rep. of	0.3	0.4	–	–
29	Barbados	0.7	0.7	–	–
30	Cyprus	2.3	6.1	–	–
31	Malta	2	-11	–	–
32	Czech Republic	–	13.4	–	1.5
33	Brunei Darussalam	–	–	–	–
34	Argentina	1.3	0.8	-1.5	-0.1

Table 4.4 continued

	Net foreign direct investment inflows (% of GDP)		Other private flows (% of GDP)	
High human development	**1990**	**2002**	**1990**	**2002**
35 Seychelles	5.5	8.8	-1.7	-0.3
36 Estonia	–	4.4	–	20
37 Poland	0.2	2.2	(.)	0.5
38 Hungary	0.9	1.3	-1.4	-1
39 Saint Kitts and Nevis	30.7	22.7	-0.3	4.7
40 Bahrain	–	–	–	–
41 Lithuania	–	5.2	–	0.3
42 Slovakia	–	16.9	–	6.1
43 Chile	2.2	2.7	5.1	1.7
44 Kuwait	0	(.)	–	–
45 Costa Rica	2.8	3.9	-2.5	-0.4
46 Uruguay	0	1.5	-2.1	-0.6
47 Qatar	–	–	–	–
48 Croatia	–	4.4	–	11.7
49 United Arab Emirates	–	–	–	–
50 Latvia	–	4.5	–	1.3
51 Bahamas	-0.6	5.2	–	–
52 Cuba	–	–	–	–
53 Mexico	1	2.3	2.7	-0.7
54 Trinidad and Tobago	2.2	7.6	-3.5	0
55 Antigua and Barbuda	–	–	–	–
Developing countries	1	2.5	0.4	-0.1
Least developed countries	0.1	2.9	0.4	–
Arab States	0.9	0.6	-0.1	0.5
East Asia and the Pacific	2.3	3.6	0.6	-0.3
Latin America and the Caribbean	0.7	2.7	0.5	-0.6
South Asia	(.)	0.6	0.3	0.3
Sub-Saharan Africa	–	2.4	0.2	-0.3

Table 4.4 continued

High human development	Net foreign direct investment inflows (% of GDP)		Other private flows (% of GDP)	
	1990	2002	1990	2002
Central and Eastern Europe and the CIS	–	3.5	(.)	1.5
OECD	1	1.9	–	–
High-income OECD	1	1.9	–	–
High human development	1	2	–	–
Medium human development	0.7	2.2	0.3	0.1
Low human development	0.5	2.9	0.3	-0.5
High income	1	1.9	–	–
Middle income	0.9	2.7	0.3	0.3
Low income	0.4	1.2	0.5	-0.5
World	1	2	–	–

Source: World Development Report.

Sweden became one of the largest recipients of FDI in the OECD area in 1999. The country absorbed almost the same amount of FDI inflows as in the previous decade put together. The record-high inflows (almost USD 60 billion) were due to an M&A deal in the chemical industry, which accounted for around two-thirds of the value of total inflows. As outflows were actually lower than in 1998, Sweden unusually became a net recipient.

The *Czech Republic* and *Poland* increased the level of FDI inflows due to large`privatisation projects. Together with *Hungary*, they are still on the net receiving end of the FDI spectrum, as the companies in each country have been able to invest only negligible amounts abroad.

Greece, Portugal and *Turkey* continued to experience low inflows. Portugal has been playing an increasingly active role on the outflow side in the last few years, effectively becoming a net investor abroad. As a new phenomenon, OECD members in Asia figured prominently as gross recipients of FDI.

Japan received a historical record of inflows driven by the acquisition of an important stake in Nissan by Renault, as well as other M&A. Inflow into Japan was almost four times that of 1998, and almost half of the amount of the inflows of the entire decade, with European (especially French and Dutch) investors taking the leading role. However, even the record inflow did not come close to the traditionally high level of outflows; meaning that Japan was still a net investor abroad.

In *South Korea*, in response to the financial crisis, regulatory changes favouring FDI continued, resulting in a further increase in the inflow of direct investments. FDI grew by more than 60% in 1999. Inflows exceeded a generally unchanged level of outflows, changing the country's position to that of a net recipient of FDI. The inflows were boosted by an ongoing process of corporate restructuring and privatisation. The growth in direct investment from the EU and Japan was particularly pronounced.

The fact that the first three countries listed in Table 4.3 account for half of the cumulated inflows and outflows indicates the high concentration of OECD FDI in the nineties. Eight of the top ten recipients of FDI are also among the top ten outward investing countries, indicating that the larger OECD countries tend to be active in both undertaking and receiving FDI. Germany, the United Kingdom and Japan were the largest net investors in the nineties, and the United States is the largest net recipient.

Tables 4.4 and 4.5 illustrate the flows of FDI and also some related economic indicators respectively. Figure 4.1 indicates the flows of FDIs for selected advanced nations. Orthodox neoliberal economic theory predicts that global integration will bring benefits to developing countries through economic convergence. Lower barriers to trade and capital flows, even without free movement of labour, will tend to equalise factor prices, productivity and incomes over time. In summary, we may conclude the following points:

- Capital will be attracted to those countries where capital is scarcest and the rate of return is highest; the resulting increase in supply will reduce the rate of return. This process should, in principle, continue until rates of return (adjusted for risk) are equalised.
- International trade will equalise the prices of tradable goods and services between countries.
- Low-wage countries will have a comparative advantage in the production of labour-intensive goods and will attract capital to finance their production. Surplus labour will be absorbed, raising real wages.
- Agricultural production will shift toward land-rich countries, raising returns.

According to the neoliberal model, freeing international markets and liberalising domestic economies allows countries to move toward specialisation in their areas of comparative advantage. For developing countries, where labour is plentiful and capital scarce, *this* implies a shift from often capital-intensive import-substituting industries to more labour intensive sectors, primarily for export.

The result, in theory, is "pro-poor growth." Contrary to the predictions of the neoliberal model, Rao (1997) finds that the overall price level in the United States, at market exchange rates, tends to be between 2.5 and 5 times than in the poorest developing countries.

Table 4.5 Main economic indicators

Human Devel. Index	GDP (US\$ bil.)	GDP PPP (US\$)	GDP per capita PPP (US\$)
High HDI			
1. Norway	161.8	134.4	29,918
2. Sweden	227.3	215.3	24,277
3. Canada	687.9	856.1	27,840
4. Belgium	226.6	278.6	27,178
5. Australia	390.1	492.8	25,693
6. United States	9,837.4	9,612.7	34,142
7. Iceland	8.5	8.3	29,581
8. Netherlands	364.8	408.4	25,657
9. Japan	4,841.6	3,394.4	26,755
10. Finland	121.5	129.4	24,996
11. Switzerland	239.8	206.6	28,769
12. France	1,294.2	1,426.6	24,223
13. United Kingdom	1,414.6	1,404.4	23,509
14. Denmark	162.3	147.4	27,627
15. Austria	189.0	217.1	26,765
16. Luxembourg	18.9	21.9	50,061
17. Germany	1,873.0	2,062.2	25,103
18. Ireland	93.9	113.3	29,866
19. New Zealand	49.9	76.9	20,070
20. Italy	1,074.0	1,363.0	23,626
21. Spain	558.6	768.5	19,472
22. Israel	110.4	125.5	20,131
23. Hong Kong, China (SAR)	162.6	171.0	25,153
24. Greece	112.6	174.3	16,501
25. Singapore	92.3	93.8	23,356
26. Cyprus	8.7	15.8	20,824
27. Korea, Rep. of	457.2	821.7	17,380
28. Portugal	105.1	173.0	17,290
29. Slovenia	18.1	34.5	17,367
30. Malta	3.6	6.7	17,273
31. Barbados	2.6	4.1	15,494
32. Brunei Darussalam	4.8	5.4	16,779
33. Czech Republic	50.8	143.7	13,991
34. Argentina	285.0	458.3	12,377

Table 4.5 continued

Human Devel. Index	GDP (US$ bil.)	GDP PPP (US$)	GDP per capita PPP (US$)
High HDI			
35. Hungary	45.6	124.4	12,416
36. Slovakia	19.1	60.7	11,243
37. Poland	157.7	349.8	9,051
38. Chile	70.5	143.2	9,417
39. Bahrain	8.0	10.1	15,084
40. Uruguay	19.7	30.1	9,035
41. Bahamas	4.8	5.2	17,012
42. Estonia	5.0	13.8	10,066
43. Costa Rica	15.9	33.0	8,650
44. Saint Kitts and Nevis	0.3	0.5	12,510
45. Kuwait	37.8	31.4	15,799
46. United Arab Emirates	46.5	48.9	17,935
47. Seychelles	0.6	–	–
48. Croatia	19.0	35.4	8,091
49. Lithuania	11.3	26.3	7,106
50. Trinidad and Tobago	7.3	11.7	8,964
51. Qatar	14.5	–	–
52. Antigua and Barbuda	0.7	0.7	10,541
53. Latvia	7.2	16.7	7,045
Medium HDI			
54. Mexico	574.5	884.0	9,023
55. Cuba	–	–	–
56. Belarus	29.9	75.5	7,544
57. Panama	9.9	17.1	6,000
58. Belize	0.8	1.3	5,606
59. Malaysia	89.7	211.0	9,068
60. Russian Federation	251.1	1,219.4	8,377
61. Dominica	0.3	0.4	5,880
62. Bulgaria	12.0	46.6	5,710
63. Romania	36.7	144.1	6,423
64. Libyan Arab Jamahiriya	–	–	–
65. Macedonia, TFYR	3.6	10.3	5,086
66. Saint Lucia	0.7	0.9	5,703
67. Mauritius	4.4	11.9	10,017

Table 4.5 continued

Human Devel. Index	GDP (US$ bil.)	GDP PPP (US$)	GDP per capita PPP (US$)
Medium HDI			
68. Colombia	81.3	264.3	6,248
69. Venezuela	120.5	140.0	5,794
70. Thailand	122.2	388.8	6,402
71. Saudi Arabia	173.3	235.6	11,367
72. Fiji	1.5	3.8	4,668
73. Brazil	595.5	1,299.4	7,625
74. Suriname	0.8	1.6	3,799
75. Lebanon	16.5	18.6	4,308
76. Armenia	1.9	9.7	2,559
77. Philippines	74.7	300.1	3,971
78. Oman	15.0	–	–
79. Kazakhstan	18.2	87.3	5,871
80. Ukraine	31.8	188.9	3,816
81. Georgia	3.0	13.4	2,664
82. Peru	53.5	123.2	4,799
83. Grenada	0.4	0.7	7,580
84. Maldives	0.6	1.2	4,485
85. Turkey	199.9	455.3	6,974
86. Jamaica	7.4	9.6	3,639
87. Turkmenistan	4.4	20.6	3,956
88. Azerbaijan	5.3	23.6	2,936
89. Sri Lanka	16.3	68.3	3,530
90. Paraguay	7.5	24.3	4,426
91. Saint Vincent and the Grenadines	0.3	0.6	5,555
92. Albania	3.8	12.0	3,506
93. Ecuador	13.6	40.5	3,203
94. Dominican Republic	19.7	50.5	6,033
95. Uzbekistan	7.7	60.4	2,441
96. China	1,080.0	5,019.4	3,976
97. Tunisia	19.5	60.8	6,363
98. Iran, Islamic Rep. of	104.9	374.6	5,884
99. Jordan	8.3	19.4	3,966
100. Cape Verde	0.6	2.1	4,863
101. Samoa (Western)	0.2	0.9	5,041

Table 4.5 continued

Human Devel. Index	GDP (US$ bil.)	GDP PPP (US$)	GDP per capita PPP (US$)
Medium HDI			
102. Kyrgyzstan	1.3	13.3	2,711
103. Guyana	0.7	3.0	3,963
104. El Salvador	13.2	28.2	4,497
105. Moldova, Rep. of	1.3	9.0	2,109
106. Algeria	53.3	161.3	5,308
107. South Africa	125.9	402.4	9,401
108. Syrian Arab Republic	17.0	57.6	3,556
109. Viet Nam	31.3	156.8	1,996
110. Indonesia	153.3	640.3	3,043
111. Equatorial Guinea	1.3	6.9	15,073
112. Tajikistan	1.0	7.1	1,152
113. Mongolia	1.0	4.3	1,783
114. Bolivia	8.3	20.2	2,424
115. Egypt	98.7	232.5	3,635
116. Honduras	5.9	15.7	2,453
117. Gabon	4.9	7.7	6,237
118. Nicaragua	2.4	12.0	2,366
119. Sao Tome and Principe	(.)	–	–
120. Guatemala	19.0	43.5	3,821
121. Solomon Islands	0.3	0.7	1,648
122. Namibia	3.5	11.3	6,431
123. Morocco	33.3	101.8	3,546
124. India	457.0	2,395.4	2,358
125. Swaziland	1.5	4.7	4,492
126. Botswana	5.3	11.5	7,184
127. Myanmar	–	–	–
128. Zimbabwe	7.4	33.3	2,635
129. Ghana	5.2	37.9	1,964
130. Cambodia	3.2	17.4	1,446
131. Vanuatu	0.2	0.6	2,802
132. Lesotho	0.9	4.1	2,031
133. Papua New Guinea	3.8	11.7	2,280
134. Kenya	10.4	30.8	1,022
135. Cameroon	8.9	25.3	1,703
136. Congo	3.2	2.5	825

Table 4.5 continued

Human Devel. Index	GDP (US$ bil.)	GDP PPP (US$)	GDP per capita PPP (US$)
Medium HDI			
137. Comoros	0.2	0.9	1,588
Low HDI			
138. Pakistan	61.6	266.2	1,928
139. Sudan	11.5	55.9	1,797
140. Bhutan	0.5	1.1	1,412
141. Togo	1.2	6.5	1,442
142. Nepal	5.5	30.6	1,327
143. Lao People's Dem. Rep.	1.7	8.3	1,575
144. Yemen	8.5	15.6	893
145. Bangladesh	47.1	209.9	1,602
146. Haiti	4.0	11.7	1,467
147. Madagascar	3.9	13.0	840
148. Nigeria	41.1	113.7	896
149. Djibouti	0.6	–	–
150. Uganda	6.2	26.8	1,208
151. Tanzania, U. Rep. of	9.0	17.6	523
152. Mauritania	0.9	4.5	1,677
153. Zambia	2.9	7.9	780
154. Senegal	4.4	14.4	1,510
155. Congo, Dem. Rep. of the	5.6	36.9	765
156. Côte d'Ivoire	9.4	26.1	1,630
157. Eritrea	0.6	3.4	837
158. Benin	2.2	6.2	990
159. Guinea	3.0	14.7	1,982
160. Gambia	0.4	2.1	1,649
161. Angola	8.8	28.7	2,187
162. Rwanda	1.8	8.0	943
163. Malawi	1.7	6.3	615
164. Mali	2.3	8.6	797
165. Central African Republic	1.0	4.4	1,172
166. Chad	1.4	6.7	871
167. Guinea-Bissau	0.2	0.9	755
168. Ethiopia	6.4	43.0	668
169. Burkina Faso	2.2	11.0	976
170. Mozambique	3.8	15.1	854

Table 4.5 continued

Human Devel. Index	GDP (US$ bil.)	GDP PPP (US$)	GDP per capita PPP (US$)
Low HDI			
171. Burundi	0.7	4.0	591
172. Niger	1.8	8.1	746
173. Sierra Leone	0.6	2.5	490
Developing countries	6,059.4	17,438.0	3,783
Least developed countries	178.5	669.4	1,216
Arab States	603.5	1,049.5	4,793
East Asia and the Pacific	2,296.3	7,855.9	4,290
Latin America and the Caribbean	1,961.2	3,679.7	7,234
South Asia	693.5	3,347.3	2,404
Sub-Saharan Africa	307.6	1,034.4	1,690
Eastern Europe and the CIS	746.8	2,746.7	6,930
OECD	25,558.2	26,525.3	23,569
High-income OECD	24,053.3	23,685.6	27,848
High human development	25,744.2	26,508.0	24,973
Medium human Development	4,960.5	16,453.9	4,141
Low human development	264.8	1,040.5	1,251
High income	24,563.2	24,227.8	27,639
Middle income	5,390.3	15,047.0	5,734
Low income	1,017.2	4,727.7	2,002
World	30,971.1	44,002.4	7,446

Sources: United Nations.

The available evidence also suggests that convergence of per capita incomes has not occurred during the current period of globalisation; it is rather *divergence* that has been observed.

- UNCTAD (1997, p. 79), considering real GDP per capita at market exchange rates, found that only Southern Europe and East Asia converged with the developed countries between 1965 and 1995, while sub-Saharan Africa's GDP per capita had halved in relative terms, and Latin America's had fallen by 30% after 1979. Overall, there was marked divergence with a "noticeable worsening" after 1980.

- Rao (1997) found divergence in GDP per capita at purchasing power parity between 1960 and 1992, accelerating between 1960-1978 and 1979-1992. Rao cites Baumol (1986), Barro and Sala-i-Martin (1992) as having found similar results. Within the OECD, UNCTAD finds strong convergence until 1973, but weaker or possibly reversed thereafter (though re-established within the EC in 1986-1990). They interpret the increase in the incomes of the top quintile of countries relative to *all* other quintiles has been interpreted as reflecting a growing polarisation toward the top and bottom of the income scale. Thus, a period of accelerating global has corresponded to an accelerating *divergence* of per capita incomes, leading UNCTAD (1997, p. 69) to conclude, "economic theory and reality diverged in a striking way." Convergence was limited to the developed countries and East Asia; and even within the OECD, it decelerated or ceased even as the pace of globalisation increased. Income divergence is not a new phenomenon or an aberration. UNCTAD (1997, p. 87) notes that "income divergence has been the dominant trend in the world economy over the past 120 years." Rao (1997, p. 8) suggests that this tendency dates back still further to around 1600. This applies equally to the previous period of globalisation in 1870-1913, when "divergence was the dominant trend", and convergence was slow and limited to a relatively small group of core countries at the upper end of the income distribution (UNCTAD 1997, p. 74).
- Rao (1997) sets out a number of alternatives to the neoliberal model of economic growth that could account for the failure of globalisation to generate economic convergence. The idea of a *convergence club* (Baumol et al 1994) suggests that convergence is limited to those countries that have sufficient human capital resources to take advantage of technological changes. This is consistent with the finding of convergence within the OECD, within a pattern of overall divergence.
- Another possible explanation for divergence is the existence of *increasing returns* to scale (Romer 1986). According to this view, greater spillovers, particularly in terms of technology and human capital, allow richer countries to grow faster. Although this could account for overall divergence in the world economy, it cannot, however, readily explain convergence among the OECD countries.
- The *contingent convergence* principle (Barro and Sala-i-Martin 1992) suggests that each country has a long-term equilibrium income path determined by its economic fundamentals (natural resources, factor endowments, geographical location, climate, etc.), around which its actual income fluctuates. In this model, each country converges on its own trend income, in the sense that its growth is faster when income is below the trend level and slower when it is above; but it will not necessarily converge with other countries.

- Woodward (1997a) raises a number of concerns about the shift toward foreign direct and equity investment as the predominant form of international capital flows.
- There are serious questions about the sustainability of FDI and portfolio flows at recent levels, due to their dependence on the privatisation process and the one-time shift associated with asset diversification by Northern financial institutions.
- Portfolio flows are highly unstable and raise the risk of destabilising national economies. While FDI is generally more stable, it has marked procyclical tendencies, and may thus tend to compound financial problems resulting from other external shocks.

It is well established that the accumulation of physical and human capital and advances in production efficiencies and technology lead to higher per capita income. Studies have typically found that approximately 60-70% of per capita growth in developing countries reflects increases in physical capital and another 10-20% is due to increases in education and human capital with the remaining 10-30% attributed to improved (total factor) productivity.

Not surprisingly, the low- and middle-income countries with declining or slowly rising per capita income had on average lower investment and saving rates than their faster-growing counterparts in recent years, confirming the importance of capital accumulation in the growth process. Causality is difficult to infer, however, because investment and saving rates were not substantially different, on average, across groups during the early 1970s except for perhaps the fastest-growing economies.

Even in this latter group of countries, investment rates rose only after the growth takeoff. In other words, it is far from obvious that high initial investment and saving rates are requirements for growth. It may indeed be that higher investment and saving rates result because of higher growth or that other factors cause both growth and investment. Low levels of schooling or investment in human capital may be impediments to growth and have delay takeoff. Secondary school enrolment rates in the 1970s were substantially lower on average in non-rapidly converging, low-income countries than in middle-income countries.

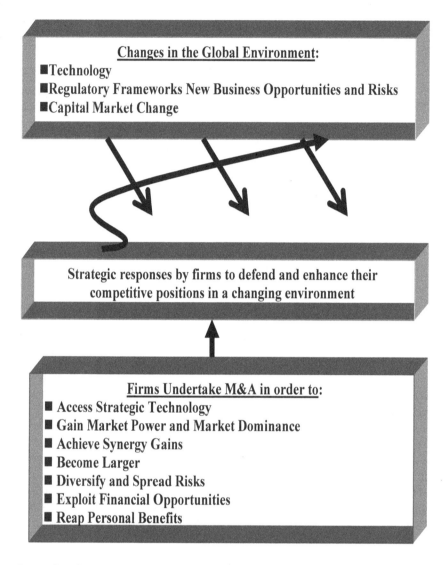

Figure 4.1 Cross border FDI and M&A activity
Source: Korres, G., 2005.

Moreover, fastest-growing, low and middle-income countries also experienced larger improvements in enrolments rates than the other developing countries did between 1975 and 1995. Although it is possible that growth induces more education as demand increases with income, it is noteworthy that among the low-income countries enrolment levels in the 1970s were highest (and similar to the levels in the middle-income countries) in the countries that subsequently grew the fastest. Basic education, including training, can contribute directly to a country's potential for growth by raising the skill level of the workforce. In addition, because physical and human capital is often complementary, education can also raise growth indirectly by inducing greater investment. While increased schooling and training alone may not be sufficient to boost growth, particularly when economic opportunities to use the acquired skills are missing, improving education will be an important part of a sustainable growth and poverty reduction strategy for developing countries. It therefore makes sense for countries to shift resources toward basic education and for the donor community to emphasise education as a high priority.

Another obstacle to a productive workforce (and society) is inadequate health care. As with school enrolment rates, life expectancy rates at birth were substantially lower on average in non-rapidly-converging, low-income countries than in the middle-income countries in the 1970s, and other health indicators show a similar pattern. Even though these health indicators have improved over time in most developing countries, they remain relatively bad in many low-income countries – for example, average life expectancy is till below 55 years for the negative- and slow-growth, low-income countries – representing an enormous loss in potential human capital. In addition, progress in improving life expectancy rates has slowed in some countries mainly due to devastating effects of the AIDS epidemic. Figure 4.1 illustrates the relationship and the effects of FDI and cross-border M&A to global socio-economic environment and at the firm level.

Inefficient investment has also been a hindrance for many countries, although, again, causality is difficult to infer. Not surprisingly, in developing countries with declining per capita growth during the last three decades, the incremental output-capital ratio (the inverse of the incremental capital-output ratio), which is a very rough proxy for the productivity of investment, was lower on average than in the countries that were growing.

Figures 4.2 to 4.5 illustrate the catching up process for some groups of selected countries, according to the income levels. In particular, Figure 4.2 illustrates the Medium rates of catch-up that corresponds to less or equal = 1.25% annually, Figure 4.3 indicates the High-income, whereas Figure 4.4 shows the catch-up and convergence process for the OECD income levels, and finally the Figure 4.5 presents the low starting point and low rates of catch-up that is less than 0.3% annually.

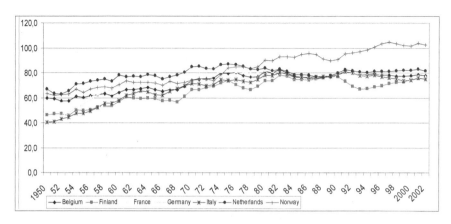

**Figure 4.2 Medium rates of catch-up (1.2% annually):
Catch-up and convergence in OECD income levels,
1950-1999 (USA = 100)**
Source: OECD data and own estimations.

This difference in financial input also has consequences in terms of innovation outputs. For example, there are over 20 times the number of patent application in Germany alone than in the four cohesion countries together (Ireland, Greece, Portugal and Spain).

The "technology gap" is a particular cause for concern with regard to the human resources for innovation, since human capital is increasingly a source of the dynamic comparative advantage which governs regional potential for innovation. In an increasingly "knowledge-based" economy, the only real capital is human capital. In terms of High Technology employment, in the 25 most advanced regions high technology accounts for an average of 14.6% of total employment, compared to just over 4% on average in the 25 least developed regions; this is compared to a community average of around 10.5%.

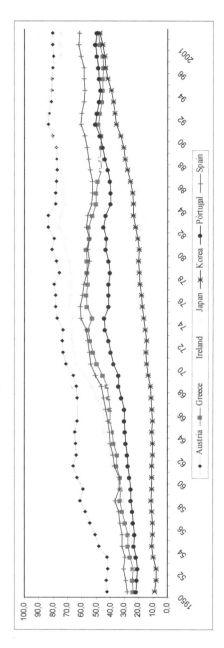

Figure 4.3 High catch-up (>1.2% annually): Catch-up and convergence in OECD income levels, 1950-1999 (USA = 100)

Source: OECD (2002) data and own estimations.

With a labour force of around 2.5 million Denmark, has almost doubled the number of innovation personnel than Portugal, with a labour force of around 4.5 million. Germany has almost doubled the number of innovation personnel per thousand labour force than Spain, three times more than Greece and four times more than Portugal.

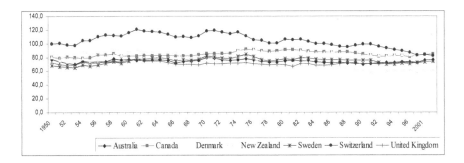

**Figure 4.4 Rapid catch-up: Catch-up and convergence in OECD income
           levels, 1950-2002 (USA = 100)**
Source: OECD (2002) data and own estimations.

If international comparison shows substantial disparities in innovation input indicators, inter-regional differences within member states are even greater in some cases. For example, in Greece over half the country's innovation expenditure takes place around Athens and over two-thirds of business innovation is located in this same region. In Spain over three-quarters of business innovation is located in three of seventeen regions (Madrid alone accounting for over 30%).

Moreover, the collection and presentation of R&D data of regional statistics implied a lot of problems in comparison with data of national statistics. For the collection of regional statistics, we should take into consideration the local differences and the difficulties. R&D units can operate in more than one region and we should allocate these activities between regions. Usually, regional statistics focused on the three first levels of NUTS (Nomenclature of Territorial Units for Statistics).

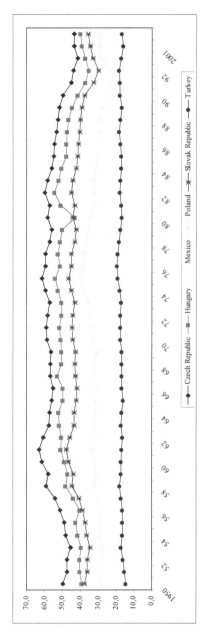

Figure 4.5 Low rates of catch-up (1.2% annually): Catch-up and convergence in OECD income level, 1950-1999 (USA = 100)

Source: OECD data and own estimations.

The reliability of R&D and innovation regional statistics is directly connected with a dependence on estimation-method and implementation of statistical technique. Another important question on R&D and innovation regional statistics is the confidentiality and the collection-method of data-set that may cover the whole or the majority of local-units. For those statistical methods focused on a regional level, we can use either "local-units" (for instance, enterprises, office, manufacturing etc.) or "local-economic-units" (NACE codes, which is a division of national codes of European member states).

The experience in most advanced countries shows that economic growth has been close related to that of technological growth and technological planning. We can see that from the history of advanced technologically countries that the technology transfer has been essential contributed to industrialisation and to modernisation of the whole economy for new industrialised countries and advanced countries. However, most advanced technological countries import a substantial part of the technology that they use (as has for instance happened with Japan and advanced technological European member states). An important question for all Less Favoured technological countries is that most of these countries continue to rely largely on imports of technology, as technological self-reliance seems neither desirable nor feasible. Policy research must be undertaken to determine approaches liable to reduce costs, increase access, select more effective technologies and ensure their integration, adoption and diffusion, both in local production system and the local innovation system.

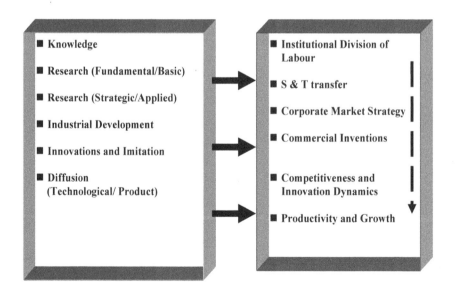

Figure 4.6 Levels of research, science and technology
Source: Korres, G., 2007.

There is a widespread belief that the declining competitive position of Europe in the world economy is related to the nation's relative level of research and development (R&D) spending and its ineffectiveness in commercialising the results of research performed in the public sector. The European Union intends to develop a coherent and an essential technological policy and planning, in order to assist the technological and economic convergence of member states; however, the technological gap is still widening and affecting negatively the economic figures. It is difficult to record and to analyse the effects from a research and technological policy. The choice of technology depends upon a large number of factors. It depends upon the availability of technologies, the availability of information to the decision maker, the availability of resources, the availability of technology itself and its capacity for successful adoption to suit the particular needs and objectives. The advanced countries which among the leaders in technological change rely on well-functioning large economies have tended to put more emphasis on these policies that aim to encourage the development of research and technological activities. Figure 4.6 illustrates the various levels of Research, Scientific and Technological activities. Mechanisms of technology and competition policies are usually complementary and both aim to increase the entrepreneur's creativity and attribute industrial and economic growth. It is important to harmonise technology "mechanisms" with competition policy. Competition policy related to research and technological activities also have an important impact on the market structure. If there is a healthy competitive environment in the market for goods and services then entrepreneurs have a greater incentive to develop new products and invest in technologies and research activities.

The analysis of system of innovations helps us understand and explain why the development of technology towards a certain direction and at a certain rate is necessary. Freeman (1987) first and Nelson (1988) later were the persons who introduced and explained the use, the concept of national systems of innovations. On the one hand, in his book for Japan Freeman (1987) refers to the nation-specific organisation of sub-systems and the interaction between sub-systems. He is also based on the interaction between the production system and the process of innovation. On the other hand, Nelson's work is based on the production of knowledge and innovation and on the innovation system in the narrow sense. According to Nelson, the national systems of innovation presume that nation states exist, and this phenomenon has two dimensions:

- the national-cultural (where all individuals belong to a nation which is defined by cultural, ethnical and linguistic characteristics); and
- the etatist-political (where there is one geographical space controlled by one central state authority without foreign nationalities). As indicated by Lundvall B. (1988) in some cases it is not even clear where to locate the borders of a "national system of innovations".

The government engages itself towards innovation policy because it has been considered that innovation is a key point for the national economic growth. In order to decide how the governments should decide to promote the innovations, it is useful to know the specific context in which the national government interferes. The first approach and definition of "system of innovations" is that, it is a social system that is constructed by a number of elements, while there is a close-relationship between these elements. These elements are "interacting" in the production, diffusion, and economic cycles. We can define "the system of innovations" from a "narrow" point of view. According to "the narrow definition" it includes organisations and institutions involved in searching and exploring the new technologies (such as technological institutes, and research departments). According to the "broad" definition, follows the theoretical perspective and includes different parts of economic structure (such as production system, and marketing system). Worldwide, when large countries change the orientation of their research activities, this affects small countries. Any improvement and technological sophistication in traditional sectors within large countries have usually pushed the firms of small countries same sectors to follow the new technologies. Development and diffusion of new technologies for a small country usually depend on the actions undertaken by private enterprises and public sector organisations and institutions. However, this is a complex and interactive process that is takes place within the national system of production and affects the competitiveness of market and economy. In literature, there are usually two different approaches analysing the international competitiveness of small countries.

Figure 4.7 shows a simple model of national systems of innovations. More specifically, we can see information, communication, legal structures and cognitive frameworks influence all activities in this above diagram. The first approach is mainly based on trade theory and the "relevant advantages" for small countries. The second approach is based on the long-term accumulation of innovative and technological capabilities and in the technological specialisation for small countries. There are a lot of reasons suggesting that a "free-enterprise market system" without government intervention (particularly for small size countries) is likely to support insufficient scientific effort and sometimes this does not allocate to an efficient pattern. We can summarise some of these reasons:

- Companies (especially SMEs) are usually unable to allocate the appropriate and adequate share of total gains in such efforts.
- Risk and uncertainties associated with such efforts that cannot be undertaken fully by private agents.
- Social problems imply the transfer of scientific and technological activities.
- Imperfections in capital markets that is in the provision of funds for scientific efforts and technological changes.
- Avoidance of wasteful duplication of scientific services.
- Consideration of national security.

- Development of large scale-economies and the importance of the markets. These reasons advocate that the government technological intervention is of importance for the development of research and scientific activities.

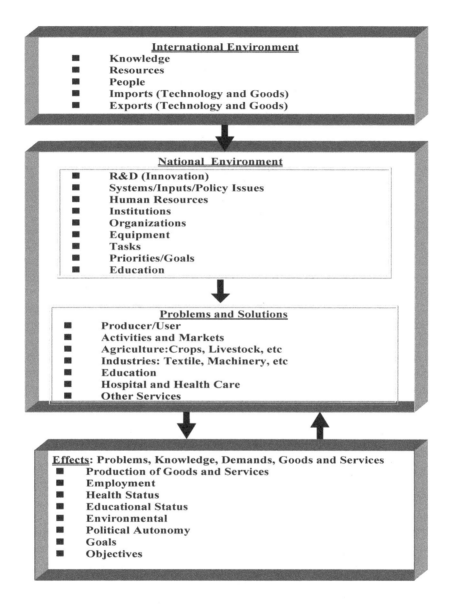

Figure 4.7 A simple model of national systems of innovation
Source: Korres, G., 2008.

On the other hand, it is usually true that small and weak technological countries have fewer resources than larger countries, thus the former being allocated to less resources for research and technological activities than the latter. Due to these reasons, small size countries are usually forced either to allocate their resources more thinly to different areas and related activities, or to select "certain areas" for research and technological priorities.

On the other hand, advanced technological countries usually invest in the development of new technologies in "associated strategic industries" that aim to increase competitiveness, economic growth and living standards. However, in practice, different countries choose different priorities for technological and economic subjects and put emphasis to these areas in which they believe they will have more potential in future. Advanced technological countries make their plans with more long-term scientific intensive criteria and usually the priorities they choose are based on the most expensive and high technology areas, while sometimes they carry out research in collaboration with other countries.

On the contrary, small countries are forced to choose those sectors that they can easily develop and compete and, furthermore, try to strengthen the technological basis in international competitive scene. The existence of specialised research and technological institutions, the amounts allocated for research and technological activities and the availability of resources in the large countries, give an additional advantage and imply that large countries usually lead in trends and fashions for different research and technological topics.

Therefore, small countries tend to follow the "direction" set by the leading large countries, and sometimes they are forced to follow even if the relevant research and technological topics are not the most appropriate and necessary to cover their specific needs. Thus, it is necessary for small countries to identify specific priorities that can exploit the particular advantages (such as natural and human resources and the increase of their research expenditures). An important thing for weak technological countries is to establish and to improve their technological infrastructure.

There are a lot of proposals and strategies that can be followed and developed from the small size and weak technologically countries. Among them, it is suggested that they should develop some "new high technology areas" that may not have been developed and expertised, but the perspective potential economic benefits may be greater so that they can develop a comparable advantage in the future.

It is also suggested that small countries should release relevant strategies to "specialisation" in some certain points for research and technological activities, in order to make an appropriate use of available resources. Alternatively, it is suggested that it might be more appropriate for small countries to abandon the idea of competing with large and more advanced technological countries; they should rather on the improvement of their technological infrastructure in order to enforce and concentrate compete mostly in medium technological sectors.

Most scenarios on national science and technological policies have been concentrated in the supply side of the science and technological system. Therefore, governments have to examine benefits and cost from technological policy and related activities. Usually, one of the main objectives of technology policy is to increase and enhance the use of new technologies. These technologies can be derived either from abroad or from domestic innovators and can be used by domestically-owned or, foreign firms. Although different countries can choose to develop the same kind of technologies, policies that usually follow can differ considerably.

Technological policies are based on the role of government's intervention and are relevant chosen priorities (such as financial support). Divergences of national policies emerge from differences among national systems and varying views in relation to the role of the government. According to different governments' policies, some countries give unfair advantage to their companies in the international competition, thus affecting the development of research activities and the technologies. The way in which priorities are combined and formulated in practice can vary according to the level of priority. For instance, a number of priorities that are not scientific and technological in a "strict sense" may have a considerable impact on the science and technology.

Technology policy implemented through technology research centres, which are often located at major research universities assist with the development of new firms and enhance the competitiveness of existing firms through increased productivity and research. These technological research centres have two main objectives: first, they are designed to attract industry research activity, primarily by attracting industry R&D labs and encouraging the expansion of existing facilities, while a second objective is to retain the benefits for the local economy. However, even if the innovation is produced locally, it is not clear that the benefits of such industry research are localised. In setting different priorities, we should take into account different conditions of each country and each regions different elements and objectives of other sectors. We should try to establish some close linkages among different priorities and the policy's objectives from other sectors.

The participation of member states in the Communities research and technological programmes can arise the opportunities for promotion and improvement of research activities and generate new research institutions in order to support the innovation and diffusion of new technologies. The EU's research and technological policy should be oriented to promote the economic and social development of the country. Particularly, the main objectives should be focused on:

- How to improve human scientific potential and how to utilise human resources;
- How incorporate in and "adjust" new and advanced technologies to local market;
- How to upgrade technical infrastructure;

- How to improve the quality of existing products and how to design the production of different and new goods;
- How to increase the level of competitiveness for the local technological products both in agricultural and industrial sectors;
- How to get an advantage from the introduction of new technologies in order to affect positively the economic and social growth. In weak technologically member states, the majority of R&D activities are initiated by the public sector and only a small part by the private sector.

4. Knowledge-based Economy and Innovation Policy

The increasing recognition by policy makers and academics of the importance of "knowledge-based economy" for future output and employment growth has yet to be reflected in any policy action. Of course, these positive employment outcomes achieved with a "painstaking" process of structural adjustment. The evidence suggests that during the 1980s all OECD countries appear to be have been confronted with a reduction and, in some cases, even with a collapse in the demand for unskilled labour, partly as a result of technical change, partly as a result of their opening up to international trade. However, different countries appear to have responded to that challenge in different ways. In the US labour market adjustment led to a substantial decline in real wages for the least-educated and least-skilled workers. Instead, in Europe, it led to much higher levels of unemployment in the unskilled labour force. In other countries, such as Canada, most of the adjustment occurred through adjustments to labour time. Whether this decline in the demand for unskilled labour can be associated with technical change and ICT in particular remains to be proved.

On the one hand, the move towards an information society is likely to lead to substantial changes in the demand for various sorts of educational and skill requirements. On the other hand, it is highly likely that large parts of the unskilled labour force will be excluded. Income distribution and inequality issues are more than ever part of the technology employment debate: efficiency gains are closely linked to access to information networks and to distribution of competence among agents. In developed countries, there is a fear that new technologies might undermine the social welfare fabric of some societies whereas, in developing countries, there is a fear that they will remain or become excluded from new opportunities. Information has rather peculiar "commodity" characteristics, while knowledge is a much broader concept, including "codified information", tacit knowledge crucially dependent on what can be best described as "accumulated knowledge", in which learning through experience is nevertheless the major critical variable. Information infrastructures provide the foundations for the exchange of goods and services in the markets of the future and generate "electronic commercial" opportunities that will affect all business practices.

The move into a creative Knowledge-based Economy (KBE) has implications for innovation policy and a number of other policy areas. It is necessary to study these implications and associated developments in order to reach the Lisbon objectives and to be prepared for innovative economic activities beyond 2010. It is important to examine the extent to which relevant policy areas have already been utilised to advance innovation policy in Europe, and how they might become more useful in this respect.

The KBE is thus at the fore of the strategy. It is both an interpretation of current socio-economic trends, an empirical hypothesis; and a vision of what Europe could become, a policy objective. Innovation is positioned as a central characteristic of a KBE that is successful in terms of being socially and environmentally sustainable.

Innovation is now recognised as a major source of competitiveness of firms and innovation systems. It's also clear that environmental problems can often best be tackled by changing the way we produce and use things, and thus innovations (of particular sorts) are required. Innovation policy has accordingly grown in significance.

It is recognised as highly relevant to economic performance and sustainability and thus has been gaining more support and attention. This does not mean that innovation policy is immune from pressures for regulatory reform, shared with other policy areas. Innovation policy also needs to draw on evidence, be evaluated to be based on the best available knowledge and to become a learning process.

Furthermore, innovation is a phenomenon that is relevant to a wide range of policies. For example, policies areas – such as education, environment, and Intellectual Property – have implications for innovation. Still policies whose fundamental concern is not innovation have effects on innovation processes. These interrelations are often poorly understood, and this may have resulted in policy designs that are sub-optimal. They need to be examined more carefully and pro-actively. Interactions between regulatory reform in all policy areas, the changing nature of innovation processes and the changing content of innovation policies need to be continually explored. In other words, it proceeds from an analysis of key features of the knowledge-based economy, and the established relations between innovation policy, innovations, and various other policy areas. On this basis it identifies emerging problems and some possible avenues solutions.

In order to specify the characteristics of a learning economy it is useful to draw a distinction between the role of knowledge (as a kind of stock) and the role of learning (as a kind of flow) in economy. The idea of knowledge and learning as central and crucial aspects of economy and economic process may be pictured, as in Figure 4.8.

All production is a process in which materials are transformed from one set of physical forms to another. The transformation of materials requires energy and is controlled by knowledge. Materials, energy and knowledge can be viewed as the basic ingredients of all production processes. In the short run production is controlled by a given stock of knowledge. In the long run the stock of knowledge is changed by various kinds of learning.

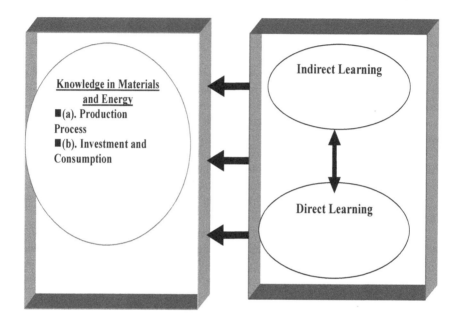

Figure 4.8 Knowledge and learning economy
Source: Korres, G., 2007.

In Figure 4.8 a distinction between learning as a deliberately organised process has been considered, for instance, some parts of the economy, for example universities, research institutes, and R&D departments are organised with the creation and utilisation of new knowledge in mind. But there is also learning going on in relation to "ordinary" economic activities.

A lot of learning may be described as more or less unintended by-products of the normal economic activities of procurement, production and marketing. These types of learning are referred to as direct learning and indirect learning, respectively. This distinction is made because heavy investments in direct learning as well as development of new ways to utilise indirect learning are characteristics of learning economy.

The distinction is also useful because there are complementarities between these two types of learning. These complementarities may take the form of virtues circles. Learning by using a new type of machine tool may produce important information for the R&D department in the machine-tool producing firm. Improvements made on the basis of this information may lead to increased diffusion of improved machinery, which again stimulates learning by using, etc.

In Figure 4.9 the role of learning and knowledge in economy is pictured in a very abstract and foot-lose way. Clearly some structures and actors are missing. In addition to being interactive, we regard learning to be partially cumulative. What one learns depends on what one has already known and therefore the production structure of economy affects its learning processes. The production structure of an economy consists not only of a tangible structure of buildings, equipment, etc., but also of a connected intangible structure of knowledge accumulated through production experiences.

Interactive learning, both direct and indirect, increases the stock of knowledge. As discussed above, this stock is diminished by different kinds of forgetting. Nevertheless, creative forgetting may create a feedback mechanism to learning and new knowledge. Entrepreneurs of different kinds use new knowledge to form innovative ideas and projects and some of these find their way into economy in the form of process and product innovations.

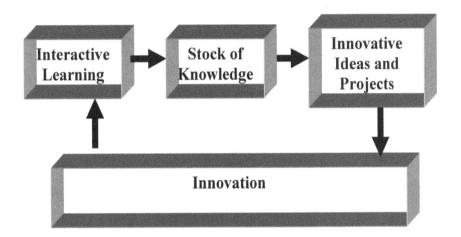

Figure 4.9 Learning and innovation
Source: Korres, G., 2007.

This means that there is a distinction to be made between production of knowledge and utilisation of knowledge. There is always a lot of knowledge around which is not put to use in economy. The ability to utilise existing knowledge is a crucial aspect of the learning economy which affects its dynamic efficiency, for example the generation of growth and employment.

The whole process is very uncertain and only a small part of the new knowledge leads to innovative ideas and projects and only some of these are actually turned into innovations. These uncertainties in the process from learning to innovation are illustrated in Figure 4.10 by the insertion of selection mechanisms at different places.

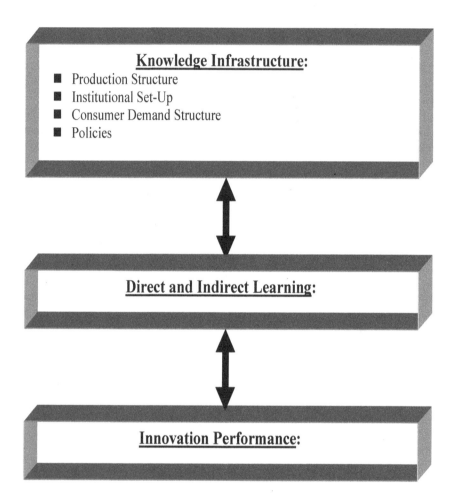

**Figure 4.10 Main factors affecting learning and innovation in a national
               system of innovation**
Source: Korres, G., 2007.

Here we would like to emphasise the distinction between variation and uncertainty. Uncertainty is often taken to be inherent to economical system we are analysing, but from another point of view, our limited knowledge itself is the sole source of uncertainty. What are uncertain are the predictions we would like to consider, and not the responses themselves – that might be with an error, which is tried to be estimated and reduced.

Moreover, the model or process under consideration should be carefully viewed. Furthermore, learning in innovation process continuously generates experiences and insights of different kinds which give feedback to it again. This process increases knowledge, thus reducing uncertainty.

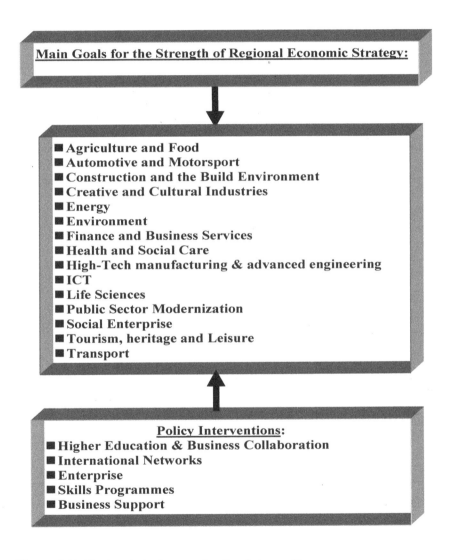

Figure 4.11 Regional strategy and policy interventions
Source: Korres, G., 2007.

Figure 4.11 illustrates the flows of regional strategy and policy interventions. *"Knowledge infrastructure"* and *"production structure"* have been mentioned above. They are distinctively different from country to country and are fairly stable over time. *Institutions* play a central role in innovation systems. As argued above, institutions form interactive learning processes in economy and fulfil several important roles in relation to innovation activities. As Freeman points out, technological trajectories are not, as sometimes believed, "natural" they are rather the results of human decisions and institutions, therefore the existence of technological trajectories, innovation avenues, technological guideposts can be documented.

5. Leading Indicators and Methodology for Measurement of Knowledge-based Economy

Knowledge has risen to the fore in social and economic analysis, in policy thought and management philosophy in recent years. This is in part a product of the trends to a knowledge-based economy. Furthermore, some practices arising from this growing awareness of the role of knowledge reinforce these trends. All human societies have, of course, relied upon knowledge and information. There are three trends underpinning contemporary knowledge-based economy (KBE), and, when combined, are used for this terminology:

- The rise of "service economy" and intangible investments;
- The emergence of new Information and Communications Technologies (ICTs) and Information Society (IS);
- New requirements for and approaches to knowledge in "learning organisations".

The Lisbon conclusions called for production of indicators (and reports) to be used to assess EU progress towards the Lisbon Summit's strategic goal that Europe should become "the most competitive and dynamic knowledge-based economy in the world" by the end of the decade. Accordingly, the Commission presented a Communication on structural indicators in September 2000 (this was adopted by the Nice Council in December 2000). This first set of indicators covered four policy domains. In December 2001 and in a synthesis report presented to the European Council in Barcelona in March 2002, a revised list of 63 indicators was adopted, covering five domains:

- employment;
- innovation and research;
- economic reform;
- social cohesion;
- environment.

KBE is also a service economy, where four elements are especially relevant:

- The bulk of economic activity, employment, and output takes place in service sectors of the economy. This is the case across industrialised countries in general, and reflects the growth of marketed services as well as public services.
- Service-type work is prevalent in all sectors. White-collar work (and higher-skilled work in general) has grown as a share of employment compared to blue-collar (and low-skilled) work within practically all sectors.
- The notion of service also extends to all sectors as an important management principle. This means that firms are oriented towards the provision of services (whether their products are raw materials, goods or intangible products) and focus increasingly on what their users are achieving. Their commercial strategies are oriented towards achieving markets and customer loyalty by responding to user requirements, which means understanding of these requirements, for instance, knowledge.
- Finally, specialised services provide critical inputs to organisations in all sectors on a vastly increased scale. One major source of growth of service sectors has been the expansion of business services. This has been reflected in part in the outsourcing of functions from "leaner" organisations, and in part in business needs to access and use new knowledge (or at least knowledge that is new to them). Some Knowledge-Intensive Business Services (KIBS) play important role in facilitating technology choice, diffusion and implementation; others support organisational innovation and adaptation to changing market and regulatory circumstances.

This Section provides an overview of progress towards this important target using two "composite indicators". In the past years, indicators relating to the high-tech and medium high-tech industries (HT/MHT industries) and knowledge intensive services (KIS) have formed part of the set of benchmarking indicators. A country's performance in knowledge-based economy is not measured simply by outputs of science and technology but must also be evaluated by increasing its competitiveness. Indeed, these different aspects of performance are interrelated.

A competitive economy is increasingly understood as an economy able to achieve sustained rises in living standards of living for its population at low levels of unemployment (European Commission 2001b). The key determinant of competitiveness is labour productivity. Gains in labour productivity are the result of increasing human capital, capital deepening and technical progress or innovation as measured by total factor productivity. The degree of innovativeness is determined not only by firms' own R&D activities leading to new products or processes and by spill-over effects that magnify the benefits of R&D efforts, but also by diffusion effects associated with imported technology and the presence of multinational firms (European Commission 2001b).

While the indicators to measure performance achieved by countries in moving towards a more knowledge-based economy are all quantitative, they are proxies for a qualitative change towards the set goal. Scientific publications are a proxy for the knowledge produced predominantly in academia, while patents inform about technological achievements. The degree of innovativeness is reflected in the importance of value added and employment in medium and high-tech industries and knowledge-intensive industries, in the technology balance of payments and in high-tech exports.

Speeding up the transition to Knowledge-based Economy has been an important objective of all European policies during the last years. These indicators attempt to capture the complex, multidimensional nature of the knowledge-based economy by aggregating a number of key variables, and expressing the result in the form of an overall index. The two composite indicators used here refer to the overall investment and performance in the transition to the knowledge-based economy. They focus on the "knowledge dimension" of that transition and, therefore, do not take into account the other dimensions (for instance, employment, sustainable development, etc.) of the Lisbon Agenda.

Table 4.6 Component indicators for the composite indicator of investment in knowledge-based economy

Sub-indicators	Type of knowledge indicator
Total R&D expenditure per capita	Knowledge creation
Number of researchers per capita	Knowledge generation
New S&T PhDs per capita	Knowledge creation
Total Education Spending per capita	Knowledge creation and diffusion
Life-long learning	Knowledge diffusion: human capital
E-government	Knowledge diffusion: information infrastructure
Gross fixed capital formation (excluding construction)	Knowledge diffusion: new embedded technology

Source: European Commission 2003.

In order to advance effectively towards a knowledge-based economy, countries need to invest in both generation and diffusion of new knowledge. The composite indicator of investment in knowledge-based economy addresses these two crucial dimensions of investment. It includes key indicators relating to R&D effort, investment in highly-skilled human capital (researchers and PhDs), the capacity and quality of education systems (education spending and life-long learning), purchase of new capital equipment that may contain new technology, and the modernisation of public services (e-government). Table 4.6 shows the sub-indicators of this composite indicator.

Investing more in knowledge is, however, only half the story. Investment also needs to be allocated in the most effective way in order to increase productivity, competitiveness and economic growth. For this to happen, and to be sustainable, investment in knowledge thus has to induce a higher performance in research and innovation and increase labour productivity, an effective use of the information infrastructure and a successful implementation of the education system. However, this relationship between investment and performance is very complex. It depends in part on favourable framework conditions and policies. Moreover, there is always a time-lag between investment and a recorded increase in performance.

The second composite indicator presented here regroups the four most important elements of the performance in the transition to knowledge-based economy: overall labour productivity, scientific and technological performance, usage of information infrastructure and effectiveness of the education system. Table 4.7 illustrates some indicators for the performance in knowledge-based economy.

Table 4.7 Component indicators for the composite indicator of performance in knowledge-based economy

Sub-indicators	Type of knowledge indicator
GDP per hours worked European and US	Productivity S&T performance S&T performance
Patents per capita Scientific publications per capita E-commerce Schooling success rate	Output of the information infrastructure Effectiveness of the education system

Source: European Commission 2003.

Basic research plays an important role in the R&D system. It generates new knowledge and understanding that provide the foundation for applied research and development. Because basic research provides reliable information about areas of future applications, more intense knowledge generation through basic research could be seen as a way to enhance innovation activities.

Generally, basic research has been under mounting pressure during the past decade or so. Due to short-term needs and economic priorities, there has been a tendency towards increasing the share of applied research and development in total R&D expenditure. However, the situation is blurring with some countries making more resources available for basic research and others less. In many countries, basic research still has a high status in the agenda of science, technology and innovation policies. There are good reasons for that. For instance, the emerging science-based areas of biotechnology and nanotechnology are promising areas for future applications and commercial activities.

Human resources are the most vital elements of R&D and of all other activities related to S&T (European Commission 2003a). If the R&D expenditure target of 3% of GDP is achieved, human resources for research will have to be available.

Education, especially at universities, is seen as a crucial factor in Europe's transition to a knowledge-based economy (European Commission 2003b). Ideally, researchers are recruited from a pool of university graduates in the fields of science and engineering. The effort and performance of the supply side of human resources in S&T are reflected in the number of new university graduates and PhDs. Additional information is provided by the numbers of female university graduates, enrolment of foreign students, expenditure on higher education, secondary educational attainment and lifelong learning.

Scientific publications are increasingly used as a measure of scientific performance. Especially at the policy level, S&T related decisions are more and more based on recent scientific performances. Scientific indicators are not perfect, but the measurement of publications, citations or scientific impact has occupied a growing number of specialists who have developed sophisticated indicators.

Patents allow inventors to protect and exploit their inventions over a given time period, and provide a valuable measure of the inventiveness of countries, regions and enterprises. Moreover, since they disclose information about new inventions, patents also play a role in the diffusion of knowledge. Patent indicators not only help shed light on patterns of technological change but also measure activities that are closely associated with competitiveness in many important international markets. Smaller Member States show the strongest growth, but patenting by acceding countries remains low.

The EU continues to be less present in the US Patent and Trademark Office (USPTO) than the US is in the European Patent Office (EPO). While around 47% of EPO patent applications come from EU-15 countries, compared with 28% and 17% from the US and Japan respectively, the EU-15 share of USPTO patents was only 16% (with the US at 52% and Japan at 21%). Since 1995, Portugal and Ireland have shown strong growth in their patent shares at both EPO and USPTO, but Austria, France, Italy and the UK have all seen their shares of patents fall in both systems over the same period. Nevertheless, there are signs that the number of patents from the Czech Republic, Hungary, Slovakia and Slovenia are increasing.

The share of so-called "knowledge workers" in a country's total employment and its ability to produce high-tech products and sell them in international markets thus constitute important indications of international economic success. The relationship between high-tech, knowledge intensive activities and compet-itiveness is in no way straightforward and should not be interpreted in a mechanistic way. However, it is clear that increasing the qualification level of the labour force, while at the same time creating and applying new knowledge, represents a requirement for future sustained growth in Europe, and for its ability to compete internationally and to keep unemployment down.

Exports of high-tech products reflect a country's ability to commercialise the results of research and technological innovation in international markets. The value added of high-tech and medium high-tech manufacturing as a percentage of total value added gives an indication of the overall importance of high-tech sectors in the economy. It would be expected that, with a gradual shift to knowledge-based economy, the value added of those industries with a higher component of R&D should grow at the cost of other, more traditional industries.

There is statistical evidence from EUROSTAT to assess the intensity of geographical variation in knowledge economy, economic activity, using the OECD guidelines for defining "knowledge economy" industries, shows alarming concentration in or near primate cities throughout the EU of such activities as "knowledge intensive services" including research, software, media, financial, medical, educational and administrative services, and "high tech manufacturing".

By the late 1990s, there was growing evidence that knowledge-based industries were outpacing general growth by up to 50%; OECD countries were spending an increasing share of resources on knowledge production (at 8% of GDP, equivalent to expenditure on physical investment); over 60% of the OECD population aged 25-64 has completed upper secondary schooling; OECD economies invested 7% of GDP on ICT; and R&D expenditure was expanding (US$500 billion by 1997, of which over 60% was spent by business).

Further evidence on major increases in patenting, human capital, and intangibles in asset valuations of firms were consistent with the picture of something of a sea change in the nature of economy. Moreover, the concept was scarcely new as the earliest work to operationalise a notion of "knowledge economy" arose from pioneering work conducted by Atkinson (1998). He sought to identify the sectors in which a heavy concentration of knowledge assets lay and map the production and distribution of knowledge sectors in the United States economy. Atkinson classified knowledge production into six major sectors: education, R&D, artistic creation, communications media, information services, and information technologies. He showed these to account for the largest sectoral share of GDP and employment in the economy, and predicted it was destined to grow absolutely and relatively over time. For Atkinson, knowledge economy is a set of sectors which intensely concentrate knowledge assets in both human and fixed capital. Hence, reducing knowledge economy disparities is a fundamental task in reducing regional disparities in prosperity for less-favoured regions. Moreover, it is no longer adequate to speak of "regional learning" from advanced knowledge centres that may already have assessed and utilised (or dismissed) such knowledge, and where the potential user in the less-favoured region lacks the infrastructure or absorptive capacity to make effective use the knowledge in question.

Table 4.8 Knowledge economies index numbers in the European Union (2000)

High	Index	Low	Index
Stockholm (S)	169.5	South Aigaio (GR)	36.7
London (UK)	166.6	Sterea Ellada (GR)	38.4
West Sweden (S)	155.2	Peloponnisos (GR)	43.9
Surrey and Sussex (UK)	153.6	East-Makedonia, Thraki (GR)	6.4
Brabant Wallonie (B)	152.4	Norte (P)	50.2
Piemonte (I)	150.7	West Greece (GR)	50.9
East Mid-Sweden (S)	150.0	Kriti (GR)	50.9
Berkshire-Oxford (UK)	149.0	Centro (P)	51.1
Berkshire-Hertford (UK)	148.9	West Makedonia (GR)	1.6
Uusima-Helsinki (FI)	148.6	Alentejo (P)	53.6
Cuter Norrland (S)	148.4	Ionia Islands (GR)	3.9
South Sweden (S)	148.1	Algrave (P)	54.7
Mid Norralnd (S)	147.6	Thessalia (GR)	5.2
Brussels (B)	145.0	Ipeiros (GR)	59.6
Paris (FR)	144.9	Castilla la Mancha (ES)	0.6
North – Mid Sweden (S)	143.9	North Aigaio (GR)	2.3
Hampshire (UK)	141.6	Central Makedonia (GR)	2.7
Stuttgart (G)	141.1	Murcia (ES)	64.1
West Midlands (UK)	140.1	Estremadura (ES)	64.9
EU	100.0	Belearics (ES)	5.3

Source: European Union.

Table 4.9 Academic entrepreneurship activities: Percentages of respondents active in a representative selection of universities for each member state

Academic entrepreneurship activities (percent active)	Sweden	Finland	Spain	Portugal	Ireland	UK
Contract research	45	50	70	43	69	57
Consulting	51	44	61	54	66	53
Scientific projects	44	42	62	42	66	46
External training	40	37	67	37	73	36
Testing trialling	15	25	22	25	40	30
Patenting licensing	12	20	7	20	26	16
Spinout firms	12	11	7	11	19	10
Research marketing	6	6	5	6	6	6

Source: European Union Technology Transfer and Spinoff Project.

In Table 4.8 some indicative data is provided showing the breakdown between typical university systems in six EU countries. The data are from a survey of representative universities in each country including traditional, technical and new or specialist universities. The results show most academic entrepreneurship activity devoted to varieties of industrial or national science council research, consultancy and external training. Table 4.9 illustrates the academic entrepreneurship activities for various member states.

The increased importance of knowledge means that the net stock of intangible capital (for instance, education and research and development) has grown faster than tangible capital (for instance, buildings, transportation, roads, and machinery). State-financed intangible capital has increased from 60% of the value of federally-financed physical capital in 1970 to 93% today. This trend is equally true in business. In the 1960s and 1970s about 25% of the difference in average stock price earnings could be attributed to change in reported earnings. By the early 1990s, this had dropped to less than 10%. Part of this change is attributable to the fact that the worth of companies is increasingly related to intangible assets (R&D, brands, employee talent and knowledge) that traditional accounting fails to measure.

In new economy, intangible capital has become at least as important as tangible capital, and a greater share of the value of tangible capital is based on intangible inputs. As we have become richer, we have increasingly consumed services and goods with higher value-added content. This trend is demonstrated by the fact that the economic output of the US economy, as measured in tons, is roughly the same as it was a century ago, yet its real economic value is 20 times greater. In other words, we have added intangible attributes to goods and services, the most important being knowledge. One example is anti-lock brakes, which are the product of a generation of research and development, and are loaded with electronics. They don't weigh any more than conventional brakes, but they certainly provide a great deal more value to drivers. The Knowledge Innovation Assessment is an integrated design of ten diverse competencies essential in an innovation system:

Collaborative Process	Products/Services
Performance Measures	Strategic Alliances
Education/Development	Market Image/Interaction
Learning Network	Leadership/Leverage
Market Positioning	Computer/Communications

It is a lack of investment in human capital, not a lack of investment in physical capital that prevents poor countries from catching up with rich ones. Educational attainment and public spending on education are correlated positively to economic growth (Barro and Sala-i-Martin 1995; Benhabib and Spiegel 1994).

School quality measured, for example, by teacher pay, student-teacher ratio, and teacher education is positively correlated to future earnings of the students.

Education is important for explaining the growth of national income. Life-long learning is also crucial (Aghion et al. 1998).

People with human capital migrate from places where education is scarce to places where it is abundant (Lucas 1988). "Human capital flight" or "brain drain" can lead to a permanent reduction in income and growth of the country of emigration relative to the country of immigration. We need more technical graduates. R&D ability to innovate is a key competitive advantage

One of the most important determining factors in knowledge-intensive economy is the speed of science and technology innovation. The world places a high value on the ability to innovate quickly. News of innovation and research is communicated around the globe in a split of a second. But how do we measure the production of new ideas? One approach is to look at a country's expenditure on research and development (R&D).

6. Information Communication Technology (ICT) and Knowledge-based Economy

The share of ICT in total non-residential investment doubled and in some cases quadrupled between 1980 and 2000. In 2001, it was particularly high in the United States, the United Kingdom and Sweden. In many countries, the share of software in non-residential investment multiplied several times between 1980 and 2000. Available data for 2001 indicate that ICT's share in total investment declined from 2000 to 2001.

In OECD countries, access to telecommunications networks has increased in recent years by more than 10% a year, especially in countries with lower penetration rates, such as Poland, Mexico and Hungary. Wireless access has grown particularly fast. The internet also continues to diffuse rapidly. Germany had 84.7 Web sites per 1000 population in 2002, followed by Denmark (71.7) and Norway (66.4). Mexico, Turkey, Greece and Japan all had less than three Web sites per 1000 population.

Broadband has diffused most widely in South Korea, Canada, Sweden, Denmark, Belgium and the United States. In Denmark and Sweden, one out of five enterprises accesses the internet through a connection faster than 2Mbps. In Italy and Greece, relatively few firms have such a rapid internet connection. In Canada, Ireland, Spain and Sweden, however, more than 40% of enterprises still connect to the internet via dial-up. In Denmark, Germany, Sweden and Switzerland, some two-thirds of households had access to a home computer in 2002. In many other OECD countries, the share is less than 50%. Data on internet access by household size shows that internet access is more frequent in households with children than in households without.

At the end of 2001, there were 77.5 million internet subscribers to fixed networks in the United States, approximately 24 million in Japan, more than 23 million in South Korea, almost 15 million in Germany and 13.6 million in the UK. A ranking in terms of internet subscribers per capita places Iceland, South Korea, Denmark, Sweden and Switzerland on the top of the list. The number of secure servers per capita increased significantly between July 1998 and July 2002, which is a sign of the growing importance of security for internet applications. Iceland has the highest number of secure servers per capita, followed by the United States, Australia, Canada and New Zealand.

Men use the internet more than women in all countries for which data is available. More than eight out of ten people in Switzerland, Austria, the United States, Denmark and Sweden use the internet for electronic correspondence. It is also commonly used to find information about goods and services, particularly in Sweden, Denmark and Finland. In the United States, almost 40% of internet users buy on line, as do many users in Denmark, Sweden and Finland. In Portugal and Sweden, about half of all internet users play games on line and/or download games and music. In Sweden and Denmark, more than half of all internet users utilise e-banking.

In many countries almost all enterprises with ten or more employees use the internet. In Finland, Denmark, Canada, Sweden and Ireland, two-thirds or more of such enterprises have Web sites. The internet is less used by smaller than by larger enterprises, and differences among countries are more striking when small enterprises are compared. Internet penetration in enterprises with ten or more employees also varies considerably across sectors. In the financial sector, almost all firms use the internet. The retail sector seems to lag behind, particularly in countries with low overall internet use by enterprises.

Internet sales range between 0.3% and 3.8% of total sales. Electronic sales, such as, sales over any kind of computer-mediated network, reach 10% or more of sales in Austria, Sweden, Finland and Ireland. In the US retail sector, the share of electronic sales in total sales grew by 70% between the fourth quarter of 2000 and the fourth quarter of 2002. Large firms use the internet more frequently than small ones to sell goods and services. It is also more common to purchase than to sell over the internet. As many as two-thirds or more of enterprises with 250 or more employees in Australia, Canada, Denmark and Finland buy goods or services via the Internet.

The ICT sector grew strongly in OECD economies over the 1990s, particularly in Finland, Sweden and Norway. In Finland, the ICT sector's share of value added doubled over 1995-2001 and now represents over 16.4% of total business sector value added. In most OECD countries, ICT services have increased their relative share of the ICT sector, owing to the increasing importance of telecommunication services and software. In 2000, the ICT sector accounted for about 6.6% of total business employment in the 21 OECD countries for which estimates are available. Over 1995-2000, OECD area employment in the ICT sector grew by more than 3 million (for instance, an average annual growth rate of over 4.3% a year), more than three times that of overall business sector employment. ICT services were the main driver of employment growth.

Investment in physical capital is important for growth. It is a way to expand and renew the capital stock and enable new technologies to enter the production process. ICT has been the most dynamic component of investment in recent years. ICT's share in total non-residential investment doubled and in some cases even quadrupled between 1980 and 2000. In 2001, ICT's share was particularly high in the United States, the United Kingdom and Sweden. Software has been the fastest-growing component of ICT investment. In many countries, its share in non-residential investment multiplied several times between 1980 and 2000. Software's share in total investment is highest in Sweden, Denmark and the United States. By 2000, software accounted for almost three quarters of total ICT investment in Denmark and Sweden. Communications equipment was the major component of ICT investment in Austria, Portugal and Spain. IT equipment was the major component in Ireland. Figure 4.12 illustrates the ICTs as a as a percentage of non-residential gross fixed capital formation.

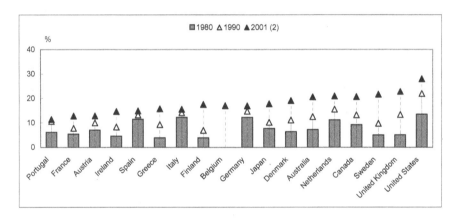

Figure 4.12 ICT investment 1980-2001, as a percentage of non-residential gross fixed capital formation, total economy
Source: Based on OECD Data.

Technology diffusion varies with business size and industry, so that indicators based on the overall "number" (proportion) of businesses using a technology can give rise to misleading international comparisons. "Share of businesses" is extremely sensitive to the size of enterprises, for instance, measured by number of employees, covered by national surveys. Moreover, international comparisons of ICT usage indicators are affected by differences in the sectoral coverage of surveys.

Table 4.10 Information and communication technologies: Concepts to data

(Primary agency)	Information needed	Current status, data gaps and measurement challenges
Electronic commerce	• Sales by product or service • Purchases by commodity or service • Electronic commerce demographics	• Recent surveys have begun to collect total e-commerce • E-commerce sales by broad product classes will be available for some sectors
Electronic business processes	• Online sales, customer service, etc. • Automated inventory control • Information Technology (IT) in production processes • Purchases of Electronic business services	• Manufacturing establishments will be surveyed on their use of several e-business processes • Determining the appropriate reporting unit and whom to contact for different e-business processes may be challenging
Electronic business infrastructure	 • Computer investment other IT • Investment stocks of IT equipment • Depreciation of IT equipment • Vintage of IT equipment • Software purchases • IT Research and Development (R&D) • Software R&D	• Some establishment and enterprise segment information available for computer and software investments • Recent enterprise segment level surveys break investment spending out by asset types including computers • No data available for stocks, vintage or depreciation • Quality-adjusted deflators not yet available for all components of IT investments

Source: Atrostic, B.K., Colecchia, A. and Pattinson, B., 2000.

Most countries use existing surveys, such as labour force, time use, household expenditure or general social surveys. Others rely on special surveys. Household surveys generally provide information on both the household and the individuals in household. Table 4.10 presents some concepts for data of ICT. Measuring the ICTs require to define it. The main definitions concerning the electronic economy consist of four key components: electronic business, electronic commerce, the infrastructure for electronic business, and the computer-mediated networks.

• *Electronic business* (*e-business*) is any process that a business organisation conducts over computer-mediated network channels. Business organisations include any for-profit, governmental, or nonprofit entity. Examples of these processes are on-line purchasing; online sales; vendor-managed inventory; production design and control; on-line logistics; customer support; employee training; and recruiting.

- *Electronic commerce* (*e-commerce*) is any transaction completed over a computer-mediated network that transfers ownership of, or rights to use, goods or services. Transactions occur within selected electronic business processes. Transactions are completed when the agreement between buyer and seller to transfer the ownership or rights to use goods or services occurs over computer-mediated networks. Only priced transactions will be measured.
- *E-business and ICTs infrastructure* are the economic infrastructure used to support electronic business processes and conduct electronic commerce transactions. It includes the capital (hardware, application software, human capital, and telecommunication networks) used in electronic business and commerce.
- *Computer-mediated networks* are electronically linked devices that communicate interactively over network channels. A variety of devices may be linked, including computers, internet-enabled cellular telephones, and telephones linked with interactive telephone systems. Such links generally involve minimal human intervention, although some businesses provide customers with on-line or internet telephony conversations with customer support representatives. Networks include internet, intranets, extranets, electronic data interchange (EDI) networks, and telecommunication networks.

Person-based data typically provide information about a number of individuals with access to a technology, those using the technology, the location at which they use it and the purpose of use. Many public-sector and private-sector organisations report on the number of "users", "people" or "households" on line.

National statistical agencies typically measure internet access on the basis of surveys of businesses, households or individuals. Some statistical offices also collect information about internet subscribers by surveying internet service providers (ISPs). These surveys are timely and provide a wide range of information, for example, about type of subscriber (business, household, government), type of technology used (dial-up, cable, etc.), and, sometimes, even the length of connection and volume of data downloaded.

An alternative approach is to compile information about internet subscribers from reports written by the largest telecommunication carriers. These provide information about the number of subscribers to their internet services and their estimates of market share.

As these carriers manage connectivity via public switched telecommunication networks, they often very well informed about subscriber numbers and associated market shares on an industry-wide basis. Moreover, the term "subscribers" has a more specific meaning than, for example, "users". For most carriers, "subscribers" implies registered Internet accounts that have been used during the previous three months. Figure 4.13 presents ICTs in both manufacturing and services sectors for selected countries.

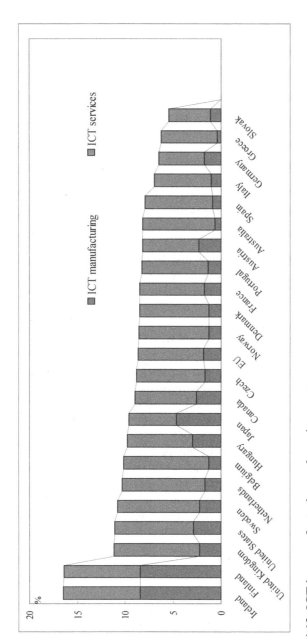

Figure 4.13 ICT in manufactoring and services sectors
Source: Based on OECD data.

Regarding data and tables of international trade in goods and services by detailed industrial activity which are compatible with the national accounts, ICT sector exports and imports at current prices have been estimated using the OECD's International Trade in Commodity Statistics (ITCS) database. Current price exports and imports for this sector have been derived from the product based data in the ITCs database by applying a standard Harmonized System Rev. 1 (HS1) to the ISIC Rev. 3 conversion key.

The trade indicators constructed here reflects trade in goods for which the ICT manufacturing sector can be considered the origin (exports) or the destination (imports) according to the UN standard conversion table. Finally, individual countries' data for both imports and exports include imported goods that are subsequently re-exported. Imports and subsequent re-exports may be in the same or in different reference periods. In the latter case, both the indicators of countries' relative trade performance and the indicators of their trade balances may be affected. The ICT sector trade balance is calculated as ICT exports minus ICT imports divided by total manufacturing trade (the average of exports and imports).

Large firms use the internet more frequently than small ones to sell goods and services. In Denmark, where e-commerce is widespread, one-fifth of enterprises with 10-49 employees sold over the internet as did more than one third of enterprises with 250 or more employees. It is more common to purchase than to sell over the internet.

As many as two-thirds or more of enterprises with 250 or more employees in Australia, Canada, Denmark, Sweden and Finland buy goods or services via the internet. Today, enterprises commonly use the internet, although there are still substantial differences between larger enterprises and the smallest, those with fewer than ten employees. For example, more than 95% of Swedish and Danish enterprises with ten or more employees now use the internet. The internet is used more frequently as a tool for ordering goods and services than for selling, particularly in countries where a large share of enterprises use the internet.

Use of the internet to sell goods or services varies among sectors. In many countries, the real estate and wholesale sectors make the most use of the internet as a sales channel. More than one-fifth of enterprises in the wholesale sector in Austria, Denmark, Finland and Japan use the internet for this purpose. Retail sales are less common, although one fifth of Canadian and Danish retail firms sell via the internet. Figure 4.14 illustrates ICTs trade by areas, as a share of total manufacturing trade.

On the other hand, statistics on ICT use by households may run into problems of international comparability because of structural differences in the composition of households (similarly, differences in countries' industrial structure affect comparability of statistics on business use of ICT). On the other hand, statistics on individuals may use different age groups, and age is an important determinant of ICT use. Household- and person-based measures yield different figures in terms of levels and growth rates.

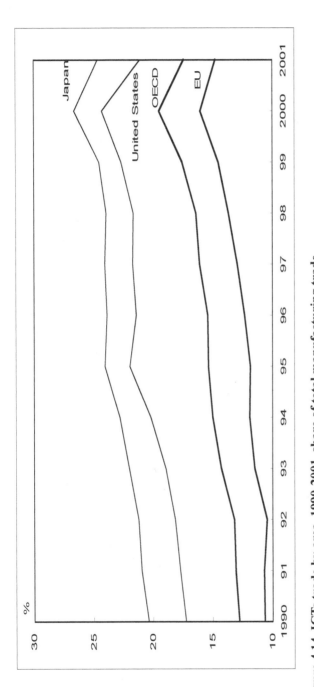

Figure 4.14 ICTs trade by area, 1990–2001, share of total manufacturing trade
Source: Based on OECD data.

Table 4.14 presents ICT and skills for both Europe and the United States Considering the data for ICT, we can summarise some of the main findings:

- Measuring the "*investment on ICTs*", we can say that the available data indicate that ICTs' share in total investment has declined from 2000 to 2001. However, while the share of IT hardware in total investment has declined everywhere, that of investment in software has grown in some countries. Only the USA produces estimates of expenditure on the three different software components (for instance, pre-packaged, own account and customised software); other countries usually provide estimates for some software components only. Data availability and measurement of ICT investment based on national accounts (SNA93) vary considerably across OECD countries, especially as measurement of investment in software, deflators applied, breakdown by institutional sector and temporal coverage. In national accounts, expenditure on ICT products is considered as investment only products can be physically isolated. For example, ICT embodied in equipment is not considered as investment but as intermediate consumption; this means that ICT investment may be underestimated and the order of magnitude of this underestimation may differ depending on how intermediate consumption and investment are treated in each country's accounts.
- *Measuring the skills of ICTs*, we can conclude that skills are difficult to measure, and proxies are often used to capture observable characteristics such as educational attainment, on the supply side, and occupations, on the demand side. The high-skilled occupations for ICTs in Europe and in the United States include the following categories:
- *Measuring of telecommunication networks*, in the past, showed that the penetration of standard access lines provided a reasonable indication of the extent to which basic telecommunications connections were available to users. Today, use of standard access lines would give a distorted view of network development, since in more than half of OECD countries, the number of standard access lines has begun to decrease as the take-up of ISDN (integrated services digital network) has increased. To appreciate overall telecommunication penetration rates across the OECD area, it is also increasingly necessary to take into account the development of mobile communication networks and "broadband" internet access. These two leading technologies currently used to provide high-speed internet access are cable modems and digital subscriber lines (DSL). Other broadband connections include satellite broadband internet access, fibre-to-home internet access, Ethernet LANs, and fixed wireless access (at downstream speeds greater than 256 kbps).
- In an attempt to a "*measure the size and the growth of the internet*", we can say that the available data on connection of enterprises to the internet cover all enterprises, except for those in the financial sector for some countries.

Small enterprises (those with fewer than ten employees) are also excluded. If they were included, the picture would probably be different. In addition, an enterprise may have various ways to connect to the internet. It should not therefore, be assumed that a certain percentage of enterprises use DSL exclusively, since they may also use other means such as a conventional dial-up connection.

Table 4.11 ICT and skills in Europe and in the United States

For Europe, high-skilled ICT-related occupations (ISCO-88) selected were:	For Europe, high-skilled ICT occupations include: computing professionals (213, including computer systems designers and analysts, computer programmers, computer engineers); computer associate professionals (312, including computer assistants, computer equipment operators, Industrial robot controllers); optical and electronic equipment operators (313, including photographers and image and sound recording equipment operators, broadcasting and telecommunications equipment operators).
For Europe, low-skilled ICT-related occupations (ISCO-88) selected were:	For Europe, low-skilled ICT occupations, the only class that could be selected was electrical and electronic equipment mechanics and fitters (ISCO-88, 724).
For the USA, data of high skilled ICT occupations include:	For the USA, high skilled ICT include: computer systems analysts and scientists (64); operations and systems researchers and analysts (65); computer programmers (229); tool programmers, numerical control (233); electrical and electronic technicians (213); broadcast equipment operators (228); computer operators (308); peripheral equipment operators (309).
For the USA, data from low skilled ICT occupations include:	For the USA, low-skilled ICT occupations include: data processing equipment repairers (525); electrical power installers and repairers (577); telephone line installers and repairers (527); telephone installers and repairers (529); electronic repairers, communications and industrial equipment (523).

Source: Based on OECD classification.

- Measuring the "*networks of telecommunications and internet infrastructure*". We can summarise some of the main findings:
- In 25 out of 30 OECD countries, inhabitants generally have access to more than one telecommunication network (fixed or wireless). Luxembourg, the Nordic countries, Switzerland and the Netherlands have the highest rates of network penetration. Telecommunications networks have grown rapidly in recent years, especially in countries with lower penetration rates, such

as Poland, Mexico and Hungary. Sweden, where penetration rates were already high, and Australia, Canada and the United States, are the only countries with average annual growth rates of under 10%.

- In 2001, most OECD countries had more than 50 fixed access channels for every 100 inhabitants. Luxembourg, Sweden, Switzerland and Denmark all had more than 70. In Mexico and Turkey penetration rates of fixed access channels are low.

- Luxembourg has the highest penetration rate for wireless networks, with close to one wireless subscriber per inhabitant. Italy, Austria, Iceland, Norway, Netherlands, Sweden and Finland also have high rates with more than 80 wireless subscribers per 100 inhabitants.

- Digital subscriber lines (DSL), cable modems and other broadband connections are an increasingly important indicator of broadband penetration, as they can carry telephony as well as large amounts of data. Broadband has diffused most widely in Korea, Canada, Sweden, Denmark, Belgium and the United States.

- The internet continues to grow rapidly. In July 2002, there were almost 36 million internet Web sites in the OECD area, almost double the 19 million in July 2000.

- Web sites per 1,000 population is an indicator of internet diffusion. In July 2002, the OECD average was 34.1 sites per 1,000 inhabitants; the EU average was 37.9. At 84.7 web sites per 1,000 inhabitants Germany had the highest number, followed by Denmark (71.7) and Norway (66.4). Mexico, Turkey, Greece and Japan all had fewer than three Web sites per 1,000 inhabitants.

- Web sites per 1,000 population grew fastest in Germany, almost doubling each year between 2000 and 2002. Denmark's annual growth rate was over 85%. Canada and the United States, which already had large numbers of Web sites in 2000, grew more slowly at approximately 20%. Business connections to the internet indicate a country's level of infrastructure development. In Denmark and Sweden, one out of five enterprises accesses the internet through a connection faster than 2Mbps. In Italy and Greece, relatively few enterprises have such a rapid internet connection.

- In many countries, and particularly in Denmark, Finland and Spain, many enterprises have digital subscriber lines (DSL). ISDN (integrated services digital network) accounts for over 30% of all connections and is the technique most commonly used to access the internet in countries for which information is available. In Austria and Luxembourg, more than half of all enterprises have an ISDN connection to the internet. The use of conventional dial-up connections is also widespread. In Canada, Ireland, Spain and Sweden, more than 40% of enterprises still connect to the internet via dial-up.

- As the number of internet subscribers increases so does its potential uses. Tracking the diffusion and use of the internet is therefore of interest, despite the few internationally harmonized measures. At the end of 2001, there were 77.5 million internet subscribers to fixed networks in the United States, approximately 24 million in Japan, more than 23 million in Korea, almost 15 million in Germany and 13.6 million in the United Kingdom.

- A ranking in terms of internet subscribers per capita places Iceland, Korea, Denmark, Sweden and Switzerland at the top of the list. Between 1999 and 2001, almost half of all OECD countries doubled the number of subscriptions per capita. Portugal, Austria and Iceland more than tripled the number.
- The number of secure servers per capita increased significantly between July 1998 and July 2002, a sign of the growing importance of secure servers for internet applications. Iceland has the highest number of secure servers per capita, followed by the United States, Australia, Canada and New Zealand.

Although the recent economic slowdown has resulted in an easing of tensions in the IT labour market, policy makers continue to need indicators relevant to the skills required for information economy. Data show that ICT-related occupations – both high-skilled and low-skilled – grew during the second half of the 1990s in the United States and Europe. In Europe, the differences between northern and southern Europe are significant. Correct measurement of ICT investment is quite important for estimating the contribution of ICT to economic growth and performance.

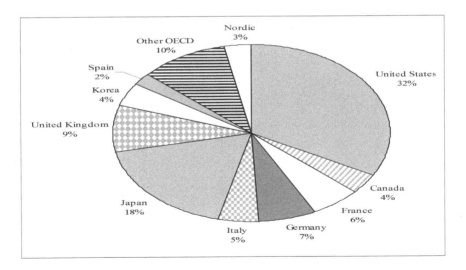

Figure 4.15 Employment in the ICT sector as a percentage share (2000)
Source: Based on OECD Data.

Figure 4.15 indicates the employment in ICTs as a percentage. Figure 4.16 illustrates the contribution of ICTs services to business sector in terms of employment growth, as an average annual growth rate.

According to an OECD's study, we can summarise the main effects o occupations and skills, as follows:

- In the mid-1990s, the share of ICT workers was around 2.7% of total occupations in both the USA and the EU. In 2001, it grow slightly faster in the USA than in the EU and reached 3.4% and 3.2%, respectively. The share of highly-skilled workers in the ICT workforce remained relatively stable between 1995 and 2001 in the USA at around 80%; it increased significantly in the EU from 48% to 63%.
- During the second half of the 1990s, highly-skilled ICT workers were the fastest-growing group of highly-skilled workers. In recent years, annual growth rates have been just under 20% in Spain and Finland. In 2001, their share in total occupations was highest in Sweden (3.8%) and the Netherlands (3.5%) and lowest in Greece (0.6%), Portugal (1.2%) and Italy (1.3%). The EU average was about 2%; the US average was 2.6%.
- Over the period 1995-2001, the number of computer workers increased substantially faster in northern than in southern Europe. In 2000, the 21 OECD countries for which estimates are available employed 16.1 million persons in the ICT sector, about 6.6% of total business employment. The United States and the EU (excluding Greece, Iceland, Ireland and Luxembourg) each represented 34% of the total; Japan employed 18% of the total.

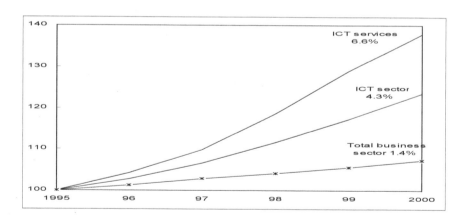

Figure 4.16 The contribution of ICT services to business sector in employment growth, as an average annual growth rate 1995-2000, index 1995 = 100

Source: Based on OECD data.

- The ICT sector has been a major source of employment growth. Over the period 1995-2000, OECD-area employment in the sector grew by more than 3 million, *for instance*, an average annual growth rate of over 4.3% a year, more than three times that of overall business sector employment. ICT services were clearly the driving force of growth, as ICT manufacturing has generally followed the decline of overall manufacturing employment, albeit to a lesser extent. Exceptions are Finland and Korea, where ICT manufacturing employment grew by over 9% a year, and Canada, the Czech Republic, the Nordic countries, Spain and the United Kingdom where it grew between 2% and 4%.
- Over 1995-2000, ICT services employment grew everywhere except in Austria. Annual growth rates in the United Kingdom (10.5%), the Netherlands (10.2%), Finland (9.8%), the United States (9.5%) and Spain (7.3%) were above the average of the 21 OECD countries for which data are available (6.6%). Employment in computer-related services, mainly software services, was the most dynamic component, growing by an average of over 11% a year in the OECD area and by over 19% in the United Kingdom.
- In 2000, ICT employment had a larger share in total business sector employment than the OECD average in Finland (10.8%), Sweden (9.2%), Canada (8.3%), the Netherlands (8%), Japan (about 8.2%), Belgium, France and the United Kingdom (about 7.3%), Hungary (7.1%) and Denmark and Norway (6.8%).
- Over 1995-2000, the contribution of ICT manufacturing to total manufacturing employment was stable in most OECD countries. It varied widely across the OECD area, ranging from 13.8% in Korea to 1.3% in Italy. The average share of ICT services employment in market services, instead, has grown over time to reach about 5.9% in the OECD area in 2000.

7. Knowledge-based Economy and the Firm

There is a difference between an organisation's ability to learn and its ability to apply learning efficiently and effectively. A good idea is a long way from a profitable product or service. Understanding the innovation process – and the concurrent role of individual and organisational learning – is fundamental to advise the strategic direction of a company. This chapter recognises the increasing importance of knowledge as both a driving force of innovation and a "product" – in its own right – to be sold or shared for competitive advantage.

The company's ability to manage knowledge must be at the heart of a strategy to create distinctive competencies, unique market positioning and sustained growth over time. The entrepreneur is considered one who not only has the capacity to invent, create and/or acquire new ideas, but can also command resources to put them in demonstrated good use. This type of behaviour needs to be encouraged throughout the organisation. Managers need to be in constant surveillance of good ideas and practices which might increase time-to-market and/or market differentiation.

Knowledge economy provides a climate of opportunities. This chapter expands current thinking and structures the dialogue for the profession. This is a very complex, timely topic. Our intent is to provide a simple framework for considering the issues and related managerial implications. There is a need for new approaches and new techniques – many of which are emerging. Although it is comprehensive in scope concerning concepts, language and world-wide thinking on the topic, it does not address specific implementation questions, such as:

- How does an organisation organise to create a knowledge strategy?
- How do organisations with limited resources participate?
- How do talent limitations impact ability to impact strategies?
- What incentives will increase the capacity for knowledge-sharing?
- How to raise current staffing ability to higher knowledge levels?
- How do organisations continue during periods of turmoil?
- What knowledge products or markets are emerging ?

Knowledge Innovation Assessment is a comprehensive dialogue tool designed to elicit the tacit knowledge resident in an organisation. It provides for a systematic analysis of the capacity and capability of organisations to create and move ideas into the marketplace profitably and expeditiously. It results in a strategy formulation document with a recommended course of action. Industrial revolution laid the foundation of the transformation of the economy from agriculture to industry; with it, not only did living standards rise, but also the location of life changed, from rural communities to metropolitan megalopolises.

Knowledge is different from other goods: it has many of the central properties of a public good, indeed of a global public good. While government has a key role in protecting all property rights, its role in intellectual property rights is far more complex; the appropriate definition of these rights is not even obvious. In knowledge economies, the dangers of monopolisation are perhaps even greater than in industrial economies. These are but three examples of the ways in which the role of government in a knowledge economy may differ markedly from that in the industrial economy with which we have become familiar over the past century. By now it should by clear that success in a knowledge economy requires a change in culture. However, knowledge, almost by definition, gives rise to a form of increasing returns to scale which may undermine competition.

Knowledge transfer also follows the trail of foreign direct investment. For instance, a major source of learning about production methods and their adaptation to American culture was Japanese direct investment in production facilities in the USA (so the knowledge flows across the Pacific have been two-way).

8. Managing Knowledge: Leaders and Laggards

What are the characteristics that distinguish organisations who are leaders in knowledge management and those who are less successful or even fail in their knowledge initiatives? In research for Creating the Knowledge-based Business, we find ten recurring characteristics that separated leaders from laggards. The report also illustrates these characteristics through case studies of 33 knowledge leaders. Ten Characteristics of Leaders are as follows:

1. They have a clearly articulated vision of what the knowledge agenda and knowledge management is about. Their thinking about their business, their business environment and their knowledge goals are clear.
2. They have enthusiastic knowledge champions who are supported by top management.
3. They have a holistic perspective that embraces strategic, technological and organisational perspectives.
4. They use systematic processes and frameworks (the power of visualisation).
5. They "bet on knowledge", even when the cost-benefits cannot easily be measured.
6. They use effective communications, using all tricks of marketing and promotion.
7. They interact effectively at all levels with their customers and external experts. Human networking takes place internally and externally on a broad front.
8. They are good team players demonstrate good teamwork, with team members drawn from many disciplines.
9. They have a culture of openness and inquisitiveness that stimulates innovation and learning.
10. They develop incentives, sanctions and personal development programmes to change behaviours.

Ten Characteristics of Laggards are as follows:

1. They simplify knowledge to information or database model, often applying the "knowledge" label without a comprehensive understanding of what knowledge is about.
2. They package and disseminate knowledge that is most readily available (vs. that which is the most useful).
3. They work in isolated pockets without strong senior management support. Thus, they may hand over responsibility for knowledge systems to one department, such as Management Information Systems, without engaging the whole organisation.

4. They focus on a narrow aspect of knowledge, such as knowledge sharing rather than all processes including new knowledge creation and innovation.
5. They blindly follow a change process.
6. They downsize or outsource without appreciating what vital knowledge might be lost.
7. They think that technology (alone) is the answer; for example, that expert systems by themselves are the way to organise and use knowledge.
8. They have a major cultural blockage, perhaps caused by a climate of "knowledge is power"
9. They "know all the answers", for instance, they are not open to new ideas.
10. They get impatient. They think knowledge management is simply another short-term project or programme. They do not allow time for new systems and behaviours to become embedded.

9. Knowledge Generation and Diffusion

Recognition of the interactive nature of innovation process has resulted in the breakdown of the earlier distinction between innovation and diffusion. The generation of knowledge and its assimilation are part of a single process. Firms need to absorb, create and exchange knowledge interdependently. In other words, innovation and diffusion usually emerge as a result of an interactive and collective process within a web of personal and institutional connections which evolve over time. Knowledge transfer may occur through disembodied or equipment-embodied diffusion. The latter is the process by which innovations spread in the economy through the purchase of technology-intensive machinery, such as computer-assisted equipment, components and other equipment. Disembodied technology diffusion refers to the process during which technology and knowledge spread through other channels not embodied in machinery (OECD 1992).

Knowledge spillovers, for instance, knowledge created by one firm can be used by another without compensation or with compensation less than the value of the knowledge, arise because knowledge and innovation are partially excludable and non-rivalrous goods (Romer 1990). Lack of exclusivity implies that knowledge producers have difficulty in fully appropriating the returns or benefits and thereby preventing other firms from utilising the knowledge without compensation (Teece 1986). Patents and other devices, such as lead times and secrecy, are a way for knowledge producers to partially capture the benefits related to their knowledge generation. It is important to recognise that even a completely codified piece of knowledge cannot be utilised at zero cost by everyone. Only those economic agents who know the code are able to do so (Saviotti 1998). By non-rivalry knowledge distinguishes itself from all other inputs in the production process. *Non-rivalry* means essentially that a new piece of knowledge can be utilised many times and in many different circumstances, for example by combining with knowledge coming from another domain. The interest of knowledge users is, thus, best served if innovations, once produced, are widely available and diffused at the lowest possible cost. This implies an environment rich in knowledge spillovers (OECD 1992).

A *system of innovation* can be thought of as consisting of a set of actors or entities such as firms, other organisations and institutions that interact in the generation, use and diffusion of new – and economically useful – knowledge in the production process. At the current stage of development, there is no general agreement as to which elements and relations are essential to the conceptual core of the framework and what is their precise content (Edquist 1997b).

A coherent system of innovation has necessarily to include a series of more or less coordinated network-like relations such as (Fischer 1999):

- *Customer-producer relations,* for instance,, forward linkages of manufacturing firms with distributors, value-added resellers and end users;
- *Producer-manufacturing supplier relations* which include subcontracting arrangements between a client and its manufacturing suppliers of intermediate production units;
- *Producer-service supplier relations* which include arrangements between a client and its producer service partners (especially computer and related service firms, technical consultants, business and management consultants);
- *Producer network relations* which include all co-production arrangements (bearing on some degree or another on technology) that enable competing producers to pool their production capacities, financial and human resources in order to broaden their product portfolios and geographic coverage;
- *Science-industry collaboration* between universities and industrial firms at various levels pursued to gain rapid access to new scientific and technological knowledge and to benefit from economies of scale in joint R&D, such as direct interactions between particular firms and particular faculty members, or joint research projects, as through consulting arrangements, or mechanisms that tie university or research programs to groups of firms.

10. Modelling the Diffusion Model in the New Growth Theory

The importance of diffusion of technology for economic growth has been emphasised by several authors. Specifically, the term *dissemination of technology* is used to include both voluntary and involuntary spread of technology. The term of *technology transfer* is defined as voluntary dissemination, while involuntary dissemination is labeled *imitation*. In literature on the diffusion process, there is considerable agreement on the time pattern of diffusion which may be expected to follow the first introduction of a new technique (or innovation).

The first important point is to distinguish between diffusion and adoption of technology. In the analysis of adoption one considers the decisions taken by agents to incorporate a new technology in their activities. A typical measure of adoption would be the proportion of eligible firms in an industry using a given technology.

By contrast, in the analysis of diffusion one is concerned with measuring the change of economic significance of a technology with the passage of time. In a sense, the analysis of diffusion is closely related to the analysis of *technological substitution* in which the displacement of one technology by another is the focus of attention. The spread of new technology occurs in a number of dimensions. The potential buyers of a technology can be public institutions, firms and households. The notion of technology diffusion must be taken today to include "the adoption by other users as well as more extensive use by the original innovator. More generally, it encompasses all those actions at the level of a firm or an organisation taken to exploit the economic benefits of the innovation" (OECD, 1989). Thus diffusion cannot be reduced in the introduction of new machinery to the factory floor or the office or the adoption by firms of new intermediate goods.

The formal model is based on Roomer specification (Romer 1990a, 1990b, and River Batiz-Rimer 1991). Let us consider a closed economy with three sectors:

- a final good sector;
- an intermediate good sector;
- the research sector.

In the first sector, final output is produced by means of physical labour (L), human capital (H) and physical capital (x). The physical capital is assumed to be the sum of an infinite number of distinct types of producer durables.

Final output can be represented by the following production function:

$$Y = g(H,L)\sum_{i=1}^{\infty} X_i \tag{a}$$

As in Romer specification, this production function is homogeneous of degree one, as g(H, L) is homogeneous of degree 1 and x of degree 0.

The research sector produces knowledge which is incorporated in designs. Each design is then sold to a single firm in the producer durables sector. Each firm in this sector produces a single capital good which is acquired by the final goods sector. The production function of the Research sector is given, as in Romer, by equation b:

$$\dot{A} = \delta H_\alpha A \tag{b}$$

where $\dot{A}$ is the number of designs produced at time t, being proportional to the existent stock of knowledge A. H_α is the amount of human capital employed in the research sector and δ is a positive parameter.

Treating it as a continuous variable, the sum on the right hand side of equation (a) can be substituted by an integral. At any time (t) a firm will use only the durables that have already been invented. The range of integration varies between 0 and A, where A is the number of capital goods invented and produced. As it will be clear later, it is assumed that A(t) is a linear function of time, this imply a constant number of invented capital goods at any time (t). Therefore, equation (a) becomes:

$$Y = g(H, L) \int_0^A x(i)^0 \, di$$

(c)

Integration by parts. Recall that:

$$\int_0^\infty f'(t)g(t)dt = f(t)g(t) - \int_0^\infty f(t)g'(t)dt$$

and $x = z$

The final output sector can be thought of in terms of a representative firm, whereas in the intermediate goods sector each capital good is produced by a single monopolistic firm. We can now consider the way in which the model behaves. To simplify and to link our discussion with the problem of diffusion, we can think of a demand and supply sector is described in terms of decisions taken by a single aggregate price taking firm. This firm represents, therefore, the demand side of the technology that is incorporated in capital good (i) produced by the supplying sector. The production function of the representative firm determines the demand size.

Therefore the only way to think of diffusion is to consider intra-firm diffusion. One can think of the representative firm as a repeating buyer of capital good (i) produced by the supplying sector. F(x) is now defined as the increase in revenues of the representative firm, determined by the additional purchase of capital good (i) in time t. Recall that the representative firm is a repeating buyer. It continues to buy until x(i)=x*; for instance, the capital stock is at its post diffusion or equilibrium level. Moreover, assume that the increase in revenue is perpetual; this implies a present value gain of f(x)/r. The cost of acquisition of capital good (i) in time t is p(t). We can now more formally represent the problem facing the representative firm. It will buy a certain level of capital good (I) in time t if two conditions hold:

$$f(x) \geq rp(t)$$

$$- \hat{p}(t) + rp(t) - f(x) \leq 0$$

Condition (1) is a simple profitability. For profit maximisation it will hold with equality. Condition (2), states that the representative firm will acquire in time t if it is not profitable to wait until time $t + dt$.

We assume that the buyer is taking into account the expectation about the future price of capital good (i). P represents buyer's expectation of the change in price, equivalent to the discrete time form:

We can now define different expectations regimes. We specify two models:

- Myopic expectations. Under this assumption $p_t = p_{t+1}^e$ or, in continuous time, $\hat{p}(t) = 0$. In other words, the price $p(t)$ is expected to hold forever. In this case condition 2 collapses into 1,

- Perfect foresight. Under this assumption $\hat{p}(t) = p(t)$ (for instance, $p_t = p_{t+1}^e$ Furthermore, if condition (2) holds as an equality condition (1) holds as well (but not vice versa). Following Ireland-Stoneman (1986), we can therefore write a generalised dynamic demand function, which incorporates both these two different expectation regimes.

$$-p + rp = \alpha_0 f_x z + \alpha_1 f(x) \tag{d}$$

where z=x represents the current acquired level of capital good (i). In other words, it represents the difference in the used level of capital good (i) at time t and $t + dt$.

Under myopia $\alpha_0 = -1/r$ and $\alpha_0 = 0$, , whereas an $\alpha_0 = 1$, under perfect foresight. Given the production function of equation (c), conditions (a) and (b) become:

$$\phi g(H, L) x^{\phi-1} \geq p \tag{a'}$$

$$-p + rp \leq \phi g(H, L) x^{\phi-1} \tag{b'}$$

The dynamic demand function under myopia becomes: these conditions hold for each capital good (i).

$$-p + rp = -\frac{1}{r} \phi(\phi - 1) g(H, L)^{\phi-2} z + \phi g(H, L) x^{\phi-1} \tag{e}$$

Under perfect foresight this equation becomes:

$$-p + rp = \phi g(H, L) x^{\phi-1} \tag{f}$$

Consider again the second sector, for instance, the sector which produces capital goods, used by the final good sector. The basic assumption here is that each capital good (i) is produced by identical monopolistic firms, which have bought the design of the capital good from the research sector. There costs for a design are sunk costs. The objective of each firm can be represented by the usual inter temporal maximisation problem. Furthermore, one must take into account that the production of each capital good takes place as soon as the capital good is invented. The profit function for the monopolistic supplier of capital good of vintage (v) is given by:

$$\Pi = \int_{\nu}^{\infty} (p(t) - \mu(t))z(t)e^{-r(t-v)}dt$$

$$(g)$$

where $p(t)$ and $u(t)$ are unit price and unit of capital good i and $z(t)$ is the current production level of capital good i. The problem can be solved by integrating by parts the integral in equation (7) and then using the dynamic demand functions (e) and (f). From this problem it is possible to determine the diffusion path (for instance, the supply trajectory). Furthermore, we need to specify that p(t) is derived from the production function (on the demand side) as an input price and $\mu(t,\nu)$ is such that $\mu < 0$; for instance, function decreases with time. This assumption is justified by considering the effect of learning economies on $\mu(t,\nu)$ (Stoneman-Ireland 1983; Ireland-Stoneman 1986), Integrating by parts (7) yields:

$$\Pi = \int_{\nu}^{\infty} (-p + rp - \mu - r\mu)xe^{-r(t-\nu)}dt$$

$$(h)$$

Consider now the simple case of myopic expectations. Substituting (e) into (h) yields:

$$\Pi = \int_{\nu}^{\infty} \left[\left(-\frac{1}{r}\phi(\phi - 1)g(H,L)x^{\phi-2}z + \phi g(H,L)x^{\phi-1} \right) + \mu - r\mu \right]xe^{-r(t-\nu)}dt$$

$$(j)$$

The problem is to maximise (9) under these constraints:

$$x = z \qquad\qquad (j')$$

$$z \geq 0 \qquad\qquad (j'')$$

Hamiltonian conditions. From the maximisation of equation (j) under conditions (j') and (j'') we get the following Hamiltonian conditions:

$$H = \left[-\frac{1}{r}\phi(\phi-1)g(H,L)x^{\phi-2}z + \phi g(H,L)x^{\phi-1} + \mu - r\mu \right]xe^{-r(t-\nu)}dt$$

$$H_x = -\lambda$$

$$H_z = 0$$

Differentiating with respect to time (c) and substituting into (b) yields equation (k). The optimal trajectory of capital good i is given in equation (k).

$$\phi g(H,L)x^{\phi-1} = r\mu - \mu \tag{k}$$

As $t \to \infty$ the diffusion of capital good i terminates and x(i)=x*. Therefore, it must be:

$$\phi g(H,L)x(t_\nu)^{\phi-1} = r\mu(t_\nu) \tag{l}$$

In order to fully characterise the diffusion path, we must define $\mu(t,\nu)$. Recall that we have assumed that this function is affected by learning economies; for instance, $\mu < 0$. Furthermore, we assume that:

$$\mu(t,\nu) = \Omega e^{-\theta(t-\nu)} + c \tag{m}$$

where Ω and θ are positive parameters and c is a positive constant which determines the production cost when $t \to \infty$.

Figure 4.17 shows different costs function for capital goods of different vintage.

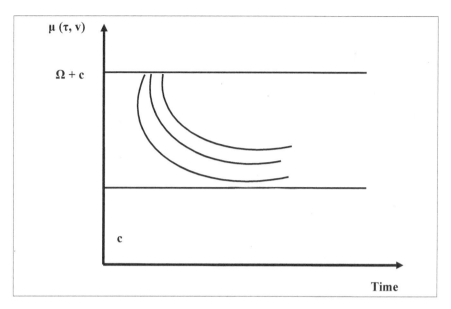

Figure 4.17 Cost functions
Source: Korres, G., 2008.

From equation (k) we get:

$$\phi g(H,L)x^{\phi-1} = (r+\theta)\Omega e^{-\theta(t-\nu)} + c \tag{n}$$

The diffusion path is then given by:

$$x(t,\nu) = \left(\frac{\phi g(H,L)}{(r+\theta)\Omega e^{-\theta(t-\nu)} + c} \right)^{\frac{1}{1-\phi}} \tag{n'}$$

the diffusion path for capital good of vintage v is also shown in Figure 4.18.

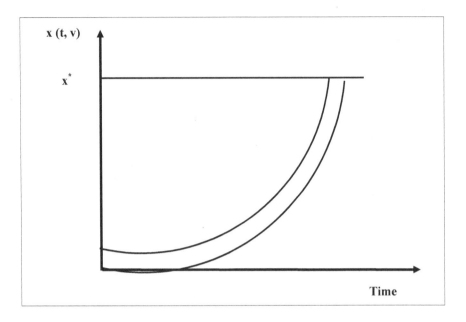

Figure 4.18 Diffusion paths
Source: Korres, G., 2008.

Given the supple trajectory we can modify the production function on the demand side, yielding:

$$Y = g(H,L)\delta H_a e^{\delta H_a t} \int_0^t e^{-\delta H_a t} \left(\frac{\phi g(H,L)}{(r+\theta)\Omega e^{-\theta r} + c} \right)^{\frac{\phi}{1-\phi}} dt \qquad (\text{n''})$$

Derivation of equation.
Let us consider equation.

$$Y = g(H,L) \int_0^A x(i)^\phi \; di$$

From product name i. consider its vistage v.

$$Y = g(H,L)\delta H_a \int_{-\infty}^t e^{\delta H_a v} x(t-v)^\phi \; dv$$

Given that: $i = e^{\delta H_a v}$

This equation can be expressed in terms of a new variable, for instance, the age of capital. We define this variable as $\tau = t - \nu$, $(\nu = [0,1])$.

Therefore, it will be:

$$Y = g(H, L)\delta H_a \int_{-\infty}^{t} e^{\delta H_a \nu} x(t - \nu)^{\phi} d\nu$$

This transformation is also used by Jovanovic and Lach (1993).

Equation (n") suggests that there are $(\delta H_a e^{\delta H_a (1-t)})$ capital goods of age t, each of them used according to the supply trajectory given by equation (n').

Given this specification, we consider the growth rate of the economy in the long run; for instance, we consider the asymptotic property of the growth rate calculated from equation (n"). It is possible to show that:

$$\frac{\dot{Y}}{Y} = \delta H_a + \frac{\left(\dfrac{\phi g(H, L)}{(r + \theta)\Omega e^{-\theta r} + c}\right)^{\frac{\phi}{1-\phi}}}{e^{\delta H_a t} \int_{0}^{t} e^{-\delta H_a t} \left(\dfrac{\phi g(H, L)}{(r + \theta)\Omega e^{-\theta r} + c}\right)^{\frac{\phi}{1-\phi}} dt}$$

Output growth in this case depends on time and on all the parameters that define the diffusion path. For instance, in the long run, as $t \to \infty$ output growth rate approaches δH_a, that is, the balanced growth rate. The second term on the right hand side of equation (n") goes to zero as $t \to \infty$. Indeed, the integral at the denominator converges as:

$$e^{-\delta H_a t} > e^{-\delta H_a t} \left(\frac{\phi g(H, L)}{(r + \theta)\Omega e^{-\theta r} + c}\right)^{\frac{\phi}{1-\phi}} dt$$

We also need to show that the growth rate of capital is equal to δH_a as $t \to \infty$. Following Romer (1990) the accounting measure of capital is given by:

$$K(t) = \int_{0}^{t} \mu(t)x(t)dt \tag{n'''}$$

Substituting the functional forms adopted into equation (n''') yields:

$$K(t) = \delta H_a e^{\delta H_a t} \int_{0}^{t} (\Omega e^{-\theta t} + c)\left(\frac{\phi g(H, L)}{(r + \theta)\Omega e^{-\theta(r)} + c}\right)^{\frac{\phi}{1-\phi}} e^{-\delta H_a t} dt$$

The growth rate of capital is given by:

$$\frac{\dot{K}}{K} = \delta H_a + \frac{(\Omega e^{-\theta t} + c)\left(\frac{\phi g(H,L)}{(r+\theta)\Omega e^{-\theta r} + c}\right)^{\frac{\phi}{1-\phi}}}{e^{\delta H_a t}\displaystyle\int_0^t (\Omega e^{-\theta t} + c)\left(\frac{\phi g(H,L)}{(r+\theta)\Omega e^{-\theta(r)} + c}\right)^{\frac{\phi}{1-\phi}} e^{-\delta H_a t} dt}$$

As $t \to \infty$ the growth rate of capital approaches δH_a.

It is worth emphasising the conclusion about the determinants of output growth rate. In Romer specification, growth rate of economy is determined either by the allocation of human capital in the research sector (Roomer 1990a, 1990b) or by the parameters that define the production function (River Batiz-Romer 1991). In the specification adopted here, growth rate is determined in the short run by the diffusion path of capital goods produced by the producer durable sector. The definition of growth rate allows to takes into account the difference between the long and the short run determinants of output growth rate.

In long run, output growth is just determined by the allocation of human capital to the research sector. In short run, together with this latter effect, there is the impact of diffusion. Indeed, output growth rate is given by the sum of the parameter δH_a and the ratio of newly diffused

capital $\left[\left(\frac{\phi g(H,L)}{(r+\theta)\Omega e^{-\theta r} + c}\right)^{\frac{\phi}{1-\phi}}\right]$ to the already diffused capital

stock $\left[e^{\delta H_a t}\displaystyle\int_0^t e^{-\delta H_a t}\left(\frac{\phi g(H,L)}{(r+\theta)\Omega e^{-\theta r} + c}\right)^{\frac{\phi}{1-\phi}} dt\right]$. The definition of output growth

allows to take into account policy intervention, as the speed of diffusion and the unit cost of investment in new capital goods (respectively parameters è and Ù) enter the short run definition of output growth.

11. Inter-country and International Diffusion Approach: The Theoretical Framework

Inter-country differences tend to be explained in terms of three groups of variables:

- the most popular is the measurement of proxies for *profitability of innovation* in different countries;
- *technological and institutional differences*, which are mentioned in a number of cases;

- *economic industrial characteristics*, such as growth and size of market, size of firms and age of existing equipment.

Literature on diffusion of technology incorporates three different approaches. The most well-known is the *inter-industry innovation approach* pioneered by Mansfield (1969). They studied diffusion in one or more innovations in a number of industries, and they attempted to explain empirically the variance of the speed of diffusion in terms of differences in the attributes of the industries and innovations concerned.

Mansfield (1969) suggested that if other things were equal, then length of time that a firm waits before using a new technique will be inversely related to its size. Large firms are more likely to have more units to replace, and conditions are usually more favourable and better for a large firm, such as financial resources, engineering and research departments. For these reasons, large firms would be expected in general to use a new technique more quickly than the small ones.

In the *inter-firm model*, at any point of diffusion process, the number of users acquiring technology is related to risk attached to acquisition, the expected profitability of acquisition and the number of potential adopters. According to the inter-firm decision theories, the most important elements that contribute to determine the actual cost of entry can be considered to be:

- fixed investment costs;
- the cost of scientific and technical knowledge required to assimilate the innovation;
- the cost of acquiring the experience required to handle it and successfully bring it to the market;
- the cost of overcoming any locational disadvantages related to the general infrastructure and other economic and institutional conditions.

For any innovation, the costs of entry for the innovator can be represented as the sum of the following components: the fixed investment cost in plant and equipments, the cost incurred by the innovator in acquiring scientific and technical knowledge which was not possessed by the firm at the beginning of innovation process; the cost incurred by the innovator in acquiring the relevant experience (know-how in organisation, management, marketing or other areas) required to carry the innovation through; and the cost borne by the innovator to compensate for whatever relevant externalites are not provided by the environment in which the firm operates. Imitators will compare the cost of buying the technology with the cost of developing it themselves, if they can.

However, the imitators' knowledge related to the entry costs will depend crucially on his/her own initial scientific and technical knowledge base in the relevant areas. Consequently, his/her entry costs may be much higher or much lower than the innovators', depending on their relative starting positions in the knowledge level of the firm.

Moreover, government regulations, taxes, tariffs and other relevant policies will affect strongly *environment* and actual cost for an innovator. Specifically, the difficulty of *catching-up* for industries/firms in the developing countries is because scientific and technical knowledge, practical experience and locational advantages may be lower than in the more advanced countries, while of technology may be higher.

In the diffusion context, two factors are critical but each works to an opposite direction; if early adopters are large, medium or small firms will depend upon the importance of cost/risk considerations relative to innovativeness considerations and upon the way in which qualities vary with the firm size. This approach can be applied so as to investigate the diffusion of the same innovation in a number of different countries and to explain the observed differentials in the diffusion performance in the terms of the characteristics of the countries and industries concerned.

11.1 The International Diffusion Approach

International diffusion of technology has been a major factor behind most industrial nation's economic growth. Information and particular characteristics of each country are key points for international diffusion of technologies through different countries. Moreover, the *international approach* attempts to explain international differences in the speed of diffusion of innovations in terms of the characteristics of the countries and industries concerned. An overall assessment of international differences in the rate of diffusion of new innovation technologies is extremely difficult to make for a variety of technical applications and for innovations that are continuously are introduced. *International diffusion* can be considered in connection with *international technology transfer* (through multinationals and licensing); including various variables (such as profitability and transfer cost). An important factor affecting the level of diffusion is the nature of competition in the user's industry. It has also been argued that firms are more likely to experiment with new products and methods during a phase of increasing competition.

The framework of international diffusion can be considered through the following approaches:

a. The *Schumpeterian approach* that tried to investigate and to explain long-waves in economic activity (*the Kondratieff cycle*). The Schumpeterian hypothesis is concerned with the implications of new technology in economy. In Schumpeterian theory, the entrepreneur introduces innovations and the resulting profits derived from new innovations give the signal and attribute to be imitated by other entrepreneurs. The introduction of new technologies would result in the reduction of factor and product prices. The change of prices will induce non-adopters to use the new technology.

b. The *vintage approach*; the great strength of the vintage model is that it is perfectly rational for entrepreneurs to use old technologies even when new best-practice techniques exist. Introduction of new technologies under perfect competition will depend on the age structure of the capital stock, improvements in new technologies over time and movements in relative prices. *Old machines* can still yield a contribution to profits if price covers operating costs. One disadvantage of the vintage models is for instance that all investment in machines involves the latest type. Moreover, these models give us no guarantee that the diffusion will be sigmoid. The length of time between an initial innovation and an imitation in another country defines the *innovation lag*.

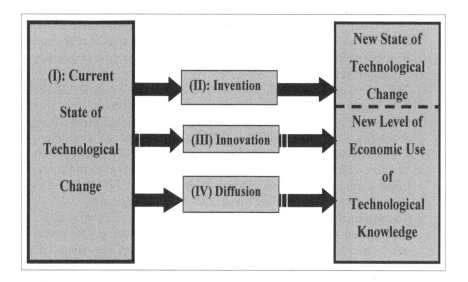

Figure 4.19 Process of technological change
Source: Korres, G., 2008.

According to the classification analysis of Posner and Soete (1988), *innovation-lag* can be viewed as a sum of the following components:

*   *Foreign reaction lag*, as the product innovations are usually introduced into foreign markets through exports from the country in which the innovation initially occurred. The length of foreign reaction lag depends on the magnitude of the threat to the foreign industry's market resulting from imports of the new innovated product; the greater the competitiveness between domestic and foreign producers for the share of the market, the shorter will be *foreign reaction-lag*.
*   *Domestic reaction lag* can be considered as the time elapsing between a positive *foreign reaction* to an innovation and the actual decision to

imitate. The length of time that an industry waits before imitating tends to be inversely related to its size. Generally, large industries produce a wide range of products and usually have better facilities and technical skills for the improvement or introduction of products.

- Finally, *learning period*, where international communications channels tend to accelerate the diffusion of innovations.

The most important determinants in diffusion lag can be considered the following:

- The *size of the country*. According to Mansfield (1969) and Metcalfe (1981), size plays a positive role in the reduction of diffusion-lags. Small countries seem to have better opportunities than large ones to adopt earlier innovations that originate abroad, and they are more receptive to innovation that originates elsewhere.
- *Technological capability* of the country. Many studies (i.e. Antonelli 1986) have suggested that the R&D influence reduces diffusion-lags.
- The *origin of technology* seems important in explaining diffusion lags. According to Metcalfe (1981), diffusion process of an innovation is affected by the characteristics of supply and demand of technology. Firms are more able to capitalise on technological opportunities when the origin of the technology is internal. Moreover, as Benvignati (1982) has shown, domestic technologies diffuse much quicker than foreign ones.
- *Multinational firms*. According to Antonelli (1986), multinational firms have played an important role in diffusion of technology. However, it seems that multinational firms can help spread product innovations rather than process innovations. In fact, product innovations are introduced to imitating countries by multinational firms that have already benefited from capitalised know-how and research spending in the innovating country.
- An economic analysis of international diffusion patterns of technological innovations distinguishes four different aspects:
- the *speed* with which a country initially tries a new product or the demand-lag;
- how quickly the use of the product *spreads* among consumers after introduction into the domestic market, as indicated by the growth in the country's consumption;
- the *speed* with which the country acquires the production technology from abroad or *imitation lag rate*;
- how quickly the domestic producers *adopt* technology, once it is transferred from abroad, as indicated by the growth of the country's output. Diffusion models have a methodological similarity with some of the models of industrial and economic growth which were developed in the 1930s by Kuznets and Schumpeter.

According to Schumpeter (1934), the diffusion process of major innovations is the driving force behind the trade cycle (the *long term Kondratieff cycle*). However, the forces driving the diffusion process per se are not made explicit. The conception is that the entrepreneur innovates and the attractiveness of attaining a similarly increased profit and cost reductions encourages others to imitate; this imitation representing a diffusion process.

Diffusion of technology can be defined as the process by which the use of an innovation spreads and grows. Diffusion is very important for the process of technological change. On the one hand, diffusion narrows the technological gap that exists between the economic units of an industry, and thus the rate of diffusion determines to a large extent the rate of technological change measured as the effect of an innovation on productivity increase in an industry. On the other hand, diffusion plays an important part in competitiveness process in the sense that diffusion deteriorates the competitive edge which is maintained by the originator of successful innovations. Schumpeter has classified technological change in the following steps:

- invention;
- innovation;
- diffusion.

Diffusion is the last step in the economic impact of a new product or process. Diffusion is the stage in which a new product or process comes into widespread use.

Figure 4.19 indicates the importance of diffusion in the process of technological change (Chen 1983). The *current state of technological knowledge* (phase I) gives rise to the second phase (II) of *invention*; however, sometimes it gives rise to *innovation* and *diffusion*. At the second phase, the results of *invention* can give rise to a *new state of technical knowledge*, where in this case a new phase is created and the cycle begins again. Most literature on diffusion is focused on the theoretical arguments underlying the traditional, *S-shaped epidemic diffusion curve*.

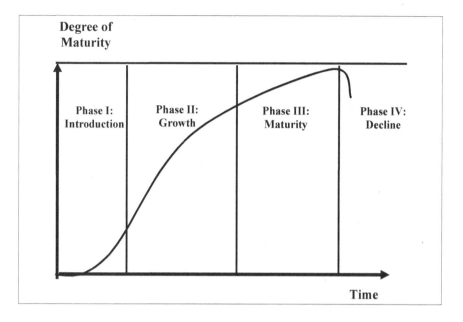

Figure 4.20 Phases of growth
Source: Korres, G., 2008.

Figure 4.20 illustrates the different phases of the diffusion process, where improvements are achieved slowly in the first stage, then accelerate and finally slow down. Figure 4.20 (Malecki 1991) shows diagrammatically the following diffusion phases:

- *phase I is the period of first introduction*, when the innovation has to perform adequately and break successfully into the market;
- *phase II is the period of rapid market growth*, once the product is basically defined and its market tested the focus shifts to the process of production;
- *phase III of maturity*, when market size and rate of growth are well known and the relationship between product and process has been optimised;
- *phase IV of decline*, when both the product and its process of production are standardised.

11.2 Epidemic Model and the Logistic Curve

Many diffusion models, i.e. Davies 1979, and Stoneman 1987, are based on the approach of the theory of epidemics. Epidemic models can be used to explain how innovation spreads from one unit to others, at what speed and what can stop it. The epidemic approach starts with assumption that a diffusion process is similar to the spread of a disease among a given population. The basic epidemic model is based on three assumptions:

- the potential number of adopters may not be in each case the whole population under consideration;
- the way in which information is spread may not be uniform and homogeneous;
- the probability to optimise innovation once informed is not independent of economic considerations, such as profitability and market perspectives.

The spread of new technology among a fixed number of identical firms can be represented as follows: Let us assume that the level of diffusion is D which corresponds to m_t number of firms in a fixed population of n which have adopted the new innovation at time t and to $(n-m_t)$ firms that remaining as the potential adopters.

Let us assume the probability of an adoption is a constant term b. Then Dm_t, the expected number of new adopters between t and Dt, will be given by the product of this probability (between one non-adopter and one adopter to lead to an adoption during the period of time D_t). The number of individuals contracting the disease between times t and t+1 is proportionate to the product of the number of uninfected individuals and the proportion of the population already infected, both at time t. The magnitude of b will depend on a number of factors, such as, the infectiousness of the disease and the frequency of social intercourse.

This is rationalised by assuming that each uninfected individual has a constant and equal propensity to catch the disease, from the contact with an infected individual and that the number of such contacts will be determined by the proportion of the population who is already infected (assuming homogeneous mixing). At each instant t, every individual can meet randomly with another member of population and then the expected number of encounters (between adopters and non-adopters) during the time Dt, is:

$$[m_t(n-m_t)]Dt \qquad (4.1)$$

It follows that Dm_t is equal to:

$$m_{t+1}-m_t=b[(n-m_t)m_t/n] \ (b>0) \qquad (4.2)$$

where, the parameter b (usually called the *speed of diffusion* or the *rate of diffusion*). This is rationalised by assuming that each uninfected individual has a constant and equal propensity to catch the disease (as given by b) from the contact with an infected individual and the number of such contacts will be determined the proportion of the population who are already infected. If the period, is very small then equation (4.2) can be rewritten, as:

$$dm_t/dt[1/(n-m_t)]=bm_t/n \tag{4.3}$$

This differential equation has the following solution (*logistic function*):

$$m_t/n=\{1+exp(-a-bt)\}^{-1} \tag{4.4}$$

where a is a constant of integration.

If one plots m_t against the time t, the profile will follow an *S-shaped curve* (or the *sigmoid curve*). This is the well known logistic time curve. As we can see from Figure 4.21 it predicts that the proportion of the population which having contacted the disease will increase at an accelerating rate until 50%, when infection is attained at time t=-(a/b). Thereafter, infection increases at a decelerating rate and 100% infection is approached asymptotically.

The upper limit of the curve will be $m = \sqrt{n}$ (which itself has a maximum of 1, when t increases infinitely which follows from the assumption that all firms were potential adopters). The logistic curve has an infection point at $m_t=1/2$, where the adoption process accelerates up to a point where the half of the population of firms have adopted and decelerates beyond. Empirical tests are straightforward using the linear transformation:

$$log[m_t/(n-m_t)]=a+bt, \tag{4.5}$$

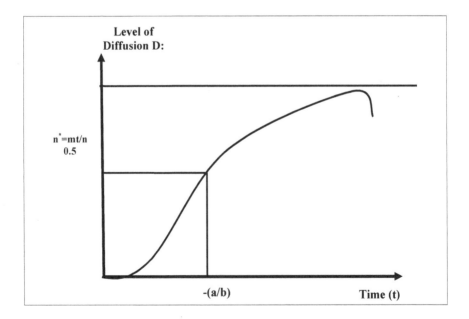

Figure 4.21 The logistic epidemic curve
Source: Korres, G., 2008.

There is a huge literature on the *law of logistic growth*, which must be measured in appropriate units. Growth process is supposed to be represented by a function of the form (4.3) with t to represent the time. Different studies on plants and animals were found to follow the *logistic law*, even though these two variables cannot be subject to the same distribution. Population theory relies on logistic extrapolations. The only trouble with this theory is that not only the logistic distribution but also the normal, the Cauchy, and other distributions can be fitted to the same material with the same or better goodness of fit. Examining the logistic curve, we can summarise the following disadvantages:

- the infectiousness of the disease must remain constant over time for all individuals; that means, b must be constant, however, in the increasing resistance on the part of uninfected or a reduction in the contagiousness of the disease suppose that b falls over the time;
- all individuals must have an equal change of catching-up the disease.

That means, b is the same for all groups within the population. There are a number of other assumptions which may prove unrealistic for the logistic solution (for instance, constant population is required).

11.3 Probit Models

The probit analysis has already been a well-established technique in the study of diffusion of new products between individuals. This approach concentrates on the characteristics of individuals in a sector and is suitable not only to generate a diffusion curve, but also gives some indications of which firms will be early adopters and which late.

Given the difficulties which are associated with the linear probability model, it is natural to transform the original model in such a way that predictions will lie between (0.1) interval for all X. These requirements suggest the use of a *cumulative probability function* (F) in order to be able to explain a dichotomous dependent variable (the range of the *cumulative probability function* is the (0.1) interval, since all probabilities lie between 0 and 1. The resulting probability distribution may be represented as:

$$P_i = F(a+bX_i) = F(Z_i) \tag{4.6}$$

Under the assumption that we transform the model using a *cumulative distribution function* (CDF), we can get the constrained version of the linear probability model:

$$P_i = a + bX_i \tag{4.7}$$

There are numerous alternative cumulative probability functions, but we will consider only two, the *normal* and the *logistic* ones. The probit probability model is associated with the cumulative normal probability function. To understand this model, we can assume that there exists a theoretical continuous index Z_i which is determined as an explanatory variable X. Thus, we can write:

$$Z_i = a + bX_i \tag{4.8}$$

The probit model assumes that there is a probability Z_i^* that is less or equal to Z_i, which can be computed with the aid of the *cumulative normal probability function*. The standardised cumulative normal function is written by the expression (4.8), that is, a random variable which is normally distributed with mean zero and a unit variance. By construction, the variable P_i will lie in the (0,1) interval, where P_i represents the probability that an event occurs. Since this probability is measured by the area under the standard normal curve, the more likely the event is to occur, the larger the value of the index Z_i will be. In order to be able to obtain an estimate of the index Z_i, we should apply in (4.8) the inverse of the cumulative normal function of:

$$Z_i = F^{-1}(P_i) = a + bX_i \tag{4.8'}$$

In the language of probit analysis, the unobservable index Z_i is simply know as *normal equivalent deviate* (n.e.d.) or simply as *normit*.

The central assumption underlying the probit model is that an individual consumer (or a firm/country) will be found to own the new product (or to adopt new innovation) at a particular time when the income (or the size) exceeds some critical level.

Let us assume that the potential adopters of technology differ according to some specified characteristic, z, that is distributed across the population as f(z) with a cumulative distribution F(z), as the above Figure 4.22 indicates. The advantage of the probit diffusion models is that relate the possibility of introducing behavioural assumptions concerning the individual firms (firms). The probit model also offers interesting insights into the slowness of technological diffusion process.

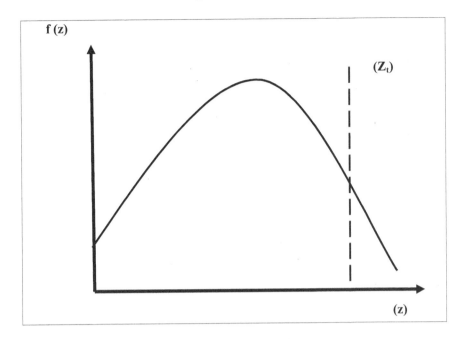

Figure 4.22 The cumulative distribution
Source: Korres, G., 2008.

Let us consider that we have two set of innovations, the first group concerns the innovation A which follow a *cumulative lognormal diffusion curve* (this can be considered as the simple and the relative cheap innovation), while the second group concerns the innovation B which follow a *cumulative normal diffusion curve* (this can be considered as the more complex and expensive innovation):

$$P_t = N(\log t / m_D, s^2_D) \tag{4.9}$$

$$P_t = N(t / m_D, s^2_D) \tag{4.9'}$$

For estimation purposes, both equations can be linearised by the following transformation:

$$P_t = N(Z_t / 0, 1), \tag{4.10}$$

where: Zt may be defined as the normal equivalent deviate or normit of Pt, where given values for Pt, Zt can be read off from the standard normal Tables.

Re-arranging the equations (4.9) and (4.9') in terms of the standard normal function, it follows that:

$$Z_t = (\log t - m_D)/s_D) \tag{4.11}$$

$$Z_t = (t - m_D)/s_D) \tag{4.11'}$$

for group (4.11), and for group (4.11'), respectively.

For empirical purposes, it must be remembered that P_t refers to a probability that a randomly selected firm has adopted the innovation at time t. This can only be measured by the proportion of firms having adopted m_t/n. However, to employ the variable Z_t as dependent variable in the regression equation, we will violate one of the assumptions of the standard linear regression model, which is the dependent variable and thus the disturbance term is not homoskedastic.

In fact, this problem is always encountered when is used the *probit analysis*. In the past, two alternative estimators have been advocated under these circumstances: the first concern the *maximum likelihood* and the second concerns the *minimum normit x^2 method*. In this context, the *minimum normit X^2 method* amounts the following weighted regressions

$$Z_t = a_1 + b_1 \log t \tag{4.12}$$

(for group A which corresponding to *cumulative lognormal*),

$$Z_t = a_2 + b_2 t \tag{4.13}$$

(for group B which corresponding to cumulative normal), where: Zi refers to the normal equivalent deviate of the level of diffusion (mt/n) in year t where diffusion is defined by the proportion of firms in the relevant industry who have adopted.

Figure 4.23 (4.23 (A), 4.23 (B), and 4.23 (C) parts), shows different possibly alternative time paths of diffusion between two group of innovations (5 A) and (5 B), which correspond to the theoretical cumulative lognormal and normal diffusion curves (Davies, 1974). Figure 4.23 (A), in general shows the theoretical forms of these two model-equations.

Figure 4.23 (B) and 4.23 (C) shows the *fast* and *slow* curves which usually are based on the maximum and the minimum observed values, while the *average* curve merely correspond to the *typical* curve. These theoretical diffusion paths correspond to the diffusion of technologies in different industries (or countries).

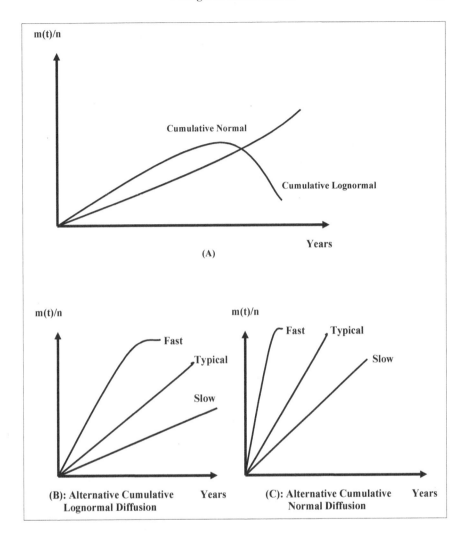

Figure 4.23 Diffusion paths
Source: Korres, G., 2008.

11.4 Technological Substitution Models

A number of economists (such as Mansfield 1969; Sahal 1977a) consider diffusion as a disequilibrium phenomenon. Usually, when a new technology or a new method is introduced, it is less developed than the older with which it competes. Therefore, it is likely to have greater potential for improvement and for reduction in cost. The introduction of a new product or process broadens the range of choice of producers and consumers, and equilibrium is altered. In the real world, there is only a *gradual adjustment* over the course of time to the new equilibrium level.

A simple formulation of this adjustment process would be to assume that the percentage adjustment in any period is proportional to the percentage difference between the actual level of adoption of innovation and the level which corresponds to the new equilibrium. The essence of the technological substitution hypothesis lies in the disequilibrium characteristic of diffusion process.

We can assume that the system-wide disequilibrium caused by the gap in the use of two techniques. The equilibrium levels of the use of two techniques can be indicated by K_1 and K_2, while intra-equilibrium gaps can be denoted by:

$$(K_1-Y)/Y \text{ and } (K_2-Y)/X. \tag{14a}$$

Particularly, we can assume that the use of one technique as a percentage of the other is some fixed proportion g of the percentage of intra-equilibrium gaps, that is:

$$\log f(t)-\log f'(t)=g[\log(X)-\log(Y)] \tag{14b}$$

or, otherwise, using the differential equation of the well-known logistic function, we can find that:

$$\log f(t)-\log f'(t)=g[\log(K_2-X)/X-\log(K_1-Y)/Y] \tag{4.15}$$

where, $\log(K_2-X)/X=a_2-b_2 t$ and $\log(K_1-Y)/Y=a_1-b_1 t$ and a is the constant depending on the initial conditions, K is the equilibrium level of growth and b is the rate of growth parameter.

Another interesting result is that the coefficient g is a *measure of the speed* with which movement from equilibrium to the other takes place. According to the previous analysis, the greater the disparity in the use of two techniques, the faster the speed the substitution will be. Using one technique as a proportion of the other, this can be indicated by f/f, and thus we can reach in the following equation:

$$\log(f/(1-f))=a_1+b_1 t \tag{4.16}$$

It can also be verified that the logistic curve is a symmetrical S-shaped curve with a point of infection at 0.5K. The higher the coefficient g, the less the difference between the rates of the adoption of the two techniques will be: $b=g(b_1-b_2)$, where: $a_1=g(a_2-a_1)$, and $b_1=g(b_1-b_2)$. For a more detailed analysis see Sahal and Nelson (1981) and Sahal (1980).

Moreover, assuming that X(t) is the adoption of new technique at the time t and Y(t) is the old technique at time t, then the fractional adoption of the new technique at time t is given by:

$$f(t)=X(t)/(X(t)+Y(t)) \tag{4.17}$$

and

$$f'(t)=Y(t)/(X(t)+Y(t)), \tag{4.17'}$$

so that $f(t)+f'(t)=1$.

Both X and Y can follow an S-shaped pattern of growth; see Sahal and Nelson (1981), and Sahal (1981). The simplicity of the model is that it contains only two parameters. Any substitution that has gained a few% of the available market has shown economic viability and hence the substitution will proceed to 100%.

The substitutions tend to proceed exponentially in the early years (as for instance, with a constant percentage annual growth increment) and to follow an S-shaped curve. The simplest curve is characterised by two constants: the early growth rate and the time, at which substitution is half complete.

Figure 4.24 illustrates a similar analysis. According to this analysis, substituted fraction can be given by the relationship:

$$f=(1/2)[1+\tanh a(t-t_0)], \tag{4.18}$$

where: a is the half annual fractional growth in the early years and where t_0 is the time at which $f=1/2$. A more convenient form of the substitution expression can be given as:

$$f/(1-f)=\exp [2\ a(t-t_0)] \tag{4.19}$$

This expression allows us to plot substitution data in the form of $f/(1-f)$ as a function of time on a *semilog function* which fit in a straight line. The slope of line is 2a, the time t_0 is found at $f/(1-f)=1$, as indicated in Figure 4.24.

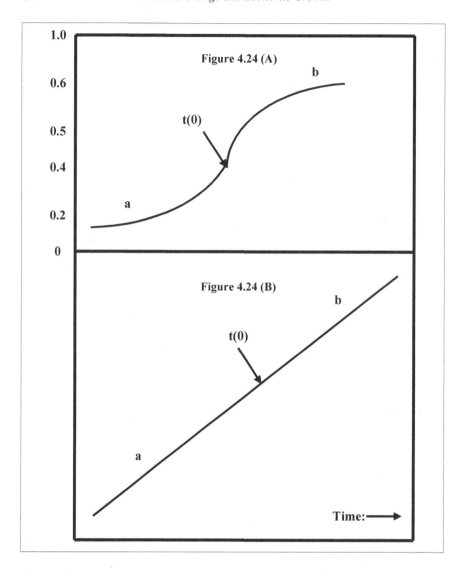

Figure 4.24 A general form of substitution model function
Source: Korres, G., 2008.

12. Policy Priorities and Summary

Technology transfer through FDI is an important factor on the process of economic development and economic performance. MNEs and FDIs are the main policy tools for the international technology transfer and the development of innovation activities in many countries. Multinationals also produce and control most of the world's advanced technology. About four fifths of the FDIs and the production of advanced technology originate in Japan, Germany, the United Kingdom, the USA and Switzerland.

Technology transfer through MNEs and FDIs lead to a geographical diffusion of technology and contribute substantially towards the development of research and innovation activities in less technologically advanced countries. Most of these countries lack the funds and opportunities to develop their own technologies, and they align on the policies of technology transfer through MNEs. However, multinationals transfer only the technologies that needed and have been developed abroad from the host laboratories. Ownership and control of new technologies from MNEs do not automatically imply the improvement and the development of research activities at a national level.

Most empirical studies have emphasised the profits, the age and the amount of new technologies transferred by MNEs. Usually, the affiliated companies operate in a monopolistic market where new technologies give their products a *quality advantage* and a higher market share.

SMEs in less favoured regions may need assistance in tapping into necessary resources (related to knowledge, in the form of technology or qualified human capital in particular), to face new forms of competition developing in global economy.

Regional innovation policy may help stimulate firms, SMEs in particular, in less favoured regions to adopt improved production methods (for instance, quality and environmentally friendly processes, incorporation of technological developments and innovation management methods, etc.), make new/different products and services (for instance, design, customisation, etc.), and exploit new economic opportunities and markets (university spin-offs, new technology-based firms, etc), thus, using their regional innovation potential to the fullest in order to compete in the global economy.

Regional policy has to cope with fresh challenges, globalisation and rapid technological change in order to provide economic opportunities and quality jobs needed in less favoured regions. Today, innovation-gap is nearly twice as great as cohesion gap. Many of the causes of disparities among regions can be traced to disparities in productivity and competitiveness. Education, research, technological development and innovation are vital components of regional competitiveness. The 25 least developed regions in Europe spend, as a percentage of GDP, less than a quarter of the EU average (0.5% compared to an EU average of 2% – 1995). On a regional level, business expenditure on innovation as a percentage of GDP in the most developed 25 regions is on average 1.9%, while in the 25 least developed regions this figure falls to around 1.1%.

Long term foreign private capital flows have a complementary and catalytic role to play in building domestic supply capacity as they lead to tangible and intangible benefits, including export growth, technology and skills transfer, employment generation and poverty eradication. Policies to attract FDI are essential components of national development strategies. Inter-regional innovation-gap is not only of a quantitative nature but also of a qualitative one. There are a number of characteristics of regional innovation systems in less advance regions which make them less efficient, that is:

- Firms may not be capable of identifying their innovation needs or maybe unaware of the existence of a technical solution.
- There may be poorly developed financial systems in the area with few funds available for risk or seed capital, which are specifically adapted to the terms and risks of the innovation process in firms.
- There may be a lack of technological intermediaries capable of identifying and "federating" local business demand for innovation (and RTD&I) and channelling it towards sources of innovation (and RTD&I) which may be able to respond to these demands.
- Co-operation between the public and private sectors may be weak, and the area may lack an entrepreneurial culture which is open to inter-firm co-operation, leading to an absence of economies of scale and business critical mass which may make certain local innovation efforts profitable.
- Traditional industries and small family firms which have little inclination towards innovation may dominate. There may be a low level of participation in international RTD&I networks and a low incidence of large, multinational firms.

Given all the above, we believe that regional policy should increasingly concentrate its efforts on the promotion of innovation to prepare regions for the new economy and close the "technology gap" if it is to be successful in creating the conditions for a sustained (and sustainable) economic development process in less favoured regions. Now, before we turn to what has been our policy response over the last decade and what our ideas about the future are, let me briefly pick up the second question.

Regional policy should evolve from supporting physical innovation infrastructure and equipment towards encouraging co-operation and a collective learning process among local actors in the field of innovation. A policy which facilitates the creation of rich, dynamic regional innovation systems and which assists in the exchange of skills and expertise which small and medium sized firms may not have available in-house.

In this context, a stable economic, legal and institutional framework is crucial in order to attract foreign investment and to promote sustainable development through investment. In this regard, a conducive international financial environment is also crucial. Promoting a conducive macro-economic environment, good governance and democracy, as well as strengthening structural aspects of the economy and improved institutional and human capacities, are important also in the context of attracting FDI and other private external flows.

Development partners would complementing LDCs' efforts need to provide a range of support measures to attract FDI. Action by LDCs (Less Developed Countries) and the development partners will be along the following lines:

(i) Action by LDCs

- Strengthening the enabling environment for private sector development and foreign investment flows; of particular importance is a supportive regulatory and legal framework for new and existing FDI along with the necessary institutional infrastructure and capacity to implement and maintain it;
- Designing and implementing policies that reduce risks which deter foreign investment, including through the negotiation of bilateral and regional investment treaties and accession to international conventions providing investment guarantees and insurance, as well as dispute settlement;
- Attracting foreign capital, especially FDI, towards the building of supply capacity;
- Encouraging linkages between domestic businesses and foreign affiliates with a view towards helping to disseminate appropriately tangible and intangible assets, including technology, to domestic enterprises;
- Taking appropriate action to avoid double taxation;
- Improving timely availability as well as reliability of investment information and statistics, including those related to investment opportunities and regulatory framework;
- Continuing efforts to establish an effective, fair and stable institutional, legal and regulatory framework in order to strengthen the rule of law and to foster effective participation of and close cooperation among all relevant stakeholders at national and local levels in the development process;
- Promoting broad-based popular participation in development, *inter alia* through decentralisation, when appropriate;
- Enabling the poor through promoting social inclusion and empowerment in order to enhance their effective participation in governance process, *inter alia* by strengthening their social networks;
- Strengthening policies and measures aimed at social, economic and political inclusion of all segments of societies;
- Continuing to promote and enhance effective measures, including fiscal and financial sector reforms for better domestic resource mobilisation, and reallocating public resources for investment in social development, *inter alia* through the appropriate reduction of excessive military expenditures, including global military expenditures;
- Strengthening human and institutional capacities for the formulation, application and evaluation of relevant policies and actions in the above areas.

(ii) Action by development partners

- Encouraging increased non-official flows, including investment flows, to LDCs;
- Supporting LDCs in devising and implementing appropriate FDI strategies and policy frameworks and institutions through the development of a comprehensive approach to FDI and actions aimed at improving the regulatory framework and the availability of reliable investment information;
- Supporting LDCs' efforts to attract foreign businesses and their affiliates, encouraging the appropriate dissemination of tangible and intangible assets, including technology, to domestic enterprises in LDCs;
- Assisting LDCs in human resource development so as to enable them to attract and benefit from FDI and to participate effectively in negotiations on international agreements in this regard;
- Supporting LDCs' efforts towards infrastructure development to attract FDI flows;
- Identifying and implementing best practices for encouraging and facilitating FDI to LDCs;
- Supporting initiatives in the development of public and private venture capital funds for LDCs;
- Assisting LDCs in establishing foreign investment advisory bodies in their own countries, as an one-stop shop which would be responsible for providing information, service and administrative support to potential foreign investors;
- Improving coordination among relevant international organisations on advisory services for investment to the LDCs, with possible participation of the private sector, *inter alia* by supporting global investment advisory services.

Technical progress (through production functions) plays a crucial role in the theory of economic growth. A production function specifies a long-run relationship between inputs and outputs and technical progress is an essential factor underlying the growth of per capita income. The promotion of technological progress has been one of the main objectives of economic policy. There are a number of ways to approach the estimation of production functions and technical progress.

A shift in production function over time is generally considered to represent technical progress through greater efficiency in combining inputs. These shifts are achieved in a variety of ways, including changes in coefficients of labour and capital. Theoretical and empirical aspects of technical progress have been extensively considered in a numerous studies. The characteristics of technical change may be shown by the shifts of unit isoquant towards origin over time. A greater saving in one input than in others will result in a bias in technical change. The relative contribution of factors to the production process is measured by the elasticity of substitution.

Then, a bias in technical change will be represented by a modification in the position of the isoquant and will lead, for example, to greater labour savings for all techniques. when i=j, then $(w_j/w_i)^{1/2}=1$, then the γ_{ij} is a constant term in the above input-output equation.

We can define productivity as the ratio of output to input. A productivity ratio may be changed when the price or unit cost of an output or input is changed. Productivity change is an important aspect of technological change, so that productivity measurement plays a crucial role in assessing the effects of technological change. Total Factor Productivity (TFP) indicates the productivity of all purchased inputs and is the most useful approach to productivity measurement. Technological change is a concept based on the physical measurements of science and engineering, while the Total Factor Productivity measures the economic impact of technological change. Any change in the quantities or qualities of inputs or outputs is classified as technological change.

This section attempts to measure the relationship between FDI, Technology and Productivity, or in other words to investigate the relation between the decline in FDI, Productivity growth and Technology (*technological and catching up models*). There is a huge literature demonstrating that R&D makes an important contribution to the growth at the firm, industry and national levels. Most of these studies have investigated the relation between productivity growth and R&D. Economists have analysed different possible views on why productivity growth has declined. These alternative explanations can be grouped into:

- the capital factor; for instance, investment (FDI) may have been inadequate to sustain the level of productivity growth;
- the technology factor affecting the productivity level, for instance a decline in innovation activities can affect productivity growth;
- the increased price of raw materials and energy;
- government regulations and demand policies that affect the productivity level;
- skills and experience of labour force may have deteriorated or moreover workers may not work as hard as they used to;
- products and services produced by economy have become more diverse; and
- productivity levels differ greatly across industries.

Technological progress has become virtually synonymous with long-run economic growth. It raises a basic question about the capacity of both industrial and newly industrialised countries to translate their seemingly greater technological capacity into productivity and economic growth. In literature, there are various explanations about the slow-down in productivity growth of OECD countries. One source of the slow-down in productivity growth may be substantial changes in FDI, and in the industrial composition of output, employment, capital accumulation and resource utilisation. The second source may be that technological opportunities have declined; otherwise, new technologies have been developed but the application of new technologies to production has been less successful. Technological factors act in a long-run way and should not be expected to explain medium-run variations in the growth of GDP and productivity.

On the basis of the previous discussion, the main conclusions and recommendations of this chapter can be summarised as follows:

- The idea that globalisation and integration in general lead to convergence may be mistaken and an alternative model may be more appropriate.
- The benefits of recent changes in international rules (primarily the Uruguay Round Agreement) may be skewed away from poorer countries.
- Differences in international tradability of factors of production may be an obstacle to the convergence of their prices.
- International capital movements may be insufficient to equalise rates of return.
- The nature of international capital movements maybe such as to benefit the countries of origin more than the recipients.
- The nature of the international transfer of technology maybe such as to limit its scope or benefits.
- National economic policies which have been pursued in the context of integration may limit the potential for convergence.
- National economic structures or circumstances may prevent poorer countries from benefiting from integration.
- Distributional effects of integration may impair development process.
- The operation of domestic capital markets may be such as to limit the resources available for investment, or its contribution to development process.
- The competitive nature of outward-oriented development may mean that the benefits of such development to each country are offset by the costs it imposes on others.
- There may be inherent asymmetries in the production of or international markets for goods, between those produced predominantly by developed and developing countries.
- Developing countries' policy responses to external shocks may be such as to extend and compound their effects.

These possible explanations are discussed in turn in the remainder of this section. It should be noted that they are by no means mutually exclusive. On the contrary, it is likely that any failure of convergence is associated with a combination of these and, possibly, others factors. However, conclusions cannot be easily drawn from simple summary measures of the extent or the rate of international compositional structural change, without having some additional information about the direction of change the path followed from the previous industrial structure and associated and institutional factors.

Most of the scenarios in national science and technological policies have been concentrated on the supply side of the science and technological system. Therefore, governments have to examine the benefits and the cost from technological policy and related activities.

Usually, a main objective of technology policy is to increase and enhance the use of new technologies. These technologies can be derived either from abroad or from domestic innovators and can be used by domestically owned, or, in owned foreign firms. Although different countries can be choose to develop the same kind of technologies, the policies that usually follow can differ considerably. Technological policies are based on the role of government's intervention and the relevant chosen priorities, such as the financial support. The divergence of national policies stem from differences between national systems and varying views on the role of the government.

According to different government's policies, some countries give unfair advantage to their companies in the international competition affecting the development of research activities and new technologies. The way in which priorities are combined and formulated in practice can vary according prioritisation criteria; for instance, a number of priorities that are not scientific and technological in a "strict sense" nonetheless have a considerable impact on the scale of science and technology. This is obviously in various priorities with economic and social aims (such as in defence, and industrial competitiveness).

In setting different priorities, we should take into account different conditions of each country and each regions as well as different elements and objectives of other sectors. We should try to establish some close linkages among different priorities and the policy's objectives from other sectors. Education and the stock of knowledge, for instance, play an important role in influencing the rate of innovation and diffusion of technology. Usually, technological policy should aim to create a favourable "psychological climate" for the development of research and innovations; for instance, different financial incentives, the support in education and training programmes, to provide technical services etc.

In technological and science policy, economic forecasting is required, if economic gains are to be a major component of science strategy; for instance, there is little point in developing a new technology for which there is no market due to changing economic conditions. Otherwise, there is little point in developing a technology in a country when there are good reasons to believe that another technology will be developed in another country and supersede the indigenous technology, possible even before it is developed.

Thus, governments should pay more attention to the following points:

- to deal with multiple policy objectives in the establishment of priorities including their quantification;
- deal with uncertainty in the ex-ante assessment of cost and benefits for the proposed government-financed programmes;

- compare the cost-effectiveness of government intervention with other alternatives solutions; and
- identify the appropriate type of government intervention.

Technological policies aim to support and promote the new technologies through different "direct and indirect measures". "Direct measures" usually include different subsidies, or different favourable tax treatments for research and technological activities. "Indirect measures" are carried out in the pursuit of other policy objectives (for instance, competition policy, monetary, fiscal policies etc.), and, consequently, affect different research and technological activities.

If there is availability of data and necessary information for research and technological activities, the safer plan is to make a separate analysis for each economic sector concerning research and technological activities and take them into account in the perspective plans. The next step is to consider and analyse some specific sectors that can be served as a guide for further government action. The final step is to choose the method for government action.

The experience in most advanced countries shows that economic growth has been close related with that of technological growth and technological planning. The history of advanced technologically countries indicate that technology transfer has been essential contributed to industrialisation and to modernisation of the whole economy in new industrialised countries and advanced countries. However, most advanced technological countries import a substantial part of the technology that they use, as it happened to Japan and other European advanced technological member states.

Finally, one important question is to examine the availability in human resources and the manner in which these resources are used. Universities and research institutes are important source that can be substantial contribute to the radical change in technological opportunities and infrastructure.

Educational institutions can contribute to the introduction and diffusion of new techniques in different sectors. For many future employees they provide the first contact with techniques they will employ in their workplace.

Educational bodies and research institutions can often play a useful role in building up a core of expertise for a new industry itself before the industry becomes commercially viable. The industries that are based upon or associated with nuclear energy provide an example.

Policies designed to alter the rate of economic growth directly tend to focus on enhancing the technological advances and the quality of labour force. The rate of technical change is affected by research expenditures and the rate of improvement of the quality of labour force is affected by investment in human capital (such as training, and education). The investment in human capital affects positively the rate of technical change.

In general (macro oriented) factors – the process of human resource formation, the inflow of foreign technologies, the government's industrial, trade and science/

technology policies that shaped industrial structure and the direction of growth, and so on – set the stage for a rapid acquisition of technological capability.

Table 4.12 illustrates the instruments of government policy that aim to support the industrial research and technological activities in Greece, in comparison to other countries.

Table 4.12 Government policy instruments used to support the industrial R&D: Policy instruments (approximate share expenditures in brackets)

United States	Tax concessions (65%), grants (35%) (procurement)
Canada	Grants (100%) (tax concessions not included)
Japan	"Consignment" subsidies (40%),tax concessions (35%), grants (25%), equity capital (2.5%)
CEC	Grants (100%) (tax concessions not included)
Denmark	Grants (some repayable) (80%), loans (20%)
France	Grants (50%), repayable grants (25%), tax concessions (2.5%)
Germany	Grants (90%), tax concessions (10%)
Greece	Grants (infrastructure development) (100%)
Ireland	Grants (100%)
Spain	Grants (100%)
United Kingdom	Grants (65%), mixed grants and loans (35%)

Note: "Consignment" subsidies involve R&T in private industry and cooperative research projects.
Source: OECD, "Industrial Policy in OECD countries, annual".

There is a great deal of confusion about the meaning of "Appropriate technology". Several times, the word of appropriate technology has been used as synonymous with the suitable or "proper" technology. Therefore, appropriate technology can be understood as a technology that may be suitable to or proper in a particular community, area, region or country. Another problem with appropriate technology is that many people have been considering appropriate technology as an approach which is relevant only to the so-called "Less Developed or Poorer countries or South".

We can distinguish two views on appropriateness of technology. The first concerns policies devoted to indigenous produced technology, whereas the second concerns policies of appropriateness for technology transfer. Appropriate technology has to meet the basic criteria of comparable efficiency, performance and general production needs. The problem of appropriate technology is closely related to relevant strategies that each government follows. The problem of appropriate technology is also related to the availability of resources and the market size.

Appropriate technology models offer many advantages for the socio-economic development particularly of developing countries, as for instance in the solution of rural employment problem, decentralisation and dispersal of industries in rural areas, encouragement of agro-industries, capital-saving and low costs, use of local resources, transfer of new skills and technical know-how, wide-dispersal of income, ecological balance, development of organisational-managerial and marketing skills. Labour intensive technologies tend to be available on a mass scale so that a large part of population can employ in these technologies. They also tend to use local resources in terms of material and energy that improve productive capacity on a sustained level of provided skills, encourage capital formation, research and technological capabilities. However, appropriateness of technology alone cannot guarantee effectiveness of small scale industries. Amongst other variables that play crucial role in determining the success of small industrial enterprises are the following: business management skills, technology use skills, resource supplies, regional and international climate, degree of monopolisation of industry areas and market volatility.

There is widespread agreement that a defining aspect of new economy is the increased importance of knowledge. But what exactly does this mean? There are two important types of knowledge industries to consider: First, there are those industries whose major product is knowledge itself; then there are industries that manage or convey information. On the one hand, the first group includes industries such as software, biotechnology, and information technology hardware; and occupations such as engineers, scientists, programmers, and designers, whose major output is research that translates into new products and services.

These industries are driven not by machinery, skilled labour force, or even capital – although these all play a role – but rather by individuals engaged in research, design, and development. While these industries make up less than 7% of the economy's output, they are in many ways key drivers of new economy. Just as capital- and machinery-intensive industries (for instance,, autos, chemicals, steel) drove growth in the 1950s and 1960s, knowledge production firms are the growth engines of new economy. On the other hand, a large share of the economy is now involved in managing, processing, and distributing information. These industries include telecommunications, banking, insurance, advertising, law, medicine, and much of government and education; and occupations such as managers, lawyers, bankers, sales representatives, accountants, and teachers. In these industries, effective handling and managing of information, rather than breakthrough knowledge generation, are the keys to success.

The various objectives of technological policy may be subsumed under five headings:

- to improve the efficiency of the transfer of technology from foreign suppliers to the local users;
- increase the efficiency of operation of technology;
- strengthen the industrial base;

- develop the indigenous technological capability; and
- smooth adjustment forced by new technologies.
- In addition, science and research policies should be oriented towards two main objectives:
- to assess the possibilities and needs of private and public enterprises with respect to research and technological activities.
- to choose those priority objectives that can delineate government technological action.

We are using the term "innovation" rather broadly in order to include processes through which firms master and practice product designs and manufacture processes that are new to them, if not to the nation or even to the universe. We are adopting "innovation" to the actors that do research and development. The term "system" indicates something that is designed and built, but this concept is far from the orientation here. The term indicates a set of institutions whose interactions determine innovative performance. The term of "system" concept is a set of institutional actors that play major role in influencing the innovative performance. We are using the term "national system of innovations" in order to indicate policies that are related to research and technological activities planning (both from a macro and micro economic view) in a country.

New technologies imply some direct and indirect effects or more specifically some micro effects (such as firms, and organisations) and macro effects (such as inter and intra-industrial and moreover regional effects) for the whole economy. New technologies play an important role is sectoral productivity, overall growth, employment, modernisation, industrialisation, socioeconomic infrastructure and to competitiveness of a country. Principal effects on technological policy can are distinguished in demand and supply.

Evaluating assertions that information and communication technologies, defined by the use of the internet and other computer networks, drive change in overall economy requires solid statistical information. Improving baseline measures of economy and developing measures specific to the electronic economy will provide the required information. Over a very short period, national statistical offices have made great progress in providing high-quality, timely indicators of the use of ICT.

On the one hand, the ICT sector grew strongly in OECD economies over the 1990s. Rapid growth was especially apparent in Finland, Sweden and Norway. In Finland, the ICT sector's share of value added doubled over 1995-2001 and now represents over 16.4% of total business sector value added. In 2000, the ICT sector represented between 5% and 16.5% of total business sector value added in OECD countries. The average share in a group of 25 OECD countries was about 9.8%; it was 8.7% in the European Union. Ireland, Finland, Korea, Japan and Mexico are specialised in the manufacturing of ICT goods. For example, in Finland, ICT accounts for almost 23% of total manufacturing value added. Except for Ireland, where computing and office equipment accounts for over 10% of manufacturing value added, the largest contribution to economic activity typically comes from manufacturing telecommunications equipment. ICT services, such as telecommunication and computer services, often constitute between 70% and 90% of total ICT sector value added.

Most OECD countries have already got a well-developed telecommunication services sector, which makes a sizeable contribution to ICT sector value added. Hungary and the Czech Republic have the highest relative share of telecommunication services. At the same time, there is a noticeable increase in the contribution of computer and related services, mainly software services. The share of computer and related services in business services value added was highest in Ireland (7% in 1999), Sweden (5.7% in 2000), and the United Kingdom (5% in 2001). Software consultancy accounts for between 60% and 80% of computer services. Looking at the most important variables and the related data of Information and Telecommunication Technologies, we can focused on the following points:

- Computers are increasingly present in homes both in OECD countries, with high penetration rates, and in those where adoption has lagged. Given differences in reference periods, survey methodologies and household structure, it is however difficult to compare the various countries.
- The picture of households with internet access is similar. On the one hand, in Denmark, Sweden and the United States, more than half of households had internet access in 2001. On the other hand, in France and Portugal, less than one-fifth had internet access in that year. Data on internet access by household size are available for the United Kingdom, Finland, Austria and Germany. They show that more households with children have internet access than households without children. Countries with the highest rates of internet use by adults are Sweden (70%), Denmark (64%) and Finland (62%). However, internet use is growing more slowly in these countries than in other OECD countries, a sign that they are reaching saturation. Men make greater use of the internet than women in all countries for which data are available. The gap is largest in Switzerland where one-half of men but only one-third of women use the internet. The internet is used for different purposes in different countries. More than eight out of ten internet users in Switzerland, Austria, the USA, Denmark and Sweden use electronic correspondence. It is also commonly used to find information about goods and services, particularly in Sweden, Denmark and Finland, small countries with high internet penetration rates.
- In many countries almost all enterprises with ten or more employees use the internet. Frequent use of the internet seems to be positively correlated with a country's number of enterprise Web sites. In Finland, Denmark, Canada, Sweden and Ireland, two-thirds or more of all enterprises with ten or more employees have Web sites.

- The internet is less used by smaller than by larger enterprises, and differences among countries are more striking when small enterprises are compared. Finland has the highest share of internet use by enterprises with 10-49 employees, almost double that of Mexico, which has the lowest share in this size class.
- A number of countries have started to measure the value of internet and electronic sales. Total internet sales range between 0.3% and 3.8% of total sales. Electronic sales, for instance, sales over any kind of computer-mediated network, reach 10% or more of sales in Austria, Sweden, Finland and Ireland. In the US retail sector, the share of electronic sales in total sales grew by 70% between the fourth quarter of 2000 and the fourth quarter of 2002.
- In 1990, trade in ICT goods, defined as the average of imports and exports, accounted for over 13% of OECD-wide trade in goods. By 2000, the share had reached almost 20%. ICT imports and exports contributed to total imports and exports by roughly the same amount (18% of imports and 17% of exports). The ICT manufacturing sector plays a particularly important role in Ireland (41% of manufacturing trade) and Korea (30%). In Hungary, the Netherlands, Mexico and Japan, it represented about a quarter of total manufacturing trade in 2001. The overall trade balance shows countries' relative comparative advantage in ICT manufacturing. Only six countries showed a positive ICT trade balance in 2001. The surplus was highest in Ireland, Korea and Japan. The main source of comparative advantage in Finland and Sweden is trade in telecommunications equipment; in Ireland, it is trade in computers.

New information specific to information and communication technologies and electronic business infrastructure – is needed for all industries and sectors. In many cases, relatively minor changes to data collection programs would provide initial information about electronic commerce transactions. A series of longer-term improvements would continue to improve baseline measures of the entire economy and would allow better assessments of the impact of electronic economy. The suggestions in this chapter are a first step in the planning process. Measuring information and communication technologies touches on almost every aspect of the economy. No single statistical agency has resources and technical expertise to independently resolve all measurement issues and fill all information gaps associated with measuring electronic economy. What is needed is the cooperation across statistical agencies.

The economic performance of the bulk of manufacturing industries and services that lie outside new technology sectors depends to a large extent on adopting ideas and products developed elsewhere A stable macro-economic environment that encourages investment in the creation and adoption of new technologies is an important requirement. More important however are micro-economic policies that induce firms to share information, develop absorptive capacity and increase rates of adoption of new technologies, either directly (through subsidies, and financial schemes) or indirectly through alteration of the institutional and regulatory environment.

Small countries are likely to need a more comprehensive and oriented policy of co-operative innovative effort in order to develop their future capabilities and make the necessary choice for technological priorities. The participation of member states in the EU research and technological programmes can increase the opportunities for promotion and improvement of research activities, creation of new research institutions so to support innovation and diffusion of new technologies and, therefore, to improve the level of economic and regional growth and induce social development. In general, debates about the political response to innovation date back at the beginning of the industrial revolution. In particular, recent debates about biotechnologies suggest that knowledge-based economy may be associated with equally vociferous debate – and action.

The governance of technological change – when it is a matter of politics rather than markets – is likely to play an important role in shaping this evolution. The issue of "governance" is a relatively new one, with the White Paper only being published in late 2001. However, it is central to thinking about policy-making and is likely to have a large impact on across all policy areas. As previous discussion has highlighted, in thinking about innovation policy it is essential that consideration is given to other policy areas, and conversely that thinking about innovation should be a consideration in the development of policy in these other areas. The direction given by the White Chapter should lead to policy-making processes becoming more open ones. It is difficult at this stage to be precise about the direct effect that this may have on innovation and innovation policy.

Consequently, many policymakers view research universities as «knowledge factories» for the new economy with largely untapped reservoirs of potentially commercialisable knowledge waiting to be taken up by firms and applied. The theoretical shift toward an emphasis on interactive learning in the production and application of knowledge carries critical implications for the processes of knowledge transfer and regional economic development in general, and for universities in particular. Knowledge frontier moves so rapidly that successful innovation requires constant learning and adaptation, and thus the emerging paradigm is more accurately described as a "learning economy" than a "knowledge-based" one. Innovation is also a *social process*, where users and producers actively learn from each other by regular "learning-through-interacting". In this context, learning refers primarily to the building of new competencies and the acquisition of new skills rather than simply accessing information of codified scientific knowledge. However, successful learning through interaction involves a capacity for *localised* learning within firms, and between firms and supporting institutions in a region. In this sense, the capacity for learning of firms in a region – the ability to develop and assess both person-embodied, tacit knowledge, and easily accessible and reproducible codified knowledge – is a critical variable in successful innovation. Much of this multi-faceted institutional behaviour that is closely engaged with the local economic community is captured in the concept of the "entrepreneurial research university".

The identification of key sectors or priority groupings must be accompanied with a framework for policy and decision-making. Interventions will differ according to the aspirations and needs of the sector. The set of interventions is likely to:

- Include rollout of a focused innovation centre and enterprise hub programme, centred on the areas of international quality expertise.
- Strength the links between enterprise and the knowledge base, through, for instance, R&D grants, spinout and licensing assistance.
- Support networks, skills initiatives and tailored business support packages, focused on needs and issues of certain sectors.
- Establish and overseeing international alliances, to ensure the international competitiveness and profile of what the region offers.
- Participate in the inter-regional initiatives, where there are sector synergies with other regions.
- Achieve the highest sustainable economic growth and employment and arising standard of living in member countries, while maintaining financial stability, and thus to contribute to the development of the world economy.
- Contribute to sound economic expansion in member as well as non-member countries in the process of economic development.
- Contribute to the expansion of world trade on a multilateral, non-discriminatory basis in accordance with international obligations.
- Ensure stable macroeconomic and framework conditions to underpin the entrepreneurial business environment.
- Ensure the reduction and simplification of administrative regulations and costs which fall disproportionately on SMEs.
- Promote an entrepreneurial society and entrepreneurial culture, in particular through education and training. Integrate entrepreneurship at all levels of the formal education system and ensure access to information, skills and expertise relating to entrepreneurship via "lifelong learning" programmes for the adult population. Promote the diffusion of training programmes by stimulating the private market's supply of such services and providing hands-on focused courses.
- Integrate the local development dimension into the promotion of entrepreneurship.
- Ensure that programmes in support of SMEs and entrepreneurship are realistic in terms of cost and are designed to deliver measurable results.
- Strengthen the factual and analytical basis for policymaking so that policy makers can take decisions in an informed manner based on empirical evidence.
- Increase the ability of women to participate in the labour force by ensuring the availability of affordable child care and equal treatment in the

workplace. More generally, improving the position of women in society and promoting entrepreneurship generally will have benefits in terms of women's entrepreneurship.

- Support the emergence and maintenance of innovative clusters. Help local actors implement the cluster strategies primarily through schemes to stimulate collaboration between public and private research institutions, improve the availability of market information and strengthen co-operation among firms, for instance in the fields of market intelligence, design and branding, and technological and human resource development.

- Promote policy coherence at regional, national and international level. Work to support whole of government approaches so that trade and investment policies and standard setting are aligned with development co-operation objectives and policies. We believe we tacked the KBE and the effect on the innovation and entrepreneurship activities, and we offer an analysis at the existent internal mechanism relating both.

Chapter 5
European Innovation Policy and Regional Cohesion

1. Introduction

Europe's overall economic performance experienced a significant weakening, after years of exceptional growth by European standards. The GDP of the European Union grew by 1.6% in 2001, a reduction of nearly 2% compared with that of 2000, when the highest growth rates of the last fifteen years were recorded. Economic growth gradually slowed down in 2002 and, more or less, stagnated in the first half of 2003. Most of the world's other main economies also experienced a slowdown and some of them even showed negative growth rates (for instance, real GDP actually declined). The US economy, after years of vigorous growth well ahead of the figures registered in the European Union, encountered near-stagnation in 2001. Japan, which had hardly recovered from the previous weak years, reported economic growth very close to zero.

Investment in research and development (R&D) rose in 2001 and into 2002, as did investment in software in several countries. Information and Communication Technology (ICT) continued to diffuse to households and businesses and electronic commerce continued to gain in importance, despite the slowdown in parts of the ICT sector. The growing role of knowledge is reflected in economic performance. In Australia, Canada, Finland, Ireland and the United States, the overall efficiency of capital and labour – Multi-Factor Productivity (MFP) – increased considerably over the 1990s, partly thanks to rapid technological progress and the effective use of ICT.

The trade-to-GDP ratio increased by about 2 percentage points over the 1990s in the United States and the European Union, although it remained stable in Japan. Over the 1990s, manufacturing, particularly high-technology industries, was increasingly exposed to international competition.

- In 1999, OECD countries made 99.268 patent applications to the European Patent Office (EPO), based on priority date, a 68% increase from 1991.
- The EU accounted for 47% of total OECD patent applications to the EPO, significantly above the United States (28%) and Japan (18%).
- Among European countries, Germany had by far the largest share with 20.5% of total EPO applications, more than the combined shares of France, the United Kingdom, Italy and the Netherlands Patent applications from

Korea, Ireland and Finland increased sharply over the 1990s (annual growth rates of 16% or more).

Researchers are viewed as the central element of the R&D system. They are defined as professionals engaged in the conception and creation of new knowledge, products, processes, methods and systems and are directly involved in the management of projects. For those countries that compile data by qualification only, data on university graduates employed in R&D are used as a proxy. The number of researchers is here expressed in full-time equivalent (FTE) on R&D (for instance, a person working half-time on R&D is counted as 0.5 person-year) and includes staff engaged in R&D during the course of one year. Underestimation of researchers in the United States is due to the exclusion of military personnel in the government sector. The business enterprise sector covers researchers carrying out R&D in firms and business enterprise sector institutes. While the government and the higher education sectors also carry out R&D, industrial R&D is more closely linked with the creation of new products and production techniques as well as to the country's innovation efforts.

The White Paper on European Governance [COM(2001)428] concerns the way in which the EU uses the powers given by its citizens. It proposes, "opening up the policymaking process to get more people and organisations involved in shaping and delivering EU policy. It promotes greater openness, accountability and responsibility for all those involved. The quality, relevance and effectiveness of EU policies depend on ensuring wide participation through the policy chain: from conception to implementation ...". Such reform must start now, so that people see changes well before further modification of EU Treaties. These considerations clearly respond to widespread expressions of dissatisfaction with remote and nontransparent policy institutions – and could be seen as another manifestation of the emergence of the knowledge-based economy and society.

The European Commission requires effort from all the Institutions, central governments, regions, cities, and civil societies in the current and future Member States. The White Paper is primarily addressed to these actors – some of whom will be responsible for initiating reforms of governance in their own countries, regions and organisations. Proposals within the White Paper indicate:

- The EU must renew the Community method by following less of a top-down approach, and by complementing its policy tools more effectively with no legislative instruments.
- Better involvement and more openness implies provision of up-to-date, on-line information on preparation of policy through all stages of decision-making.
- There is a need to be a stronger interaction with regional and local governments and civil society. Member States bear the principal responsibility for achieving this, but the Commission has a role to play.

- This kind of development (in Governance) does not initially appear to have a direct bearing on innovation propensity. Nevertheless, it could influence the culture of public and private sector organisations, and the way they work together. It could stimulate the creation and growth of new kinds of knowledge-based companies, offering information, advice and support in new enhanced democratic or stakeholder processes.
- To improve the quality of its policies, the EU must first assess whether action is needed and, if it is, whether it should be at the EU level. Thus, the EU obligation ought to clarify and simplify proposed regulations and support schemes and determine if support can be decentralised.

This chapter aims to analyse and examine the evaluation of the knowledge-based economy and the development of the EU's policy, and how it can be implemented to the member states and the effects on economic growth and integration. It also attempts to examine the role of knowledge-based economy and innovation policy and their effects on sustainable development and, more specifically, on economic integration, and regional development.

2. The Framework of European Innovation Policy

Innovation requires, first and foremost, a state of mind combining creativity, entrepreneurship, willingness to take calculated risks and an acceptance of social, geographical or professional mobility. Being innovative also demands an ability to anticipate needs, rigorous organisation and a capacity of meeting deadlines and controlling costs.

Greater priority should be given at both national and Community level to disseminate organisational innovations and use information and communication technologies in this field. The Commission aims to favour the use the instruments at its disposal (the framework programme, the Structural Funds and the training programmes) to this end.

The EU and the member states should first of all make efforts to improve the European patent system, making it more efficient, more accessible and less expensive. The public debate has confirmed the needs of users in this field. Many of the defects in the current situation stem from the coexistence of three patent systems in the EU: national, European and Community. The Commission recommends that Member States put in place instruments for assisting SMEs and universities in the event of litigation, to raise awareness in SMEs and to develop training schemes in this area.

The Commission needs to work on propagating good practice, facilitating its adoption – particularly with the support of pilot projects- and mobilising the Structural Funds and newer instruments such as the European Investment Fund (EIF).

This action should be guided by three objectives:

- First, investment in risk capital and equity needs encouragement. This applies particularly to start-up investment and innovative, high-growth firms, which are a major source of new jobs. Long term sources of funding (pension funds, life insurance, "business angels" and save-as-you-earn schemes) should be directed more towards risk investment.
- Secondly, the conditions within which European capital markets for innovative, high-growth companies (such as the New Market Federation or EASDAQ) develop must be secured.
- Thirdly, interfaces between technological innovation and financial circles need to be strengthened. Support is needed for the transnational dissemination of good practice and the testing of new methods in this area. Furthermore, closer links between Community research and risk capital should improve the exploitation of the results of the research. Information and guidance service on this topic will be set up for those taking part in the framework programme.

2.1 Human Resources, Education and Training

Education, vocational training, further training, and concern for the skills level of the entire labour force are strong elements in innovation policies. However, educational budgets in member states are more decentralised than budget lines of most other innovation policy relevant actions. The observation that science subjects trail in popularity among school children and young people has become a concern to most member state governments.

The linkages between university level education and the enterprise sector: in this field most policies and measures aim to support the mobility of university graduates into their first jobs and promote the exchange of research staff.

2.2 Entrepreneurship and Innovation Finance

Recent national White Papers and Action Plans show the need to rationalise the framework conditions to support SMEs and industrial competitiveness. The following examples are categorised according to entrepreneurship and innovation finances. The excessive costs of patent protection in Europe compared with patent costs in the United States are addressed in most member states. The variety of measures demonstrates the difficulty in combining the benefits of protection (allowing a pay-back to the inventor/innovator) with the benefits of wider exploitation of new products, processes (in particular in biotechnology), or services.

European Norms and Standards

There is an uneven presence of adequate infrastructures to promote recent years' advances in the use of high quality norms and standards, not least in the field of services and in the application of total quality standards or design as a competition parameter.

Priorities differ among countries according to the current situation of the science, technology and innovation system in each country. The size of individual economies, industrial structure, and specific economic problems are likewise factors that determine priorities at national and regional level. Reallocation of government portfolios and departmental responsibilities are another indicator of policy development. The trend in several countries has been to maintain or raise the level at which R&D expenditure is co-ordinated with other industry relevant budgets.

Re-organisation at government level has been accompanied by restructuring of institutions as well. Intermediary institutions for the support of technology transfer and the co-operation among major research institutions are often organised as private non-profit entities outside the public sector.

2.3 Innovation, Growth and Employment

The new theories of growth (known as "endogenous") stress that development of know-how and technological change – rather than the mere accumulation of capital – are the driving force behind lasting growth. According to these theories, authorities can influence the foundations of economic growth by playing a part in the development of know-how, one of the principal mainsprings of innovation. Authorities can also influence the "distribution" of know-how and skills throughout economy and society, for instance, by facilitating the mobility of persons and interactions between firms and between firms and outside sources of skills, in particular universities, as well as ensuring that competition is given free rein and by resisting corporatist ideas.

The relationship between innovation and employment is complex. In principle, technological progress generates new wealth. Product innovations lead to an increase in effective demand which encourages an increase in investment and employment. Process innovations, for their part, contribute to an increase in productivity of the factors of production by increasing production and/or lowering costs. In the course of time, the result is another increase in purchasing power, which promotes increased demand and, here again, employment.

Table 5.1 Some of the factors explaining American and Japanese success

United States	Japan
• A more important research effort	• –
• A larger proportion of engineers and scientists in the active population	• –
• Research efforts better coordinated, in particular with regard to civilian and defence research (in particular in the aeronautic, electronic and space sectors)	• A strong ability to adapt technological information, wherever it comes from. A strong tradition of cooperation between firms in the field of R&D
• A close University - Industry relationship allowing the blossoming of a large number of high technology firms	• An improving cooperation between University / Industry, especially via the secondment of industrial researchers in Universities
• A capital risk industry better developed which invests in high technology. NASDAQ, a stock exchange for dynamic SMEs	• Stable and strong relationships between finance and industry fostering long term benefits and strategies
• A cultural tradition favourable to risk taking and to enterprise spirit, a strong social acceptance of innovation	• A culture favourable to the application of techniques and on-going improvement
• A lower cost for filing licenses, a single legal protection system favourable to the commercial exploitation of innovations	• A current practice of concerted strategies between companies, Universities and public authorities
• Reduced lead time for firms creation and limited red tape	• A strong mobility of staff within companies

Source: OECD, STAN database.

2.4 Innovation and Cohesion

Innovation is particularly important for regions which lag behind in development. The SMEs, which make up virtually the entire economic fabric, encounter special difficulties, particularly with regard to financing. For instance, the actual interest rates are often 2-3 points higher than in more developed regions, this is a frequent occurrence with cooperation opportunities; access to sources of technical or management skills, etc. The handicaps mount up, indicating shortcomings in the operation of markets which can justify intervention by authorities. Table 5.2 illustrates the index of industrial specialisation of high to medium and low industries.

Table 5.2 Index of industrial specialisation for high, medium and low tech industries

OECD = 100	Japan		United States		European community	
	1970	1992	1970	1992	1970	1992
High technology	124	144	159	151	86	82
Medium technology	78	114	110	90	103	100
Low technology	113	46	67	74	103	113

Source: OECD, STAN database.

The effort channelled towards developing innovation as part of the Community's regional policy needs to be seen as an opportunity for two reasons. On the one hand, it is an effort to target regions and fields which have a special need, and, therefore, this should be seen as a priority in innovation development. On the other hand, it is a means by which the laggard regions can move immediately alongside the developed regions, not by attempting to imitate what the latter have already achieved but by trying to lay the groundwork, in accordance with their own features and requirements and together with the developed regions to adapt the conditions of competitiveness of a global economy. Figure 5.1 illustrates scientific and technological performance for the EU vis-à-vis the US and Japan.

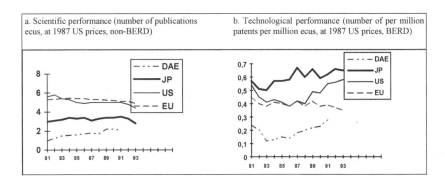

Figure 5.1 Propensity of the EU, US, and Japan to produce results
Source: Data from European report on science and technology indicators (summary, author's elaboration).

These are exciting times for the economics of information and knowledge. Industry in developed countries is moving from metal-bashing to knowledge generation. The information or ICT revolution is pushing to eliminate the effects of "weight" and distance. The fact that knowledge is, in central ways, a public good and that there are important external means that exclusive or excessive reliance on the market may not result in economic efficiency. At national level, several types of action are necessary, depending on the member state; the Commission may give assistance where appropriate:

• *Firstly, develop a strategic foresight vision of research and its application*

Exercises such as "key technologies", "Delphi" or "Foresight" can contribute to directing collective efforts to sectors, areas or technologies, which are the most relevant the future. Member States which do not have any experience in that area ought to consider the opportunity of this type of approach. The Commission will act to:

- facilitate the exchange of experiences between Member states and exploit the results of these exercises in order to identify relevant leads at the Community level;
- reinforce technology watch at a European level within the framework of the European Science and Technology Observatory, set up by the RCC's Institute for Prospective Technological Studies as focal point for the Member states observatories.

• *Secondly, strengthen the research carried out by industry, in both absolute and relative terms*

Member states are requested to draw up quantitative and ambitious objectives aiming to increase the share on the Gross Internal Product dedicated to research, to development and to innovation, in particular by encouraging research undertaken by industry (especially the one financed by enterprises or by governments within the limits allowed by article 92 of the Treaty). In Europe, the share of GDP devoted to research financed by industry, which offers more opportunities for exploitation, is on average 38% below that of the USA and 55% below that of Japan.

• *Thirdly, encourage strongly the start-up of technology-based firms ("campus companies", spin-offs, etc.)*

The Commission recommends that member states step up the action they have been taking in this area and exploit the structures which have proved effective in the field. Since 1997, it has been organised a thorough exchange with member states on this topic, involving leading players in the field. This will concentrate on measures to facilitate this spin-off process (covering intellectual property rights, social rights, financial arrangements, etc.) and national or regional promotion schemes. It will back up the dissemination of best practice through pilot projects involving, for example, university technology-transfer departments, regional institutions concerned, venture capital companies and technology brokers.

• *Fourthly, intensify the cooperation between public, university and industrial research*

The Commission recommends that member states establish a legal and practical framework which will foster this cooperation by:

- providing opportunities for universities and researchers to spend some of their time developing companies;
- enabling universities and public research centres to incorporate exclusive contracts with industry so to take advantage of exploiting results, including through financial holdings.

• *Lastly, strengthen the capacity of SMEs so to absorb new technologies and know-how, whatever their origin*

Substantial effort needs to be made in this area. Member states should extend the scope of their measures to include the transfer of technologies of international origin. Companies, particularly SMEs, should have easier access to expertise at the highest level, European or worldwide, in technological, organisational or management methods.

Moreover, at national and regional level, the drive to rationalise innovation support organisations, as mentioned above, needs to be accompanied by measures empowering them to achieve critical mass and the necessary degree of professionalism. The Commission will intensify activities to create improved links among various national and regional innovation-support systems. Working with the players concerned, it will help to professionalise or, where appropriate, certify new professions which may emerge out of this context.

The EU must make full use of the international dimension of innovation. Two-thirds of world innovations and scientific discoveries are made outside the EU, and most expanding markets are to be found outside Europe. In particular, this means:

- closer interaction of the framework programme with the COST and EUREKA cooperation frameworks;
- support for international industrial cooperation;
- intensified international cooperation on research and development with non-Member countries;
- stronger encouragement of entities in the countries concerned, through the possibilities offered by instruments such as TACIS, PHARE,

MEDA, etc. in order to search for a stronger synergy with community research projects; and

- continued vigilance in international negotiations for aspects liable to affect European innovation and its outlets (such as intellectual property rights and anti-counterfeit measures).

In the three main fields identified, the Commission has put forward those measures whose priority, expected impact or urgency has been confirmed by the debate. At a Community level, these measures can be financed from existing or planned budgets.

The main effort must nevertheless be made at a local, regional or national level. The Commission proposes to analyse in more detail those activities which are the province of the member states, in collaboration with local governments, in order to establish a joint reference framework and so help them identify priority options and opportunities for cooperation.

2.5 Innovation and Public Action

The Commission has clearly identified – first in the White Paper on Growth, Competitiveness and Employment, and then in its 1994 communication on An Industrial Competitiveness Policy for the European Union – that firms' capacity for innovation, and support for it from the authorities, are essential for maintaining and strengthening this competitiveness and employment. This Green Paper makes use of, adds to and extends that work with a view to arriving at a genuine European strategy for the promotion of innovation. While respecting the principle of subsidiarity, it has proposed the measures to be taken at both national and Community levels.

"In exercising their responsibilities, the authorities must promote the development of future-oriented markets and anticipate changes rather than react to them (...). The European Union must place its science and technology base at the service of industrial competitiveness and the needs of the market more effectively. Greater attention must be paid to dissemination, transfer and industrial application of research results and to bringing up to date the traditional distinction between basic research, pre-competitive research and applied research which, in the past, has not always allowed European industry to benefit from all the research efforts made." The Commission has paid attention to this aspect of updating in the new arrangements on research aid adopted in December 1995.

Strengthening the capacity for innovation involves various policies: industrial policy, RTD policy, education and training, tax policy, competition policy, regional policy and policy on support for SMEs, environment policy, etc. Ways must therefore be identified, prepared and implemented – in a coordinated fashion – the necessary measures covered by these various policies.

There is widespread agreement on the need for a global approach to the problem, incorporating technological aspects, training, venture capital development and the legal and administrative environment. According to the European Innovation-Summit (Florence, 21 and 22 June 1996), "the European council has clearly indicated that the fight for employment must remain the main priority for the Union and its Member States and within the framework of a strategy to achieve that objective has requested the Commission to establish a plan of action for the measures to be undertaken in the field of innovation.

The White Paper should be commended for its treatment of the many facets of public policy for a knowledge-economy. A key to success in knowledge-economy is a trained labour force. It is not surprising that so many countries have focused on improving their educational systems. Furthermore, we may observe the following points:

- First, in the long run, success in the knowledge economy requires creativity, higher order cognitive skills in addition to basic skills. Those countries that find ways of fostering this kind of creativity will, in the long run, be more successful in a competitive knowledge-economy.
- Second, also key to success in knowledge-economy is training in science and technology. There are good grounds for government subsidies to science education.
- Thirdly, one of the reasons that the education sector may not be as strong is due to limited competition.

Thus as regard SMEs, the Commission has outlined a new policy strategy in its report, "Small and Medium-sized Enterprises, a Dynamic Source of Employment, Growth and Competitiveness in the European Union", which has been presented to the Madrid European Council in December 1995. These priority policies and measures to be undertaken, both by the European Union and the Member States, will form the basis of the next Multi-annual Programme in Favour of SMEs and the Craft Sector for the period 1997 to 2008.

First and foremost, the authorities must establish a common strategy. This is a matter of ongoing monitoring and raising awareness. The Green Paper contributes to these two objectives by it wide-ranging debate, aiming to encourage the economic and social, public and private players. It touches upon the following:

- the *challenges of innovation* for Europe, its citizens, its labour force and its firms, against a background of globalisation and rapid technological changes;
- a *revaluation of the situation* of innovation policies and *the many obstacles to innovation*;
- *proposals or lines of action,* while respecting the principle of subsidiarity, for government, regions and the European Union, aimed at removing the obstacles and contributing towards a more dynamic European society which is a source of employment and progress for its citizens.

This mobilisation gets more and more necessary as Europe suffers from a paradox. Compared with the scientific performance of its principal competitors, but over the last fifteen years its technological and commercial performance in high-technology sectors such as electronics and information technologies has deteriorated. One of Europe's major weaknesses lies in its inferiority in terms of transforming the results of technological research and skills into innovations and competitive advantages.

3. New Economy and Knowledge-society in Europe

The meaning and scope of Innovation are defined in that Green Paper on Innovation (COM(95)688, which opened up a number of pathways. For the sake of efficiency, this *"First Action Plan"* refers to a limited number of priority initiatives to be launched very soon at Community level and includes a number of schemes put into action or announced since the launch of the Green Paper, identified as essential to the innovation process.

On 20 November 1996, the Commission adopted the First Action Plan for Innovation in Europe following the wide ranging public debate stimulated by the Green Paper on Innovation. The Action Plan provides a general framework for action at the European and member state level to support innovation process. A limited number of priority measures to be launched immediately by the Community, are identified. The plan also sets out these measures which have already been underway or which have been announced since the launch of the Green Paper. Two main areas for action have been identified:

- *Fostering an innovation culture:* education and training, easier mobility for researchers and engineers, demonstration of effective approaches to innovation in economy and in society, propagation of best management and organisational methods amongst businesses, and stimulation of innovation in the public sector and in government;
- *Establishing a framework conducive to innovation:* adaptation and simplification of the legal and regulatory environment, especially with respect to Intellectual Property Rights, and providing easier access to finance for innovative enterprises;

Gearing research more closely to innovation at both national and Community level: as far as action at the Community level is concerned, the Commission proposes to establish within the Research Framework a single, simplified horizontal framework to integrate "innovation" and "SME" dimensions. Outside of the Framework Programme, all Community instruments are to be mobilised to support innovation.

On the one hand, the Commission continues to investigate some of the long-term schemes identified in the Green Paper. On the other hand, it proposes to carry out a more detailed analysis of activities of the member states and of applicant countries, with their collaboration, with the aim of establishing, in a second phase, a common reference framework which will help to identify priority options and opportunities for cooperation.

Nevertheless, the Union's overall innovation performance continues to be disappointing. Europe as a whole must become more innovative if the strategic goal set at the Lisbon Summit of the European Council in March 2000 – the Union to become the most competitive and dynamic knowledge-based economy in the world – is to be achieved. The Commission targets five objectives:

- Coherence of innovation policies
- A regulatory framework conducive to innovation
- Encouragement of the creation and growth of innovative enterprises
- Improvement a key interfaces in the innovation system
- A society open to innovation

Action at Community level, while respecting the rules of subsidiarity is necessary to draw up and enforce the rules of the game, particularly those on *competition, intellectual property rights* and the *internal market*. Lastly, the Commission should show an example by mobilising its own instruments, above all the Framework Programme for Research and Development, and the Structural Funds.

Innovation requires, first and foremost, a state of mind combining creativity, entrepreneurship, willingness to take calculated risks and an acceptance of social, geographical or professional mobility. Being innovative also demands an ability to anticipate needs, rigorous organisation and a capacity of meeting deadlines and controlling costs.

In particular, the means to act are:

(i) Education and training

At national level, continue reviewing courses and teaching methods, above all for their ability to stimulate creativity and a spirit of enterprise from the earliest age, and think about any changes which may be necessary for trainers' training. Member states should also continue to develop life long training. The Commission's contribution will be to set up a permanent "training and innovation" forum to stimulate the exchange of experience and best practice in this area. It will continue to implement the White Paper on Education and Training, particularly where apprenticeship (Erasmus apprenticeship, European apprentice statute) and continuing training are concerned. It will foster links between schools as part of the *"Learning in the Information Society"* initiative.

(ii) Easier mobility of researchers and engineers to firms

In the orientations the Framework Programme for Research, the Commission proposes a wide programme with the main objective to enhance human potential. It should in particular boost the efforts of the framework programme to arrange for transnational secondments of young researchers and engineers to businesses, in particular SMEs, to help with their innovation or technology transfer projects. Member states are invited to adopt similar measures and to set up the conditions in order to make this mobility a reality.

(iii) Demonstrate effective approaches to innovation in the economy and in society

It is easier to make innovation acceptable and hence successful in the long run if citizens, industry, and their representatives are involved in the debate on the major technological choices to be made, and if employees, users and consumers take part in the process. The dissemination of good practice in this field should be strengthened. Moreover, the future framework programme for research should open up new approaches to demonstration, including technical, economic and social aspects, management and organisation, as well as fostering participation.

(iv) Propagate the best management and organisational methods amongst businesses

More and more of the firms that succeed are "agile", pro-active and likely to forge cooperative links with external centres of expertise. At both national and Community level greater priority should be given to disseminate organisational innovations and use information and communication technologies in this field. The Commission will see in favour the use the instruments at its disposal (the framework programme, the Structural Funds and the training programmes) to this end. Quality promotion policy contributes to steer business and public administrations towards that direction. Emulation amongst firms, such as comparative evaluation or benchmarking is an effective way of propagating good practice and enables them to compare themselves with the international leaders in their field.

(v) Finally, stimulate innovation in the public sector and in government

At national level, innovation training or awareness schemes for decision-makers and managers of projects and funds in the public domain need to be developed. The Commission will stimulate exchanges of experience on ways of promoting and propagating innovation in government departments and authorities. This may culminate in the issue of a Green Paper in 1998. It will also compile a permanent trend chart of innovation performance and policies in Europe, forming the basis for a regular report on innovation in the EU. Finally, member states are requested to pursue their schemes to foster competition in public invitations to tender and the use of performance standards.

The EU and the member states should first of all make efforts to improve the European patent system, making it more efficient and accessible but less expensive. Many of the defects in the current situation stem from the coexistence of three patent systems within the EU: national, European and Community. Since the European patent system provides for no European-level tribunal with jurisdiction over disputes in this area, there is a danger that competent Courts in the member states may deliver conflicting decisions.

The Community patent is still not effective, it has yet to be ratified by all member states, and has already fallen behind the changing requirements and the construction of Europe. The Commission will pursue its plan with the member states, that is to harmonise and complete legislation (especially with regard to the information society, design or employment), and will reinforce the role that it can play in the action against counterfeits. It will also implement information and support service for participants in the research framework programme. The Commission recommends that member states put in place instruments to assist SMEs and universities to raise awareness of SMEs and to develop training schemes in this area. Suitable legal structures (European companies, joint undertakings) must be adopted, and the promotion of existing instruments (EEIGs) will be actively pursued.

In knowledge-based economies, the efficient systems are those which combine the ability to produce knowledge, those mechanisms which can disseminate it as widely as possible and the aptitude of the individuals, companies and organisations concerned to absorb and use it. The crucial factor for innovation is thus the link between research (the production of knowledge), training, mobility, interaction (the dissemination of knowledge) and the ability of firms, particularly SMEs, to absorb new technologies and know-how.

At the *national level*, several types of action are necessary, depending on the member state; the Commission may give assistance, where appropriate, by acting to:

- Facilitate the exchange of experiences between Member states and exploiting the results of these exercises in order to identify relevant leads at the Community level.
- Reinforce technology watch at European level within the framework of the European Science and Technology Observatory, set up by the RCC's Institute for Prospective Technological Studies as focal point for the Member states observatories.
- The Commission recommends that Member States establish a legal and practical framework which will foster this cooperation by:
- providing opportunities to universities and researchers to spend some time in developing companies;

- enabling universities and public research centres to exclusive contracts with industry so to take advantage results, including through financial holdings.

Accepting that large companies have an important role to play in the innovation process, especially with smaller firms, this action should give more SMEs access to all research work and its results, develop technology transfer and stimulate innovation. In consequence, it would be desirable to improve at Community level:

- the incentive character of participation in the work of Task forces, by taking innovation more into account as a selection criterion for projects within the Fifth and Sixth framework programmes; and
- the efficiency of procedures by planning simultaneous or integrated calls for proposals for the various programmes of priority research.

4. An Evaluation of European Technological Policy

During the past quarter of a century or so, many arrangements for international economic integration have come into existence. The most important for the European Community is in reality an amalgamation of three separate communities: the European Coal and Steel Community (ECSC) established by the Treaty of Paris in 1952 and valid for fifty years. The European Economic Community (EEC) created in 1957 by the Treaty of Rome for an unlimited period and the European Atomic Energy Community (EURATOM) founded by another Treaty of Rome in 1957 and also of an unlimited duration.

The Treaty of Rome states that the aim of establishing the EEC is "to promote throughout the Community a harmonious development of economic activities, a continuous and balanced expansion, an increased stability, an accelerated raising of the standard of living and closer relations between its member states: (Article 2). In order to achieve this aim the EEC member states will consider their economic policy as a matter of common interest. They will consult with each other and with the Commission on measures to be taken in response to current circumstances (Article 103). With the EEC, the European integration reached a decisive stage in development providing a drastic form of integration: First of all, complete the customs union, the free movement of persons and capital, and finally, an integrated policy in a number of areas such as, agricultural policy, transportation, research and technological policies.

For many years, technological change has been widely considered as an *engine of growth* and an important factor in development process. Today, there is keen technological competition among the EEC, the USA and Japan. The aim is to reinforce technological capabilities and international competitiveness. European technology policy also aims to increase convergence among member states and to reduce disparities of the Community's less favoured regions. European technological policy is implemented through various rolling framework research programmes, which consist of various research projects and cover various sectors and scientific subjects.

Today, there is a large technological gap between advanced and less favoured regions within the EU. The countries of Europe have a long cultural and scientific tradition. Major scientific discoveries and the main developments in technology are products of European civilisation. The Treaty of Rome did not endow the Commission with explicit power to conduct research and technology policy. The Commission operated only through unanimous decisions of the Council of Ministers. In the first phase of the Community's research policy only eight articles from Euratom treaty were devoted to the promotion of research activities.

This treaty did not provide a framework for a general research policy. However, the Community's research activities were developed within this framework and provided the basis for the work is being done today. The ECSC and EEC treaties do not contain such detailed provisions as the Euratom treaty. During the first period 1953-1974 there was thus no clear common framework for Community's research policy. The Community's research programmes for this period concentrated mainly in the nuclear, steel and agricultural sectors. Only the Single European Act extended the Commission's competence in technological subjects and strengthened the Commission's role in these fields.

In 1965 three Communities (European Coal and Steel Community, Euratom and European Economic Community) set up a joint committee of their executive bodies to examine the merits of a Community for co-ordinated research and development programmes and to get prepared for a proposed meeting of the Councils of Ministers on this subject. In 1966, the Vice-president of EEC (M. Marjolin) addressed the issue of the importance of technology in the European Parliament. He proposed that scientific research should be regarded as an integral part of economic policy. At the same time, there was another proposition for a *technological Marshall aid* scheme that would have been based on NATO. Both aimed to fill out the existing technological gap. Finally, the *European Technological Community* was preferred.

Figure 5.2 illustrates the Gross Domestic Expenditures on Research and Development in relation to Gross Domestic Product for the mean of European Union, whereas Figure 5.3 illustrates the Business contribution to Gross Domestic Expenditures on Research and Development for the mean of European Union. However, the percentage of funds allocated for technological activities was still very low and corresponded only to 2% of the total Community's budget expenditures.

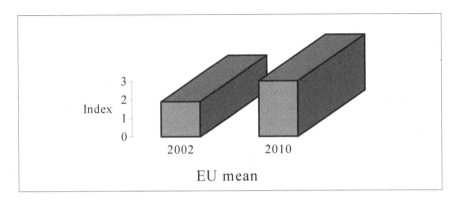

Figure 5.2 Gross domestic expenditures on research and development in relation to GDP for the EU mean
Source: Korres, G., 2008.

During the 1960s, several attempts were made to develop cross national research groupings. For instance, in 1962, Siemens, Olivetti, Elliott Automation (these later formed the core of ICL) and Bull tried to create a cross European research grouping. However, this attempt was unsuccessful. In 1969, the Eurodata consortiums (ICL, CII, Philips, AEG, Telefuken, Saab and Olivetti), established the European Space Research Organisation (ESRO) for computer requirements, but this also failed.

In 1960s, nuclear power was one of the most important areas of new technology; the Commission's power in this field derived from the Euratom treaty of 1957. At this period, four research centres were established and the areas of research extended to high temperature gas-reactors, nuclear ship propulsion and nuclear applications in medicine and agriculture. Later, in the early 1970s, the research that was undertaken at JRC (Joint Research Centres) focused on other fields, such as the environment, solar energy and materials. The most successful story in European collaboration during the 1960s and 1970s was in aerospace. In the 1970s, the European Space Agency (ESA) was developed with participation of all Western European countries. This helped create a *research space community* of scientists, engineers, policy makers and industrialists. In November 1971, the COST European programme in the field of Cooperation in Scientific and Technical research) was established. It consisted of nineteen OECD western European members (including Switzerland). COST was a useful framework to prepare and carry out pan-European projects in applied scientific research.

During 1974-1982, there was an unsteady technological policy without any apparent results. In this period, there was a tendency to increase the allocation of funds to R&T activities. In July 1978, the Commission launched FAST (Forecasting and Assessment in the field of Science and Technology) experimental programme. The main objective of FAST was to define the long-term priorities and objectives of the Community's technological policy. European technology slowed down after the energy crises of the 1970s, but it came into its own in the 1980s.

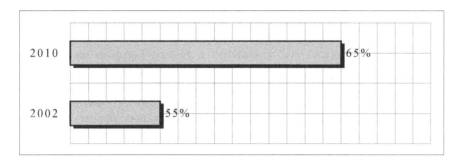

Figure 5.3 Business contribution to gross domestic on R&D (EU mean)
Source: Korres, G., 2008.

The EUREKA project was launched in 1985, and by 1990 it had already reached total committed investment by governments, companies and research institutes of more than 8 billion €, deriving from almost 500 projects. Eureka membership encompasses the EC and EFTA countries and Turkey.

The Community's research programmes and EUREKA are complementary. In June 1991, there were 470 ongoing EUREKA projects in nine technology areas, which varied greatly in their scope and financial impact. Some EUREKA projects have through their size gained widespread awareness and have created a favourable image for initiative, as for example, JESSI, HDTV, and PROMETHEUS. However, the percentage of funds allocated for technological activities was still very low and corresponded only to 2% of the total Community's budget expenditures. The Community's expenditures allocated to JRC were about 25% of the Community's total research budget, these funds were allocated mostly to the four countries where the JRCs (Joint Research Centres) are located. In addition, the Community's *direct-order* research programmes are *more suitable* for the advanced technological member states.

Until the end of the late 1980s, the Community's research policy was orientated mainly towards co-ordination of the national technology policies of member states rather than to pursue a coherent technology policy. Most of the criteria used by Community research policy were based on quality rather than our needs. However, during 1982-1990, a more coherent and clear technology policy began to develop. The European Single Act and the Treaty of Maastricht worked towards this direction. In 1987, things changed; the Single European Act (SEA) explicitly legitimised the Community dimension in scientific and technical co-operation within Europe by giving the Community formal power in the fields of research and technology. Articles 130f-130g of SEA embody a research and technology policy that enjoys equal status with other Community areas, such as economic, social and competition policy.

The SEA makes substantial amendments to the Treaty of Rome. It contains provisions that are intended to speed up European integration by completing the single market, strengthening economic and social cohesion and co-operation in financial matters. The European Single Act aims to develop the social and environment policies and to establish a genuine European research and technological Community.

The principles introduced by the Single European Act are repeated, confirmed and extended in the text agreed at Maastricht. The Treaty of Maastricht (1992) gives a double perspective to technological policy. The co-ordination of national technological policies essentially ceases to be entrusted solely to the good intentions of member states. Now, there should be mutual consistency between national and Community policies.

The Community's research policy is implemented with specific programmes. In the 1980s, the first step towards the direction of Community research policy was the formulation of the first framework program (1984-1987). This introduced the medium term planning of research activities at an EC level. The Community's research programs concern the following:

- research and technological programs of JCR centres;
- *direct order* research programs which are in collaboration and in co-financing with governments of the member states;
- training research programs; and
- international research programs.

The research framework programs aim to strengthen the international competitiveness of European industry in high technology sectors and more specifically as against the USA and Japan. The first framework programme covered seven high priority areas, and these formed the basis for a large number of projects in industry, universities and research centres.

Table 5.3 EU's framework research programmes

Focal areas	Sum in m €	Proportion of total budget
First framework programme (1984-1987):		
(1). Agricultural Competitiveness:	130	3.50
(2). Industrial Competitiveness:	1060	28.20
(3). Improving raw materials:	80	2.10
(4). Improving energy resources:	1770	47.20
(5). Stepping up development aid:	150	4.00
(6). Improving working conditions:	385	10.30
(7). Improving the S/T potential:	85	2.30
(8). Horizontal action:	90	2.40
Total Budget:	3750	100
Second framework programme (1987-1991):		
(1). Quality of Life:	375	
(2). Towards an Inf. society:	2275	6.90
(3). Modernisation of industry:	845	42.30
(4). Biological resources:	1173	15.60
(5). Energy:	280	5.20
(6). S/T for development:	80	21.70
(7). Exploiting marine resources	80	1.50
(8). Improvement of S/T co-operation:	288	1.50
Total Budget (1)-(8):	5396	5.30
R&D Programme already adopted or in hand:	1084	100
Total Budget:	6840	
Third framework programme (1990-1994):		
Enabling Technologies:		
(1). Information Technology and Communications:	3000	38.90
(2). Industrial and material technologies:	1200	15.60
Management Industrial Resources:		
(1). Environment:	700	9.10
(2). Life Sciences and Technologies:	1000	13.00
(3). Energy:	1100	14.30
Management of Intellectual Resources:		
(1). Human capital and mobility:	700	9.10
Total Budget:	7700	100
Fourth framework programme (1994-1998):		
Area I: Technology and demonstration of R&D programmes:		
Area II: Cooperation of non-EC countries and Intern. Organisation:	11600	78.91
Area III: Circulating and exploiting research funding:	1400	9.52
Area IV: Improving training and mobility for researchers:	700	4.76
Horizontal support measures:	1000	6.80
Total Budget:	(1600)	
	14700	100

Table 5.3 continued

Focal areas	Sum in m €	Proportion of total budget
Fifth framework programme (1999-2002):		
Research, technological development and demonstration activities:	10843	72.4
Confirming the International Role of Community's Research:	475	3.2
Promotion of Innovation and Encouragement of SME participation:	363	2.5
Improving human research potential and the socio-economic knowledge base:	1280	8.6
Joint Research Centre (JRC):	739	4.9
Indirect Actions: Research and Training in the Field of Nuclear Energy:	979	6.6
Direct Actions: Joint Research Centre (JRC):	281	1.8

Note: Horizontal support measures can be applied to four activities. The framework programmes aimed to promote the international competitiveness of European industry and to reinforce economic and social cohesion.
Source: Own elaboration based on EU classification.

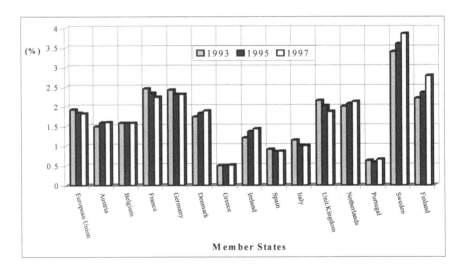

Figure 5.4 Gross domestic expenditures of R&D (percent of GDP)
Source: Korres, G., 2008.

The second framework programme started in September 1987. About 60% of the funds of the second framework programme were allocated to industrial research. However, most funds were intended to promote the introduction of new technologies to traditional industrial sectors (such as engineering and construction. The decisive breakthrough to a comprehensive political strategy on technology sectors came with the second and third framework programmes. The second (1987-1991) and the third (1990-1994) research framework programmes were based on the Single European Act. In April 1990, the Council of Ministers adopted the third framework programme (1990-1994), which overlapped the second framework programme by two years. The total appropriation of ECU 5.7 billion falls for the third framework programme into two parts: (a) 2.5 b € for 1990-1992 and (b) 3.2 b € for 1993-1994.

Table 5.3 indicates a sectoral breakdown for the Community framework research programmes. Since 1984, there has been rapid growth of the Community's research expenditures. The amount which is included in these figures corresponds to the previous proposed resource allocation of four activities: evaluation, co-ordination, concentration and JRC (Joint Research Centre). It should be noticed that the representative budget figures in the framework programmes correspond to the Community's financial contribution only. If we take into account national contributions, then the total budget would be approximately doubled. The research framework programmes consist of various projects that work on a competitive basis, which implies that the participation of each country depends upon the criteria of *quality and strength of applicants*.

The Commission proposed a total amount of 14,700 m € for the fourth research programme (1994-1998). The fourth programme complies with the provisions Treaty of Maastricht and therefore covers all the Community's research and demonstration activities. International scientific co-operation will now be part of the program, and some research activities that were outside the third framework program will be included in the new one. Figure 5.4 presents the Gross Domestic Expenditures of R&D as a percentage of GDP for European member states.

The objectives of the Community's framework programmes are to:

a. enhance European industrial competitiveness;
b. set up a vast unified market by promoting standardisation and open procurement;
c. improve the effectiveness of the Community's scientific and technical co-operation;
d. promote agricultural competitiveness;
e. speed up the marketing of new technologies by carrying out programmes for the application of information technologies;
f. help the least favoured regions of Community (LFR) obtain access to new technologies;
g. encourage SMEs and continuing education and training.

Table 5.4   Framework programmes of R&T activities: A comparison (percentages)

	1984-1987	1987-1991	1990-1994
Information and communication technologies	25	42	39
Industrial and materials technologies	11	16	16
Environment	7	6	9
Life science and technologies	5	9	13
Energy	50	23	14
Human capital	2	4	9
Total (%):	100	100	100

Source: Own elaboration based on EU classification.

Table 5.4 compares the first, second and third research framework programmes. As we can see on the one hand, information technologies receive more attention and account for about 40% of the total budget. On the other hand, research in the energy sectors has declined from 50% in the first programme to only 14% for the third. In addition, life sciences and industrial and material technologies have increased their participation and account for about 13% and 16% respectively. In the 1990s, the Community's research plans are to enforce *joint research*. In the long-term, these plans aim to change the approach of co-operation between theoretical and industrial research, by providing a *new learning environment*. The main problem for less favoured member states is the poor rate of diffusion of new technologies and lack of access to information networks related to new techniques and to new technologies. The Community aims to emphasise these points and to accelerate the diffusion of technologies between and within the member states.

For instance, the SPRINT programme was established in order to reinforce dissemination activities. SPRINT accounted for 90 m € during 1989-1993. However, in reality, SPRINT represented a total expenditure of 180 m € as it supported the total cost of an activity up to a maximum level of 50%, while the remaining expenditures were contributed by participants. Similarly, the research framework programmes have specific sections concentrated on dissemination of information and diffusion of new technologies. Table 5.5 illustrates the emerging technologies for the EU vis-avis USA and Japan. Tables 5.6 and 5.7 indicate the allocation of the whole funds by objective and the allocation of funds by member states, respectively.

Table 5.5 Emerging technologies

Europe	Vis-à-vis the USA	Vis-à-vis Japan
Ahead	Digital imaging technology Flexible computer-integrated manufacturing	Flexible computer-integrated manufacturing Software engineering technologies
Level	Advanced semiconductors High-density data storage Sensor technology Advanced materials Software engineering technologies	Artificial intelligence Digital imaging technology Sensor technology Superconductors Biotechnology Medical equipment
Behind	Artificial intelligence High-performance computers Optoelectronics Biotechnology Medical equipment	Advanced semiconductors High-performance computers High-density data storage Optoelectronics Advanced materials

Source: Korres, G., 2003.

Table 5.6 Allocation of community structural funds for various objectives

	Allocation in billions of Euro	% of the Structural Funds budget	% reserved for transitional support
Objective 1	135.9	69.70	4.30
Objective 2	22.5	11.50	1.40
Objective 3	24.05	12.30	–
Fisheries: (outside of Objective 1)	1.11	0.60	–

Source: European Union.

Table 5.7 Allocation of community structural funds for the member states

Member state	Objective 1	Transitional support ex-objective 1	Objective 2	Transitional support ex-objective 2 and 5b	Objective 3	Fisheries instrument (outside obj. 1)	Total
Belgium	0	625	368	65	737	34	1829
Denmark	0	0	156	27	365	197	745
Germany	19229	729	2984	526	4581	107	28156
Greece	20961	0	0	0	0	0	20961
Spain	37744	352	2533	98	2140	200	43087
France	3254	551	5437	613	4540	225	14620
Ireland	1315	1773	0	0	0	0	3088
Italy	21935	187	2145	377	3744	96	28484
Luxembourg	0	0	34	6	38	0	78
Netherlands	0	123	676	119	1686	31	2635
Austria	261	0	578	102	528	4	1473
Portugal	16124	2905	0	0	0	0	19029
Finland	913	0	459	30	403	31	1836
Sweden	722	0	354	52	720	60	1908
UK	5085	1186	3989	706	4568	121	15635
EUR15	127 543	8411	19733	2721	24050	1106	183 564
	Mill. €	Mill. €	Mill. €	Mill. €	Mill. €	Mill. €	Mill. €

Note: (1) Including PEACE (2000-2004). (2) Including the special programme for the Swedish coastal areas.
Source: European Union, www.eu.int/eurostat.

Since the beginning of the European integration process, three structural funds have been set up to promote harmonious economic and social development in Europe: the European Social Fund (ESF) in 1958, the Guidance Section of the European Agricultural Guidance and Guarantee Fund (EAGGF) in 1964 and the European Regional Development Fund (ERDF) in 1975. In 1986, the Single European Act provided close co-operation between the three funds, so that they may contribute effectively to the achievement of five priority objectives. The main *objectives* of CSFs are delineated briefly below:

- objective 1 refers to regions which lags in their economic development;
- objective 2 refers to industrial regions with high unemployment;
- objectives 3 and 4 concern long term and youth unemployment;
- objective 5a concerns agricultural restructuring; and
- objective 5b refers to rural regions which have a high level of income but face difficulties with development.

We can say that positive effects are mainly because of financial transfers (through CSFs). What is really necessary for the Community technological policy is that more attention should be paid to specific strategies which will take into account the particular needs and conditions of less favoured regions. The participation of member states in the Community's research framework programmes through different research institutes, organisations, universities and enterprises can give a *push* to technological flows in these countries. The Community's research framework programmes can create opportunities for costless and easy access by enterprises and scientists to new technologies and know-how.

To sum up, we can say that there were at least three major benefits from technological collaboration within European Community:

- cost savings for both research and production
- reinforced competitiveness as against USA and Japan
- technological convergence of member states.

5. European Innovation Policy and Lisbon Strategy towards Knowledge-based Economy

The European Council of Barcelona (March 2002) emphasised the importance of research and innovation by setting the goal of increasing the level of expenditure in research and development to 3% of GDP by 2010. While investing more in R&D is one part of the equation, another is better co-ordination of European research. This has been initiated through the creation of the European Research Area (ERA) and related policy actions, such as the "benchmarking of national research policies". The ERA is the broad heading for a range of linked policies attempting to ensure consistency of European research and facilitate the research policies of individual member states in order to improve the efficiency of European research potentialities.

The Lisbon strategy becomes all the more important (Spring Report: European Commission 2003d, p. 29). As decided by the Heads of State and Governments at the Lisbon Summit in 2000, this strategy aims to transfer the European Union by 2010 into "the most competitive and dynamic knowledge-based economy in the world capable of sustainable economic growth with more and better jobs and greater social cohesion". The set of measures and decisions taken then, better known as "the Lisbon strategy", entail reforms in three main dimensions:

- Further consolidation and unification of the European economic environment;
- Improvement of the creation, absorption, diffusion and exploitation of knowledge; and
- Modernisation of the social model.

Thus not only does the Lisbon strategy remain Europe's overall roadmap to higher and sustainable economic growth but also do European policy-makers acknowledge that the progress needs to be accelerated for growth recovery. This year's Spring Report, for instance, states that "The Union's priority for the next 12 months must be to stimulate investment in knowledge and innovation alongside faster structural changes in order to boost productivity and employment" (European Commission 2003d, p. 33). More recently, the European Council of Thessaloniki (European Council 2003) asked the European Commission to launch an initiative in cooperation with the Investment Bank to support growth by increasing overall investment and private sector involvement in infrastructures and in research and development (European Council 2003, p. 17; European Commission 2003e, 2003f).

Enlargement also reinforces the acceleration of the process. Integrating new Member States does not imply a rewriting of the Lisbon strategy: the targets for the whole of the Union remain the same for the EU-25. The Lisbon strategy forms a common basis for reforms needed in the new Member States as well as in the EU-15, and therefore is a sound tool for integration. However, enlargement also means that additional efforts are needed from member states in order for the Union to be kept on track in its transition to a knowledge-based economy.

Education, research and innovation are some of the main means to achieve the overall Lisbon objective. Recognising the pivotal role of education and training, the European Council invited Ministers of Education "to reflect on the concrete future objectives of education systems" and to concentrate on "common concerns and priorities". Hereby the Lisbon Council launched an unprecedented process in the area of education and training helping member states to develop their own policies progressively by spreading best practice and achieving greater convergence towards the main EU goals.

Both from a theoretical and empirical point of view, there is a broad recognition among economists and policy-makers of the impact of human capital, R&D, technological progress and innovation on productivity and economic growth. Research recently carried out for the European Commission suggests that one additional year of schooling can increase the aggregate productivity by 6.2% for a typical European country (European Commission, 2002). Countries where R&D expenditure by the business sector in relation to GDP has increased most from the 1980s to the 1990s have typically experienced the largest increase in the growth of multi-factor productivity (MFP) (OECD, 2001b).

Europe is, however, still under-investing in knowledge and skills. The EU-25 is still lagging far behind the US and Japan in R&D investment and the exploitation of technological innovations; in many domains the gap is still widening. If we are to consolidate economic recovery and enhance long-term competitiveness, efforts should therefore be maintained and increased. All Member States except Sweden registered a declining growth rate in this period compared with 1995-2000. In Germany, investment growth even became negative in 2001. The relative position of countries remains more or less unchanged since the mid-1990s. One can broadly distinguish three groups within the EU-15 in terms of efforts made to speed up the transition to the knowledge-based economy. The data go up to 2001 and show the recent progress made by the EU-15. In the United States, investment in knowledge – the sum of investment in R&D, software and higher education – amounted to almost 7% of GDP in 2000, well above the share for the EU or Japan. The OECD average was about 4.8% of GDP, of which almost half for R&D. In most OECD countries, investment in knowledge has grown more rapidly than investment in fixed assets; the United States, Canada and Australia are the major exceptions.

In 2001, OECD countries allocated about USD 645 billion (accounted with PPP, current purchasing power parity) to R&D. The United States accounted for approximately 44% of the OECD total, the European Union for 28% and Japan for 17%. R&D expenditure in the OECD area rose annually by 4.7% over 1995-2001. R&D expenditure has risen faster in the United States (5.4% a year) than in the European Union (3.7%) and Japan (2.8%). In 2001, the R&D intensity of the European Union reached 1.9% of GDP, its highest level since 1991, still well below the Lisbon target of 3% in 2010. In 2001, Sweden, Finland, Japan and Iceland were the only OECD countries in which the R&D to GDP ratio exceeded 3%.

During the second half of the 1990s, the share of business funding of R&D increased significantly in the United States, moderately in Japan and only slightly in the EU. R&D expenditure by the higher education sector increased in the first half of the 1990s and then stabilised. R&D by the government sector has declined in recent years, partly owing to the reduction in defense R&D and the transfer of some public agencies to the private sector.

In 2000, services accounted for about 23% of total business sector R&D in the OECD area, an increase of 8 percentage points from 1991. More than 30% of all R&D is carried out in the services sector in Norway, Denmark, Australia, Spain and the

United States but less than 10% in Germany and Japan. High-technology industries accounted for more than 52% of total manufacturing R&D in 2000, ranging from over 60% in the United States to 47% and 44% in the European Union and Japan, respectively. Greece, Portugal, Spain and Italy were still lagging behind in 2001. These four countries had an investment level below EU average and a growth of investment comparable to the average growth in 2000-2001 (Greece being slightly above average in terms of investment growth). However, compared to the second half of the nineties, their catching up with the rest of Europe appeared to have slowed down in 2001. A second group consisting of France, United Kingdom, Germany, Austria, Ireland, Belgium and the Netherlands occupied an average position in terms of both their investment level and growth in 2001, although the cohesion of this group is less obvious than in the 1995-2000 period.

Turning to the EU's performance in the knowledge-based economy growth was also lower, but the slowdown was less pronounced than for investment. While EU growth in 2001 was positive, its progress was not as fast as in the second half of the 1990s. This deceleration in performance growth occurred for all EU countries except United Kingdom, The Netherlands and Greece. Greece had a relatively high growth rate in all fields of the performance indicator in 2000-2001. The United Kingdom's improved growth was due to a relatively high growth in overall productivity (GDP/hour worked) whereas the Netherlands showed a high growth in technological performance (patents). Two broad groups can be distinguished within the EU-15. Portugal, Spain, Greece and Italy were below the EU average. Greece and Spain improved their positions, but Italy and Portugal registered a decline in their performance level in 2001. The second group, consisting of the remaining 10 EU countries was slightly above-average in terms of performance level (especially Sweden and Finland) in 2001 and around average in terms of growth rate. During the period in question Ireland caught up with the European average.

In terms of performance in the knowledge-based economy the Acceding countries were all below the EU-15 average performance level in 2001. This was especially pronounced for technological performance (patents). When one looks only at scientific performance or overall productivity growth, the picture was less negative for these countries, although they were still far below the average EU level.

In 2000-2001, Bulgaria recorded below-EU-average growth rates for all the sub-indicators of the performance indicator, whereas Turkey had a low growth of overall productivity. Estonia and Cyprus recorded under-average growth rates in scientific and technological performance, but had an average growth of overall productivity. Slovenia had above-average growth in technological performance in 2000-2001, but underscored notably in scientific performance. In 2001, 8.4% of the EU-15's value added originated from high-tech and medium high-tech industries, while for the EU-25 the figure was marginally lower. Ireland is at the top of the group, with almost twice the level of the next country – Malta. It is also worth noting that among the top performing countries there are both countries with a high overall share of manufacturing in their economic base

(Germany, Hungary, Czech Republic).In EU-15, about 972,500 researchers were employed in the year 2000. This number has shown an average annual growth rate of 3.9% since 1996. In the enlarged EU with 25 member states, the number will be 110,000 higher, but still about 175,000 lower than the US. Japan is on a similar level to Germany, France, the UK and Spain grouped together. Poland is the largest employer among the new Member States; the other Acceding countries each employ between 300 and 15,000 researchers.

Whereas in EU-15 about 50% of researchers are employed by the private sector and in EU-25 even less, this share increases to about 64% for Japan and about 80% for the US. In Europe, only Ireland has a similar share to Japan, and only Austria, Sweden and Switzerland are above 60%. The higher education sector is the most important employer for researchers in Spain, Portugal, Hungary, Poland, Slovakia and Turkey. The EU-15 as a whole had a lower level of overall investment in the knowledge-based economy in 2001 than the US and Japan. The decrease in investment growth during the 2000-2001 period was much stronger for the US than for the EU-15 or Japan. The fall in investment growth for both the US and Japan was due mainly to a sharp decrease in capital formation in 2000-2001. In addition, the US also recorded lower growth than EU-15 in the number of researchers; however, the growth of US research spending was close to that of the EU.

The composite indicator of performance in knowledge-based economy was lower for EU-15 than for the US in 2001, although Germany's position was marginally above that of the US. More specifically, the US still had a higher level of technological performance than the EU-15, whereas overall productivity and scientific performance in 2001 were very close to the EU level. In terms of performance growth, one can observe a similar small decrease in both the EU and the US. The interest in the contribution of R&D and human resources to growth and creation of a knowledge-based economy has reached new heights in the EU in recent years.

Today, it is widely agreed that research and technological advancement together with the availability of a highly skilled labour force are among the key factors for innovation, competitiveness and socio-economic welfare. Likewise, the capacity to exploit knowledge has become a crucial element for the production of goods and services. In 2000, the Lisbon European Council agreed upon the objective to make Europe the most competitive and dynamic knowledge based economy in the world. To reach the objective, the Barcelona Council in March 2002 set the specific target to increase the average level of R&D expenditure in the EU from 1.9% of GDP to 3% by 2010, of which two thirds should be funded by the private sector. By 2003, most Member States had taken action to boost R&D investment and set national targets in line with the 3% objective. In April 2003, the Commission adopted a strategic Action Plan ("Investing in research"; COM (2003) 226) to accelerate progress towards the goal set by the Barcelona Council. The objectives and plans are challenging, among other reasons because of the economic difficulties experienced in Europe. Economic growth in the euro region slowed down in 2002 and stagnated in the first half of 2003.

Table 5.8 R&D expenditure (in 1000 current €) per researcher (FTE), 2001

	Totals	Business enterprise	Higher education	Government
Belgium	153	201	90	127
Denmark	188	254	121	132
Germany	199	236	121	186
Greece	54	101	38	86
Spain	78	172	41	74
France	180	239	94	205
Ireland	139	151	111	130
Italy	188	239	150	165
Netherlands	186	223	145	170
Austria	180	183	168	228
Portugal	58	121	41	59
Finland	125	156	76	103
Sweden	227	291	128	132
UK	145	164	92	214
Cyprus	81	67	47	140
Czech Rep.	55	87	31	41
Estonia	14	30	11	15
Hungary	37	54	24	30
Lithuania	9	55	5	12
Latvia	10	15	7	13
Poland	23	49	12	39
Slovenia	76	131	40	57
Slovakia	16	45	3	15
Bulgaria	8	13	4	8
Romania	9	10	7	9
Turkey	60	125	50	35
Iceland	140	180	95	123
Norway	154	165	137	144
Switzerland	266	312	171	222
US	182	169	171	361
Japan	212	245	103	404

Source: European Commission, 2003.

In EU-15, every research post was funded by an average of 171,000 € in 2001. This is lower than both the US average (182,000 €) and the Japanese average (212,000 €). After the enlargement, the new EU-25 will have an average of 156,000 €. In EU-15, the R&D expenditure per researcher varies between 225,000 € in the Business Enterprise Sector (BES) and 103,000 € in the Higher Education Sector (HES). The Governmental institutions are at the average of all sectors. Sweden is the EU Member State which spent the largest amount of money per researcher with 227,000 €, followed by Germany (199,000 €). In the rest of Europe, Switzerland was highest with 266,000 €. Bulgaria, Poland and the Baltic States, all below 15,000 €, were lowest. Figures on investment are derived from the data on gross domestic expenditure on R&D (GERD). It provides an overall picture of the level of commitment to the creation of new knowledge and to the exploitation of research results in different countries. The volume of R&D investment is a proxy for countries' innovation capacity, and reflects the magnitude of both accumulation and application of new knowledge. Table 5.8 indicates the R&D expenditure (in 1,000 current €) per researcher as a full-time equivalents.

The "R&D intensity' indicator compares countries" R&D expenditure with their GDP. It also facilitates comparisons of the R&D activities between countries. R&D expenditure broken down by main sources of funds reveals information on the structure of financing and the relative importance of different sources in the national R&D system. The section also deals with the role of government in R&D financing, and expenditure on basic research. In terms of the absolute volume of R&D investment compared to the three economic blocks (EU-15, US, Japan), both the EFTA countries (€10 billion; PPS 7 billion, in 2001) and the 13 Acceding countries (€5 billion; PPS 9 billion) are comparatively small investors. For instance, the 10 Acceding countries only spent an amount equivalent to less than 2% of the total EU-15 investment in research in current terms. In addition, in the period 1998-2001, the real growth rate recorded for the Acceding countries (16%) was less than one percentage point higher than that of the EU-15. Despite the recent favourable development in the EU-15, the R&D investment gap between the EU and the US has continued to increase in favour of the US. In 2001, the gap was PPS 87 billion in real terms, and €141 billion in current terms.

Between 1997 and 2001, the growth rate was highest in the small economies and amongst the catching-up countries with relatively low absolute volumes of R&D activities and R&D intensities. The highest growth rates were recorded, in the EU, in Greece (17% per year), Finland (9%) and Sweden (8%), in EFTA, in Iceland (14%), and in the Acceding countries, in Estonia (13%), Hungary (12%), Turkey (11%) and Cyprus (10%). The figure recorded for Israel was also exceptionally high (14%). At the opposite end of the scale, the figure for Switzerland (1.3% per year) was the lowest. Only three of the countries, Bulgaria, Romania and Slovakia (each with negative growth rates) were ranked below Switzerland. Table 5.9 illustrates the R&D expenditure as a percentage, by main sources of funds.

Table 5.9 R&D expenditure by main sources of funds (percent), 2001

Countries	Business enterprise	Government	Other national sources	Abroad
Denmark	58.0	32.6	3.5	5.3
Germany	66.0	31.5	0.4	2.1
Greece	24.2	48.7	2.5	24.7
Spain	47.2	39.9	5.3	7.7
France	52.5	38.7	1.6	7.2
Ireland	66.0	22.6	2.6	8.9
Italy	43.0	50.8	–	6.2
Netherlands	50.1	35.9	2.6	11.4
Austria	39.0	42.1	0.3	18.6
Portugal	32.4	61.2	2.1	4.4
Finland	70.8	25.5	1.2	2.5
Sweden	71.9	21.0	3.8	3.4
UK	46.2	30.2	5.7	18.0
Cyprus	17.5	66.5	6.5	9.4
Czech Republic	52.5	43.6	1.7	2.2
Estonia	24.2	59.2	3.9	12.7
Hungary	34.8	53.6	0.4	9.2
Latvia	29.4	41.5	na	29.1
Poland	30.8	64.8	2.0	2.4
Slovenia	54.7	37.1	1.1	7.2
Slovakia	56.1	41.3	0.8	1.9

Source: European Commission, 2003.

In 2001, R&D intensity of the EU-15 reached a record figure of 1.98%. In spite of this achievement – the highest figure recorded ever for the EU-15 – the EU average was lagging well behind the intensity of the US and Japan and even more so than ever before. The gap was over 0.8 percentage points below the value for the US and 1.1 percentage points behind Japan. If we take into account the 10 Acceding countries, R&D intensity for the EU-25 in 2001 comes out slightly lower (1.93%) than that of the EU-15.

The small difference between figures was due to the fact that the combined volumes of both GDP and R&D expenditure in the Acceding countries are very low compared to those of the EU-15. The share of basic research in total R&D expenditure shows considerable variation between countries. The share of basic research is highest in three Acceding countries: the Czech Republic (40%), Poland (38%), and Hungary (29%). The share recorded for Switzerland was also comparatively high, 28%. Within the EU-15, Portugal's figure was the highest, followed at some distance by France, Denmark and Italy, all these in the range 22-28%. While the figure for the US was also above 20%, the share of basic research in total R&D was very low in Japan, at only 12%.

Since 1997, the share of R&D expenditures allocated to basic research, which reflects the relative importance of basic research for R&D and innovation activities, has increased significantly in many countries. For instance, during 1997-2001, in the US, expenditure on basic research grew in real terms by almost 50%, while total R&D spending increased at the same time by less than 24%. The growth rate of expenditure on basic research was also clearly higher than that of total R&D expenditure in the Czech Republic, France and Poland.

The rate of growth of expenditure on basic research has been clearly lower than that of the total R&D spending in certain countries such as Spain and Portugal. In terms of expenditure on basic research as a percentage of GDP, Switzerland (0.7%), the US (0.6%), and the Czech Republic (0.5%) put more emphasis on basic research than others.

At the other end of the scale, figures recorded for Spain, Slovakia, Portugal, Hungary and the Netherlands were all very low, below 0.2%. A key determinant of the future competitiveness of an economy is the level and intensity of overall expenditure on R&D. But it is also important to look at the sectors in which this R&D is performed. The business sector is probably the most important in this regard. It is closest to consumers and best positioned to significantly improve or develop new products based upon new combinations of existing knowledge or knowledge newly developed through research in-house or elsewhere and to commercialise them.

In the mid-1990s, the EU-15 took over from the US as being the largest producer of scientific literature in absolute terms as well as in world share. By the end of the century, the gap between the EU-15 and the US had grown to more than six percentage points in favour of the EU-15.

In 2001 Europe had to face a small decline of its share, although total publication numbers were still growing. From 2001 to however, the situation deteriorated for the EU-15 in terms of share (-2.1%), and its total number of publications also fell. With high growth rates during the latter half of the 1990s, the situation was similar for Japan. However, in terms of publication share Japan experienced a small loss in 2002 (-1.2%) but still managed to increase its total publication numbers. Table 5.10 illustrates the Relative Activity Index (RAI) by EU-15 for the time-span 1996-1999.

Table 5.10 Relative activity index (RAI) by EU-15, 1996-1999

	Engineering	Physics, Astrophysic Astronomy	Mathematics, Statistics and Computer Sciences	Chemistry	Earth and Environmental Sciences	Life Sciences
Greece	+		+		+	
Poland		+		+		
Bulgaria		+		+		
Latvia		+		+		
Italy		+				
Slovenia	+			+		
Cyprus						
Tu rkey	+					
Germany		+		+		
Russia		+		+		
Estonia		+			+	
Slovakia				+		
Spain				+		
Czech Republic				+		
France						
Japan+			+			
Israel						
UK						
US						
Austria						
Switzerland						
Denmark					+	
Belgium						
Norway					+	+
Ireland						
Iceland					+	+
Finland						+
Sweden						-1-

Source: European Commission, 2003.

The situation has certainly improved for the US. While the US suffered from diminishing publication numbers and shares during the late 1990s, it has managed to grow in both categories since 2000. It may be too early to speculate about changes in trends. However, the capabilities of the US in terms of scientific production should not be underestimated.

While the current EU-15 decrease is still minor, it may well foreshadow something worse and result from a relative decline in R&D investment in the EU-15 during the 1990s. Table 5.11 shows the activities, in terms of scientific publications, in 27 countries of the European Research Area as well as important competitors and partners. It shows the relative specialisation of each country in six main science and technology fields. Business expenditure on R&D (BERD) accounted for most of total domestic R&D expenditure (GERD) in Japan (73.7%), the US (72.9%), the EU-15 (65.6%) and the EU-25 (65.3%). The shares for both the EU-15 and the EU-25 are quite high, but substantially lower than the US and Japanese shares. However, growth rates for the period 1997-2001 of 0.9% for the EU-15 and 0.8% for the EU-25, as compared to -0.3% for the US and 0.6% for Japan, point to possible convergence in the future.

Table 5.11 R&D expenditure by top 300 international business R&D spenders by trade zone

	Number of firms	% of total R&D		Average annual growth rate of R&D investment %	Average annual growth rate of R&D investment %
	2002	1998	2002	1998-2002	1998-2002
US	127	42.8	40.9	3.1	-12.6
Japan	73	22.7	21.7	3.2	4.0
Belgium	–	0.1	0.2	19.3	16.1
Denmark	2	0.2	0.3	11.2	9.0
Finland	1	0.6	1.3	24.5	24.5
France	22	5.9	6.8	8.2	0.0
Germany	24	11.9	12.4	5.4	19.5
Ireland	1	0.6	0.1	-27.4	-10.0
Italy	3	1.2	1.1	1.4	2.9
Sweden	5	2.1	1.7	-1.0	-16.8
Netherlands	6	1.4	2.5	19.5	3.2
UK	15	4.1	5.0	9.5	0.3
Other countries	19	6.3	6.1	3.5	14.0
Total	300	100.0	100.0	4.3	-2.2

Source: European Commission, 2003.

Table 5.12 Export market shares by type of industry* and RCA in manufacuring exports**

	Total man.	High tech***	Medium tech	Low tech	Resour. intens.	Labour intens.	Scale intens.	Special. supplier	Science based
USA									
1970:	17.8	28 (159)	19 (110)	11.9 (67)	14.1 (79)	10.2 (58)	15.5 (97)	21 (123)	34 (194)
1980:	15.7	25 (160)	16 (106)	11.0 (70)	12.2 (78)	12.6 (80)	12.5 (79)	18 (118)	32 (204)
1990:	14.8	23 (161)	13.2 (89)	11.0 (74)	13.3 (90)	9.3 (63)	11.5 (78)	16 (110)	26 (181)
Japan									
1970:	9.7	12 (124)	7.6 (78)	10 (113)	3.2 (33)	12 (132)	13 (139)	10 (105)	6.1 (63)
1980:	11.7	15 (130)	12 (106)	8 (75)	2.6 (22)	8.6 (73)	17 (151)	15 (135)	6.6 (56)
1990:	12.8	19 (149)	14 (113)	5 (44)	2.3 (18)	6.2 (48)	16 (125)	19 (156)	12.2 (95)
Bel./Lux									
1970:	5.5	2.4 (44)	5.2 (95)	7.0 (127)	6.0 (109)	7.4 (135)	7.1 (129)	2.9 (52)	2.3 (42)
1980:	5.4	2.6 (49)	5.5 (102)	6.6 (123)	6.6 (122)	8.0 (149)	6.2 (115)	2.7 (50)	3.1 (58)
1990:	5.0	2.0 (40)	5.8 (116)	6.2 (124)	5.6 (113)	7.9 (159)	6.6 (132)	2.3 (47)	2.6 (53)
Denmark									
1970:	1.5	1.1 (73)	0.9 (62)	2.2 (149)	2.9 (197)	1.4 (97)	0.7 (50)	1.5 (97)	1.0 (69)
1980:	1.4	1.0 (77)	0.8 (58)	2.2 (161)	2.6 (195)	1.5 (111)	0.6 (46)	1.2 (92)	1.0 (77)
1990:	1.4	1.1 (78)	0.8 (59)	2.4 (171)	2.7 (195)	1.8 (128)	0.7 (51)	1.3 (92)	1.1 (82)
Greece									
1970:	0.2	0.0 (15)	0.1 (60)	0.3 (174)	0.4 (221)	0.2 (115)	0.2 (96)	0.0 (10)	0.1 (35)
1980:	0.4	0.1 (18)	0.2 (39)	0.3 (210)	1.0 (247)	0.7 (184)	0.2 (43)	0.1 (15)	0.2 (44)
1990:	0.3	0.1 (18)	0.1 (33)	0.8 (252)	0.8 (250)	0.9 (294)	0.1 (39)	0.1 (18)	0.1 (18)
Ireland									
1970:	0.4	0.3 (72)	0.1 (22)	0.7 (191)	1.0 (274)	0.5 (136)	0.1 (25)	0.1 (26)	0.3 (85)
1980:	0.7	0.8 (117)	0.4 (58)	1.0 (143)	1.3 (183)	0.7 (109)	0.4 (58)	0.4 (53)	1.0 (145)
1990:	1.0	1.8 (181)	0.5 (54)	1.1 (107)	1.5 (150)	0.7 (66)	0.5 (48)	0.7 (68)	2.3 (232)

Table 5.12 continued

	Total man.	High tech ***	Medium tech	Low tech	Resour. intens.	Labour intens.	Scale intens.	Special. supplier	Science based
Italy									
1970:	6.5	5.0 (78)	6.4 (99)	7 (109)	4.8 (74)	11 (185)	5.1 (78)	7.5 (117)	4.5 (69)
1980:	7.0	4.6 (66)	6.3 (91)	8 (128)	5.9 (84)	13 (199)	5.7 (81)	7.4 (106)	4.0 (57)
1990:	7.3	4.6 (63)	6.6 (90)	10 (140)	6.4 (87)	16 (227)	5.4 (74)	7.7 (106)	4.1 (56)
Spain									
1970:	1.0	0.4 (37)	0.6 (63)	1.6 (163)	1.8 (184)	1.3 (132)	0.8 (82)	0.6 (56)	0.3 (32)
1980:	1.7	0.8 (47)	1.5 (86)	2.5 (142)	2.3 (133)	1.9 (112)	2.1 (120)	1.1 (62)	0.7 (42)
1990:	2.3	1.2 (53)	2.4 (102)	3.0 (132)	3.1 (134)	2.4 (104)	3.1 (134)	1.3 (59)	1.2 (52)
UK									
1970:	9.2	9 (105)	10 (117)	7.4 (81)	7.1 (78)	10 (115)	8.6 (94)	10 (112)	10 (118)
1980:	8.8	11 (127)	9 (109)	7.1 (80)	7.8 (88)	10 (115)	7.1 (81)	9 (104)	14 (163)
1990:	7.5	9 (123)	7 (97)	6.9 (91)	6.3 (83)	7 (97)	7.0 (93)	7 (98)	11 (147)

Notes: * Calculated on the basis of US dollars. ** Revealed Comparative Advantage (RCA) for a particular industry (or industry grouping) is defined as the ratio of the shares of the country's exports in that industry in its total manufacturing exports to the share of total exports by that industry (or industry grouping) in OECD manufacturing exports. With exports denoted by X for a country k, the RCA of an industry i is given by: $100 \cdot [X_{ik}/\Sigma X_{ik}]/[\Sigma X_{ik}/\Sigma\Sigma X_{ik}]$). *** The definition of high-technology sectors depends upon the following three criteria: (a) R&D expenditure; (b) scientific and technical employment staff; and (c) the nature of the sector products.

Source: OECD, "Industrial Policy OECD countries", annual review chapter III.

There exists substantial diversity among EU Member States. Greece (28.5%) and Portugal (40.5%) remain quite far below the 50% level, while Italy (50.1%) and Spain (52.4%) find themselves at levels only just above the 50% level. On the other hand, the UK (67.4%), Ireland (68.5%), Germany (70.0%), Finland (71.1%) and Belgium (71.6%) are closer to the US, and Sweden (77.6%) even higher than Japan. With the exception of Slovakia (67.3%), none of the Acceding countries have values higher than those for the EU-25, the EU-15, the US or Japan. And only Slovakia, Romania (61.6%), the Czech Republic (60.2%) and Slovenia (57.8%) exceed the 50% level.

Data on patents with foreign co-inventors provide an indication of the extent to which countries co-operate internationally in inventive activities. To some extent such cooperation is a function of country size, with smaller countries tending to engage more often in foreign collaboration. Thus one sees Luxembourg with 57% of its patents involving foreign co-inventors, followed by Belgium and Ireland with over 30%. The Czech Republic and Hungary also have quite high rates (31% and 27%). The larger countries tend to have lower rates of overseas collaboration – for example, France has 13% and Germany 10% – although the UK with nearly 20% foreign co-inventors shows a comparatively high degree of internationalisation for its size. Taken as a whole, and excluding intra-EU collaborations, the EU-15 has a slightly lower proportion of foreign co-inventors than the US (7% versus 11%), but is higher than Japan (3%). For most countries the trend since the early 1990s has been towards an increase in foreign co-invention.

High technology products represented almost one-third of American exports in 1990 (31%), more than one-quarter of Japanese exports (27%) and less than one-fifth of European exports (17%). Table 5.12 illustrates the development of export market shares between 1970 and 1990 on the basis of two broad industry groupings, as well as for total manufacturing trade. The first grouping reflects *technological intensity* and the second the major factors that affect the *competitiveness* of particular industries.

In total manufacturing, except for the early 1980s, Germany has had the highest overall export market share during the past two decades, fluctuating between 16% and 18%, slightly above that of the United States. The United Kingdom has lost ground steadily from over 9% in the early 1970s to 7.5% in 1990.

The shares of Italy and Belgium remained stable at about 7% and 5%, respectively. Greece nearly doubled its export market share for total manufacturing but remains at 0.3% of the OECD market. Share of export markets provide a description of the evolving structure of OECD exports, the pattern of international specialisation, however is best examined through indicators such as *revealed comparative advantage* (RCA). Table 5.1 shows in brackets *revealed comparative advantage* for the period between 1970 and 1990. RCA is an indicator showing the relative specialisation and performance. It provides information about the export specialisation of a country and about comparative advantage in the past. It can be defined as the share of the exports of the industry in the total manufacturing exports of the country divided by the share of total OECD exports of the industry in total OECD manufacturing exports. With exports denoted by X for a country k, the RCA of an industry i is given by:

$$100.([X_{ik}/\Sigma X_{ik}]/[\Sigma X_{ik}/\Sigma X_{ik}])$$

However, Revealed Comparative Advantage neglects intrafirm exchanges. By definition, the average value of RCA for a particular industry in the OECD area is 100. Values greater than 100 indicate that the country's exports are specialised in that industry.   In the high technology industrial groups, only four countries had a relative specialisation in 1990, United States (161), Japan (149), United Kingdom (123) and Ireland (181); Ireland has increased its specialisation in computers, while the United States specialised in aerospace. Japan, Belgium, Germany and UK are specialised in the medium technology industries, while the small economies such as Greece and Portugal have a comparative advantage in the low technology group and in the labour intensive industries. On a sectoral basis, the Community was well placed in 1989 in the fields of medicine, electrical and non-electrical equipment and chemicals.

6. European Policy and the Regional Systems of Innovation

Regional differences remain the prime sources of competitive advantage. A long-term approach to development of regional knowledge economies must therefore combine local (regional) bottom-up approaches with global or European top-down approaches. There is no contradiction between global and local approaches to development of knowledge- economy. Regional policy should evolve from supporting general R&D efforts towards innovation promotion. It should also change the emphasis from a "technology-push" a "demand-pull" approach, to identify and understand the demand for innovation in firms in the less favoured regions. Technological transfer is essential for regions which lag behind. It might even be more important than the development of indigenous R&D activities in the weaker regions. Regional policy should facilitate the identification, adaptation and adoption of technological developments elsewhere in a specific regional setting. It might be less costly, avoid duplicating previous errors and reinventing the wheel. Regional policy should facilitate technology transfer and the flow of knowledge across regions, maximising the benefit of the European dimension by facilitating access from less favoured region's economic actors to international networks of "excellence" in this field. They encourage regions to take actions such as:

- Promoting innovation, new forms of financing (for instance, venture capital) to encourage start-ups, specialised business services, technology transfer,
- interacting between firms and higher education/research institutes,

- encouraging small firms to carry out R&D for the first-time,
- networking and co-operating in industry,
- developing human skills.

The theoretical framework for the concept can be found mainly in the work of Cooke and his colleagues. According to the author the first references to the term appeared at the beginning of the nineties and their evolution has its origin in two major theoretical currents. The first current originates in research on technological innovation, particularly that which refers to National Systems of Innovation (Lundvall 1992); the second results from advances in theories of regional development. The discussion of National Systems of Innovation emphasises the importance of innovations on national processes of development. These innovations are the result of the interaction between firms, clients, and government and research institutions, constituting an environment that is favourable to the learning of new ways of producing and of organising production. One of the matters that is emphasised in this type of research are the processes through which this learning takes place and the roles carried out by the different actors that are involved.

The concept of innovation that is used in this research is a broad one. It goes beyond new discoveries in activities and products on the frontiers of technological progress, to refer as well to changes in the production of less-elaborated products and to human behaviour, including changes in cultural values, routines and habits. At the same time, there are according to the authors several elements that indicate that the issues dealt with in this discussion can be better understood and analysed within a more restricted territorial environment, such as the region. This is where the second formative element of the concept of Regional Systems of Innovation enters the scenario. Through their discussion of national systems of innovation and on regionalism within regional development, we can move toward the construction of a concept of regional systems of innovation. Consequently, the formation of knowledge can be seen as made up through two levels of learning. The first is the one that establishes competence – the ability to carry out a particular task – and the second, which establishes capability – the comprehension of the underlying mechanisms for the solution of a problem that the task involves. (Cooke and Morgan 1998)

Evidently, a learning system that develops capability is much more onerous than one that merely supplies competence. Thus, a regional system of learning cannot restrict itself to mere transferring competence coming from elsewhere. From the perspective of economic development, we can not imagine that this whole framework to increase the capability of countries/regions can dispense with intense action on the part of the State. To the extent that this regional learning system interacts formally or informally with universities, research institutes, vocational training agencies, technology transference, technological parks and firms in general, it tends to become a Regional System of Innovation (Cooke and Morgan 1998).

In 1997, the OECD proposed a more general strategy set for all (not just for less favoured) regions. Although this was not specifically focused on Information Society issues, it has clear and direct relevance with knowledge-economy. The OECD study (1997) looked at the concept of *regional competitiveness* to explain why some regions successfully develop clusters and networks, a wide variety of manufacturing activities and of services for businesses and consumers, along with educational, research and cultural institutions, and why some must grapple with industrial and institutional imbalance and a lack of resources necessary to adapt. A territory's indigenous capacity of development is linked with the productivity of enterprises, their ability to join networks, the skills of the labour force and the strength of institutional resources. Such an approach stresses the (mainly) endogenous task of creating networks, partnerships and cooperation within the region, and five important strategies are recommended in this context:

a. To use regional policies for human resource development;
b. To give a demand-driven focus to human resource development;
c. To base competitiveness on the development of partnerships;
d. To reinforce economic efficiency by policies of equity; and
e. To develop regional governance in order to consolidate national policies.

Strategies (a) and (b) were subsequently refined into one of the most important current policy and strategy approaches to the development of regions in a knowledge-economy context, the *learning region* (OECD 2001a). This emphasises the essential role of skills and competencies in enhancing innovative capacity and regional competitiveness. The *learning region* concept is seen as a heuristic framework for analysing key relationships and developing effective strategies for regional policy.

At base, economic competitiveness at the regional level is determined by the quality of social capital, defined as institutions, relationships, and social norms impinging upon the quality and quantity of social interactions within a society. In a broad sense, it includes the social and political framework that shapes both these norms and relevant social structures. Social capital, in turn, moulds the types of learning and use and creation of knowledge which take place, resulting not only in economic competitiveness but also in social inclusion, if long term sustainability is to be ensured.

Figure 5.5 presents regional and innovation policies for the learning economy. Morgan (1997) and Maskell and Törnqvist (1999) define a *learning region* as one where an industrial cluster becomes a collective learning system, a concept drawing heavily on Lundvall's concept of national systems of innovation, fleshed out at local and regional levels. Morgan (1997) and Maskell and Törnqvist argue that in such regions, learning organisations develop at three levels:

• at an intra-firm level,
• at an inter-firm level between firms interacting within a cluster,

- at the institutional level, through public intervention to support organisational innovation in business services, research and training.

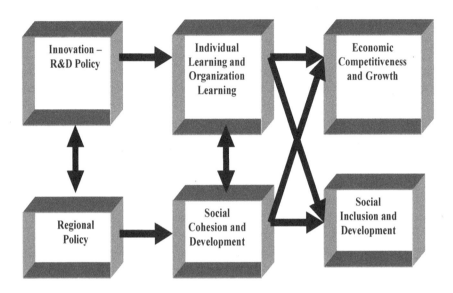

Figure 5.5 Regional and innovation policies towards the learning economy
Source: Korres, 2008.

It is argued that a *learning region* need not necessarily be high-tech (Maskell and Törnqvist 1999), and that it can be based upon one or more traditional manufacturing sectors. Malmberg and Maskell (1999) argue that the *learning region* permits the acquisition of monopoly rents, so that they become the basis of comparative advantage based on the local available resources and resource immobility.

The EU is one of the most prosperous economic areas in the world but the disparities between its member states are striking, even more so if we look at the EU's various 250 regions. To assess these disparities, we must first of all measure and compare the levels of wealth generated by each country, as determined by their gross domestic product (GDP). For instance, in Greece, Portugal and Spain, average per capita GDP is only 80% of the Community average. Luxembourg exceeds this average by over 60 percentage points. The ten most dynamic regions in the Union have a GDP almost three times higher than the ten least developed regions. The European Union's regional policy is based on financial solidarity inasmuch as part of member states' contributions to the Community budget goes to the less prosperous regions and social groups. For the 2000-2006 period, these transfers will account for one third of the Community budget, or €213 billion. More analytically:

- € 195 billion will be spent by the four Structural Funds (the European Regional Development Fund, the European Social Fund, the Financial Instrument for Fisheries Guidance and the Guidance Section of the European Agricultural Guidance and Guarantee Fund);
- € 18 billion will be spent by the Cohesion Fund.
- 70% of the funding goes to regions whose development is lagging behind. They are home to 22% of population of the Union (Objective 1);
- 11.5% of the funding assists economic and social conversion in areas experiencing structural difficulties. 18% of the population of the Union lives in such areas (Objective 2);
- 12.3% of the funding promotes the modernisation of training systems and the creation of employment (Objective 3) outside the Objective 1 regions where such measures form part of the strategies for catching up.
- There are also four Community Initiatives seeking common solutions to specific problems, namely Interreg III for cross-border, transnational and interregional cooperation, Urban II for sustainable development of cities and declining urban areas, Leader for rural development through local initiatives, and Equal for combating inequalities and discrimination in access to the labour market .

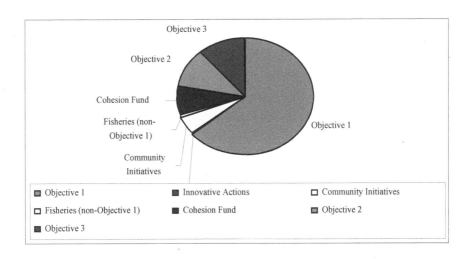

Figure 5.6 Total budget allocations for structural and cohesion funds, 2000-2006 (1999 prices)

Source: Own elaboration based on EU data.

Figure 5.6 presents the allocation of total budget for the structural and the Cohesion Fund for the period 2000-2006, whereas, Figure 5.7 depicts the GNP and the operating budgetary balances.

The estimated results illustrate that there is an increase of real GDP in 2006 by around 6% in Greece and Portugal and by 2.4% in Spain as compared with the situation without intervention. The effect is relatively modest in Ireland (1.8%), where the Structural Funds only account for under 10% of total public expenditure.

The CSF will increase investment by much more, especially in Portugal (by 23%) and Greece (14%), which will add to effective demand via multiplier effects and, over time, also tend to increase productivity, through improved infrastructure and human capital as well as the use of more modern, and therefore efficient, plant and equipment.

The effect on employment is likely to be significant, but will tend to decline after 2006, because of higher productivity. The principal effect is higher growth, which is estimated to continue beyond the programming period as a result of investment strengthening the supply-side, or the productive potential of the economy.

The added growth in GDP averages between 1-1.5% a year for Greece and Portugal, 0.8% for Spain and 0.5% for Ireland. The relatively small multiplier in Ireland and Portugal reflects the openness of the two economies, which means that a large part of the increased demand goes to imports, as well as the assumed 'crowding-out' effects on the private sector of higher public investment. Finally, Figure 5.8 presents some of the most popular objectives of regional policy.

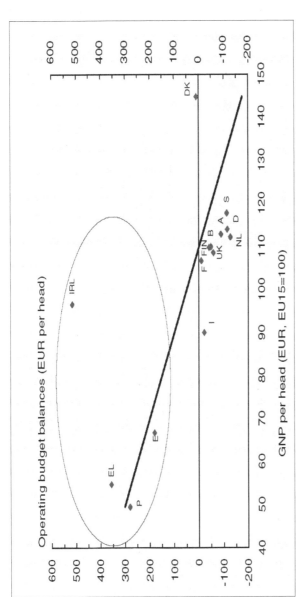

Figure 5.7 GNP and operating budgetary balances, 1999
Source: Own elaboration based on EU data.

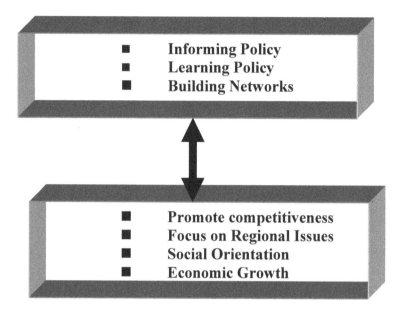

Figure 5.8 Main objectives for the regional policy planning
Source: Korres, G., 2008.

In recent years, considerable experience with practices related to the planning of regional policies in LDRs (Less Developed Regions) has built up with support from the EU, national and regional governments and local authorities. At a European level, starting from the Structural funds reform in 1988, and more recently with the new regulations for the period 2000-2007, a new development planning methodology has been promoted which is inspired by the principles of greater responsibility for local institutions and greater interaction with and involvement of local actors.

7. Conclusions

One of the most interesting results of the analyses in this chapter is the indication of a process of convergence between the included EU countries. Convergence is found in three ways. First, relatively poor countries tend to have relatively large welfare growth, whereas the growth rates of GDP per capita in relatively rich countries are often relatively small. Second, the sectoral distributions of value added have showed convergence among the EU countries. Smaller than average sectors tend to have growth rates that are larger than average and vice versa. Third, there is an indication of technological convergence. Although, the number of sectors with significant structural convergence is very small, it exceeds the number of sectors with significant structural divergence.

Despite the fact that the evidence is not very strong, the empirical analyses are in line with most theoretical expectations. On the country level, the outcomes sometimes contradict the theoretical expectations. Furthermore, the general increase in specialisation together with the general increase in intra-industry trade is a paradox, since theoretically there should be a negative relation between changes in specialisation and intra-industry trade. Therefore, based on the analyses in this study, the trade theories seem to offer a reasonable but rough explanation of economic changes of countries in a process of economic integration. They are a simplification of detailed developments. The empirical analyses indicate that actual processes are much more complex than those described by trade theories.

There is considerable empirical evidence that investment in research and technological development and innovation (R&D) has a positive correlation with the level of economic development. Efforts in the area of R&D have been associated with higher growth rates, increases in exports and trade, gains in productivity, growth in income and output, bigger business profits and lower inflation, international competitiveness, etc. in economic literature. Given the correlation between innovation and R&D efforts, and regional economic development, closing the interregional R&D gap in the EU becomes a requirement for reducing the cohesion gap, which is the primary objective of regional policy. Less favoured regions spend comparatively lower levels of public funds on innovation and, on top of this, having greater difficulties in absorbing these funds than more developed regions. Regional advantage will go to those places which can attract and quickly mobilise the best people ("knowledge workers"), resources and capabilities required to turn innovations into new business ideas and commercial products. This is precisely why regional policy should help the less advanced regions to anticipate and prepare for new economy through a new type of regional policy.

Moreover, the European research and innovation policy has adopted an approach oriented more towards innovation than technological excellence as such, better addressing the deficiencies of less favoured regions as a result. An improvement in the interaction between the deployment of the Structural Funds and research policy is important for acceleration of the "catching up" of lagging regions. Structural Funds can provide the necessary support for firms and research institutes in the latter to participate on equal terms in future research programmes. We have reviewed and developed a model in order to show how to discriminate empirically among the following three hypotheses:

- convergence due to capital deepening with technology levels uniform across economies, as in Mankiw, Romer and Weil (1992);
- convergence due to capital deepening with stationary differences in individual technologies, as in Islam (1995);
- convergence due to both catch-up and capital deepening (non-stationary differences in individual technologies.

This chapter has analysed the situation of EU member states from the perspective of indicators, showing their relative position in respect of the knowledge-based economy as well as their competitive position. It has been argued that in order to make Europe more competitive - or even simply maintain its current competitive position, sustained growth and employment levels - Europe needs to invest in production of new knowledge, in application of new technology, and ultimately in the people that will be able to put the new knowledge and technology to use. The current state of affairs has been described using various indicators of scientific and technological output, as well as general competitiveness indicators.

New technologies imply some direct and indirect effects or more specifically some micro effects (such as firms, and organisations) and macro effects (such as inter and intra-industrial and moreover regional effects) for the whole economy. New technologies play an important role to sectoral productivity, overall growth, employment, modernisation, industrialisation, socioeconomic infrastructure and to competitiveness of a country. The principal effects for technological policy can be distinguished in demand and supply sides. Technical change and innovation activities have an important role for growth and sustainable development. There is a huge literature on the role and economic impact of invention and innovation activities; many studies investigate the relationship between productivity, technical change, welfare, growth and regional development. Local produced technologies may affect and determine the rate of regional growth.

In the literature there are various explanations for the slow-down in productivity growth for OECD countries. One source of the slow-down may be substantial changes in the industrial composition of output, employment, capital accumulation and resource utilisation. The second source of the slow down in productivity growth may be that technological opportunities have declined; otherwise, new technologies have been developed but the application of new technologies to production has been less successful. Technological factors act in a long run way and should not be expected to explain medium run variations in the growth of GDP and productivity. The countries that are technologically backward have a potentiality to generate more rapid growth even greater than that of the advanced countries, if they are able take advantage of new technologies which have already employed by technological leaders.

The Community's technology policy has the following objectives:

- industrial modernisation and competitiveness;
- quality and productivity improvements in agriculture;
- dissemination of new technologies;
- exploitation of human and natural resources;
- a better quality of life;
- regional convergence.

The Community's research programmes also attempt to establish co-operation between *theoretical research* through the different research bodies of the public sector (such as research institutes and universities) and *industrial research* through private enterprises.

We can summarise the main conclusions and policy implications of this chapter as follows: technology policy has been heavily concerned with the external gap of the EEC vis-a-vis Japan and USA. However, the same size of gap also exists among EC countries. It is true that technological competition among Japan, the USA and European Community is intense. According to the Community's plans, the following criteria are essential for the selection and implementation in technological policy:

a. research must contribute to strengthen the economic performance, social cohesion and competitiveness of the Community's areas and moreover to secure their *convergence*;
b. research must contribute to the achievement of the common market and to unification of European scientific and technical areas, in order to establish uniform norms and standards.

Decision making in technology policy has been largely transferred to the Community level; the scope for national decision making has been reduced, while the responsibility of Community has increased correspondingly. The Community's action for small member states in technological activities should be reconsidered carefully, in order to achieve a higher level of efficiency. They should be more targeted and concentrated. The various *research measures* can be combined with other financial instruments and institutional regulations to create a significant size of action and to have a more favourable effect on the productive capabilities of these countries.

The Community's research framework programmes have been launched to meet the specific needs of the weaker member states. Financial and technological flows through the CSFs and the Community's research programmes should be expected to reduce the disparities between member states and to expand the opportunities for the LFRs (Less Favoured Regions).

Extracting sufficient benefits from public investment in science and R&D is a core task for governments. Links between science and industry are not equally developed across countries. Science is also of increasing importance if countries want to benefit from the global stock of knowledge. It is particularly important for government-funded research to continue to provide the early seeds of innovation. The shortage of private-sector product and R&D cycles carries the risk of under-investment in scientific research and long-term technologies with broad applications. Governments, particularly of small countries, cannot fund all fields of science.

The Commission's "middle way" industrial policy has had mixed results. Economic growth returns to Europe after the widespread recession of the early

1990s, but unemployment still persists at double digit levels. The interaction between European business and the Community greatly influenced the creation of a tailored policy that met efficiency needs (the Single Market Program) but also gave European industry a fair chance (in the form of trade protection) to catch up. It is too early to tell whether this policy will survive the economic fluctuations and political changes of the future. According to the previous analysis, we can summarise the following main results:

- Industrial policy is a highly controversial issue. It is justified because of the existing market failures. Formulating a coherent industrial policy is a highly complicated venture since there is a number of conflicts that are hard to resolve. Performance in terms of growth, employment and competitiveness and the respective contribution made by research, technological development and innovation. One of the findings is that in 1999, the high-technology sectors and knowledge intensive services contributed significantly to the improvement in both growth and the employment situation in Europe.
- The EU justifies its industrial policy on the grounds of common problems across countries, its capacity to coordinate and reduce duplication of efforts, its capacity to control and limit member state subsidies to industries.
- Industrial policy in Europe should aim to correct market failures, particularly in the field of R&D and environmental damage, at strengthening specialised factors in industrial locations, and at managing industrial adjustment. While the EU Commission has an obvious role to play in the first and third field, it should leave locational policy to local and regional governments.
- Investment in knowledge – research and development expenditure, education, software – and venture capital investment, for instance, spending patterns in the perspective of the knowledge economy.
- Human resources in and for science and technology, including certain figures of mobility and attractiveness. This difference is even more marked if one looks only at the number of researchers employed in industry.
- Scientific and inventive "output", innovation and high-tech trade, including a number of regional indicators. Patterns of co-operation in innovation activities between European companies vary considerably from one member state to another.
- Technology policy has been relatively successful in certain fields like telecommunications or traffic control systems. In other fields, like microelectronics and computers, the results have been mixed.

In the light of these remarks, Community technological policy has to be reinforced and oriented on several fronts:

a. to establish a coherent technological policy;
b. to target and concentrated more effectively on the technological capabilities of the small member states. A co-ordination with the broader Community

instruments and resources (CSFs) can create a much more favourable effect on the productive capabilities of these countries.

c. the traditional industries that are quite an important factor for the weaker states should be supported by appropriate research and technological programmes;

d. the Community could envisage specific programmes for technological diffusion in the small member states;

e. human capital formation should have a particular position in the Community policies vis-a-vis the smaller countries. The Community's technological policy aims to enhance the international demand for research activities and consequently to reinforce the weak internal market demand of the small member states. This creates the opportunity to expand activities that otherwise would probably have remained at much lower levels.

Looking first at scientific and technological output, the EU is still ahead of the US and Japan in its share of scientific publications, but lags behind in most of the other performance indicators, especially patents. There is, nonetheless, a substantial variation within the EU and certain EU Member States often score better than the US and Japan (most notably Sweden and Finland), yet the overall situation in the EU-15 is far from satisfactory.

Moreover, one tends to find most of the Acceding countries in a position of catching up from relatively low levels of S&T output. Although there are some noticeable encouraging tendencies in several Acceding countries, one can expect that with the enlargement of the European Union the "European Paradox" will be, at least temporarily, further accentuated. In other words, in relation to its enlarged population, the EU-25's strong performance in science will contrast increasingly with its weaker development and commercialisation of technology.

However, Europe still needs to exploit better its scientific and technological output, notably in terms of selling its high-tech goods on world markets. While its share of high-tech exports has grown slightly since the mid-1990s, the EU still had a lower market share than the US in 2001. Indeed, 2001 was a difficult year for the high-tech sector, and the ability of industry to withstand this correction will be a crucial factor in a number of countries. Moreover, this is a highly competitive market no longer restricted to the major developed countries. Over the past decade, we have seen developing Asian producers emerge as important players in high-tech market niches. A number of Acceding countries are also growing rapidly in their exports of high-tech, due in part to inflows of foreign investment.

The slowing down of EU-15 investment in the knowledge-based economy is likely to be reflected sooner or later in a significant decline in its performance. This trend underlines the urgency of implementing the Lisbon Strategy. In particular, the EU needs to increase its efforts, so as to give renewed impetus to the catching up of some countries with the rest of the EU-15 and to close the gap as soon as possible with the US.

- In 2000, approximately 3.4 million researchers were engaged in research and development (R&D) in the OECD area. This corresponds to about 6.5 researchers per thousand employees, a significant increase from the 1991 level of 5.6 researchers per thousand.
- Among the major OECD regions, Japan has the highest number of researchers relative to total employment, followed by the United States and the European Union. However, around 38% of all OECD-area researchers reside in the United States, 29% in the European Union and 19% in Japan.
- In 2000, approximately 2.1 million researchers (about 64% of the total) were employed by the business sector in the OECD area.
- In the major economic zones, the share of business researchers in the national total differs widely. In the United States, four out of five researchers work in the business sector but only one out of two in the European Union.
- Finland, the United States, Japan and Sweden are the only countries where business researchers in industry exceed 6 per thousand employees; in the large European economies, they are only 3 or 4 per thousand employees.
- Portugal, Greece and Poland have a low intensity of business researchers (fewer than 1 per thousand employees in industry). This is mainly due to national characteristics; in these countries, the business sector plays a much smaller role in the national innovation system than the higher education and government sectors. Business sector R&D expenditure in these countries accounts for only 25-35% of total R&D expenditure.
- Countries in Central and in the previous Eastern Europe have been affected by the reduction in numbers of business researchers in the 1990s, although the trend has reversed in the Czech Republic and Hungary in the past few years.

Large investments in education over the past decades have led to a general rise in the educational attainment of the employed population. On average, 28.2% of employed persons in OECD countries have a tertiary-level degree. The United States (36.8%) and Japan (36.5%) rank far ahead of the European Union (24.0%), which also has large cross-country disparities. Employment growth of tertiary-level graduates ranged between 2% and 6% a year over 1997-2001, substantially faster than aggregate employment growth. Unemployment rates are generally much lower for university graduates than for the overall population, although they are higher for women than for men. Professional and technical workers represent between 20% and 35% of total employment in most OECD countries, and over 35% in Sweden and Denmark.

We can summarise some of the main findings:

- In terms of scientific publications Europe's strong growth seems to have halted. Actual numbers are still rising, but the EU share of world publications is declining, whereas the US share is recovering.

- Per head of population, the EU generates fewer patents with a high economic value (so-called 'Triadic patents') than the US and Japan.
- The EU is lagging behind the US in its share of patents in biotechnology and information and communications technology.
- There has been a slight increase in the EU share of global exports of high-tech products in value terms between 1996 and 2001. Japan's share fell sharply in 2001 hit by falling sales of electronic goods.
- Since the middle of the 1990s, the EU has stopped catching up with the US in terms of labour productivity, reflecting a relatively weaker innovation performance.
- Large disparities persist among EU countries in both high-tech manufacturing and KIS. Japan outperforms the EU in high-tech manufacturing indicators while the Central European Acceding countries perform better than the EU average.
- The production of scientific research and technological know-how increasingly depends on research conducted in other countries. Indicators of cross-border co-authorship of scientific articles and co-invention of patents seek to shed light on this trend.
- Scientific collaboration with advanced countries is generally much more widespread than with smaller ones. Researchers in 160 countries co-authored at least 1% of their internationally co-authored papers with US researchers. The United Kingdom, France and Germany also play a leading role in international scientific collaboration.
- By the late 1990s, about 6% of patents of OECD residents were the result of international collaborative research. Several factors may affect the degree of a country's internationalisation in science and technology: size, technological endowment, geographical proximity to regions with high research activity, language, industrial specialisation, existence of foreign affiliates, etc.
- Internationalisation tends to be higher in smaller European countries. For example, 56% of Luxembourg's patents have foreign co-inventors and 30% of Iceland's and Belgium's. International cooperation in science and technology is also relatively high in Poland, the Czech Republic and the Slovak Republic.
- When intra-EU co-operation is factored out, international collaboration in patenting is lower in EU than in USA. In Japan, international co-operation in science and technology is rather limited.

Appendix
Glossary of Definitions and Measurements

Innovating Firm, Technological Product and Process	A technological product and process innovating firm is one that has implemented technologically new or significantly technologically improved products or processes during the period under review. A technological product innovation is the implementation/commercialisation of a product with improved performance characteristics such as to deliver objectively new or improved services to the consumer. A technological process innovation is the implementation/adoption of new or significantly improved production or delivery methods. It may involve changes in equipment, human resources, working methods or a combination of these.
Innovation Activities, Technological Product and Process	Technological product and process innovation activities are all those scientific, technological, organisational, financial and commercial steps which actually, or are intended to, lead to the implementation of new or improved products or processes. Some may be innovative in their own right, others are not novel but are necessary for implementation.
Innovation Expenditure, Technological Product and Process	Expenditure on technological product and process innovation includes all expenditure related to those scientific, technological, commercial, financial and organisational steps which are intended to lead, or actually lead, to the implementation of technologically new or improved products and processes.
Innovation Implementation Technological Product and Process	Technological product and process innovation has been implemented if it has been introduced on the market (product innovation) or used within a production process (process innovation).
Innovation, Diffusion	Diffusion is the way in which technological product and process (TPP) innovations spread, through market or non-market channels, from their first worldwide implementation to different countries and regions and to different industries/markets and firms.
Technical Change Disembodied	Disembodied technical change is the shift in the production function (production frontier) over time. Disembodied technical change is not incorporated in a specific factor of production.
Technical Change Embodied	Embodied technical change refers to improvements in the design or quality of new capital goods or intermediate inputs.

Technical Co-operation	There are two basic types of technical cooperation: (1) free-standing technical cooperation (FTC), which is the provision of resources aimed at the transfer of technical and managerial skills or of technology for the purpose of building up general national capacity without reference to the implementation of any specific investment projects; and (2) investment-related technical cooperation (IRTC), which denotes the provision of technical services required for the implementation of specific investment projects.
Technical Co-operation	Includes both: (a) grants to nationals of aid recipient countries receiving education or training at home or abroad, and (b) payments to consultants, advisers and similar personnel as well as teachers and administrators serving in recipient countries (including the cost of associated equipment). Assistance of this kind provided specifically to facilitate the implementation of a capital project is included indistinguishably among bilateral project and programme expenditures, and not separately identified as technical co-operation in statistics of aggregate flows.
Technicians and Equivalent Staff (for R&D)	Technicians and equivalent staff are persons whose main tasks require technical knowledge and experience in one or more fields of engineering, physical and life sciences, or social sciences and humanities. They participate in resarch and development (R&D) by performing scientific and technical tasks involving the application of concepts and operational methods, normally under the supervision of researchers. Equivalent staff perform the corresponding R&D tasks under the supervision of researchers in the social sciences and humanities.
Technological Innovations	Technological innovations comprise new products and processes and significant technological changes of products and processes. An innovation has been implemented if it has been introduced on the market (product innovation).
Technological Process Innovation	Technological process innovation is the adoption of technologically new or significantly improved production methods, including methods of product delivery. These methods may involve changes in equipment, or production organisation, or a combination of these changes, and may be derived from the use of knew knowledge. The methods may be intended to produce or deliver technologically new or improved products, which cannot be produced or delivered using conventional production methods, or essentially to increase the production or delivery efficiency of existing products.

Technologically Improved Product	A technologically improved product is an existing product whose performance has been significantly enhanced or upgraded. A simple product may be improved (in terms of better performance or lower cost) through use of higher-performance components or materials, or a complex product which consists of a number of integrated technical subsystems may be improved by partial changes to one of the subsystems.
Technologically New Product	A technologically new product is a product whose technological characteristics or intended uses differ significantly from those of previously produced products. Such innovations can involve radically new technologies, can be based on combining existing technologies in new uses, or can be derived from the use of new knowledge.
Technology	Technology refers to the state of knowledge concerning ways of converting resources into outputs.
Technology Balance of Payments (TBP)	The technology balance of payments (TBP) registers the commercial transactions related to international technology and know-how transfers. It consists of money paid or received for the use of patents, licences, know-how, trademarks, patterns, designs, technical services (including technical assistance) and for industrial rsearch and development (R&D) carried out abroad, etc. The coverage may vary from country to country and the TBP data should be considered as only partial measures of international technology flows.
Research and Development, OECD	Research and development is a term covering three activities: basic research, applied research, and experimental development.
Research and Development, SNA (OECD-UNESCO)	Research and development by a market producer is an activity undertaken for the purpose of discovering or developing new products, including improved versions or qualities of existing products, or discovering or developing new or more efficient processes of production.
Research and Development, UNESCO	Research and development services in natural sciences and engineering; social sciences and humanities and interdisciplinary. Any creative systematic activity undertaken in order to increase the stock of knowledge, including knowledge of man, culture and society, and the use of this knowledge to devise new applications. Includes fundamental research, applied research in such fields as agriculture, medicine, industrial chemistry, and experimental development work leading to new devices, products or processes.

Research and Development and Scientific and Technological Innovation	Scientific and technological innovation may be considered as the transformation of an idea into a new or improved product introduced on the market, into a new or improved operational process used in industry and commerce, or into a new approach to a social service. The word "innovation" can have different meanings in different contexts and the one chosen will depend on the particular objectives of measurement or analysis.
Research and Development Expenditure, OECD	Research and development expenditure is the money spent on creative work undertaken on a systematic basis to increase the stock of knowledge and the use of this knowledge to devise new applications.
Research and Development Personnel	Research and development personnel includes all persons employed directly on research and development [activities], as well as those providing direct services such as research and development managers, administrators and clerical staff. Those providing an indirect service, such as canteen and security staff, should be excluded, even though their wages and salaries are included as an overhead cost when measuring expenditure.
Research and Experimental Development	Research and experimental development (R&D) comprises creative work undertaken on a systematic basis in order to increase the stock of knowledge, including knowledge of man, culture and society, and the use of this stock of knowledge to devise new applications (as defined in the Frascati Manual).
Research Co-efficients	Research coefficients are fractions or proportions applied to statistics describing the total resources of the higher education sector. They are derived in a number of ways, ranging from informed guesses to sophisticated models. Whatever the method used, they are a useful alternative to the more costly large-scale surveys of researchers and/or higher education institutions.
Researchers	Researchers are professionals engaged in the conception or creation of new knowledge, products processes, methods, and systems, and in the management of the projects concerned. Researchers are all persons in the International Standard Classification of Occupations-88 (ISCO-88) Major Group 2 "Professional Occupations" plus "Research and Development Department Managers" (ISCO- 88 1237). By convention, any members of the Armed Forces with similar skills performing R&D should also be included in this category.
Gross Domestic Expenditure on Research and Development (GERD)	Gross domestic expenditure on research and development (GERD) is total intramural expenditure on research and development performed on the national territory during a given period.

Rate of Change – Six Month (OECD CLIS)	The annualised 6-month rate of change of OECD composite leading indicators (CLIs) is calculated by dividing the figure for a given month m by the 12-month moving average centred on m-6.5. It is easier for users to interpret the annualised 6-month rate of change since the volatility in the CLI has been smoothed out. At the same time, the annualised 6-month rate of change provides earlier signals for the turning points.
Rate of Change – Twelve Month (OECD Composite Leading Indicators)	The 12-month rate of change at annual rate smoothed used in the OECD composite leading indicator is calculated by dividing the figure for a given month m by the 12-month moving average centred on m-12.
Human Capital	Human capital is productive wealth embodied in labour, skills and knowledge.
Human Development	Human development is the process of enlarging people's choices. Their three essential choices are to lead a long and healthy life, to acquire knowledge and to have access to the resources needed for a decent standard of living. Additional choices, highly valued by many people, range from political, economic and social freedom to opportunities for being creative and productive and enjoying personal self-respect and guaranteed human rights.
Full-Time Equivalent Employment	Full-time equivalent employment is the number of full-time equivalent jobs, defined as total hours worked divided by average annual hours worked in full-time jobs.
Meta-Analysis	Quantitative study of published results relating to a particular problem. Conclusions about heterogeneity and overall significance are usually based on published values of test estimates.
Metadata	Metadata is data that defines and describes other data.

Sources: http://www.oecd.org/dataoecd/35/61/2367580.pdf, http://www.oecd.org/glossary/0,2586,en_2649_33721_1965693_1_1_1_1,00.html, http://www1.oecd.org/dsti/sti/stat-ana/prod/eas_fras.htm.

Bibliography

Abbing, M.R. and Schakernaad, J. (1990), *Joint R&D Activities of Firms in European Cost-Sharing Programmes*, Maastricht: MERIT.

Abramovitz, M. (1956), Resource and Output Trends in the United States Since 1870, *American Economic Review*, Vol. 46, pp. 5-23.

———— (1986), "Catching-up, Foreign Ahead and Falling Behind", *Journal of Economic History*, Vol. 46.

Acs, Z.J., FitzRoy, F. and Smith, I. (1999), "High Technology Employment, Wages and University R&D Spillovers: Evidence from US Cities", *Economics of Innovation and New Technology*, Vol. 8, No. 1-2, pp. 57-78.

Aghion, P. and Howitt, P. (1992), "A Model of Growth through Creative Destruction", *Econometrica*, Vol. 60, No. 2, pp. 323-351.

———— (1998), *Endogenous Growth Theory*, Cambridge, MA: MIT Press.

Ahmad, N. (2003), "Measuring Investment in Software", STI Working Paper 2003/6, OECD, Paris <www.oecd.org/sti/working-papers>.

Aked, N.H. and Gummett, P.J. (1976), "Science and Technology in the European Communities: The History of the Cost Projects", *Research Policy*, 5, pp. 270-294.

Alesina, A. (1996), "Budget Deficits and Budget Institutions", *National Bureau of Economic Research*, Working Paper No. 5556, May.

Amable, B. (1994), "Endogenous Growth Theory, Convergence and Divergence", in G. Silverberg and L. Soete (eds), *The Economics of Growth and Technical Change*, Cambridge, MA: MIT Press.

Amendola, G. and Perrucci, A. (1985), "The Diffusion of an Organizational Innovation. International Data Telecommunications and Multinational Industrial Firms", *International Journal of Industrial Organisation*, Vol. 3, pp. 109-118.

———— (1986), "The International Diffusion of New Information Technologies", *Research Policy*, Vol. 15, pp. 139-147.

———— (1988), *New Information Technology and Industrial Change: The Italian Case*, Dordrecht: Kluwer.

———— (1989a), "A Failure Inducement Model of Research and Development Expenditures, the Italian Evidence in the Early Eighties", *Journal of Economic Behaviour and Organization*.

———— (1989b), "The Role of Technological Expectations in a Mixed Model of International Diffusion of Process Innovations", *Research Policy*, October.

———— (1990), "Profitability and Imitation in the Diffusion Process of Innovations", *Rivista Internazionale di Science Economiche e Commerciali*, February.

Amemiya, T. (1985), *Advanced Econometrics*, Basic Blackwell.

———— (1990), *Specialization and Competitiveness of Italian Industry in High Technology Products*, Rome: ENEA.

———— (1992), "European Patterns of Specialization in High Technology Products: A New Approach", in *Proceedings of the Joint EC-Leiden Conference on Science and Technology Indicators*, Leiden: DSWO Press.

American Association for the Advancement of Science (2003), "Long-delayed '03 Budget Provides Historic Increases for R&D", *Science* and *Technology in Congress*, Vol. 1, No. 6-7, March.

Amin, A. and Wilkinson, F. (1999), "Learning, Proximity and Industrial Performance: An Introduction", *Cambridge Journal of Economics*, Vol. 23, pp. 121-125.

Armstrong, H. (1995), "An Appraisal of the Evidence from Cross-sectional Analysis of the Regional Growth Process within the European Union", in Armstrong, H. and Vicherman, R.W. (eds), *Convergence and Divergence Among European Regions, European Research in Regional Science*, Vol. 5, pp. 40-65, London: Pion Limited.

Andersen, B., Howells, J., Hull, R., Miles, I. and Roberts, J. (eds) (2000), *Knowledge and Innovation in the New Service Economy*, Aldershot: Elgar.

Antonelli C., Petit, P. and Tahar, G. (1990), "The Diffusion of Interdependent Innovations in the Textile Industry", *Structural Change and Economic Dynamics*.

Antonelli C., Petit, P. and Tahar, G. (1992), *The Economics of Industrial Modernization*, Academic Press.

van Ark, B. (1993), "Comparative Levels of Manufacturing Productivity in Postwar Europe: Measurement and Comparisons", *Oxford Bulletin of Economics and Statistics* Vol. 52, pp. 343-374.

van Ark, B. and Pilat, D. (1993), "Productivity Levels in Germany, Japan, and the United States: Differences and Causes", *Brookings Papers Microeconomics*, Vol. 2, pp. 1-69.

Arnold, L.G. (1998), "Growth, Welfare and Trade in an Integrated Model of Human-Capital Accumulation and Research", *Journal of Macroeconomics*, Vol. 20, No. 1, pp. 81-105.

Arrow, K.J., Hollis, B., Chenery, Minhas B.S. and Solow, R.M. (1961), "Capital-Labour Substitution and Economic Efficiency", *Review of Economics and Statistics*, Vol. 63, No. 3, August, pp. 225-247.

Arrow, K.J. (1962), "The Economic Implications of Learning by Doing", *Review of Economic Studies*, Vol. 29, No. 1, pp. 155-173.

Artis, M. (1996), "Alternative Transitions to EMU", *The Economic Journal*, Vol. 106, No. 437, pp. 1005-1015.

ASEAN (1999), *ASEAN Investment Report 1999: Trends and Developments in Foreign Direct Investment*, ASEAN Secretariat, Jakarta.

Atkinson R.D. and Jarboe, K.P. (1998), *The Case for Technology in the Knowledge Economy: R&D, Economic Growth, and the Role of Government*, Washington, DC: Progressive Policy Institute.

Atrostic, B.K., Gates, J. and Jarmin, R. (2000a), "Measuring the Electronic Economy: Current Status and Next Steps", US Census Bureau.

Atrostic, B.K., Colecchia, A. and Pattinson, B. (2000b), "Defining and Measuring *Electronic Commerce:* A Discussion Paper", Paper presented to the Working Group on Statistics on the Information Society, Eurostat, January.

Auerbach, A.J. (1979), "Wealth Maximization and the Cost of Capital", *Quarterly Journal of Economics*, August, pp. 433-66.

―――― (1983), "Corporation Taxation in the United States", *Brookings Papers on Economic Activity*, Vol. 2, pp. 451-513, Washington, DC: Brookings Institution.

Baily, M.N. and Chakrabarti, A.K. (1988), *Innovation and the Productivity Crisis*, Washington, DC: Brooking Institution.

Barro, R.J. (1991), "Economic Growth in a Cross Section of Countries", *Quarterly Journal of Economics*, 106, pp. 407-443.

Barro, R.J. and Sala-i-Martin, X. (1992), "Convergence", *Journal of Political Economy*, 100, pp. 223-251.

―――― (1995), *Economic Growth*, New York: McGraw-Hill.

―――― (1997), "Technological Diffusion, Convergence and Growth", *Journal of Economic Growth*, Vol. 2, pp. 1-26.

Battese, G.E. and Coelli, T.J. (1988), "Prediction of Firm-Level Technical Efficiencies with a Generalized Frontier Production Function and Panel Data", *Journal of Econometrics*, 38, pp. 387-399.

Baumol, W. (1986), "Productivity Growth, Convergence and Welfare", *American Economic Review*, Vol. 76, pp. 1072-1085.

Baumol, W., Nelson, R. and Wolff, N. (eds) (1988), *Convergence of Productivity: Cross-National Studies and Historical Evidence*, New York: Oxford University Press.

Belsley, D., Kuh, E. and Welsch, R. (1980), *Regression Diagnostics: Identifying Influential Data and Sources of Collinearity*, New York: John Wiley & Sons.

Benassy, J.P. (1998), "Is there Always too Little Research in Endogenous Growth with Expanding Product Variety?", *European Economic Review*, Vol. 42, No. 1, pp. 61-69.

Ben-David, D. (1994), "Convergence Clubs and Diverging Economies", CEPR, No. 922, London.

Benhabib, J. and Jovanovic, B. (1991), "Externalities and Growth Accounting", *American Economic Review*, Vol. 81, No. 1, pp. 82-113.

Benhabib, J. and Spiegel, M. (1994), "The Role of Human Capital in Economic Development: Evidence from Aggregate Cross-country Data", *Journal of Monetary Economics*, Vol. 34, pp. 143-73.

Benvignati, A.M. (1982), "The Relationship between the Origin and Diffusion of Industrial Innovation", *Economica*, Vol. 49, pp. 313-323.

Bergsman, J. and Shen, X. (1997), "Foreign Direct Investment in Developing Countries: Progress and Problems", *Finance and Development* Vol. 32, No. 4, pp. 6-8.

van Bergeijk, P.A.G., van Hagen, G.H.A., de Mooij, R.A. and van Sinderen J. (1997), "Endogenizing Technological Progress: The MESEMET Model", *Economic Modelling*, 14, pp. 341-367.

Berkhout, A.J. (2000), *New Science in a New Society, Cyclic Interaction between Knowledge and Innovation*, T.U. Delft, December 2000.

Bernard, A.B. and Jones, C.I. (1996a), "Comparing Apples to Oranges: Productivity Convergence and Measurement Across Industries and Countries", *American Economic Review*, Vol. 86, pp. 1216-1238.

——— (1996b), "Technology and Convergence", *The Economic Journal*, 106, pp. 1037-1044.

——— (1996c), "Productivity Across Industries and Countries: Time Series Theory and Evidence", *Review of Economics and Statistics*, Vol. 78, pp. 135-146.

Berndt, E.R. (1976), "Reconciling Alternative Estimates of the Elasticity of Substitution", *Review of Economics and Statistics*, Vol. 58, No. 1, February, pp. 59-68.

——— (1980), "U.S. Productivity Growth by Industry, 1947-1973: Comment" in J.W. Kendrick and B.N. Vaccara (eds), New Development in Productivity Measurement and Analysis, Chicago: The University of Chicago Press for the National Bureau of Economics Research, pp. 124-136.

——— (1991), *The Practice of Econometrics: Classic and Contemporary*, Addison-Wesley Publishers.

Berndt, E.R. and Christensen, L.R. (1973), "The Translog Function and the Substitution of Equipment, Structures, and Labour in U.S. Manufacturing 1929-68", *Journal of Econometrics*, Vol. 1, pp. 81-114.

Berndt, E.R. and Jorgenson, D.W. (1973), "Production Structure", in D.W Jorgenson and H.S. Houthakker (eds), *U.S. Energy Resources and Economic Growth*, Energy Policy Project, Washington, DC.

Berndt, E.R. and Savin, N.E. (1975), "Estimation and Hypothesis Testing in Singular Equation Systems with Autoregressive Disturbances", *Econometrica*, Vol. 43, September/November, pp. 937-957.

Berndt, E.R. and Wood, D.O. (1975), "Technology, Prices and the Derived Demand for Energy", *Review of Economics and Statistics*, Vol. 56, No. 3, August, pp. 259-268.

Berndt, E.R. and Khaled, M.S. (1979), "Parametric Productivity Measurement and Choice Among Flexible Functional Forms", *Journal of Political Economy*, Vol. 87, pp. 1220-45.

Berndt, E.R. and Waverman, L. (1979), *Empirical Analysis of Dynamic Adjustment Models of the Demand for Energy in U.S. Manufacturing Industries 1947-1974*, Final Report, Electric Power Research Institute, Palo Alto, CA.

Berndt, E.R. and Field, F.C. (1981), *Modelling and Measuring Natural Resource Substitution*, Cambridge, MA: MIT Press.

Berndt, E.R. and Triplett, J. (1990), "Productivity and Economic Growth", in D. Jorgenson (ed.), *Fifty Years of Economic Measurement Studies in Income and Wealth*, NBER, pp. 19-119.

Berndt, E.R. and Morrison, K. (1995), "High-tech Capital Formation and Economic Performance in U.S. Manufacturing Industries: An Exploratory Analysis", *Journal of Econometrics*, Vol. 65, pp. 9-43.

Bernstein, J.I. (1989), "The Structure of Canadian Inter-Industry R&D Spillovers and the Rate of Return to R&D", *Journal of Industrial Economics*, 37, pp. 315-28.

Bernstein, J.I. and Nadiri, M.I. (1988), "Interindustry R&D Spillovers, Rates of Return and Production in High-tech Industries", *The American Economic Review*, Vol. 78, No. 2, pp. 429-34.

——— (1991), "Product Demand, Cost of Production, Spillovers, and the Social Rate of Return to R&D", NBER Working Paper No. 3625.

Bergson (Burk), A. (1936), "Real Income, Expenditure Proportionality, and Frisch's New Method of Measuring Utility", *Review of Economic Studies*, Vol. 4, No. 1, October, pp. 33-52.

Bhalla, A. and Fluitman, A. (1985), "Science and Technology Indicators and Socio-economic Development", *World Development*, Vol. 13, No. 2.

Biehl, D. et al. (1986), "The Contribution of Infrastructure to Regional Development", *Comisión de las Comunidades Europeas*, Luxemburg.

Bienaymé, A. (1986), "The Dynamics of Innovation. International", *Journal of Technology Management*, Vol. 1, pp. 133-159.

Binswanger, H.P. (1974), "The Measurement of Technical Change with Many Factors of Production", *American Economic Review*, Vol. 64, No. 6, pp. 964-976.

Binswanger, H.P. and Vernon, W.R. (1978), *Induced Innovation: Technology, Institutions and Development*, Johns Hopkins University Press.

Bitros, G. and Korres, G. (2002), *Economic Integration: Limits and Prospects*, London: Macmillan-Palgrave Press.

Blinder, A. (2000), "The Internet and the New Economy", *The Internet Policy Institute*, January.

Boskin, M.J. and Lau, L.J. (1992), "Capital, Technology and Economic Growth", in Rosenberg, Landau and Mowery (eds), *Technology and the Wealth of Nations*, Stanford, CA: Stanford University Press.

Boulding, K.E. (1981), *Evolutionary Economics*, Beverly Hills: Sage Publications.

——— (1985), *The World as a Total System*, Beverly Hills: Sage Publications.

——— (1991), "What is Evolutionary Economics?", *Journal of Evolutionary Economics*, Vol. 1, No. 1.

Bovenberg, A.L. and de Mooij, R. (1997), "Environmental Tax Reform and Endogenous Growth", *Journal of Public Economics*, 63, pp. 207-237.

Bovenberg, A.L. and Smulders, S.A. (1996), "Transitional Impacts of Environmental Policy in an Endogenous Growth Model", *International Economic Review*, Vol. 37, No. 4, pp. 861-893.

Braczyk, H.-J., Cooke, P. and Heidenreich, M. (eds) (1998), *Regional Innovation Systems. The Role of Governances in a Globalised World*, London: UCL Press.

Breschi, S. and Malerba, F. (1997), "Sectoral Innovation Systems-Technological Regimes, Schumpeterian Dynamics and Spatial Boundaries", in C. Edquist, (ed.)

(1997), *Systems of Innovation: Technologies, Institutions and Organizations*, Pinter Publishers/Cassel Academic.

Breschi, S. and Livoni, F. (2001), "Localised Knowledge Spillovers vs. Innovative Milieux: Knowledge 'Tacitness' Reconsidered", *Papers in Regional Science*, Vol. 80, pp. 255-273.

Brown, D.K. (1991), "Tariffs and Capacity Utilization by Monopolistically Competitive Firms", *Journal of International Economics*, Vol. 30, pp. 371-381.

Brown, L.A. (1981), *Innovation Diffusion: A New Perspective*, Methuen Publishers.

Brown, R.S. and Christensen, L.R. (1981), "Estimating Elasticities of Substitution in a Model of Partial Static Equilibrium: An Application to U.S. Agriculture 1947 to 1974" in Berndt and Field (eds), *Modelling and Measuring Natural Resources Substitution*.

Brynjolfsson, E. and Hitt, L. (1995), "Computers as a Factor of Production: The Role of Differences Among Firms", *Economics of Innovation and New Technology*, Vol. 3, May, pp. 183-199.

Brynjolfsson, E. and Yang, S. (1996), " Information Technology and Productivity: A Review of the Literature", *Advances in Computers*, Vol. 43, pp. 179-214.

Buigues, P. and Sapir, A. (1993), Community Industrial Policies, in P. Nicolaides (ed.), *Industrial Policy in the European Community: A Necessary Response to Economic Integration?* pp. 21-37, Dordrecht: Nijhoff.

Bureau of Labor Statistics (1997), *Handbook of Methods: Productivity Measures: Business Sector and Major Subsectors*, Chapter 10, BLS Bulletin 2490, April 1997, pp. 89-102 <www. stats.bls.gov/mprhome.htm>.

Burton-Jones, A. (1999), *Knowledge Capitalism*, Oxford: Oxford University Press.

Camagni, R. (1985), "Spatial Diffusion of Pervasive Process Innovation", *Papers of the Regional Science Association*, Vol. 58.

Caracostas, P. and Soete, L. (1997), "The Building of Cross-Border Institutions in Europe: Towards a European System of Innovation?", in C. Edquist (ed.), *Systems of Innovation. Technologies, Institutions and Organizations*, London: Pinter, pp. 395-419.

Carlsson, B. (ed.) (1995), *Technological Systems and Economic Performance: The Case of Factory Automation*, Dordrecht: Kluwer.

Carlsson, B. and Stankiewicz, R. (1995), "On the Nature, Function and Composition of Technological Systems", in B. Carlsson (ed.) (1995), *Technological Systems and Economic Performance. The Case of Factory Automation*, Dordrecht: Kluwer.

Castells, M. (1996), *The Rise of the Network Society*, Oxford: Blackwell.

Castro, E.A. and Jensen-Butler, C.N. (1991), *Flexibility and the Neo Classical Model in the Analysis of Regional Growth*, Institute of Political Science, University of Aarhus, Denmark.

——— (2002), "Demand for Information and Communication Technology Based Services and Regional Economic Development", *Papers in Regional Science*, 2002.

Caves, R.E. (1998), "Industrial Organization and New Findings on the Turnover and Mobility of Firms, *Journal of Economic Literature*, Vol. XXXVI, December, pp. 1947-1982.

Caves, D.W., Christensen, L.R. and Diewert,W.E. (1982a), "The Economic Theory of Index Numbers and the Measurement of Input, Output and Productivity", *Econometrica*, Vol. 50, pp. 1393-1414.

———— (1982b), "Multilateral Comparisons of Output, Input, and Productivity Using Superlative Index Numbers", *The Economic Journal*, Vol. 92, pp. 73-86.

Caves, D.W., Christensen, L.R. and Swanson, J.A. (1980), "Productivity in U.S. Railroads, 1951-1974", *Bell Journal of Economics*, Vol. 11, No. 1, pp. 166-181.

Caves, D.W., Christensen, L.R. and Tretheway M.W. (1984), "Economics of Density versus Economics of Scale: Why Truck and Local Airline Costs Differ", *Rand Journal of Economics*, Vol. 15, No. 4, pp. 471-489.

Centre for Economic Planning and Research (CEPR), *The Financing of Greek Manufacture* (by Tsoris).

———— (1985), *Innovation in Greek Manufacturing* (by Skoumai and Kazis), Athens.

———— (1986a), *Foreign Investment in Greece* (by Georganta and Manos), Athens.

———— (1986b), *Licensing and Industrial Development: The Case of Greece* (by Kazis and Perrakis), Athens.

Chambers, R.G. (1988), *Applied Production Analysis*, New York: Cambridge University Press.

Chen, E. (1983), "The Diffusion of Technology", Chapter 4 in *Multinational Corporations, Technology and Employment*, Macmillan Press.

Chenery, H. (1986), "Growth and Transformation" in Y. Kubo, S. Robinson and M. Syrquin (eds), *Industrialization and Growth: A Comparative Study*, Oxford University Press.

Chenery, H., Lewis, J., De Melo, J. and Robinson, S. (1986), "Alternative Routes to Development", Chapter 11 in Y. Kubo, S. Robinson and M. Syrquin (eds), *Industrialization and Growth: A Comparative Study*, Oxford University Press.

Chenery, H., Shishido S. and Wtanabe, T. (1962), The Pattern of Japanese Growth, 1914-1954, *Econometrica*, Vol. 30, No. 1, January.

Chenery, H. and Srinivasan (1989), *Handbook of Development Economics*, Vol. 2 (Chapter 30), Amsterdam, Holland.

Chesnais, F. (1988), Technical Co-operation Agreements Between Firms, STI Review, OECD, Paris.

Christensen, L.R. and Greene, W.H. (1976), "Economies of Scale in U.S. Electric Power Generation", *Journal of Political Economy*, Vol. 84, No. 4, Part 1, pp. 655-676.

Christensen, L.R., Jorgenson, D.W. and Lau, L.J. (1970), "U.S. Real Product and Real Factor Input 1929-1967", *Review of Income and Wealth*, Vol. 16, pp. 19-50.

———— (1971), "Conjugate Duality and the Transcendental Logarithmic Function", *The Review of Economics and Statistics*, Vol. 53, pp. 255-56.

———— (1975), "Transcendental Logarithmic Production Frontiers", *Review of Economic Studies*, Vol. 55, February, pp. 28-45.

Clarysse, B. and Muldur, U. (2001), "Regional Cohesion in Europe? An Analysis of How EU Public RTD Support Influences the Techno-economic Regional Landscape", *Research Policy*, Vol. 30, No. 2, pp. 275-296.

Cobb, C.W. and Douglas, P.H. (1928), "A Theory of Production", *American Economic Review*, Supplement, Vol. 18, No. 1, March, pp. 139-165.

Coe, D.T. and Helpman, E. (1993), "International R&D Spillovers", NBER Working Paper No. 4444, August, Cambridge, MA.

——— (1995), "International R&D Spillovers", *European Economic Review*, Vol. 39, No. 5, pp. 859-887.

Cohen, W.M. and Levinthal, D.A. (1989), Innovation and Learning: The Two Faces of R&D, *Economic Journal*, Vol. 99, pp. 569-596.

Commission of the European Communities, CEC (1980), *The European Community's Research Policy*, Brussels, Belgium.

——— (1982), *The Current State of European Research and Development*, Brussels, Belgium.

——— (1983a), *Towards a European Research and Science Strategy*, Brussels, Belgium.

——— (1983b), *The Community and Small and Medium Sized Enterprises*, Brussels, Belgium.

——— (1983c), *The Europe, United States and Japan Controversy*, Brussels, Belgium.

——— (1983d), *European Economy No. 15-18*, July, Brussels, Belgium.

——— (1984), *The European Community and New technologies*, Brussels, Belgium.

——— (1985a), *European Research Policy*, Brussels, Belgium.

——— (1985b), *The European Community and Culture*, Brussels, Belgium.

——— (1985c), *The European Community Research Policy*, Brussels, Belgium.

——— (1985d), *Community R&D Policy up to 1984*, Brussels, Belgium.

——— (1985e), *ERDF in Figures*, Brussels, Belgium.

——— (1985f), *The Regional Location Pattern of New Information Technology Production in the Community: National and Regional Report-Greece* (by Tsipouri, L.), Brussels, Belgium.

——— (1986a), *New Technologies in Europe*, Brussels, Belgium.

——— (1986b), *National Regional Development Aid*, Economic and Social Consultative Assembly, Brussels, Belgium.

——— (1986c), *Incentives for Industrial R&D and Innovation*, 2nd ed., Brussels, Belgium.

——— (1986-1987), *Research and Technological Development in Less Favoured Regions of the Community* (STRIDE), final reports (two volumes), Brussels, Belgium.

——— (1987a), *The Single European Act*, Brussels, Belgium.

——— (1987b), *Research and Technological Development for Europe*, Brussels, Belgium.

——— (1988a), *Research and Technological Development Policy*, Brussels, Belgium.

—— (1988b), *Technology in Europe*, 1988-1991, Eurotech, Brussels.

—— (1988c), *Science, Research and the European Community*, Brussels, Belgium.

—— (1988d), *Science and Technology in EEC Member States*, Brussels, Belgium.

—— (1988e), *Science and Technological Policy, Scientific Potential Policies in EEC Member States*, Brussels, Belgium.

—— (1988f), *Small Countries, Science and Technology and EC Cohesion*, FAST Programme II (1984-1987), exploratory dossier 14, Brussels, Belgium.

—— (1988g), *Comparison of Scientific and Technological Policies of Community Member States-Greece* (by Fragakis), CREST, copol, Brussels, Belgium.

—— (1989a), *Science and Technology for Europe*, JRC, Brussels, Belgium.

—— (1989b), *Managing Technological Change: A Key Element in Technology Transfer*, Brussels, Belgium.

—— (1989c), *Statistical Analysis of Extra-EUR12 Trade in High Technology Products*, Eurostat, Brussels, Belgium.

—— (1989d), *First Survey on State Aid in the European Community*, Brussels, Belgium.

—— (1989e), *Guide to the Reform of the Community's Structural Funds*, Brussels, Belgium.

—— (1989f), *European Economy No. 41*, July, Brussels, Belgium.

—— (1989g), *Science, Technology and Society in Europe*, FAST II, report, Brussels, Belgium.

—— (1989h), *European Communities-Financial Reports 1986-1990*, different issues, Brussels, Belgium.

—— (1989i), *The Regional Impact of Community Policies*, European parliament papers, Brussels, Belgium.

—— (1989j), *Enterprises in the European Community*, Brussels, Belgium.

—— (1989-1990), *The Community Budget in Figures*, Brussels, Belgium.

—— (1990a), *SPRINT-innovation and Technology Transfer-Fifth Annual Report 1988*, Brussels, Belgium.

—— (1990b), *Trends in Scientific R&TD in the EEC* (by Quinn, A.), Brussels, Belgium.

—— (1990c), *Community Support Framework 1989-1993, Greece (objective 1)*, Brussels, Belgium.

—— (1990d), *An empirical assessment of factor shaping regional competitiveness-the problem regions*, Brussels, Belgium.

—— (1990e), *The Regional Impact of Community Policies*, European parliament papers, Brussels, Belgium.

—— (1990 and 1991), *EC Research Funding*, 2nd and 3rd edns, Brussels, Belgium.

—— (1991a), *European Community Direct Investment 1984-1988*, Eurostat, Brussels, Belgium.

—— (1991b), *Globalisation and the Small Less Advanced Countries: The Case of Greece*, FAST, Vol. 21 (by Giannitsis, T.), University of Athens, April, Brussels, Belgium.

———— (1991c), *A New Strategy for Social and Economic Cohesion after 1992*, European Parliament Papers, Brussels, Belgium.

———— (1991d), *Government Financing of R&D 1980-1990*, Eurostat, Brussels, Belgium.

———— (1991e), *Guide to Community Initiatives 1990*, 1st ed., Brussels, Belgium.

———— (1991f), *Second Survey on State Aid in European Community in the Manufacturing and Certain other Sectors*, Brussels, Belgium.

———— (1991g), *Annual Report of the Implementation of the Reform of the Structural Funds-1989*, Brussels, Belgium.

———— (1991h), *European Scenarios on Technological Change and Social and Economic Cohesion*, FAST, Vol. 16 (by Cadmos), June, Brussels, Belgium.

———— (1991i), *Aid Element of Government R&D Contracts*, Brussels, Belgium.

———— (1991j), *Prospects for Anthropocentric Production Systems in Greece*, FAST/MONITOR, Vol. 17 (by Papadimitriou, Z.), July.

———— (1991k), *Archipelago Europe-islands of Innovations: The Case of Greece*, FAST/MONITOR, Vol. 28 (by Halaris, G., Kyrtsoudi, M., Nikolaidis, E. and Philippopoulos, P.), December.

———— (1991), *General Reports on the Activities of European Communities*, 1989, 1990 and 1991, Brussels, Belgium.

———— (1992a), *Information and Communications Technologies in Europe 1991*, Brussels, Belgium.

———— (1992b), *Research after Maastricht: An Assessment – A Strategy*, Brussels, Belgium.

———— (1992c), *IMP-Progress Report for 1990*, SEC(92)690 Final, Brussels, Belgium.

———— (1992d), *SPRINT-The European Network for Technological Inter-firm Co-operation*, Brussels, Belgium.

———— (1992e), *A Specific Programme for R&D and Demonstration in the Field of Agriculture and Agro-industry, a List of Financed Projects*, Brussels, Belgium.

———— (1992f), *The Community's Structural Interventions*, Statistical Bulletin No. 3, Brussels, Belgium.

———— (1992g), *Second Annual Report on the Implementation of the Reform of the Structural Funds*, Brussels, Belgium.

———— (1992h), *European Economy*, 25, Chapter 4, Brussels, Belgium.

———— (1993), *An Integrated Approach to European Innovation and Technology Diffusion Policy – A Maastricht Memorandum*, Brussels/Luxembourg.

———— (1995), *Small and Medium-Sized Enterprises, a Dynamic Source of Employment, Growth and Competitiveness in the European Union*, report at European Council, December, Brussels/Luxembourg.

Commission of the European Communities, International Monetary Fund, Organisation for Economic Co-operation and Development, United Nations, World Bank (1993), *System of National Accounts – SNA 1993*, Brussels/ Luxembourg, New York, Paris, Washington, DC.

Commission on Intellectual Property Rights (2002), Integrating Intellectual Property Rights and Development Policy, London: Department for International Development, available at <http://www.iprcommission.org>.

Commission Staff Working Paper (2000), Report on the Implementation of the Action Plan to Promote Entrepreneurship and Competitiveness Terms of Reference SEC(2000), 1825 Brussels, European Commission.

Cooke, P. (1992), "Regional Innovation Systems: Competitive Regulation in the New Europe", *Geoforum*, Vol. 23, No. 3, pp. 365-382.

———— (1998), "Introduction: Origins of the Concept", in H.-J. Braczyk, P. Cooke, M. Heidenreich (eds), *Regional Innovation Systems. The Role of Governances in a Globalised World*, London: UCL Press, pp. 2-25.

Cooke, P. and Morgan, K. (1998), *The Associational Economy: Firms, Regions and Innovation*, London: Oxford University Press.

Cooke, P. and Uranga, M.G. et al. (1997), "Regional Innovation Systems: Institutional and Organizational Dimensions", Research Policy, Vol. 26, pp. 685-699.

Cooke, P., Clifton, N. and Huggins, R. (2001), *Competitiveness and the Knowledge Economy*, ESRC "Social Capital and Economic Performance", Project Research Paper 1, Centre for Advanced Studies, Cardiff University, UK, January.

Cornwell, C., Schmidt, P. and Sickle, R.C. (1990), "Production Frontiers with Cross-Sectional and Time-Series Variation in Efficiency Levels", *Journal of Econometrics*, 46, pp. 185-200.

Costello, A., Watson, F. and Woodward, D. (1994), *Human Face or Human Facade? Adjustment and the Health of Mothers and Children*, London: Institute of Child Health Occasional Paper.

Costello, D.M. (1993), "A Cross-Country, Cross-Industry Comparison of Productivity Growth", *Journal of Political Economy*, Vol. 101, pp. 207-222.

Cowles, M.G. (1994), "Organizing Industrial Coalitions", Paper presented at the Sussex European Institute Seminar "Industrial Networks in the EC", 13-15 October.

Crauser, G. (2000), "Regional Innovation Policy under the new Structural Funds", in *Innovating Regions in Europe* (RIS-RITTS Network), II Plenary Meeting, Madrid, Director General, DG Regional Policy, European Commission 15 June 2000.

Cuadrado, J.R. (1994), "Regional Disparities and Territorial Competition in the EC", in J.R. Cuadrado, P. Nijkamp, P. Salva (eds), *Moving Frontiers: Economic Restructuring, Regional Development and Emerging Networks*, Hants, UK, pp. 3-23.

Dalum, B., Johnson, B. and Lundvall, B.-Å. (1992), "Public Policy in the Learning Society", in B.-Å. Lundvall (ed.), *National Systems of Innovation*, London: Pinter Publishers.

Dasgupta, P. and Stiglitz, J.E. (1980a), "Industrial Structure and the Nature of Innovative Activity", *Economic Journal*, Vol. 90, June, pp. 266-293.

―――― (1980b), "Uncertainty, Market Structure and the Speed of R&D", *Bell Journal of Economics*, Vol. 11, No. 1, Spring, pp. 1-28.

―――― (1988), "Potential Competition, Actual Competition and Economic Welfare", *European Economic Review*, Vol. 32, May, pp. 569-577.

Davenport, T. and Prusak, L. (1998), *Working Knowledge*, Boston: Harvard Business School Press.

David, P.A. (1969), "A Contribution to the Theory of Diffusion", Research Center in Economic Growth, Stanford University.

―――― (1975), *Technical Choice, Innovation and Economic Growth*, New York and London: Cambridge University Press.

David, P.A. and van de Klundert, T. (1965), "Biased Efficiency Growth and Capital-Labour Substitution in the U.S., 1899-1960", *American Economic Review*.

Davidson, R. and Mackinnon, G.J. (1993), *Estimation and Inference in Econometrics*, Oxford University Press.

Davies S. (1974), *The Diffusion of Process Innovations*, Cambridge University Press.

―――― (1979), "Diffusion Innovation and Market Structure" in D. Sahal (eds), *Research, Development and Technological Innovation*, Lexington, Massachussetts.

De Bresson, C. and Amesse, F. (1991), Networks of Innovators: A Review and Introduction to the Issue, *Research Policy*, Vol. 20, pp. 363-379.

Dedrick, J. and Kraemer, K.L. (1999), "Compaq Computer: Information Technology in a Company in Transition", *Working Paper, Center for Research on Information Technology and Organizations*, University of California at Irvine, available at <www.crito.uci.edu>.

Dedrick, J., Kraemer, K.L. and Tsai, T. (1999), "Acer: An IT Company Learning to use Information Technology to Compete", Working Paper, Center for Research on Information Technology and Organizations, University of California at Irvine, available at <www.crito.uci.edu>.

De la Fuente (1995), "Catch-up, Growth and Convergence in the OECD", CEPR, Discussion Paper No. 1274, London.

―――― (1997), "The Empirics of Growth and Convergence", *Journal of Economic Dynamics and Control*, Vol. 21, pp. 23-77.

Deming, W.E. (1982), *Out of the Crisis*, Cambridge: MIT Center for Advanced Engineering Study.

―――― (1994), *The New Economics for Industry, Government, Education*, Cambridge: MIT Center for Advanced Engineering.

Denison, E.F. (1962), *The Sources of Economic Growth in the United States*, Washington, Committee for Economic Development.

―――― (1967), *Why Growth Rates Differ: Post-war Experience in Nine Western Countries*, Washington, DC: Brookings Institution.

Denny, M. and Fuss, M. (1983), "A General Approach to Intertemporal and Interspatial Productivity Comparisons", *Journal of Econometrics*, Vol. 23, No. 3, December, pp. 315-330.

Denny, M. and Pinto, C. (1978), "An Aggregate Model with Multi-product Technologies", in M. Fuss and D. McFadden (eds), *Production Economics: A Dual Approach to Theory and Applications*, Amsterdam, North Holland.

Denny, M., Fuss, M. and Waverman, L. (1981), "The Substitution Possibilities for Energy: Evidence from U.S. and Canadian Manufacturing Industries", in E.R. Berndt and B.C. Field (eds), *Modelling and Measuring Natural Resource Substitution*, Cambridge, MA: MIT Press.

Department for Trade and Industry (1998a), *Our Competitive Future: Building the Knowledge-Driven Economy*, London: Cm 4176.

―――― (1998b), *Our Competitive Future: Building the Knowledge-Driven Economy: Analytical Background*, London.

Dicken, P. (1998), *Global Shift: Transforming the World Economy*, 3rd ed., New York: The Guilford Press.

Diewert, W.E. (1971), An Application of the Shepard Duality Theorem: A Generalised Linear Production Function", *Journal of Political Economy*, Vol. 79, No. 3, May/June, pp. 482-507.

―――― (1974), "Applications of Duality Theory", in M. Intriligator and D.A. Kendrick (eds), *Frontiers of quantitative economics*, Vol. 2, Amsterdam, North Holland.

―――― (1976), "Exact and Superlative Index Numbers", *Journal of Econometrics*, Vol. 4, pp. 115-145.

―――― (1982), "Duality Approaches to Microeconomic Theory" in K.J. Arrow and M.D. Intriligator (eds), *Handbook of Mathematical Economics*, Vol. 2, Amsterdam, North Holland.

―――― (1992), "The Measurement of Productivity", *Bulletin of Economic Research*, Vol. 44, pp. 163-198.

Diewert, W.E. and Wales, T.J. (1987), "Flexible Functional Forms and Global Curvature Conditions", *Econometrica*, Vol. 55, No. 1, January, pp. 43-68.

―――― (1995), "Flexible Functional Forms and Tests of Homogeneous Separability", *Journal of Econometrics*, Vol. 67, pp. 295-302.

Dixit, A. and Stiglitz, J. (1977), "Monopolistic Competition and Optimum Product Diversity", *American Economic Review*, 67, pp. 297-308.

Dixit, A.K. (1996), *The Making of Economic Policy: A Transaction-Cost Politics Perspective*, Cambridge: MIT Press.

Dluhosch, B. (2000), *Industrial Location and Economic Integration*, Cheltenham: Edward Elgar.

Dollar, D. and Wolff, E.N. (1993), *Competitiveness, Convergence, and International Specialization*, Cambridge, MA: MIT Press.

Dosi, G. (1982), "Technological Paradigms and Technological Trajectories: A Suggested Interpretation of the Determinants and Directions of Technical Change", *Research Policy*, Vol. 11, No. 3.

―――― (1984), *Technical Change and Industrial Transformation: The theory and the Application to the Semiconductor Industry*, Macmillan Press.

———— (1988), "Sources, Procedures, and Microeconomic Effects of Innovation", *Journal of Economic Literature*, Vol. XXVI, September, pp. 1120-1171.

Dosi, G., Freeman, C., Nelson, R., Silverberg, G. and Soete, L. (1988), *Technical Change and Economic Theory*, London: Pinter Publishers.

Dosi, G. and Orsenigo, L. (1988), "Coordination and Transformation: An Overview of Structures, Behaviours and Change in Evolutionary Environments", in G. Dosi, C. Freeman, R. Nelson, G. Silverberg and L. Soete (eds), *Technical Change and Economic Theory*, London and New York: Pinter Publishers.

Dosi, G., Pavitt, K. and Soete, L. (1990), *The Economics of Technical Change and International Trade*, London: Harvester Wheatsheaf.

Dowrick, S. (1992), "Technological Catch Up and Diverging Incomes: Patterns of Economic Growth 1960-1988", *Economic Journal*, Vol. 102, pp. 600-610.

Dowrick, S. and Nguyen, D.T. (1989), "OECD Comparative Economic Growth 1950-85: Catch-Up and Convergence", *American Economic Review*, Vol. 79, pp. 1010-1030.

Drakopoulos, S. (2002), "A Model for Regional Development and the Learning Economy", *Archieve of Economic History*, Vol. 14, No. 2, Athens.

———— (2004), "Community Structural Funds and Regional Cohesion in Europe", *Archieve of Economic History*, Athens.

Dunning, J.H. (1993), "Governments and Multinational Enterprises: From Confrontation to Co-operation?", in L. Eden and E.H. Potter (ed.), *Multinationals in the Global Political Economy*, New York: St. Martins Press, pp. 59-83.

———— (2000) (ed.), *Regions, Globalisation and the Knowledge-based Economy*, Oxford: Oxford University Press.

Durlauf, S.N. and Quah, D.T. (1999), "The New Empirics of Economic Growth", *Centre for Economic Performance Discussion Paper*, 384, Final version, February.

EBRD (1999), *Transition Report Update*, April, Luxembourg.

ECLAC (1999), *Foreign Investment in Latin America and the Caribbean*, ECLAC, Santiago.

Edlin, A. and Stiglitz, J.E. (1995), "Discouraging Rivals: Managerial Rent-Seeking and Economic Inefficiencies", *American Economic Review*, Vol. 85 No. 5, December, and also NBER Working Paper No. 4145, 1992.

Edquist, C. (1997a), *Systems of Innovation. Technologies, Institutions and Organizations*, London: Pinter Publishers.

Edquist, C. (1997b), "Systems of Innovation Approaches – Their Emergence and Characteristics", in Edquist, C. (ed.), *Systems of Innovation. Technologies, Institutions and Organizations*, London: Pinter/Cassell Academic, pp. 1-35.

Edquist, C. and Johnson, B. (1997), "Institutions and Organizations in Systems of Innovation", in Edquist, C. (ed.) (1997), *Systems of Innovation: Technologies, Institutions and Organizations*, London: Pinter/Cassell Academic.

Edquist, C., Hommen, L. and McKelvey, M. (2001), *Innovation and Employment – Process versus Product Innovation*, Cheltenham, UK: Edward Elgar.

El Elj, M. (1997), "Specific R&D, Domestic and Foreign Technological Spillovers and Productivity in Major OECD Countries: Causality Tests and Estimation Based on Heterogenous Panel Data", E3ME-Working Paper No. 1.2, Work Package 4.3, CCIP/ERASME.

Elam, M. (1995), "The National Imagination and Systems of Innovation", Paper prepared for the Systems of Innovation Research Network Meeting, Söderköping, Sweden, 7-10 September.

Enterprise DG (2002), "Business Impact Assessment Pilot Project – Final Report: Lessons Learned and The Way Forward", Enterprise Working Paper at <http://europa.eu.int/comm/enterprise/regulation/bia/ppbia_en.htm>.

Epstein, G. (1995), "International Profit Rate Equalization and Investment: An Empirical Analysis of Integration, Instability and Enforcement", in G. Epstein and H. Gintis (eds), *Macroeconomic Policy After the Conservative Era: Studies in Investment, Saving and Finance*, Cambridge: Cambridge University Press.

Ergas, H. (1987), "Does Technology Policy Matter?", in B.R. Guile and H. Brooks (eds), *Technology and Global Industry. Companies and Nations in the World Economy*, pp. 191-245. Washington, DC: National Academy Press.

Ethier, W. (1982), "National and International Returns to Scale in the Modern Theory of International Trade", *American Economic Review*, Vol. 72, pp. 389-405.

European Commission (1994), *The European Report on Science and Technology Indicators 1994*, Report EUR 15897 EN, Luxembourg.

——— (1997), *Green Paper on the Community Patent and Patent System in Europe*, COM (97), 314 final 24/06/97.

——— (2000a), *Towards a European Research Area: Communication from the Commission*, COM(2000)6, European Commission, Luxembourg.

——— (2000b), *The Regions in the New Economy – Guidelines for Innovative Measures under the ERDF in the Period 2000-06*, Draft Communication from the Commission to the Member States, Brussels 11/07/00.

——— (2000c), *The Regions in the New Economy*, Fact Sheet, Brussels 14/07/00.

——— (2000d), *The New Programming Period 2000-2006: Methodological Working Papers*, Working Paper No. 3, "Indicators for Monitoring and Evaluation: An Indicative Methodology", *DG Regional Policy*, Brussels.

——— (2000e), *11th Annual Report on the Structural Funds, 1999*, Brussels, 13/11/00, COM(2000)698 final.

——— (2001a), *Competitiveness Report 2001*, Commission Staff Working Paper, SEC (2001), 1705, available at <http://europa.eu.int/comm/enterprise/enterprise_policy/competitiveness/doc/competitiveness_report_2001/>.

——— (2001b), "Environment 2010: Our future. Our Choice", The Sixth Environment Action Plan, *Proposal for a Decision of the European Parliament and of the Council*, COM(2001)31 final European Commission (2001c), The Regions and the New Economy, COM(2001), 60-005.

———— (2001c), "A Mobility Strategy for the European Research Area", *Communication from the Commission*, COM(2001), 331, European Commission, Brussels.

———— (2001d), *European Competitiveness Report 2001*, European Commission, Brussels.

———— (2001e), "On Implementation of the Risk Capital Action Plan (RCAP)", *Communication from the European Commission*, COM(2001), 506, European Commission, Brussels.

———— (2001f), *Second Report on Economic and Social Cohesion*, European Commission, Brussels.

———— (2002), *Human Capital in a Global and Knowledge-based Economy*, European Commission, Brussels.

———— (2003a), Investing in Research: An Action Plan for Europe, *Communication from the Commission*, COM(2003), 226, European Commission, Brussels.

———— (2003b), "Researchers in the European Research Area: One Profession, Multiple Careers", *Communication from the Commission*, COM(2003), 436, European Commission, Brussels.

———— (2003c), "The Role of the Universities in the Europe of Knowledge", *Communication from the Commission*, COM(2003), 58, European Commission, Brussels.

———— (2003d), *Employment in Europe*, European Commission, DG Employment, Brussels.

———— (2003e), "Choosing to Grow: Knowledge, Innovation and Jobs in a Cohesive Society", *Report to the Spring European Council, 21 March 2003 on the Lisbon Strategy of Economic, Social and Environmental Renewal*, COM(2003), 5, European Commission, Brussels.

———— (2003f), Commission's Paper Launching an Initiative for Growth on 9 July 2003 SEC(2003), 813, European Commission, Brussels.

———— (2003g), *Communication from the Commission: An Initiative for Growth for the European Union through Investment in Networks and Knowledge. Interim Report to the European Council* (26 September 2003), European Commission, Brussels.

European Commission/DG Research (2003a), *Third European Report on Science and Technology Indicators 2003: Towards a Knowledge-based Economy*, European Commission, Brussels.

———— (2003b), *"She Figures" Women and Science Statistics and Indicators*, European Commission, Brussels.

———— (2004), *Key Figures 2003-2004: Towards a European Research Area Science, Technology and Innovation*, European Commission, Brussels.

European Council (2003), *Presidency Conclusions of the Thessaloniki European Council, 19 and 20 June 2003*, European Council, Brussels.

European Science Foundation (2003), "New Structures for the Support of High-Quality Research in Europe", *An ESF Position Paper*, April 2003.

European Investment Bank (EIB), *Annual Reports*, different issues, Luxembourg.

Eurostat (1991), *R&D and Innovation Statistics: Lena Tsipouri's Paper on the Regional Dimension of R&D and Innovation Statistics*, Brussels, Belgium.

—— (1991), *R&D and Innovation Statistics: Final Draft Report by Dr. David Charles on the Regional Dimension of R&D and Innovation Statistics*, Brussels, Belgium.

—— (1995), *European System of Accounts – ESA 1995*, Luxembourg.

—— (1996), *Regional Statistics of R&D and Innovation*, Brussels, Belgium.

—— (1996), *Research and Development*, Brussels, Belgium.

—— (2002a), *Research and Development: Annual Statistics, Data 1990-2000*. Eurostat, Luxembourg.

—— (2002b), *Science and Technology in Europe. Statistical Pocketbook, Data 1990-2000* (2002), Luxembourg, Eurostat.

Eurostat/OECD (1995), *Manual on the Measurement of Human Resources Devoted to S&T*, Canberra Manual, Paris.

Evans, P. and Karras, G. (1994), "Are Government Activities Productive? Evidence from a Panel of U.S. States", *The Review of Economics and Statistics*, Vol. 1, pp. 1-11.

Fabricant, S. (1954), *Economic Progress and Economic Change*, Princeton, NJ: Princeton University Press.

Fageberg, J. (1987), "A Technology Gap Approach to Why Growth Rates Differ", in *Research Policy*, Vol. 16, pp. 87-99.

—— (1988), "Why Growth Rates Differ", Chapter 20 in G. Dosi, C. Freeman, R. Nelson and L. Soete (ed.), *Technical Change and Economic Theory*.

—— (1991), "Innovation, Catching-up and Growth", in OECD (ed.), *Technology and Productivity – The Challenge for Economic Policy*, Paris.

—— (1994), "Technology and International Differences in Growth Rates", *Journal of Economic Literature*, Vol. XXXII, No. 3, September.

—— (1995), "User-producer Interaction, Learning and Comparative Advantage", *Cambridge Journal of Economics*, Vol. 19, pp. 243-256.

—— (1996), "Technology, Policy Growth – Evidence and Interpretation", NUPI Working Paper No. 546, March 1996.

Fagerberg, J. and Verspagen, B. (1996), "Heading for Divergence. Regional Growth in Europe Reconsidered", *Journal of Common Market Studies*, Vol. 34, pp. 431-48.

Fagerberg, J., Verspagen, B. and Caniëls, M. (1996), "Technology, Growth and Unemployment Across European Regions", NUPI Working Paper No. 565, December, Oslo.

Faini, R., Clavijo, F. and Senhadj-Semlali, A. (1989), "The Fallacy of Composition Argument: Does Demand Matter for LDCs' Manufacturers Exports?" Centro Studi Luca d'Agliano/Queen Elizabeth House Development Studies Working Paper No. 7.

Fischer, M.M. (1999), "The Innovation Process and Network Activities of Manufacturing Firms", in M.M. Fischer, L. Suarez-Villa and M. Steiner (eds), *Innovation, Networks and Localities*, Berlin: Springer, pp. 11-27.

Foray, D. and Lundvall, B.-Å. (1996), "The Knowledge-based Economy: From the Economcs of Knowledge to the Learning Economy", in *Employment and Growth in the Knowledge-based Economy*, OECD Documents, OECD, Paris.

Førsund, F. and Hjalmarsson, L. (1974), "On the Measurement of Productive Efficiency", *Swedish Journal of Economics*, Vol. 76, No. 2, pp. 141-154.

―――― (1987), "Analyses of Industrial Structure: A Putty-Clay Approach", The Industrial Institute for Economic and Social Research, Almqvist and Wiksell International, Stockholm.

Foster, L., Haltiwanger, J. and Krizan, C.J. (1998), "Aggregate Productivity Growth: Lessons from Microeconomic Evidence", NBER Working Paper No. 6803, November.

Freeman, C. (1974), *The Economics of Industrial Innovation*, Penguin.

―――― (1984), *Long Waves in the World Economy*, London: Pinter.

―――― (1987), *Technology and Economic Performance: Lessons from Japan*, London: Pinter Publishers.

―――― (1987), *Innovation*, New Palgrave Dictionary.

―――― (1990), *The Economics of Innovation*, Aldershot: Elgar.

―――― (1991), Networks of Innovators: A Synthesis of Research Issues, *Research Policy*, Vol. 20, pp. 499-514.

―――― (1992a), *Economics of Hope. Essays on Technical Change, Economic Growth and the Environment*, London: Pinter Publishers.

―――― (1992b), "Technology, Progress and the Quality of Life", in *The Economics of Hope. Essays on Technical Change, Economic Growth and the Environment*, London and New York: Pinter Publishers.

―――― (1994), "The Economics of Technical Change: A Critical Survey, *Cambridge Journal of Economics*, Vol. 18, pp. 463-514.

―――― (1995), "The National System of Innovations in Historical Perspective", *Cambridge Journal of Economics*, Vol. 19, pp. 5-24.

Freeman, C. and Foray, D. (1993), *Technology and the Wealth of Nations*, London: Pinter Publishers.

Freeman, C. and Lundvall, B. (1988a), *Small Countries Facing the Technological Revolution*, London: Pinter Publishers.

Freeman, C. and Perez, C. (1988b), "Structural Crises of Adjustment, Business Cycles and Investment Behaviour", in Dosi et al. (eds), *Technical Change and Economic Theory*, London: Pinter Publishers.

Freeman, C. and Soete, L. (1990), *New Explorations in the Economics of Technical Change*, London: Pinter Publishers.

Frisch, R. (1935), "The Principle of Substitution: An Example of its Application in the Chocolate Industry", *Nordisk Tidsskrift for Teknisk Okonomi*, Vol. 1, No. 1, pp. 12-27.

Fuss, M., McFadden, D. and Mundlak, Y. (1978), "A Survey of Functional Forms in the Economic Analysis of Production", Chapter II in M. Fuss and D. McFadden, et al. (eds), *Production Economics: A Dual Approach to Theory and Applications*, Amsterdam, North Holland.

Gallant, A.R. (1987), *Nonlinear Statistical Models*, New York: John Willey and Sons.

Giannitsis, T. (1991), "Licensing in a Newly Industrializing Country: The Case of Greek Manufacturing", *World Development*, Vol. 19, No. 4.

Gilbert, R.J. and Newbery, D.M.G. (1982), "Preemptive Patenting and the Persistence of Monopoly", *American Economic Review*, Vol. 72, pp. 514-526.

Gillespie, A., Richardson, R. and Cornford, J. (2001), "Regional Development and the New Economy", Paper presented to the European Investment Bank Conference, Luxembourg, January.

Gittleman, M. and Wolf, E.N. (1995), "R&D Activity and Cross-country Growth Comparisons", *Cambridge Journal of Economics*, Vol. 19, pp. 189-207.

Godin, B. (2004), "The Knowledge-based Economy: Conceptual Framework or Buzzword?" *The Journal of Technology Transfer*, Vol. 29.

Goel, R. (1990), "The Substitutability of Capital-Labour and R&D in US Manufacturing", *Bulletin of Economic Research*, Vol. 42, No. 3.

Gollop, F.M. and Roberts, M.J. (1981), "The Sources of Growth in the U.S. Electric Power Industry", in T.G. Cowing and R.E. Stevenson (eds), *Productivity Measurement in Regulated Industries*, New York: Academic Press, pp. 107-143.

Gomulka, S. (1971), *Incentive Activity, Diffusion and the Stages of Economic Growth*, Institute of Economics, Aarhus.

———— (1990), *The Theory of Technological Change and Economic Growth*, London: Routledge.

Grahl, J. and Teague, P. (1988), "The EUREKA Project and the Industrial Policy of the European Community", *International Review of Applied Economics*.

———— (1990), *1992 – The Big Market: The Future of European Community*, Lawrence and Wishart Publishers.

Greenan, N. and Mairesse, J. (1996), "Computers and Productivity in France: Some Evidence", NBER Working Paper No. 5836.

Greenwald, B. and Stiglitz, J.E. (1986), "Externalities in Economics with Imperfect Information and Incomplete Markets", *Quarterly Journal of Economics*, May, pp. 229-264.

Gregersen, B. and Johnson, B. (1997), Learning Economies, Innovation Systems and European Integration, *Regional Studies*, Vol. 31, No. 5, pp. 479-490.

Gregersen, B., Johnson, B. and Kristensen, A. (1994), "Comparing National Systems of Innovation. The Case of Finland, Denmark and Sweden", in S. Vuori and P. Vuorinen (eds), *Explaining Technical Change in a Small Country*, Heidelberg: Physica-Verlag.

Griliches, Z. (1973), "Research Expenditures and Growth Accounting" in B.R. Williams (ed.), *Science and technology in economic growth*, New York: John Wiley & Sons.

———— (1979), "Issues in Assessing the Contribution of R&D in Productivity Growth", *Bell Journal of Economics*, Vol. 10, pp. 92-116.

———— (1980), "R&D and the Productivity Slow Down", *American Economic Review*, Vol. 70, No. 2, May.

—— (1988a), *Technology, Education and Productivity*, Oxford: Blackwell.

—— (1988b), "Productivity Puzzles and R&D: Another Explanation", *Journal of Economic Perspectives*, Vol. 2, No. 4, pp. 9-21.

—— (1992), "The Search for R&D Spillovers", *Scandinavian Journal of Economics*, 94, pp. 29-48.

Griliches, Z. and Jorgenson, D.W. (1966), Sources of Measured Productivity Change: Capital-Input, *American Economic Review*, Vol. 56, pp. 50-61.

Griliches, Z. and Lichtenberg, F. (1984), "R&D and Productivity Growt at the Industry Level: Is There Still a Relationship?", Chapter 21 in Griliches, Z. (ed.), *R&D, Patents and Productivity*, Harvard University Press.

Grossman, G.M. and Helpman, E. (1989), "Endogenous Product Cycles", NBER Working Paper No. 2913, Cambridge, MA.

—— (1991a), "Quality Ladders in the Theory of Growth", *Review of Economic Studies*, 58, pp. 43-61.

—— (1991b), *Innovation and Growth in the Global Economy*, Cambridge, MA: MIT Press.

—— (1994), "Endogenous Innovation in the Theory of Growth", *Journal of Economic Perspectives*, Vol. 8, No. 1, pp. 23-44.

Grossman, H.J. and Lucas, R.F. (1974), "The Macroeconomic Effects of Productive Public Expenditures", *The Manchester School of Economics and Social Studies*, Vol. 42, pp. 162-170.

Håkansson, H. (1987), *Industrial Technological Development: A Network Approach*, London: Croom Helm.

Hall, H.P. (1988), "The Theory and Practice of Innovation Policy: An Overview", *Greek Economic Review*.

Hall, R.E. and Jones, C.I. (1999), Why Do Some Countries Produce So Much More Output Per Worker Than Others?, *Quarterly Journal of Economics*, Vol. 114, pp. 83-116.

Hall, V.R., Bergstrom, T.C. and Hal, R. (1993), *Workouts in Intermediate Microeconomics* 3rd ed., New York: W.W. Norton.

Halter, A.N., Carter, H.O. and Hocking, J.G. (1957), "A Note on the Transcendental Production Function", *Journal of Farm Economics*, pp. 466-74.

Haltiwanger, J. and Jarmin, R. (1999), "A Measuring the Digital Economy", in E. Byrnjolfsson and B. Kahin (eds), *Understanding the Digital Economy*, Cambridge, MA: MIT Press.

Hanoch, G. (1975), "The Elasticity of Scale and the Shape of Average Costs", *American Economic Review*, Vol. 65, pp. 492-7.

Hariolf, G. (1995), "Science, High Technology and the Competitiveness of EU Countries", *Cambridge Journal of Economics*.

Harrigan, J. (1995), "Factor Endowments and the International Location of Production: Econometric Evidence for the OECD, 1970-1985", *Journal of International Economics*, Vol. 39, pp. 123-141.

———— (1997a), "Technology, Factor Supplies and International Specialization: Estimating the Neoclassical Model", *The American Economic Review*, Vol. 87, pp. 475-494.

———— (1997b), "Cross-Country Comparisons of Industry Total Factor Productivity: Theory and Evidence", *Federal Reserve Bank of New York Research Paper*, No. 9734

Harrison, G., Rutherford, T. and Tarr, D. (1995), "Quantifying the Uruguay Round", in W. Martin and A. Winters (eds), *The Uruguay Round and the Developing Countries*, Washington, DC, World Bank Discussion Paper No. 307.

Hayami, Y. and Ruttan, V.M. (1970), Agricultural Productivity Differences Among Countries, *American Economic Review*, Vol. 60, pp. 895-911.

———— (1985), *Agricultural Development: An International Perspective*, Baltimore: Johns Hopkins University Press.

Heady, E. and Dillon, J.L. (1961), *Agricultural Production Functions*, Ames, Iowa: Iowa State University Press.

Hellenic Industrial Development Bank (1991), "Incentives for Investments in Greece-Law 1892/90".

Helpman, E. and Krugman, P. (1985), *Market Structure and Foreign Trade*, Cambridge, MA: MIT Press.

Herzenberg, S.A., Alic, J.A. and Wial, H. (1999), "Toward a Learning Economy", in *Issues in Science and Technology*, Winter 1998-1999, pp. 55-62.

Hicks, J.R. (1935), "A Suggestion for Simplifying the Theory of Money", *Econometrica*, Vol. 2, pp. 1-19.

———— (1946), *Value and Capital*, Oxford University Press.

———— (1963), *The Theory of Wages*, 2nd ed. (1st ed. 1932), London: Macmillan.

———— (1965), *Capital and Growth*, Oxford University Press.

———— (1994), "Adjusting to Technological Change", *Canadian Journal of Economics*, Vol. 27, No. 4, pp. 763-775.

Hirschman, A.O. (1981), *Essays in Trespassing: Economics to Politics and Beyond*, Cambridge: Cambridge University Press.

Hjalmarsson, L. (1973), "Optimal Structural Change and Related Concepts", *Swedish Journal of Economics*, Vol. 75, No. 2, pp. 176-192.

Hodbay, M. (1989), "The European Semiconductor Industry: Resurgence and Rationalisation", *Journal of Common Market Studies*, Vol. XXVIII, No. 2.

Hoen, A.R. (1999), *An Input-Output Analysis of European Integration*, Capelle aan de IJssel: Labyrint Publication.

Hooper, P. and Larin, K.A. (1989), "International Comparisons of Labor Costs in Manufacturing", *Review of Income and Wealth Series*, Vol. 35, No. 4, December.

Hotelling, H. (1932), "Edgeworth's Taxation Paradox and the Nature of Demand and Supply Functions", *Journal of Political Economy*, Vol. 40, pp. 577-616.

Hudson, R. (1999), 'The Learning Economy, the Learning Firm and the Learning Region: A Sympathetic Critique of the Limits to Learning', *European Urban and Regional Studies*, Vol. 6, No. 1, pp. 59-72.

IMF (2000), *Balance of Payments Statistics*, Washington.

IMF/OECD (1999), *Report on the Survey of Implementation of Methodological Standards for Direct Investment*, Washington.

Informal Seminar of Industry and Research Ministers (2002), "Fostering Innovation: The European Research and Innovation Area", S'Agaró-Girona, 1-2 February 2002.

Ioannides, Y.M. and Caramanis, M.C. (1979), "Capital-labour Substitution in a Developing Country: The Case of Greece", *European Economic Review*, Vol. 12.

Ireland, N. and Stoneman, P. (1986), "Technological Diffusion, Expectations and Welfare", *Oxford Economic Papers*, Vol. 38, pp. 283-304.

Islam, N. (1998), Growth Empirics: A Panel Data Approach – A Reply, *Quarterly Journal of Economics*, Vol. 113, pp. 325-9.

———— (1995), Growth Empirics: A Panel Data Approach, *Quarterly Journal of Economics*, Vol. 110, pp. 1127-70.

Jefferson, T. (1984), "No Patent on Ideas: Letter to Isaac McPherson, 13 August, 1813", in *Writings. New York, Library of America*, pp. 1286-94.

Johannisson, B. (1991), "University Training for Entrepreneurship: Swedish Approaches", *Entrepreneurship and Regional Development*, Vol. 3, pp. 67-82.

Johansen, L. (1972), *Production Functions*, Amsterdam, North Holland.

Johnson, B. (1997), "Systems of Innovation: Overview and Basic Concepts", in C. Edquist (ed.), *Systems of Innovation, Technologies, Institutions and Organizations*, London: Pinter Publishers, pp. 36-40.

Johnson, B. and Gregersen, B. (1995), "Systems of Innovation and Economic Integration", *Journal of Industry Studies*, Vol. 2, No. 2, pp. 1-18.

Johnson, B., Kristensen, A., Christensen, J.L., Mulvad, M. and Storgaard, L. (1991), "Modes of Usage and Diffusion of New Technologies and New Knowledge – The Case of Denmark", FAST Programme, Commission of the European Comunities.

Jones, C.I. (1995), "Time Series Tests of Endogenous Growth Models", *Quarterly Journal of Economics*, 110, pp. 495-525.

———— (1995), "R&D-Based Models of Economic Growth", *Journal of Political Economy*, 103, pp. 759-784.

———— (1997), "Convergence Revisited", *Journal of Economic Growth*, 2, pp. 131-153.

———— (1997), "Population and Ideas: A Theory of Endogenous Growth", NBER Working Paper No. 6285.

Jones, C.I., Williams, J.C. (1996), "Too Much of a Good Time? The Economics of Investment in R&D", Standford University Working Paper (unpublished).

Jorgenson, D.W. (1988), "Productivity and Economic Growth" (mimeo), *Washington Meeting of the Conference on Research and Income and Wealth, National Bureau of Economic Research*, Cambridge, MA.

———— (1990), "Productivity and Economic Growth", in E.R. Berndt and J.E. Triplett (eds), *Fifty Years of Economic Measurement*, Chicago: University of Chicago Press.

Jorgenson, D.W. and Fraumeni, B.M. (1983), "Relative Prices and Technical Change", in *Quantitative Studies on Production and Prices*, Wurzburg-Wien.

Jorgenson, D.W., Gollop, F.M. and Fraumeni, B.M. (1987), "Productivity and U.S. Economic Growth", Chapter 9, *Growth in Aggregate Output*, Harvard University Press.

Jorgenson, D.W. and Griliches, Z. (1967), The Explanation of Productivity Change, *Review of Economic Studies*, Vol. 34, pp. 249-183.

Jorgenson, D.W. and Kuroda, M. (1990), "Productivity and International Competitiveness in Japan and the United States, 1960-1985", in C.R. Hulten (ed.), *Productivity Growth in Japan and the United States*, Chicago: University of Chicago Press.

Jorgenson, D.W., Kuroda, M. and Nishimizu M. (1987), "Japan-U.S. Industry-Level Productivity Comparisons, 1960-1979", *Journal of the Japanese and International Economies*, Vol. 1, pp. 1-30.

Jorgenson, D.W. and Laffont, J. (1974), "Efficient Estimation of Non-linear Stimultaneous Equations with Additive Disturbances", *Annals of Economic and Social Measurement*, October, pp. 615-640.

Jorgenson, D.W. and Landau, R. (1989), *Technology and Capital Formation*, Cambridge, MA: MIT Press.

Jorgenson, D.W. and Stiroh, K. (1995), "Computers and Growth", *Economics of Innovation and New Technology*, Vol. 3, May, pp. 295-316.

Jorgenson, D.W. and Wilcoxen, P.J. (1990), "Environmental Regulation and U.S. Economic Growth", *Rand Journal of Economics*, Vol. 21, pp. 314-340.

Jovanovic, B. and Lach, S. (1993), *Diffusion Lags and Aggregate Fluctuations*, NBER Working Paper No. 4455.

Judge, G.G., Griffiths, W.E., Hill, R.C. and Lee, T.C. (1980), *The Theory and Practice of Econometrics*, New York: John Wiley & Sons.

Kalt, J.P. (1978), "Technological Change and Factor Substitution in the United States: 1929-1967", *International Economic Review*, Vol. 19, No. 3, October, pp. 761-773.

Kamien, M.I. and Schwartz, N.L. (1969), "Induced Factor Augmenting Technical Progress from a Microeconomic Viewpoint", *Econometrica*, Vol. 37, No. 4, pp. 668-684.

Kaplinsky, R. (1990), *The Economies of Small: Appropriate Technology in a Changing World*, London: Intermediate Technology Publications.

Kaufman, L. (1999), "A Big Names Lead in Holiday Internet Sales", *The New York Times* on the web, Technology <http://www.nytimes.com/library/tech99/12/biztech/articles/02shop.html>.

Kearns, D. and Nadler, D. (1992), *Prophets in the Dark*, New York: Harper Business.

Keller, A. (1990), "Econometrics of Technical Change: Techniques and Problems", in P. Hackl (ed.), *Statistical Analysis and Forecasting of Economic Structural Change*, Chapter 23, International Institute for Applied Systems Analysis.

Kendrick, J.W. (1961), *Productivity Trends in the United States*, Princeton University Press.

———— (1984), *International Comparisons of Productivity and Causes of the Slowdown*, Cambridge, MA: Ballinger.

———— (1991), "Total Factor Productivity – What it Does Not Measure: An Overview", in OECD, *Technology and Productivity: The Challenge for Economic Growth*, Paris: OECD, pp. 149-57.

———— (1992), "The Translog Production Function and Variable Returns to Scale", *Review of Economics and Statistics*, Vol. 74, No. 3, August, pp. 546-552.

———— (1977), "Capital-Labour Substitution in a Developing Country: The Case of Greece: Comments and Some New Results", *European Economic Review*, Vol. 9, pp. 379-382.

———— (1978), "Specification of the Elasticity of Substitution Function Within a Cost-minimization CES Production Function Framework", *Economic Appliquee XXIX*, April 1-28.

———— (1978), "Biased Efficiency Growth and Capital-Labour Substitution in Greek Manufacturing", *Quarterly Review of Economics and Business*, pp. 27-37.

———— (1979), *Patterns and Sources of Growth in Greek Manufacturing*, Athens, Greece.

Kim, H.Y. (1992), "The Translog Production Function and Variable Returns to Scale", *Review of Economics and Statistics*, Vol. 74, No. 3, pp. 546-552, August.

Kirat, T. and Lung, Y. (1999), "Innovations and Proximity. Territories as Loci of Collective Learning Processes", *European Urban and Regional Studies*, Vol. 6, No. 1, pp. 27-38.

Kitsos, C.P., Hadjidema, S. and Korres, G. (2005), The Determinant Factors of the Female Entrepreneurship in Greek Enterprises, *18th Greek Statistical Meeting*, Greece.

Kitsos, C.P. and Hatzikian, J. (2005), *Sequential Techniques for Innovation Indexes. ISPIM, Porto*, Portugal, May.

Kitsos, C.P., Korres, G. and Hatzikian, J. (2005), Innovation Activities in Greece: A Statistical and Empirical Approach, *18th Greek Statistical Meeting*, May, Greece.

Kline, S.J. and Rosenberg, N. (1986), "An Overview of Innovation", in R. Landau and N. Rosenberg (eds), *The Positive Sum Strategy*, National Academy Press, Washington, pp. 275-305

Kmenta, J. (1986), *Elements of Econometrics*, New York: Macmillan.

Kokkelenberg, E.C. and Nguyen, S.V. (1987), "Forecasting Comparison of Three Flexible Functional Forms", Proceedings of the Business and Economic Statistics Section, *American Statistical Association*, pp. 57-64.

——— (1989), "Modelling Technical Progress and Total Factor Productivity: A Plant Level Example", *Journal of Productivity Analysis*, pp. 21-42.

Koopmans, T.C. and Montias, J.M. (1971), "On the Description and Comparison of Economic Systems", in Eckstein, A. (ed.), *Comparison of Economic Systems*, Berkeley, LA: University of California Press.

Korres, G.M. (1996), *Technical Change and Economic Growth: Empirical Eidence from European Countries*, London: Avebury/Ashgate.

——— (1996), "Sources of Structural Change: An Input-output Decomposition Analysis", *Journal of Applied Economic Letters*, Vol. 3, No. 11, November.

——— (1998), "An Overview on Theory of Diffusion Models", *Journal of Science, Technology and Development*, University of Strathclyde Management School, Vol. 16, No. 1, May.

——— (1998), "Productivity and Technical Change on EEC Countries", *Cyprus Journal of Science and Technology*, Vol. 1, No. 4, February.

——— (1999), "An Implementation of Generalized Production Function to Greek Industry", *Journal Southwestern Economic Review*, Vol. 26, No. 1, Spring, University of Arkansas.

——— (2000), "Some Insights of Endogenous Technical Change and Economic Growth", *Journal Archives of Economic History*, Special Issue, pp. 63-71.

——— (2001), "An Estimation of Technical Change and Productivity Using a Translog Function for Greek Industrial Sectors", *Journal Southwestern Economic Review*, Vol. 28, No. 1, pp. 55-75, Spring.

——— (2002), "Technical Change, Diffusion and Innovation in a Context of a Growth Model", in Paraskevopoulos et al. (ed.), *Globalization and Economic Growth*, University of Toronto and APF/ Press Canada, pp. 111-122.

——— (2002), "The Institutional Development and the Harmonization of Technological Policy on the European Community", in G. Bitros and G. Korres (eds), *Economic Integration: Limits and Prospects*, Basingstoke: Macmillan-Palgrave Press.

——— (2002), "Technical Change and Productivity in European Member States: an Explanation of Why Growth Rates are Different", in G. Bitros and G. Korres (eds), *Economic Integration: Limits and Prospects*, London: Macmillan-Palgrave Press.

——— (eds) (2007), *Regionalization, Growth and Economic Integration*, Germany: Springer-Physica-Verlag Press.

——— (2007), "Industrial and Innovation Policy in Europe: The Effects on Growth and Sustainability", *Bulletin of Science, Technology and Society*, forthcoming.

Korres, G. and Bitros, G. (2002), *Economic Integration: Limits and Prospects*, London: Macmillan-Palgrave Press.

Korres, G., Chionis, D. and Tsamadias, C. (2004), "An Inter-Comparison Study of Labour Productivity in the European Union and the United States, 1979-2001", *Applied Econometrics and Quantitative Studies, IJAEQS*, Vol. 1-4.

Korres, G. and Drakopoulos, S. (2002), "Globalization, Foreign Direct Investment (FDI), and International Inequality", *Applied Research Review*, Vol. 7, No. 1, pp. 201-222.

Korres, G., Drakopoulos, S. and Polychronopoulos, G. (2004), "Regional Cohesion and Innovation Activities: A Measurement on the Capacity of E.U. States", *Review of Economic Science*.

Korres, G. and Iwsifidis, T. (2002), "The Impact of Foreign Direct Investment and Technical Change on Regional Growth", in *CD of the European Regional Science Association (ERSA)*, University of Dortmund, Germany.

———— (2003), "Technical Change, Productivity and Economic Growth", in *CD of the European Regional Science Association (ERSA)*, University of Jyvaskyla, Finland.

———— (2006), "Meta-Production Function: A Review on Theory and Evidence", in *Journal of Statistical Review*, Vol. 1.

———— (2007), "A Note for the Role of Foreign Direct Investment, and Technical Change in Regional Growth", in *Journal Management Sciences and Regional Development*, forthcoming.

———— (2007), "Foreign Direct Investment, Technical Change and Regional Growth", in the *Journal Management Sciences and Regional Development*, forthcoming.

Korres G., Kitsos, C. and Chatsidima, S. (2005), "Inside to the Knowledge Based Economy: Looking for the Effects of Innovation and the Entrepreneurship Activities on Regional Growth", in *International Journal of Knowledge, Culture and Change Management*, Vol. 5, No. 4.

———— (2006), "Innovation Activities: A Study for the Determinant Factors and the Role of Female Entrepreneurship in Greek Enterprises", in *Sixth Conference Proceedings of the International Statistical Association*.

Korres, G., Liargkovas P. and Tsamadias, C. (2007), "Regional Disparities and the Effects of Innovation Activities on Regional Integration", in Korres, G. (ed.), *Regionalisation, Growth and Economic Integration*, Germany: Springer, forthcoming.

Korres, G., Lionaki, I. and Polychronopoulos, G. (2003), "The Role of Technical Change and Diffusion in the Schumpeterian Lines", in Backhaus, J. (ed.), *Joseph Alois Schumpeter: Entrepreneurship– Style and Vision*, Kluwer Academic Publishers, pp. 293-312.

Korres, G. and Paraskevopoulos, Y. (1996), "The Role and the Impact of Community's Technological Policy to European Economic Integration", in C. Paraskevopoulos, R. Grinspun and T. Georgakopoulos (eds), *Economic Integration and Public Policy in the European Union*, York University in Toronto/Canada: Edward and Elgar.

Korres, G., Paraskevopoulos, Y. and Geraniotakis, E. (1997), "European Mediterranean and Technological Policy and the Effects on Growth and Employment", in *International Conference Proceedings of the European Association of Labour Economics*, Vol. VI.

Korres G., Patsikas, S. and Polychronopoulos, G. (2002), "A Knowledge Based Economy, the Socio-economy Impact and the Effects on Regional Growth", in *International Journal of Informatica Economica*, 1, pp. 5-12.

Korres, G. and Polychronopoulos, G. (2003), "A Review on Theory of Productivity, Technical Change and Growth", in *A Conference Proceedings of the Quantitative Methods in Industry and in Commercial Firms, Technological Educational Institute of Athens*, pp. 279-291.

——— (2003), "Looking at the Framework of Statistical Measurement on Innovation Activities", in *A Conference Proceedings of the Quantitative Methods in Industry and in Commercial Firms, Technological Educational Institute of Athens*, pp. 435-450.

——— (2004), "Some Aspects for the Measurement of the Development Process: The Human Development Index", in *An International Conference Proceedings of Europe and the Regional Inequalities, Technological Educational Institute of Epirus*, pp. 58-80.

——— (2007), "Entrepreneurship and the Role of Information Economy", in *Journal of Archieves of Economic History*, forthcoming.

Korres, G., Polychronopoulos, G. and Rigas, C. (2001), "A Note on the Choice of a Flexible Functional Form", in *Fourteenth Conference Proceedings of the International Statistical Association*, pp. 605-612.

Korres, G. and Rigas, C. (1997), "Technological Substitution Models, Diffusion Policy and Economic Integration in EEC Countries", in *International Conference Proceedings of the Maastricht ISINI-Papers*, Vol. II, edited by G. Meijer, W.J.M. Heijman, J.A.C. Van Ophem and B.H.J. Verstegen, pp. 321-337.

——— (1999), "Research and Development, Statistical Measurement and the Regional Dimension of Innovation Activities", in *Twelveth Conference Proceedings of the International Statistical Association*.

Korres, G. and Tsombanoglou, G. (2003), "National System of Innovations in E.U., Institutional Harmonization and the Effects on Sustainable Development", in *CD – Proceedings, Defining and Measuring Knowledge, New Economy Statistical Information System (NEsis Project)*, Luxemburg.

——— (2005), "The Knowledge Based Economy and the European National Policy of Innovation", in *The Cyprus Journal of Sciences*, Vol. 3.

——— (2005), *Technical Change, Social Policy and Development: Innovation Activities and Employability in Europe*, Gutenberg Publishers (in Greek), Athens.

Kraemer, K.L., Dedrick, J. and Yamashiro, S. (1999), "Refining and Extending the Business Model with Information Technology: Dell Computer Corporation", Working Paper, *Center for Research on Information Technology and Organizations*, University of California at Irvine, available at <www.crito.uci.edu>.

Krugman, P.R. (1979), "A Model of Innovation, Technology Transfer, and the World Distribution of Income", *Journal of Political Economy*, 87, pp. 253-266.

Kubo, Y. (1985), "A Cross-country Comparison of Interindustry Linkages and the Role of Imported Intermediate Inputs", *World Development*, Vol. 13, December, pp. 1287-1298.

Krieger, L., Mytelka and Delapierre, M. (1987), "The Alliance Strategies of European Firms in the Information Technology Industry and the Role of ESPRIT", *Journal of Common Market Studies*, Vol. 25, No. 2.

Kubo, Y. and Robinson, S. (1984), *Sources of Industrial Growth and Structural Change: A Comparative Analysis of Eight Economies*, in UNIDO (ed.), The Proceedings of the Seventh International Conference on Input-Output Techniques.

Kumbhakar, S., Heshmati, A. and Hjalmarsson, L. (1997), "Temporal Patterns of Technical Efficiency: Results from Competing Models", *International Journal of Industrial Organisation*, Vol. 15, pp. 597-616.

Kumbhakar, S.C. and Lovell, C.A.K. (2000), *Stochastic Frontier Analysis*, Cambridge University Press.

Kuznets, S.S. (1971), *Economic Growth of Nations*, Cambridge, MA: Harvard University Press .

——— (1973), *Population, Capital and Growth: Selected Essays*, New York: W.W. Norton.

Lahiri, K. and Moore, G.H. (1992), *Leading Economic Indicators: New Approaches and Forecasting Records*, Cambridge University Press.

Landau, D. (1986), "Government Expenditure and Economic Growth in the Less Developed Countries: An Empirical Study for 1960-1980", *Economic Development and Cultural Change*, Vol. 35, October, pp. 35-75.

Landau, R. (1989), "Technology and Capital Formation", Chapter 12 in D. Jorgenson and R. Landau (eds), *Technology and Capital Formation*, MIT Press.

Landau, R. (1983), "Government Expenditure and Economic Growth: A Cross Country Study", *Southern Economic Journal*, January, pp. 783-792.

Lau, L.J. (1978), "A Note on the Compatibility of a System of Difference Equations and a Time-independent Linear Equation", *Economic Letters*, Vol. 1, No. 3, pp. 243-247.

Lau, L.J., Jamison, D.T. and Louat, F.F. (1990), "Education and Productivity in Developing Countries: An Aggregate Production Function Approach" (mimeo), Stanford University.

Lau, L.J., Lin, W. and Yotopoulos, P.A. (1978), "The Linear Logarithmic Expenditure System", *Econometrica*, Vol. 46, pp. 840-868.

Lau, L.J. and Yotopoulos, P.A. (1989), "The Meta-production Function Approach to Technological Change in World Agriculture", *Journal of Development Economics*, Vol. 31, October, pp. 241-269.

Leamer, E.E. (1978), *Specification Searches*, New York: John Wiley & Sons.

Lehmann, J.P. (1992), "France, Japan, Europe, and Industrial Competition: The Automotive Case", *International Affairs*, Vol. 68, No. 1.

Lee, K., Pesaran, M.H. and Smith, R. (1998), "Growth Empirics: A Panel Data Approach – A Comment", *Quarterly Journal of Economics*, Vol. 113, pp. 319-24.

Lee, Y.H. and Schmidt, P. (1993), "A Production Frontier Model with Flexible Temporal Variation in Technical Efficiency", in Chapter 8 of H. Fried, C.A.K. Lovell and S.S. Schmidt (eds), *The Measurement of Productive Efficiency Techniques and Applications*, Oxford Academic Press, pp. 237-255.

Lengrand, L. (2002), *Innovation Tomorrow*, Office for Official Publications of the European Communities.

Leontief, W. (1953), "Dynamic Analysis", Chapter 3 in *The Studies in the Structure of the American Economy*, Oxford University Press.

Lequiller, F., Ahmad, N., Varjonen, S., Cave, W. and Ahn, K.H. (2003), "Report of the OECD Task Force on Software Measurement in the National Accounts", Statistics Directorate Working Paper, 2003/1, OECD, Paris.

Levin, R.C. (1988), "Appropriability, R&D Spending and Technological Performance", *American Economic Review*, Vol. 78, pp. 424-428.

Levine, R. and Renelt, D. (1990), *Cross-country Studies of Growth and Policy: Methodological, Conceptual and Statistical Problems*, World Bank, Washington.

Lianos, T.P. (1976), "Factor Augmentation in Greek Manufacturing 1958-1968", *European Economic Review*, pp. 15-31.

Lichtenberg, F., van Pottelsberghe de la Potterie, B. (1996), "International R&D Spillovers: A Re-examination", NBER Working Paper No. 5668.

Link, A.N. (1987), *Technological Change and Productivity Growth*, Chur, Switzerland: Harwood Academic Publisher.

López-Bazo, E., Vayá, E., Mora, A. and Suriñach, J. (1999), "Regional Economic Dynamics and Convergence in the European Union", *The Annals of Regional Science*, Vol. 22, No. 3, pp. 1-28.

Lucas Jr., R.E. (1967), "Tests of a Capital-Theoretic Model of Technological Change", *Review of Economic Studies*, pp. 175-189.

——— (1969), "Labour-Capital Substitution in U.S. Manufacturing" in A.C. Harberger and M.J. Bailey (eds), *The Taxation of Income from Capital*, Washington, DC: The Brooking Institution, pp. 223-274.

——— (1988), "On the Mechanics of Economic Development", *Journal of Monetary Economics*, 22, pp. 3-42.

Lundvall, B.-Å. (1988), "Innovation as an Interactive Process: From User-producer Interaction to the National System of Innovations", in G. Dosi, C. Freeman, R. Nelson, G. Silverberg, L. Soete (eds), *Technical Change and Economic Theory*, London: Pinter Publishers, pp. 349-369.

——— (1992a), "User-Producer Relationships, National Systems of Innovation and Internationalization", in B.-Å. Lundvall (ed.) (1992), *National Systems of Innovation*, London: Pinter Publishers.

——— (ed.) (1992b), *National Systems of Innovation*, London: Pinter Publishers.

——— (1992c), *National Systems of Innovations: Towards a Theory of Innovation and Interactive Learning*, London: Pinter Publishers.

Lundvall, B.-Å. and Johnson, B. (1994), "The Learning Economy", *Journal of Industry Studies*, Vol. I, No. 2.

Luther, M. (1523), "Concerning Secular Authority", in F.W. Coker (ed.), *Readings in Political Philosophy*, New York: Macmillan, pp. 306-29.

Maddala, G.S. (1987), "Limited Dependent and Quality View Variables in Econometrics", *Econometric Society Monographs*, Cambridge University Press.

Maddison, A. (1987), "Growth and Slowdown in Advanced Capitalist Economies", *The Journal of Economic Literature*, Vol. 25, pp. 649-698.

Malecki, E.J. (1991), *Technology and Economic Development: The Dynamics of Local Regional and National Change* (eds), Longman Scientific and Technical.

———— (1997), *Technology and Economic Development*, 2nd ed., Longman, Essex.

Malecki, E.J. and Oinas, P. (eds) (1999a), *Making Connections: Technological Learning and Regional Economic Change*, Aldershot: Ashgate.

Malecki, E.J., Oinas, P. and Ock Park, S. (1999b), "On Technology and Development", in E.J. Malecki and P. Oinas (eds), *Making Connections. Technological Learning and Regional Economic Change*, Aldershot: Ashgate, pp. 261-275.

Mankinw, N.G., Romer, D. and Weil, D.N. (1992), "A Contribution to the Empirics of Economic Growth", *Quarterly Journal of Economics*, Vol. 107, No. 2, pp. 407-437.

Mansfield, E. (1968), *Economics of Technological Change*, New York.

———— (1969), *Industrial Research and Technological Innovation: An Econometric Analysis* (eds), Longman and Green Publishers.

———— (1977), *The Production and Application of New Industrial Technology*, W.W. Norton Publishers.

———— (1988), "The Speed of Cost of Industrial Innovation in Japan and the United States: External vs. Internal Technology", *Management Science*, Vol. 34, No. 10.

Mansfield, E., Romeo, A., Schwartz, M., Teece, D., Wagner, S. and Brach, P. (1982), *Technology Transfer, Productivity and Economic Policy*, New York: Norton and Co.

Maskell, P. and Malmberg, A. (1999), "The Competitiveness of Firms and Regions. 'Ubiquitification' and the Importance of Localized Learning", *European Urban and Regional Studies*, Vol. 6, No. 1, pp. 9-25.

Maskell, P. and Malmberg, A. (1999), "Localised Learning and Industrial Competitiveness", *Cambridge Journal of Economics*, Vol. 23, pp. 167-185.

Maskus, K.E. (1991), "Comparing International Trade Data and Product and National Characteristics Data for the Analysis of Trade Models", in P. Hooper and J.D. Richardson (eds), *International Economic Transactions: Issues in Measurement and Empirical Research*, University of Chicago Press for the NBER, Chicago.

May, K.O. (1966), "Quantitative Growth of the Mathematical Literature", *Science*, Vol. 154, pp. 1672-1673.

McAleavey, P.C. (1994), "Who is the Operative Subject of EC Regional Policy? The Cases of Scotland and North Rhine-Westphalia" in U. Bullmann (ed.), *Die Politik der dritten Ebene: Regionen im Europa der Union*, Baden-Baden: Nomos, pp. 79-90.

McFadden, D. (1978), *Production Economics: A Dual Approach to Theory and Applications*, Vol. 1, Amsterdam, North Holland.

—— (1978a), "Cost Revenue and Profit Functions", Chapter I.I in M. Fuss and D. McFadden (eds), *Production Economics: A Dual Approach to Theory and Applications*, Vol. 1, Amsterdam, North Holland, pp. 1-109.

—— (1978b), "The Genear Linear Profit Function", Chapter II.2 in M. Fuss and D. McFadden (eds), *Production Economics: A Dual Approach to Theory and Applications*, Vol. 1, Amsterdam, North Holland, pp. 269-286.

Mera, K. (1973), "Regional Production Functions and Social Overhead Capital: An Analysis of the Japanese Case", *Regional and Urban Economics*, Vol. 3, pp. 157-186.

Merton, R. (1981), "Fluctuations in the Rate of Industrial Invention", *Quarterly Journal of Economics*, Vol. 49, pp. 454-474.

Mesenbourg, T.L. (2000), *Measuring Electronic Business*, presentation to COPAFS, 10 March <http://www.census.gov/econ/www/index.html>.

Metcalfe, J.S. (1981), "Impulse and Diffusion in the Study of Technical Change", *Futures*, Vol. 18, No. 4.

—— (1990), "The Diffusion of Innovation: An Interpretative Survey", in Dosi et al. (eds), *Technical Change and Economic Theory*.

Metcalfe, J.S. and Gibbons, M. (1991), "The Diffusion of the New Technologies a Condition for Renewed Economic Growth", in *Technology and Productivity-the Challenge for Economic Policy*, OECD, Paris.

Middlemas, K. (1994), "Informal Politics: Power without Sovereignty", Paper presented at the Sussex European Institute Seminar 'Industrial Networks in the EC, 13-15 October.

Millard, J. (1999), "New Methods of Work: Experience from the Fourth Framework Programme", Paper given to the Socio-Economic Preparatory Conference for the Fifth Framework Programme, Paris, 23 February.

Ministry of Education and Science (2000), *A Summary of Government Bill "Research and Renewal"*, 2000/01:3. Ministry of Education and Science, Stockholm.

Ministry of Education, Culture, Sports, Science and Technology of Japan (2002), *Science and Technology Basic Plan* <http://mext.go.jp/english/org/science>.

Mizen, P. and Tew, B. (1996), "Proposals to Ensure a Smooth Transition to European Monetary Union by 1999", *The World Economy*, Vol. 19, No. 4, July, pp. 387-406.

Mohnen, P. (1994), "The Econometric Approach to R&D Externalities", in Cahiers de Recherche du Departement des Sciences Economiques de l'UQAM, No. 9408.

Molle, W. (1990), *The Economics of European Integration: Theory, Practice, Policy*, England: Dartmouth Publishing Company Ltd., pp. 417-438.

Morgan, K. (1997), "The Learning Region: Institutions, Innovation and Regional Renewal", *Regional Studies*, Vol. 31, No. 5, pp. 491-503.

Morrison, C.J. (1987), "Quasi-fixed Inputs in U.S. and Japanese Manufacturing: a Generalized Leontief Restricted Cost Function Approach", *The Review of Economics and Statistics*.

Morrison, C.J. (1993), *A Microeconomic Approach to the Measurement of Economic Performance*, New York: Springer-Verlag.

Morrison, C.R. and Diewert, W.E. (1987), "New Techniques in the Measurement of Multifactor Productivity", Paper presented at the National Bureau of Economic Research Spring Meeting of the Productivity Workshop, 20 March.

Myers, M.B. and Rosenbloom, R.S. (1996), *Rethinking the Role of Industrial Research*, in R.S. Rosenbloom and W.J. Spencer (eds), *Engines of Innovation: US Industrial Research at the End of an Era*, Boston: Harvard Business School Press, pp. 209-228.

Mytelka, L.K. (1993), "Strengthening the Relevance of European Science and Technology Programmes to Industrial Competitiveness: The Case of ESPRIT", in M. Humbert (ed.), *The Impact of Globalization on Europe's Firms and Industries*, pp. 56-63, London: Pinter Publishers.

Nasbeth, L. and Ray, F.G. (eds) (1974), *The Diffusion of New Industrial Processes: an International Study*, Cambridge University Press.

National Science Foundation (2002), *National Science Board, Science and Engineering Indicators 2002*, Vol. 1, National Science Foundation, Arlington, VA.

Naxakis, C. (1996), "The Globalization on Products, Markets and Technology", *Oikonomika Xronika*, 94.

Nelson, R. (1981), "Research on Productivity Growth and Productivity Differences: Dead Ends and New Departures", *Journal of Economic Literature*, Vol. XIX, September, pp. 1209-1064.

——— (1993), *National Innovation Systems: A Comparative Analysis*, Oxford University Press.

——— (1995), "Recent Evolutionary Theorizing About Economic Change", *Journal of Economic Litterature*, Vol. XXXIII, No. 1, March.

Nelson, R.R., Peck, M.J. and Calacheck, E.D. (1987), *Technology, Economic Growth, and Public Policy*, Washington, DC: Brookings.

Nelson, R. and Winter, S.G. (1982), *An Evolutionary Theory of Economic Change*, Cambridge, MA: Harvard University Press.

Nerlove, M. (1963), "Returns to Scale in Elasticity Supply" in C. Christ (ed.), *Measurement in Economics: Studies in Mathematical Economics and*

Econometrics in Memory of Yehuda Grunfeld, Stanford, CA: Stanford University Press, pp. 167-198.

—— (1967), "Recent Empirical Studies of the CES and Related Production Functions" in M. Brown (ed.), *The Theory and Empirical Analysis of Production*, Studies in Income and Wealth, Vol. 32, New York: Columbia University Press for the National Bureau of Economic Research, pp. 55-122.

Nicolaides, P. (1993), "Industrial Policy: The Problem of Reconciling Definitions, Intentions and Effects", in P. Nicolaides (ed.), *Industrial Policy in the European Community: A Necessary Response to Economic Integration?*, pp. 1-17, Dordrecht: Nijhoff.

Noisi, J., Saviotti, P., Bellon, B. and Crow, M. (1993), "National Systems of Innovation", in *Search of a Workable Concept, Technology in Society*, Vol. 15, No. 2, pp. 207-227.

Nonaka, I. and Takeuchi, H. (1995), *The Knowledge-Creating Company. How Japanese Companies Create the Dynamics of Innovation*, New York, Oxford: Oxford University Press.

Norworthy, J.R. (1984), "Growth Accounting and Productivity Measurement", *Review of Income and Wealth*, Vol. 30, No. 3, pp. 309-329.

—— (1990), "Cost Function Estimation and the Additive General Error Model", Unpublished Working Paper, April, Renssalaer Polytechnic Institute, Department of Economics, Troy.

Norworthy, J.R. and Malmquist, D.H. (1983), "Input Measurement and Productivity Growth in Japanese and U.S. Manufacturing", *American Economic Review*, Vol. 73, pp. 947-967.

Norworthy, J.R. and Jang, S.L. (1992), *Empirical Measurement and Analysis of Productivity and Technical Change: Applications in High technology and Service Industries*, in series of Tinbergen, J., Jorgenson, D.W. and Laffont, J.J., Contributions to Economic analysis, North Holland Publications.

OECD (1963), *Proposed Standard Practice for Surveys of Research and Development: The Measurement of Scientific and Technical Activities*, Directorate for Scientific Affairs, DAS/PD/62.47, Organisation for Economic Co-operation and Development, Paris.

—— (1968a), *Statistical Tables and Notes* ("International Statistical Year for Research and Development: A Study of Resources Devoted to R&D in OECD Member countries in 1963/64"), Vol. 2, Organisation for Economic Co-operation and Development, Paris.

—— (1968b), *Fundamental Research and the Universities*, Organisation for Economic Co-operation and Development, Paris.

—— (1970), *Proposed Standard Practice for Surveys of Research and Experimental Development: The Measurement of Scientific and Technical Activities*, DAS/ SPR/70.40, Directorate for Scientific Affairs, Organisation for Economic Co-operation and Development, Paris.

—— (1976), *Proposed Standard Practice for Surveys of Research and Experimental Development: "Frascati Manual"*, The Measurement of

Scientific and Technical Activities Series, Organisation for Economic Co-operation and Development, Paris.

——— (1979), *Trends in Industrial R&D in Selected OECD Member Countries 1967-1975*, Organisation for Economic Co-operation and Development, Paris.

——— (1981a), *Proposed Standard Practice for Surveys of Research and Experimental Development: "Frascati Manual 1980"*, The Measurement of Scientific and Technical Activities Series, Organisation for Economic Co-operation and Development, Paris.

——— (1981b), *The Measurement of Scientific and Technical Activities: Frascati Manual 1980*, Organisation for Economic Co-operation and Development, Paris.

——— (1981c), *New Technologies in the 1990s: a Socio-Economic Strategy*, Organisation for Economic Co-operation and Development, Paris.

——— (1984), *OECD Science and Technology Indicators: No. 1 – Resources Devoted to R&D*, Organisation for Economic Co-operation and Development, Paris.

——— (1986), *OECD Science and Technology Indicators: No. 2 – R&D, Invention and Competitiveness*, Organisation for Economic Co-operation and Development, Paris.

——— (1988), *Industrial Revival Through Technology*, Organisation for Economic Co-operation and Development, Paris.

——— (1989a), *OECD Science and Technology Indicators, No. 3 – R&D, Production and Diffusion of Technology*, Organisation for Economic Co-operation and Development, Paris.

——— (1989b), *R&D Statistics and Output Measurement in the Higher Education Sector: "Frascati Manual" Supplement*, The Measurement of Scientific and Technological Activities Series, Organisation for Economic Co-operation and Development, Paris.

——— (1990), "Proposed Standard Method of Compiling and Interpreting Technology Balance of Payments Data: TBP Manual 1990", *The Measurement of Scientific and Technological Activities Series*, Organisation for Economic Co-operation and Development, Paris.

——— (1991a), *Industrial Policy in OECD Countries: Annual Review 1990*, Organisation for Economic Co-operation and Development, Paris.

——— (1991b), *Technology and Productivity – The Challenge for Economic Growth*, Organisation for Economic Co-operation and Development, Paris.

——— (1991c), *Economic-Outlook: Historical Statistics, 1960-1990*, Organisation for Economic Co-operation and Development, Paris.

——— (1991d), *Basic Science and Technology Statistics*, Organisation for Economic Co-operation and Development, Paris.

——— (1991e), *Choosing Priorities in Science and Technology*, Organisation for Economic Co-operation and Development, Paris.

—————— (1992a), *OECD Proposed Guidelines for Collecting and Interpreting Technological Innovation Data– Oslo Manual*, Organisation for Economic Co-operation and Development, Paris.

—————— (1992b), *TEP–Technology in a Changing World*, Organisation for Economic Co-operation and Development, Paris.

—————— (1992c), *TEP–Technology and Economy: The Key Relationships*, Organisation for Economic Co-operation and Development, Paris.

—————— (1992d), *Science and Technology Policy: Review and Outlook 1991*, Organisation for Economic Co-operation and Development, Paris.

—————— (1992e), *The OECD STAN Database for Structural Analysis*, Organisation for Economic Co-operation and Development, Paris.

—————— (1994a), *Proposed Standard Practice for Surveys of Research and Experimental Development, "Frascati Manual 1993"*, The Measurement of Scientific and Technological Activities Series, Organisation for Economic Co-operation and Development, Paris.

—————— (1994b), *Using Patent Data as Science and Technology Indicators – Patent Manual 1994: The Measurement of Scientific and Technological Activities*, OCDE/GD(94)114, 1994, Organisation for Economic Co-operation and Development, Paris.

—————— (1994c), *National Systems of Innovation: General Conceptual Framework*, DSTI/STP/TIP94(4), Organisation for Economic Co-operation and Development, Paris.

—————— (1994d), *Canberra Manual. Manual on the Measurement of Human Resources Devoted to S&T*, Organisation for Economic Co-operation and Development, Paris.

—————— (1996a), *The Knowledge Economy*, Organisation for Economic Co-operation and Development, Paris.

—————— (1996b), *ISDB 96: International Sectoral Database, 1960-1995*, Organisation for Economic Co-operation and Development, Paris.

—————— (1997a), *The OECD Report on Regulatory Reform: Synthesis*, Organisation for Economic Co-operation and Development, Paris.

—————— (1997b), *The Oslo Manual: Proposed Guidelines for Collecting and Interpreting Technological Innovation Data*, Organisation for Economic Co-operation and Development, Paris.

—————— (1997c), *Technology and Industry: Scoreboard of Indicators*, Organisation for Economic Co-operation and Development, Paris.

—————— (1997d), *Manual for Better Training Statistics – Conceptual, Measurement and Survey Issue*, Organisation for Economic Co-operation and Development, Paris.

—————— (1997e), *Revision of the High-technology Sector and Product Classification*, STI Working Papers 2/1997, Organisation for Economic Co-operation and Development, Paris.

—————— (1997f), *Regional Competitiveness and Skills*, Organisation for Economic Co-operation and Development, Paris.

———— (1999a), *The Response of Higher Education Institutions to Regional Needs*, Organisation for Economic Co-operation and Development, Paris.

———— (1999b), *Defining And Measuring E-Commerce: A Status Report*, DSTI/ICCP/ IIS (99)4/FINAL, Organisation for Economic Co-operation and Development, Paris.

———— (2000), *Economic Outlook*, Organisation for Economic Co-operation and Development, Paris.

———— (2001a), *Economics Department Working Paper*, No. 248 (Scarpetta et al.), Organisation for Economic Co-operation and Development, May 2001.

————(2001b), *Towards a Knowledge-based Economy OECD Science, Technology and Industry Scoreboard 2001* <http://www1.oecd.org/publications/e-book/92-2001-04-1-2987/> Organisation for Economic Co-operation and Development, Paris.

———— (2001c), *Basic Research: Statistical Issues*, OECD/NESTI Document DSTI/ EAS/STP/NESTI(2001)38, Organisation for Economic Co-operation and Development, Paris.

———— (2001d), *The New Economy: Beyond the Hype*, Final Report on the OECD Growth Project, Meeting of the OECD Council at Ministerial Level, 2001, Organisation for Economic Co-operation and Development, Paris.

———— (2001e), *Innovative Networks. Co-operation in National Innovation Systems*, Organisation for Economic Co-operation and Development, Paris.

———— (2001f), *Science, Technology and Industry Scoreboard. Towards a Knowledge-based Economy*, Organisation for Economic Co-operation and Development, Paris.

———— (2001g), "Special Issue on Fostering High-tech Spin-offs: A Public Strategy for Innovation. STI Science Technology Industry", Review No. 26, Organisation for Economic Co-operation and Development, Paris.

———— (2002a), *Frascati Manual. Proposed Standards Practice for Surveys on Research and Experimental Development*, Organisation for Economic Co-operation and Development, Paris.

———— (2002b), *Special Issue on New Science and Technology Indicators. STI Science Technology Industry*, Review No. 27. Organisation for Economic Co-operation and Development, Paris.

———— (2002b), *Public Funding of R&D – Trends and Changes*, OECD Document DSTI/STP(2002)3/REV1 prepared by the ad hoc working group on "Steering and Funding of Research Institutions", Organisation for Economic Co-operation and Development, Paris.

———— (2002c), *Research and Development Expenditure in Industry 1987-2000*, Organisation for Economic Co-operation and Development, Paris.

———— (2002d), *Bibliometric Indicators and Analysis of Research Systems, Methods and Examples*, Working Paper by Yoshika Okibo, Organisation for Economic Co-operation and Development, Paris.

———— (2002e), *Manual of Economic Globalisation Indicators*, Organisation for Economic Co-operation and Development, Paris.

―――― (2002f), *Manual for Better Training Statistics: Conceptual Measurement and Survey Issues*, Organisation for Economic Co-operation and Development, Paris.

―――― (2003a), *Main Science and Technology Indicators* – 2003/1, Organisation for Economic Co-operation and Development, Paris.

―――― (2003b), *Communications Outlook 2003*, Organisation for Economic Co-operation and Development, Paris.

OECD/Eurostat (1995), *The Measurement of Human Resources Devoted to Science and Technology – Canberra Manual: The Measurement of Scientific and Technological Activities*, Organisation for Economic Co-operation and Development, Paris.

―――― (1997a), *Proposed Guidelines for Collecting and Interpreting Technological Innovation Data – Oslo Manual*, The Measurement of Scientific and Technical Activities Series, Organisation for Economic Co-operation and Development, Paris.

―――― (1999), *Classifying Educational Programmes, Manual for ISCED-97 Implementation in OECD Countries*, Organisation for Economic Co-operation and Development, Paris.

―――― (2001), *Measuring Expenditure on Health-related R&D*, Organisation for Economic Co-operation and Development, Paris.

―――― (2002), *Measuring the Information Economy*, Organisation for Economic Co-operation and Development, Paris.

―――― (Biannual), *Main Science and Technology Indicators*, Organisation for Economic Co-operation and Development, Paris.

―――― (every second year), *Basic Science and Technology Statistics*, Organisation for Economic Co-operation and Development, Paris.

―――― (every second year), *OECD Science, Technology and Industry Scoreboard*, Organisation for Economic Co-operation and Development, Paris.

―――― (every second year), *OECD Science, Technology and Industry Outlook*, Paris.

―――― (every second year), *OECD Information Technology Outlook*, Organisation for Economic Co-operation and Development, Paris.

OECD, STAN and National Accounts databases, Organisation for Economic Co-operation and Development, May 2001.

Ohmae, K. (1995), *The End of the Nation State*, New York: Free Press.

Ohta, M. (1974), "A Note on the Duality Between Production and Cost Functions: Rate of Returns to Scale and Rate of Technical Progress", *Economic Studies Quarterly*, 25, pp. 63-65.

Oliner, S. and Sichel, D.E. (2000), *The Resurgence of Growth in the Late 1990s: Is Information Technology the Story?*, Federal Reserve Board, March 2000 (mimeo).

Olson, M. (1982), *The Rise and Decline of Nations: Economic Growth*, Stagflation, and Social Rigidities, New Haven: Yale University Press.

Paci, R. and Pigliaru, F. (1999), "Technological Catch-up and Regional Convergence in Europe", *Contributi di Ricerca Crenos*, Vol. 9.

Page, S. and Davenport, M. (1994), *World Trade Reform: Do Developing Countries Gain or Lose?* London: Overseas Development Institute.

Panas, E.E. (1986), "Biased Technological Progress and Theories of Induced Innovation: The Case of Greek Manufacturing, 1958-1975", *Greek Economic Review*, Vol. 8, No. 1, November, pp. 95-119.

Paraskevopoulos, C.C. (1992), "Competitiveness and Productivity between Canadian and US Manufacturing Industries", Department of Economics, York University, Toronto (mimeo).

Paci, R. and Pigliaru, F. (1999), Technological Catch-up and Regional Convergence in Europe, *Contributi di Ricerca Crenos*, 99/9.

Parente, S.L. and Prescott, E.C. (1994), "Barriers to Technology Adoption and Development", *Journal of Political Economy*, Vol. 102, pp. 298-321.

Pavitt, K. and Walker, W. (1976), "Government Policies Towards Industrial Innovations a Review", *Research Policy*.

Pedler, R.H. (1994), "The Fruit Companies and the Banana Trade Regime (BTR)", in R.H. Pedler, van Schendelen, M. (eds), *Lobbying the European Union*, Hants: Dartmouth, pp. 67-92.

Perez, C. (1985), "Microelectronics, Long Waves and World Structural Change", *World Development*, Vol. 13, No. 3.

Perez, C. and Soete, L. (1988), "Catching-up in Technology: Entry Barriers and Windows of Opportunity", in Dosi et al. (eds), *Technical Change and Economic Theory*.

Peterson, J. (1991), "Technology Policy in Europe: Explaining the Framework Programme and Eureka in Theory and in Practice", *Journal of Common Market Studies*, Vol. XXIX, No. 3.

———— (1993), *High Technology and the Competition State. An Analysis of the Eureka Initiative*, London, New York: Routledge.

Petit, P. and Tahar, G. (1989), "Dynamics of Technological Change and Schemes of Diffusion", *The Manchester School*, December.

Petrocholis, G. (1989), *Foreign Direct Investments and Implications to Greece*, London: Avebury.

Phelps. E.S. (1966), "Models of Technical Progress and the Golden Rule of Research", *Review of Economic Studies*, 33, pp. 133-146.

Pindyck, R. (1978), "Interfuel Substitution and the Industrial Demand for Energy: an International Comparison", *The Review of Economics and Statistics*.

Pindyck, R. and Rotemberg, J.R. (1983), "Dynamic Factor Demands and the Effects of Energy Price Shocks", *American Economic Review*, Vol. 75, No. 5, December, pp. 1066-1079.

Pindyck, R. and Rudinfeld, D. (1991), *Econometric Models and Economic Forecasting*, McGraw-Hill Publishers.

Polanyi, M. (1966), *The Tacit Dimension*, London: Routledge and Kegan Paul.

Porter, M.E. (1990), *The Competitive Advantage of Nations*, New York: The Free Press.

Porter, M.E. and Fuller M.B. (1986), "Coalitions and Global Strategy", in Porter, M.E. (ed.), *Competition in Global Industries*, Boston: Harvard Business School Press, pp. 315-343.

Powell, W.W. (1990), "Neither Market nor Hierarchy: Network Forms of Organization", in Staw, B.M. and Cummings, L.L. (eds), *Research in Organizational Behavior*, Greenwich, CT: JAI Press, pp. 295-335.

Prasad, H. (1981), *Research in International Business and Finance: Technology Transfer and Economic Development*, Vol. 2.

Price, A., Morgan, K. and Cooke, P. (1994), *The Welsh Renaissance: Inward Investment and Industrial Innovation*, Cardiff: CASS.

Quinn, A. (1990), *Trends in Scientific R&TD in the EEC* (Brussels: CEC).

Rao, M. (1997), "Development in the Time of Globalization", Paper for the Workshop on Globalization, Uneven Development and Poverty, 25-25 October, UNDP, New York.

Rasmussen, P.N. (1956), *Intersectoral Relations*, Amsterdam, North Holland.

Ray, G.F. (1969), "The Diffusion of New Technology: A Study of Ten Processes in Nine Industries", *National Institute Economic Review*, Vol. 48, pp. 40-83.

Richonnier, M. (1984), "Europe's Decline is not Irreversible", *Journal of Common Market Studies*, Vol. 22, No. 3.

Ridker, R. (1994), *The World Bank's Role in Human Resource Development: Education, Training and Technical Assistance*, Washington, DC: World Bank Operations Evaluation Study.

River-Batiz, L.A. and Roomer, P. (1991), Economic Integration and Endogenous Growth, *Quarterly Journal of Economics*, Vol. 106, pp. 531-556.

Robertson, T. and Gatignon, H. (1987), "The Diffusion of High Technology Innovations: a Marketing Perspective", Chapter 8 in J.M. Pennings and A. Buitendam (eds), *New Technology as Organizational Innovation: The Development and Diffusion of Microelectronics*, Ballinger Publishing Company.

Robson, M., Townsend, J. and Pavitt, K. (1988), "Sectoral Patterns of Production and Use of Innovations in the UK: 1945-1983", *Research Policy*, 17, pp. 1-14.

Romer, D. (1986), "Increasing Returns and Long Term Growth", *Journal of Political Economy*, Vol. 94, No. 5, pp. 1002-1037.

——— (1987b), "Growth Based on Increasing Returns Due to Specialization", *American Economic Review*, Vol. 77, No. 2, May, pp. 56-62.

——— (1989), "What Determines the Rate of Growth of Technological Change?", PPR Working Paper, The World Bank, 279, Washington, DC.

——— (1990a), Endogenous Technological Change, *Journal of Political Economy*, Vol. 98, pp. 71-102.

——— (1990b), Capital, Labor and Productivity, *Brookings Papers on Economic Activity, Macroeconomics*, pp. 337-420.

——— (1990c), "Human Capital and Growth: Theory and Evidence", NBER Working Paper.

———— (1994), "The Origins of Endogenous Growth", *Journal of Economic Perspectives*, Vol. 8, No. 1, pp. 3-22.

———— (1996), *Advanced Macroeconomics*, McGraw-Hill.

Rosenberg, N. (1963), "Technological Change in the Machine Tool Industry: 1840-1910", *Journal of Economic History*, Vol. 23, No. 4, December, pp. 414-446.

———— (1976), *Perspectives on Technology*, Cambridge: Cambridge University Press.

———— (1982), *Inside the Black Box*, Cambridge: Cambridge University Press.

Rosenberg, N. and Birdzell, L.E. (1986), *How the West Grew Rich: The Economic Transformation of the Industrial World*, New York: Basic Books.

Rosenberg, N., Landau, R. and Mowery, D.C. (1992), *Technology and the Wealth of Nations*, Stanford, CA: Stanford University Press.

Ross, G. (1993), "Sidling into Industrial Policy: Inside the European Commission", *French Politics and Society*, Vol. 11, No. 1, pp. 20-43.

Rothwell, R. and Dodgson, M. (1992), "European Technology Policy Evolution: Convergence Towards SMEs and Regional Technology Transfer", *Technovation*, Vol. 12, No. 4, pp. 223-38.

Sabel, C.F. (1994), "Flexible Specialisation and the Re-emergence of Regional Economies" in A. Amin (ed.), *Post Fordism: A Reader*, Oxford, UK and Cambridge, USA.

Sah, R. and Stiglitz, J.E. (1986), "The Architecture of Economic Systems: Hierarchies and Polyarchies", *The American Economic Review*, Vol. 76, No. 4, September, pp. 716-727.

Sahal, D. (1975), "Evolving Parameter Models of Technology Assessment", *Journal of the International Society for Technology Assessment*, Vol. 1, pp. 11-20.

———— (1977a), "Substitution of Mechanical Corn Pickers by Field Shelling Technology – An Econometric Analysis", *Technological Forecasting and Social Change*, Vol. 10, pp. 53-60.

———— (1977b), "The Multidimensional Diffusion of Technology", *Technological Forecasting and Social Change*, Vol. 10, pp. 277-298.

———— (1980), *Research, Development and Technological Innovation: Recent Perspectives on Management*, Lexington, MA.

Sahal, D. and Nelson, R.R. (1981), *Patterns of Technological Innovation*, Chapter 5, Boston, MA: Addison-Wesley.

Sakurai, N., Papaconstantinou, G. and Ioannidis, E. (1997), "Impact of R&D and Technology Diffusion on Productivity Growth: Empirical Evidence of 10 OECD Countries", *Economic Systems Research*, Vol. 9, pp. 81-109.

Sala-i-Martin, X. (1996), "The Classical Approach to Convergence Analysis", *The Economic Journal*, 106, pp. 1019-1069.

Sargan, J.D. (1971), "Production Functions", Part V of R.G. Layard, J.D. Sargan, M.E. Ager, and D.J. Jones (eds), *Qualified Manpower and Economic Performance*, London: The Penguin Press, pp. 145-204.

Sato, R. (1970), "The Estimation of Biased Technical Progress and the Production Function", *International Economic Review*, Vol. 11, No. 2, June, pp. 179-208.

―――― (1975), *Production Functions and Aggregation*, Amsterdam, North Holland.

Sato, R. and Suzawa, G. (1983), *Research and Productivity*, Boston, MA: Auburn House Publishing Company.

Saviotti, P. (1988), Information, Entropy and Variety in Technoeconomic Development, *Research Policy*, Vol. 17, pp. 89-103.

―――― (1998), On the Dynamics of Appropriability of Tacit and of Codified Knowledge, *Research Policy*, Vol. 26, pp. 843-856.

Scherer, F.M. (1982a), "Inter-industry Technology Flows and Productivity Growth", *Review of Economic and Statistics*, Vol. 64, No. 4, November, pp. 627-34.

―――― (1982b), "Inter-industry Technology Flows in the United States", in *Research Policy*, Vol. 6, pp. 227-45.

Schmidt, P. and Sickles, R.C. (1984), "Production Frontiers and Panel Data", *Journal of Business and Economic Statistics 2*, pp. 367-374.

Schmitz, H. and Misyck, B. (1993), *Industrial Districts in Europe: Policy Lessons for Developing Countries?*, Brighton, Institute of Development Studies.

Schmookler, J. (1966), *Invention and Economic Growth*, Cambridge, MA: Harvard University Press.

Schumpeter, J.A. (1912), *The Theory of Economic Development*, Leipzing: Duncker and Humblot.

―――― (1934), *The Theory of Economic Development*, Cambridge, MA: Harvard Economic Studies.

―――― (1939), *Business Cycles: A Theoretical, Historical and Statistical Analysis of the Capitalist Process*, 2 Volumes, New York: McGraw-Hill.

―――― (1942), *Capitalism, Socialism and Democracy*, New York: Harper.

Shapiro, C. and Varian, H. (1999), *Information Rules*, Boston, MA: Harvard Business School Press.

Sharp, M. (1985), *Europe and the New Technologies*, London: Pinter Publishers.

―――― (1991), *Technology and the Future of Europe*, edited by M. Freeman, K. Pavitt, M. Sharp and W. Walker, London: Pinter Publishers.

―――― (1993), "The Community and the New Technologies", in J. Lodge, *The European Community and the Challenge of the Future*, London: Pinter Publishers, pp. 202-220.

Sharp, M. and Pavitt, K. (1993), "Technology Policy in the 1990s: Old Trends and New Realities", *Journal of Common Market Studies*, Vol. 31, No. 2, pp. 129-51.

Shell, K. (1966), "Towards a Theory of Incentive Activity and Capital Accumulation", *American Economic Review*, Vol. 56, No. 2, May, pp. 62-68.

―――― (1967), "A Model of Inventive Activity and Capital Accumulation" in K. Shell (ed.), *Essays on the Theory of Optimal Economic Growth*, Cambridge: MIT Press.

———— (1973), "Incentive Activity, Industrial Organisation and Economic Growth" in J.A. Mirrlees and N. Stern (eds), *Models of Economic Growth*, London: Macmillan, pp. 77-100.

———— (2000), "The Production Recipes Approach to Modeling Technological Innovation: An Application to Learning by Doing" *Journal of Economics Dynamics and Control*, Vol. 24, pp. 389-450.

Shephard, R.W. (1953), *Cost and Production Functions*, Princeton University Press.

Silverberg, G. (1987), "Technical Progress, Capital Accumulation and Effective Demand, a Self Organisation Model", in D. Batten, J. Casti and B. Johanson (eds), *Economic Evolution and Structural Adjustment*, Germany: Springer Verlag.

Sinn, H.W. (1993), *How Much Europe? Subsidiarity, Centralization and Fiscal Competition*, CEPR, London.

Skountzos, T. and Mathaios (1995), *Statistical Data for Capital Stock: Greek Economy*, CEPR (Center of Planning and Research), Athens, Greece.

Smith, K. (1997), "Economic Infrastructures and Innovation Systems", in C. Edquist (ed.) (1997), *Systems of Innovation: Technologies, Institutions and Organizations*, London: Pinter Publishers/Cassell Academic.

Snowdown, B. and Vane, H. (eds) (1999), *Conversations with Economists. Interpreting Macroeconomics*, Cheltenham: Edward Elgar.

Soete, L. (1985), "International Diffusion of Ttechnology, Industrial Development and Technological Leapfrogging", *World Development*, Vol. 13, No. 3, pp. 409-422.

Soete, L. and Turner, R. (1984), "Technology Diffusion and the Rate of Technical Change", *The Economic Journal*, Vol. 94, pp. 612-623.

Solow, R. (1956), "A Contribution to the Theory of Economic Growth", *Quarterly Journal of Economics*, Vol. 70, February, pp. 65-94.

———— (1957), "Technical Change and the Aggregate Production Function" *Review of Economics and Statistics*, Vol. 39, pp. 312-320.

———— (1962), "Technical Progress, Capital Formation and Economic Growth", *American Economic Review*, Vol. 52, No. 2, May, pp. 72-86.

———— (1963), *Capital Theory and the Rate of Return*, Amsterdam, North Holland.

———— (1964), "Capital, Labour and Income in Manufacturing", in *The Behaviour of Income Shares, Studies in Income and Wealth*, NJ: Princeton University Press.

———— (1967), "Some Recent Developments in the Theory of Production", in M. Brown (ed.), *The Theory and Empirical Analysis of Production*, New York: Columbia University Press.

———— (1970), *Growth Theory*, Oxford University Press, Oxford.

———— (1988), "Growth Theory and After", *American Economic Review*, Vol. 78, No. 3, June.

———— (1994), "Perspectives on Growth Theory", *Journal of Economic Perspectives*, Vol. 8, No. 1, pp. 45-54.

Stamer, J.M. (1995), "Industrial Policy in Europe – New Options", Paper for Eurokolleg Series, Friedrich-Ebert-Foundation, Bonn.

Stiglitz, J.E. (1969), "The Effects of Income, Wealth and Capital Gains Taxation on Risk-Taking", *Quarterly Journal of Economics*, Vol. 83, May, pp. 263-283.

―――― (1987), "Learning to Learn, Localized Learning and Technological Progress", in P. Dasgupta and P. Stoneman (eds) *Economic Policy and Technological Performance*, Cambridge University Press, pp. 125-153.

―――― (1988), "Technological Change, Sunk Costs, and Competition", *Brookings Papers on Economic Activity*, Vol. 3.

―――― (1995), "The Theory of International Public Goods and the Architecture of International Organizations", United Nations Background Paper 7, Department for Economic and Social Information and Policy Analysis, July.

―――― (1998a), "Knowledge as a Global Public Good", Paper written as chapter in a UNDP book Global Public Goods.

―――― (1998b), *Towards a New Paradigm for Development: Strategies, Policies, and Processes*. Given as Raul Prebisch Lecture at United Nations Conference on Trade and Development (UNCTAD), Geneva, 19 October.

―――― (1999), *On Liberty, The Right to Know, and Public Discourse: The Role of Transparency in Public Life*. Given as 1999 Oxford University Amnesty International Lecture.

Stokey, N.L. (1979), "Intertemporal Price Discrimination", *Quarterly Journal of Economics*, 93, pp. 355-371.

―――― (1988), "Learning by Doing and the Introduction of New Goods", *Journal of Political Economy*, 96, pp. 701-717.

―――― (1995), "R&D and Economic Growth", *Review of Economic Studies*, 62, pp. 469-489.

Stoneman, P. (1983), *The Economic Analysis of Technological Change*, Oxford University Press.

―――― (1986), "Technological Diffusion: The Viewpoint of Economic Theory", *Richerche Economiche*, Vol. XL, No. 4, pp. 585-606.

―――― (1987), *The Economic Analysis of Technology Policy*, Oxford University Press.

―――― (1995), *Handbook of the Economics of Innovations and Technological Change*, Oxford: Blackwell,

Stoneman, P. and Ireland, N.J. (1983), "The Role of Supply Factors in the Diffusion of New Process Technology", *The Economic Journal*, Supplement, March, pp. 65-77.

Storper, M. (1997), *The Regional World: Territorial Development in a Global World*, New York and London: The Guilford Press.

Summers, L.H. (2000), *The New Wealth of Nations*, Treasury News, Washington DC, The Department of Treasury.

Syrquin, M. (1989), "Productivity Growth and Factor Reallocation" Chapter 8, in Y. Kubo, S. Robinson and M. Syrquin (eds), *Industrialization and Growth: A Comparative Study*, Oxford: Oxford University Press.

Swan, P. (1973), "The International Diffusion of an Innovation", *The Journal of Industrial Economics*, Vol. 22, September, pp. 61-70.

Sweeney, G.P. (1987), *Innovation, Entrepreneurs and Regional Development*, London: Frances Pinter.

Teece, D.J. (1986), "Profiting from Technological Innovation: Implications for Integration, Collaboration, Licensing and Public Policy", *Research Policy*, Vol. 15, pp. 285-305.

Terleckyj, N. (1974), "Effects of R&D on the Productivity Growth Industries an Exploratory Study", National Planning Association, Report No. 140, Washington.

———— (1980), "What Do R&D Numbers Tell Us About Technical Change?" *American Economic Review Papers and Proceedings*, 70, pp. 55-61.

———— (1983), "R&D as a Source of Growth of Productivity and of Income", in R.H. Franke and Associates (eds), *The Science of Productivity*, San Francisco: Jossey-Bass.

———— (1984), "R&D and Productivity Growth at the Industry Level: Is There Still a Relationship: Comment", in Z. Griliches (ed.), *R7D, Patents and Productivity*, Chicago: The University of Chicago Press for the National Bureau of Economic Research, pp. 496-502.

Tijssen, R.J.W. (1998), "Quantitative Assessment of Large Heterogeneous R&D Networks: The Case of Process Engineering in the Netherlands", *Research Policy*, Vol. 26, pp. 791-809.

Thomas, K.P. (1993), *EU Regulation of State Aid to Industry: Lessons for North America*, St. Louis (mimeo).

Thomas, R.L. (1993), *Introductory Econometrics: Theory and Applications*, 2nd ed., Longman Press.

Toda, Y. (1974), "Capital-labour Substitution in a Production Function: The Case of Soviet Manufacturing for 1950-1971", in Altmann et al. (eds), *On the Measurement of Factor Productivity: Theoretical Problems and Empirical Results*, Vandenhoeck and Ruprecht Publishers.

Törnqvist, G. (1990), *Towards a Geography of Creativity*, in A. Shachar and S. Öberg (eds), pp. 103-127.

Trefler, D. (1993), "International Factor Price Differences: Leontief was Right", *Journal of Political Economy*, Vol. 101, pp. 961-987.

———— (1995), "The Case of the Missing Trade and Other Mysteries", *American Economic Review*, Vol. 85, pp. 1029-1046.

Trimble, J. (1999), *A Redesigning the Service Statistics Sector Program*, Presentation to the Census Advisory Committee of Professional Associations Meeting, 21-22 October.

Triplett, J. (1999), "The Solow Productivity Paradox: What do Computers do to Productivity?" *Canadian Journal of Economics*, Vol. 32, No. 2, pp. 309-334.

Triplett, J.E. and Bosworth, B. (2000), "Productivity in the Services Sector", presented at the *American Economic Association Meetings*, January.

Tsipouri, L. (1989), *Accession to the EC and the Greek Technological Policy: The Experience 1981-1986*, Institute of Mediterranean Studies, Athens, Greece.

UNCTAD (2000), *World Investment Report*, New York and Geneva, United Nations.

UNESCO (1969), *The Measurement of Scientific and Technological Activities*, Paris.

——— (1983), *Manual for Statistics on Scientific and Technological Activities*, New York and Geneva, United Nations.

——— (1984), *Transnational Corporations in World Development*, Third Survey, New York and Geneva, United Nations.

——— (1992), *Scientific and Technology in Developing Countries: Strategies for the 1990s*, Paris.

United Nations (1983), *Transnational Corporations in World Development*, Third Survey, New York and Geneva, United Nations.

United Nations Conference on Trade and Development (UNCTAD) (1994), *World Investment Report*, New York and Geneva, United Nations.

——— (1996), *World Investment Report*, New York and Geneva, United Nations.

——— (1997a), *Trade and Development Report, 1997: Globalization, Distribution and Growth*, New York and Geneva, United Nations.

——— (1997b), *World Investment Report, Transnational Corporations, Market Structure and Competition Policy*, New York and Geneva, United Nations.

——— (1998), *World Investment Report*, New York and Geneva, United Nations.

——— (1998), *Globalisation, Underdevelopment and Poverty: Recent Trends and Policy*, David Woodward, Working Paper Series, United Nations, UNDP, New York and Geneva, United Nations, February.

——— (1999), *World Investment Report*, New York and Geneva, United Nations.

——— (2003), *Human Development Report*, United Nations, UNDP, June, New York and Geneva, United Nations.

Urata, S. (1992), "Economic Growth and Structural Change in the Soviet Economy 1959-1972", in M. Ciaschini (ed.), *Input-Output Analysis*.

US Department of Commerce (1998), *The Emerging Digital Economy*, US Department of Commerce.

——— (1999), *The Emerging Digital Economy II*, US Department of Commerce.

——— (2000), *Falling Through the Net: Toward Digital Inclusion*, US Department of Commerce, October.

US Standard Occupational Classification (SOC) <http://stats.bls.gov/soc>.

Uzawa, H. (1962), "Production Functions with Constant Elasticities of Substitution", *Review of Economic Studies*, Vol. 29, pp. 291-9.

——— (1964), "Duality Principles in the Theory of Cost and Production", *International Economic Review*, Vol. 5, pp. 216-220.

——— (1965), "Optimal Technical Change in as Aggregative Model of Economic Growth", *International Economic Review*, 6, pp. 12-31.

——— (1969), "Time Preference and the Penrose Effect in a Two-class Model of Economic Growth", *Journal of Political Economy*, Vol. 77, No. 4, July/August, pp. 628-652.

Uzawa, H. and Watanabe, H. (1961), "A Note on the Classification of Technical Inventions", *Economic Studies Quarterly*, September, pp. 68-72.

Van Schendelen, M.P.C.M. (1994), "Studying EU Public Affairs Cases: Does it Matter?" in R.H. Pedler and M. Van Schendelen (eds), *Lobbying the European Union*, Hants: Dartmouth, pp. 3-20.

Vaucleroy, G. (2000), *European Business Summit*, June, Brussels, Belgium.

Vernardakis, N. (1992), "Structural and Technological Imperatives in the Light of Development Prospects for the Greek Economy", Chapter 14 in (eds), "Issues in Contemporary Economics: the Greek Economy, Economic Policy for the 1990s", by Thanos Skouras (proceedings of the ninth world congress of the international economic association, Vol. 5).

Vernon, R. (1966), 'International Investment and International Trade in the Product Cycle', *Quarterly Journal of Economics*, Vol. 80, No. 2, pp. 190-207.

Verspagen, B. (1992), "Endogenous Innovation in Neo-Classical Growth Models: A Survey", *Journal of Macroeconomics*, Vol. 14, No. 4, pp. 613-662.

——— (1994), "Technology and Growth: the Complex Dynamics of Convergence and Divergence, in G. Silverberg and L. Soete (eds), *The Economics of Growth and Technical Change: Technologies, Nations, Agents*, Cheltenham: Edward Elgar.

Young, A. (1993), "Invention and Bounded Learning by Doing", *Journal of Political Economy*, Vol. 101, No. 3, pp. 443-472.

——— (1998), "Growth without Scale Effects", *Journal of Political Economy*, pp. 41-63.

Yuill, D. and Allen, K. (1989), *European Regional Incentives: A Review to Member States*, published by Bower-Saur in association with the European Policies Research Centre, University of Strathclyde.

Wallsten, S. (1998), "Rethinking the Small Business Innovation Research Program", in *Investing in Innovation: Creating A Research and Innovation Policy That Works*, L. Branscomb and J. Keller (eds), Cambridge, MA: MIT Press.

Warda, J. (2001), "Measuring the Value of R&D Tax Treatment in OECD Countries", STI Review, No. 27, OECD, Paris.

Watanabe, H. (1961), "A Note on the Classification of Technical Inventions", *Economic Studies Quarterly*, September, pp. 68-72.

WIIW-WIFO (2000), *Database on FDI in Central and Eastern Europe and FSU Countries*, February.

Williams, R. (1973), *European Technology*, Croom Helm Publishers.

Williamson, J. (1996), "Globalization, Convergence and History", *Journal of Economic History*, Vol. 56, No. 2.

Willoughby, K. (1990), "Technology Choice: A Critique of the Appropriate Technology Movement".

Wolfensohn, J. (1996), *Annual Meetings Address*, Washington: World Bank <www.worldbank.org/html/extdr/extme/jdwams96.htm>.

——— (1997), *Annual Meetings Address: The Challenge of Inclusion*, Hong Kong: World Bank <www.worldbank.org/html/extdr/am97/jdw_sp/jwsp97e.htm>.

Woodward, D. (1992), *Debt, Adjustment and Poverty in Developing Countries*, London: Pinter Publishers/Save the Children (UK).

——— (1993a), "Regional Trade Arrangements in Latin America and the Caribbean" (mimeo), Oxfam (UK/I), Oxford.

——— (1993b), "Regional Trade Arrangements in Sub-Saharan Africa" (mimeo), Oxfam (UK/I), Oxford.

——— (1996a), "Effects of Globalization and Liberalization on Poverty: Concepts and Issues", in *UNCTAD: Globalization and Liberalization: Effects of International Economic Relations on Poverty*, New York and Geneva, United Nations.

——— (1996b), "Debt Sustainability and the Debt Overhang in Heavily Indebted Poor Countries: Some Comments on the IMF's View", in *Eurodad: World Credit Tables, 1996: Creditors' Claims on Debtors Exposed*, Brussels, European Network on Debt and Development.

——— (1997a), "The Next Crisis? Direct and Portfolio Investment in Developing Countries" (mimeo), European Network on Debt and Development, Brussels.

——— (1997b), "The HIPC Initiative: Presentation to the EURODAD Annual Conference, November 1997" (mimeo), European Network on Debt and Development, Brussels.

——— (1997c), "Submission to the House of Commons Select Committee on International Development: The Highly Indebted Poor Countries (HIPC), Initiative" (mimeo).

——— (1997d), "The HIPC Initiative: Effects of Changes to the Rules Governing the Fiscal Criterion" (mimeo), Jubilee 2000 Coalition, London.

——— (1998), "Fiscal Criteria for Debt Reduction: a Human Development-Based Approach" (mimeo), Catholic Fund for Overseas Development.

Woolcock, S. (1984), "Information Technology: the Challenge to Europe", *Journal of Common Market Studies*, Vol. 22, No. 4.

World Bank (1990), *Adjustment Lending Policies for Sustainable Growth*, Washington, DC: World Bank.

——— (1996), *Poverty Reduction and the World Bank: Progress and Challenges in the 1990s*, Washington, DC: World Bank.

——— (1998), *Knowledge for Development: World Development Report*, New York: Oxford University Press.

——— (2000), *World Development Report: Cross-Border Mergers and Acquisitions and Development: An Overview*, New York and Geneva: United Nations.

Zander, U. (1991), *Exploiting a Technological Edge-voluntary and Involuntary Dissemination of Technology*, Institute of International Business (IIB), Stockholm School of Economics.

Zellner, A., Kmenta, J. and Dreze, J. (1966), "Specification and Estimation of Cobb-Douglas Production Function Models", *Econometrica*, Vol. 34, No. 3, October, pp. 784-795.

Index